Praise for The Future of the Professions

'Everyone interested in the future well-being of society must read this thoroughly researched and compelling book—to understand how technology can and will be used to enable the public to do far more for themselves. In reshaping our system of justice so that it can more cost-effectively underpin our democratic society and its prosperity, I have had the benefit of the Susskinds' core thesis—how to use technology not simply to enable the legal professions to do better what they now do, but to reshape justice for the benefit of the public.'

Lord Thomas of Cwmgiedd, the Lord Chief Justice of England and Wales

'If the Susskinds are right we are at the start of a social revolution. Technology has begun to transform social class, economic activity, political discourse, working life and the limits of human activity. In the *Future of the Professions* they relentlessly and unyieldingly but also entertainingly and elegantly set about proving their point. I started knowing that their argument was important, I finished convinced that it was right. This is a necessary book. It was necessary that it be written and necessary that you read it.'

Daniel Finkelstein, *The Times*

'I know of no better book for anyone interested in the future of skilled jobs and society. Drawing on an astounding range of sources and the latest research, *The Future of the Professions* offers

vital insights into the unprecedented disruption facing all the professions.'

Professor Ian Goldin, Professor of Globalisation and Development, University of Oxford

'In this magisterial survey Richard and Daniel Susskind demolish each profession's faith in its immutable uniqueness. Instead they trace inexorable and universal forces that will drive disintermediation, deconstruction and disruption. Written with scholarly thoroughness, this is an urgent manifesto and practical blueprint for the leaders of every professional firm.'

Philip Evans, Senior Partner & BCG Fellow, The Boston Consulting Group

'A thought-provoking account of the unthinkable: a world where automation, off-shoring, contingent work, and relentless market competition dissolve not middle-class jobs, but the privileged professional elites of yesteryear. A necessary read for anyone who cares about the future of the professions and work.'

Professor Yochai Benkler, Harvard University, author of *The Wealth of Networks*

'The authors are undoubtedly right that the professions will change more in the next quarter-century than they have in the previous three.'

The Economist

'A swashbuckling journey through the professions, this book makes sense of sweeping changes going on today and helps us see what it will mean to be a professional in an era of ubiquitous knowledge and increasingly capable machines. The authors' rigorous skepticism reveals an astounding future.'

Hugh Verrier, Chairman, White & Case

'Many books about the future are shallow and unnecessarily alarmist. This book is neither. We are behaving like ostriches in the developed world, refusing to see that technology is on the cusp of fundamentally reshaping professions. The future is bright, but only if we start embracing, rather than shunning, the future which the Susskinds show is hurtling towards us.'

Sir Anthony Seldon, Vice-Chancellor, University of Buckingham, and former Master of Wellington College

'If you want to know how technology will continue to transform our lives, read this book! Well researched, beautifully written, comprehensive, insightful, and encouraging, the authors convincingly make the case that no profession is immune to these monumental changes, and that they provide an unprecedented opportunity for those who embrace rather than resist them.'

Professor Nichola s F. LaRusso, MD, Founding Medical Director of the Mayo Clinic Center for Innovation

'In the tax profession we have seen transformational change, striking at the very foundations of what we do and how we do it. In this compelling work, the Susskinds help us think more clearly about the crucial issues and opportunities we face and set clear insight as to the way in which we must respond. Essential reading for anyone interested in the future of a professional organization.'

Conrad Young, Deloitte Global Leader, Tax Management Consulting

'Professions beware! In this insightful and thought-provoking book, Richard and Daniel Susskind capture the essence of today's changing environment where, whilst the destination may not be certain, it is clear the status quo will not survive. Technology in particular is having a profound impact across the professions and no group seems exempt. The future has never been so ripe with challenges and opportunities.'

Richard Sexton, Vice Chairman, Global Assurance, PwC

Professor Richard Susskind OBE FRSE is an author, speaker, and independent advisor to international professional firms and national governments. He is President of the Society for Computers and Law, IT Adviser to the Lord Chief Justice, and Chair of the Advisory Board of the Oxford Internet Institute. His books include the best-sellers, *The End of Lawyers?* (OUP, 2008) and *Tomorrow's Lawyers* (OUP, 2013), his work has been translated into 18 languages, and he has been invited to speak in over sixty countries.

Daniel Susskind is a Fellow in Economics at Oxford University and a Research Professor at King's College London. Previously, he worked for the British Government—in the Prime Minister's Strategy Unit, in the Policy Unit in 10 Downing Street, and also as a Senior Policy Adviser at the Cabinet Office. He was a Kennedy Scholar at Harvard University.

THE FUTURE OF THE PROFESSIONS

HOW TECHNOLOGY WILL TRANSFORM THE WORK OF HUMAN EXPERTS

RICHARD SUSSKIND

AND

DANIEL SUSSKIND

OXFORD UNIVERSITY PRESS

OXFORD
UNIVERSITY PRESS

Great Clarendon Street, Oxford, OX2 6DP,
United Kingdom

Oxford University Press is a department of the University of Oxford. It furthers the University's objective of excellence in research, scholarship, and education by publishing worldwide. Oxford is a registered trade mark of Oxford University Press in the UK and in certain other countries

First Edition published in 2015
Updated Edition published in 2022

Impression: 2

Published in the United States of America by Oxford University Press
198 Madison Avenue, New York, NY 10016, United States of America

British Library Cataloguing in Publication Data
Data available

Library of Congress Control Number: 2022933853

ISBN 978–0–19–884189–0

Printed and bound by
CPI Group (UK) Ltd, Croydon, CR0 4YY

We dedicate this book to the memory of
Shirley Susskind (1935–2015)
a very loving mother and grandmother

PREFACE TO ORIGINAL EDITION

It is unusual for a father and son to write a book together. Before thanking the many people who helped us with this book, we thought readers would be interested to learn a little about the background to our collaboration.

A Note from Richard

For more than thirty years, I have been working on transforming the way that lawyers and courts work. I have written eight related books, and many of my theories about the future of legal services are no longer considered outrageous. Over the years, and around the world, at the end of my lectures to lawyers, I have been approached by stray doctors, auditors, architects, and many others who have said that my ideas apply equally to their own professions. I have had similar feedback in my consulting work with leading tax and audit specialists, and from my work as a university professor and school governor in the education sector. The starting-point for the research underpinning the book, therefore, is a well-tested and substantially corroborated set of ideas about the future of legal services that other professionals say resonates beyond law. One main purpose of the book is to test and extend this hypothesis about the law and lawyers to the professions more generally.

Above all, the project that led to this book has allowed me to work intensely with my son, Daniel. Very few fathers have this opportunity. It has been the high point of my working life.

A Note from Daniel

Five years have passed since my Dad and I first sat down to talk about this book. He had spent most of his career thinking about the future of the legal profession. But, for a while, he had sensed that his thinking applied equally well elsewhere. At the time I was working in the Policy Unit in 10 Downing Street. As we talked, it became very clear that my experience in government confirmed his suspicions. And so we decided to set off on a project, together, to think about the future of the professions. It has been an extraordinarily happy five years, and a great privilege.

As Co-Authors

This book is written in the first person plural. This reflects the fact that our views are shared views, so that when we say that 'we believe', 'we see', or 'we predict', then our positions are indeed aligned. However, we accept that our use of 'we' in the past tense is sometimes anomalous. For example, where we speak of what we wrote in the mid-1980s, one of us (Daniel) was not yet alive. Nonetheless, as a convention throughout the book, when we speak of 'we', we may be referring, variously, to our joint views or experience or those of either one of us.

ACKNOWLEDGEMENTS

We have been fortunate to have had the help of a large number of people while writing this book. The following list comprises the many individuals who gave generously of their time to be interviewed, alongside numerous friends, colleagues, and clients who supported us throughout. To each and every one of you we extend our warmest thanks: David Agus, David Barnes, George Beaton, Lukas Biewald, Nick Birks, Bruce Braude, Jonathan Brayne, Steven Brill, Tim Brown, Simon Carne, Mark Chandler, Stacey Childress, Keith Coleman, Richard Collier-Keywood, Charles Conn, Dan Cooperman, Jim Dabney, John Danner, Ian Davis, Robin Downie, Matthew Edwards, Neville Eisenberg, Philip Evans, Alice Fermor-Hesketh, Gi Fernando, Cam Findlay, Daniel Finkelstein, Joshua Foer, Howard Gardner, Josh Glancy, Tom Goetz, Ian Goldin, Colin Gounden, Muir Gray, Ashok Gupta, Ben Hammersley, Mark Harris, Mike Hess, Silvia Hodges, Jonathan Hughes, Will Hunter, Michael Ingram, Ari Kaplan, Hanif Kara, John Kerr, Daphne Koller, Daniel Kraft, Kieran Kumaria, Adrian Lajtha, Nick LaRusso, Bill Liao, Paul Lippe, Ian Lloyd, Jay Lorsch, George Lowder, Bruce MacEwen, David Maister, James Manyika, Helen Margetts, Chris McKenna, Christopher Michel, Christopher Millard, Michael Mills, John Moore, David Morley, Tim Morris, Alastair Morrison, Gary Nelson, Howard Nichols, Cory Ondrejka, Chris Outram, Jonathan Oviatt, Alan Paterson,

David Pester, Richard Punt, Stephen Rabinowitz, Chas Rampenthal, Paul Robinson, Joel Rose, Mari Sako, Viktor Mayer-Schönberger, Dov Seidman, Anthony Seldon, Richard Sennett, Richard Sexton, Tom Standage, Janet Stanton, Paloma Strelitz, Ziona Strelitz, Matt Sucherman, Stephen Swensen, Gideon Sylvester, Eric Topol, Darrel Untereker, David Vines, Vivek Wadhwa, Kent Walker, Ted Wang, Anthony Warrens, Rachel Whetstone, David Wilkins, Tom Wright, and Conrad Young.

A very big thank-you also to Darcy Hill for helping us so diligently with the bibliography, and to Patricia Cato and Suzanne Richmond for their assistance with early drafts of the book.

Our friends at Oxford University Press have been notably patient. David Musson has been an ongoing source of encouragement and of wise counsel; and we are grateful also at OUP to Kim Behrens, Kate Farquhar-Thomson, Phil Henderson, and Clare Kennedy for their enthusiasm and professionalism. Thank you also to Jeff New for his superb copy-editing.

The epigraph by John Maynard Keynes, *The General Theory of Employment, Interest and Money* (1936), © The Royal Economic Society, published by Cambridge University Press, is reproduced with permission.

Alan Susskind reviewed the entire manuscript. His observations and his ongoing support were very much appreciated. At the same time, Werner Susskind merits special mention for keeping us fully supplied with relevant articles from the *BMJ*.

Jamie Susskind deserves the largest thank-you of all. He was there for us constantly—to brainstorm, to motivate, to advise, and, occasionally, to mediate. He read two versions of the manuscript, and his detailed analysis and critique were invaluable.

Grace—I (Daniel) fear this will not be the last time. With all the love there is in the world, thank you for being there for me.

Alexandra—we thank you for your warmth, your smile, and your love. Michelle (our wife/mother)—you have been remarkable in your support of our work and your belief in us as co-authors. We cannot thank you enough for your love and endurance.

Finally, we dedicate this book to the memory of Shirley Susskind, our mother and grandmother. Very sadly, she passed away just a few weeks before we completed the manuscript. We know she would have been proud of us.

Richard Susskind
Daniel Susskind
Radlett, England
30 March 2015

Hitherto [1848] it is questionable if all the mechanical inventions yet made have lightened the day's toil of any human being. They have enabled a greater population to live the same life of drudgery and imprisonment, and an increased number of manufacturers and others to make fortunes. They have increased the comforts of the middle classes. But they have not yet begun to effect those great changes in human destiny, which it is in their nature and in their futurity to accomplish. Only when, in addition to just institutions, the increase of mankind shall be under the deliberate guidance of judicious foresight, can the conquests made from the powers of nature by the intellect and energy of scientific discoverers become the common property of the species, and the means of improving and elevating the universal lot.

John Stuart Mill

The difficulty lies, not in the new ideas, but in escaping from the old ones, which ramify, for those brought up as most of us have been, into every corner of our minds.

John Maynard Keynes

CONTENTS

PART III. IMPLICATIONS

LIST OF BOXES AND FIGURES

Boxes

Figures

NEW PREFACE – AN UPDATE

The central claims of the first edition of this book can be stated simply. Machines are becoming increasingly capable and are taking on more and more of the tasks that were once the exclusive province of human professionals. While new tasks will no doubt arise in years to come, machines are likely in time to take on many of these as well. In the medium term, during the 2020s, this will not mean unemployment for professionals. But there will be widespread redeployment and a need for extensive retraining. In the long run, however, we find it hard to avoid the conclusion that there will be a steady decline in the need for traditional flesh-and-blood professionals working as they do today.

We stand by this line of thinking. And advances, since we first published in 2015, fortify our thesis. We decided in mid-2019 that it would be useful to provide an update on these recent developments in a revised version of the book. We resolved to leave the original version intact and to prepare this update in the form of a new preface. We were almost ready to submit this when, in the middle of March 2020, we watched with alarm the rapid spread of Covid-19. We decided to delay publication, to give ourselves the time to evaluate its impact on the professions. As we write, we are no longer in lockdown in the United Kingdom. Nor are we restricted in most of our activities. Other countries are less fortunate and will be fettered for some time yet. In truth, given the possibility of new variants and the challenges of global vaccination, the future remains uncertain. Nonetheless, we have given thought to the overall impact of Covid-19 on our original arguments and claims. We have come to the conclusion, and we expand on this shortly, that because of the remarkable development of vaccines, the emergence of quick and inexpensive testing, and better treatment at all stages, that although the effects of Covid-19 are tragic and pervasive, and although it has brought some accelerating and decelerating effects with respect to technology, we do not expect the virus and illness will alter the long-term course for the professions that is laid out in this book. Before we say more on this, however, we reflect more generally on relevant developments in the professions since the first edition of this book appeared and on some striking ways in which technology has evolved in the past few years. After our discussion of Covid-19, we identify and respond to a set of recurrent questions that have been put to us in our travels. Then, we report back on the extent to which we have seen innovation in the professional firms to which we have been exposed. And we conclude by providing a new framework to help professionals think about and categorize their innovations.

Relevant Developments (2015 onwards)

In the four years following the original publication of our book in October 2015, we had the opportunity to test our thinking on audiences of professionals around the world. We presented in person in more than 30 countries, at over 200 events, to around 50000 people. The response has been mixed. When it comes to individuals, our work seems to have a polarizing effect—with equal gusto, there are those who agree fervently with our thesis, and there are those who wholeheartedly reject it. People feel very strongly in both camps. This division corresponds in many ways with current views on artificial intelligence (AI)—some argue that we are entering an entirely new era, while others dismiss this as hype, maintaining that we have been through similar transitions before. Within particular professions, speaking in the broadest of terms, we have found that doctors tend to be dismissive of non-doctors having a view on their future, teachers are conspicuously outspoken—if divided—on social media, the clergy has been notably silent, lawyers are mostly conservative, journalists appear to be resigned, management consultants see greater need for change in other professions and businesses than in their own, accountants are largely receptive, while architects express great interest in the new possibilities. Nor have professional bodies responded in unison. Some, such as in law, have gathered protectively around their members while others, in accountancy for instance, seem more inclined to join our call for some fundamental re-thinking. And all of this has taken place in the context of a general upsurge of public interest in AI and the future of white-collar work.

More substantively, there has been a steady flow of significant advances in each of the professions. Many of these took place before the pandemic began. But the unique challenges of the last twelve months have prompted significant further developments. We can only give a flavour here but the trajectory is clear.

In health, achievements in medical diagnostics have continued apace. AI-based systems can now often outperform human experts in everyday activities like detecting cancers, diagnosing eye problems, and analysing scans. In mental health, new applications have also emerged, for example to help identify people at risk of suicide; Crisis Text Line, a US charity, developed a system that scanned more than 100 million texts to spot the language used by those most in need (those who use a crying face emoji, for instance, are said to be 11 times more likely to need serious help than a person who uses the word 'suicide').[1] Medical advances have not been confined to diagnostics. DeepMind made a 'gargantuan leap' in solving one of the biggest unresolved challenges in biology, known as the 'protein folding problem'. This, it is said, will transform drug discovery in the future.[2] The first AI-developed drug entered clinical testing, designed to help those suffering from OCD.[3] And new partnerships were formed across traditional disciplinary boundaries: Microsoft and Novartis, for instance, struck one of the biggest agreements between Big Tech and Big Pharma, the latter turning to the former to help them use AI across their business.[4]

The prospects for greater use of technology in health care are succinctly captured by Eric Topol (the author of *Deep Medicine: How Artificial Intelligence Can Make Healthcare Human Again*)[5] who was invited to produce a report for the NHS in the United Kingdom on preparing the healthcare workforce for a digital future.[6] He begins as follows: 'We are at a unique juncture in the history of medicine, with the convergence of genomics, biosensors, the electronic patient record and smartphone apps, all superimposed on a digital infrastructure, with artificial intelligence to make sense of the overwhelming amount of data created. This remarkably powerful set of information technologies provides the capacity to understand, from a medical standpoint, the uniqueness of each individual—and the promise to deliver health-care on a far more rational, efficient and tailored basis.'[7] And he concludes, tellingly for all professions that, '(t)he greatest challenge is the culture shift in learning and innovation, with a willingness to embrace technology for system-wide improvement.'[8]

Various technological trends in education were accelerated by the pandemic. Overnight, virtual education become the norm in most countries. Worldwide investment in ed-tech start-ups increased more than two-and-a-half-fold during the pandemic. In the United States, the delivery of laptops and tablets to primary and secondary schools almost doubled.[9] 'Massive-Open-Online-Courses' (or MOOCs), for instance, which had been dismissed by many as a failure, have enjoyed a pandemic-induced surge in use (Udacity, for instance, one influential platform, saw their enrollment double).[10] More ambitious work is underway. Consider Dreamscape Learn, a Los Angeles-based company that Peter Diamandis, one of its investors, describes as bringing together 'the power of Hollywood storytelling and immersive VR technology to disrupt how we teach and learn'. He concludes that, '(w)hen AI and VR converge with wireless 5G networks, our global education problem moves from the nearly impossible challenge of finding teachers and funding schools for the hundreds of millions in need, to the much more manageable puzzle of building a fantastic digital education system that we can give away for free to anyone with a headset.'[11]

As for the clergy, there was modest technological experimentation before the pandemic. One noticeable trend was the growing use of religious robotics: the Buddhist android Mindar that delivers 25-minute sermons on religious scripture,[12] the Catholic robot SanTO that reports the Pope's homilies and cites verse,[13] and the Protestant robot BlessU2 that offers prayers in seven languages (in a trial, most recorded interactions were positive).[14] While cases like these might sound a little playful, their use prompted serious reflection: one Catholic Theologian, for instance, argued that 'gender-neutral' robot priests might be a useful solution to a 'very male, very patriarchal' institution.[15]

The pandemic, though, has been technologically transformative. In a world where personal contact was curtailed, the profession found itself immersed in a fundamental and fractious debate about which religious rituals must necessarily be carried out with other human beings in a physical place—and which ones, through technology, could be undertaken very differently. Some activities have proven adaptable: many people, most obviously, were able to pray remotely. And on balance, there are signs this shift was a success: in the United States, for instance, more than 9 out of 10 people who worshipped virtually during the pandemic were either 'very' or 'somewhat' satisfied;[16] in England, churches found that more people were participating in their online services than used to meet in person (a website designed to help people track down churches—AChurchNearYou.com—now has more than 20,000 online services and events, whereas before the pandemic it had none).[17]

More surprising adaptations have taken place, too. One Rabbi, in interviews for the first edition of this book, joked with us that his ancestral colleagues were so clever they had designed their profession to be 'automation-proof'—Jewish Law forbids the use technology on Shabbat (Sunset on Friday to Sunset on Saturday), so there will always be jobs for Rabbis, he smiled. Yet even that sort of prediction frayed at the edges: during the pandemic, certain uses of technology were permitted for even the most strictly observant Jews.[18] Inevitably, though, certain practices did not change: 'drive-thru' confessions that maintained human contact, for instance, were a staple for many Catholics during lockdown, and *tarawih* prayers for Muslims during Ramadan were held in empty mosques and not live streamed for those at home.[19]

At the same time, a growing issue for the clergy and followers has been the use and misuse of technology in sharing religious ideas. In particular, fears have intensified about the role of the internet in enabling religious radicalization: in one survey of US extremists, for instance, social media appeared to play a role in radicalizing about one quarter of them between 2005 and 2010, but three-quarters of them between 2011 and 2016 (and almost 90 percent in 2016).[20]

In the legal world, much of the work of the courts went online during the pandemic. In more than 160 countries, hearings have now been conducted remotely, largely by video.[21] Meanwhile, major law firms seemed to have achieved greater profitability while the virus spread—overheads were reduced, and more hours were clocked up at the kitchen table than in the open plan office. One senior lawyer confessed to us recently that his working hours had increased to the extent that he no longer had the time to commute.

Other advances in law had little to do with the crisis. Work continues on machine learning systems that can predict judicial decisions as accurately as human lawyers,[22] extract key terms from agreements, identify significant documents in litigation bundles and in due diligence exercises, and forewarn organizations of impending legal risks.[23] In the criminal area, computer algorithms were claimed to 'beat humans in predicting re-offending rates'[24] and, in the same spirit, JP Morgan announced the development of a system called COIN, standing for 'contract intelligence', which scans commercial loan agreements, doing in a matter of seconds what, it is said, would have required up to 360,000 hours of traditional lawyers' time.[25] Most leading global law firms are now taking client technology seriously. In 2016, for example, Allen & Overy, in collaboration with Deloitte, launched an online system, MarginMatrix, to help banks cope with the documentation challenges arising from the new rules governing the global derivatives markets. This system has enjoyed great commercial success, spawning kindred solutions and confirming that online legal service can be at once beneficial for clients and profitable for firms.[26]

Meanwhile, in the world of law but outside the world of law firms, a company called LegalZoom, founded 20 years ago, an online service that helps non-lawyers to draft legal documents, aimed for a valuation of more than $5 billion in its initial public offering (IPO).[27] It is clear that in jurisdictions that permit such investment, venture capital and private equity are finding their way into the burgeoning legal technology start-up industry. This will likely lead to more investment in systems for non-lawyers (citizens and in businesses). In contrast, today, the main buyers and users of legal technology are law firms.

The Big 4 accounting firms have continued their incursion into the legal market, each growing huge teams of traditional lawyers but also keen to differentiate by using advanced technologies developed for their other service lines, most notably tax.

Governments are also recognizing the strategic relevance of legal technology—the UK government, for example, has funded a work programme that aims to transform the UK legal sector through technology.[28] And, slowly but perceptibly, law schools around the world are acknowledging that a legal education would be incomplete without exposure to developments in technology. Courses, centres, and professorships are now being dedicated to legal technology and transformation.

In journalism, familiar patterns continued to unfold. Print media, on several measures, continued its collapse and digital media its rise, prompting the UK industry auditor, the Audit Bureau of Circulations, to stop requiring newspapers to publish their monthly figures in 2020 in a foolhardy attempt to halt a 'negative narrative of decline'.[29] But these well-known headline numbers also masked subtler underlying trends. To begin with, the rise of digital media has been extremely bumpy: for instance, many of the early digital-only news platforms, like BuzzFeed and The Huffington Post, had difficulty maintaining the trajectory of their initial ascent. And while certain parts of the print media have struggled—local newspapers, for instance, continued to fold, with one in five being lost in the United States since 2004[30]—other areas of the traditional profession have flourished. Several national newspapers, for instance, have performed extremely well: at the start of 2021, *The New York Times* reported 7.8 million subscribers—almost three-and-half times the number of subscribers it had in 2015 when this book was first published—and earned more revenue from digital than print subscriptions in 2020.[31] Similar success stories at other national papers in different countries have prompted a re-evaluation of the feasibility of the online business model, dispelling some of the early skepticism directed at mechanisms like the paywall.

In turn, other funding innovations have recently played a role in rejuvenating early forms of bottom-up online journalism: platforms like Substack and Patreon, which streamline the process of setting up online subscriptions, have allowed the writers of basic blogs and simple newsletters to make an income from their work. But, the last few years have also seen the emergence of new challenges. More than any other profession, journalism has been preoccupied by the rise of what we called 'new gatekeepers': platforms like Facebook and Twitter, for instance, have taken on more of the roles and responsibilities that once fell to traditional media institutions, shaping and filtering the news and opinion to which we are exposed—with very mixed success. With respect to the pandemic, on balance, it appears it has rendered technological challenges and opportunities more acute: in a 2021 survey of media leaders, for instance, 76 per cent said that Covid-19 has 'accelerated their plans for digital transition'.[32]

In the field of management consulting, there have been notably fewer calls for revolution. It is ironic that those who advocate so strongly for disruption across the business community direct their transformational urges at their clients rather than themselves.

Focusing here on the larger management consulting businesses, one area of significant recent growth has been the management and execution of major technology projects and change programmes. This is labour-intensive and technology-intensive work, well suited to the global firms. During the pandemic, many of these firms were able, in this vein, to provide armies of consultants, well versed in process and technology, to help governments cope with the logistical and operational challenges of tracking the virus and distributing the vaccinations. We see a related shift in consulting over the past decade that we call the move from 'curves' to 'sleeves'—from cerebral strategic thinking (delivered as curves plotted cleverly on grids) to consulting as harder graft (rolling up sleeves and delivering).

Looking forward, the consulting market is rapidly coalescing around *data*—on the development and deployment of increasingly sophisticated tools, not least machine learning systems, for data collection and analysis.[33] Historically, consulting firms brought brainpower to bear on complex problems. Now they also bring tools to capture and work with relevant datasets. Accordingly, the leading players are gearing up. Each of the Big 4 already has thousands of data scientists. McKinsey too has legions of data specialists and, in 2015, they acquired QuantumBlack, an advanced analytics business. BCG and Bain are operating in the same spirit.

Technology here, though, simply extends rather than changes the traditional consulting service. The emphasis in most of these consulting practices is still on selling the time of human specialists (now data experts rather than, say, strategists). This shift to data will, however, bring stiff competition, whether from major technology companies (like IBM), new players (such as Palantir), or indeed suitably resourced in-house strategy units.

AI may well represent the biggest competitive threat. A paper in *Harvard Business Review* argues that 'a great deal of what is paid for with consulting services is data analysis and presentation.

Consultants gather, clean, process, and interpret data from disparate parts of organizations. They are very good at this, but AI is even better'.[34] Here as elsewhere in the professions is the prospect of building AI-based systems that replace traditional service. McKinsey Solutions is an example; they call it 'asset-based consulting'.[35] We see it as a shift from advisory service to pre-packaged, online tools and solutions.

Turning now to auditors, Sir Donald Brydon undertook an independent review of the quality and effectiveness of audit for the UK government in 2019. He notes on his first page, inauspiciously, that 'audit is not broken but it has lost its way'.[36] Much of the current disquiet about the *quality* of audit has its roots, no doubt, in a succession of high-profile corporate collapses where there was clear evidence of poor audit practice. Market leaders and professional bodies agree that public trust needs to be restored in the competence and independence of auditors.

Brydon indeed proposed that auditing 'should be an independent profession in its own right, with its own governing principles, qualifications and standards'.[37] He also recommended that audit should *inform* the markets as well verify (or not) the accuracy of financial reporting, echoing a wider sentiment that stakeholders would value assurance beyond the figures—on non-financial factors, such as risk.

Meanwhile, in relation to the *process* of auditing, it is increasingly conceded that technology is poised to revolutionize the statutory financial audit.[38] Long-term strategic thinkers do not generally expect that today's audit—characterized by annual sampling and the gut instincts of seasoned practitioners—will last the decade. In a bold public statement, a KPMG audit partner speaks of 'digital transformation, which revamps the auditing process into something entirely new—a reimagined audit experience' and anticipates the need 'to move from statistical sampling to actually reviewing 100 per cent of a client's transactions in real time'. He concludes that the future of audit will involve 'real-time auditing, in which clients record transactions on a blockchain and the auditor is alerted if there are any unusual interactions' and AI-based systems that 'can flag additional anomalies or risky transactions based on parameters that it "learns" on its own'.[39]

The field of tax has played host recently to heated public debate. One issue has been the ethics of tax paying. In the United Kingdom at least, the government has questioned the moral fibre of those who seek too diligently to reduce their tax liabilities. Tax planners have in turn been perplexed, torn between doing the best for their clients and exposing themselves to censure and perhaps worse. A related global controversy has also raged over the apparent ease with which major tech companies seem able to pay very little tax in countries in which they trade copiously.

As for the daily administration and practice of tax, the discipline of tax compliance (broadly, preparing and filing tax returns), continues to be transformed through technology. For individual citizens, online submission of tax forms has become one of many examples of digital interaction with the state. Readily available tax software helps simplifies the process—in the United States, a recent survey suggested that as much as one-half of the population uses such systems (and, by implication, not human tax advisers) in helping file their tax returns.[40]

At the business end of the spectrum, enabled by advances in 'big data' and cloud technology, the Big 4 continue to invest hugely in tax technology, integrating and internationalizing their corporate tax compliance systems. As part of an alliance with Microsoft, for instance, EY has developed its 'Global Tax Platform'. Other collaborations are significant. GE, for example, has transferred most of its in-house tax team to PwC under a major outsourcing arrangement, while Deloitte was appointed by Amazon as a tax service provider, to support 'VAT services on Amazon', an online service that helps Amazon sellers comply with new EU rules for VAT reporting.[41] This service itself built on Deloitte's collaboration with tax technologists, Taxamo—together they built a fully automated tax compliance service that enables digital marketplaces and online sellers to register for VAT and file compliant returns.[42]

Tax authorities around the world are also embracing technology. The UK government, for example, is committed to 'making tax digital' and so transforming tax administration,[43] while in Norway, the Norwegian Tax Administration has simplified the tax process for employees by collecting data from third parties and using this to produce prefilled tax returns.[44]

Bolder visions are emerging, most notably from the OECD, whose recent paper, 'Tax Administration 3.0,' argues that digitization provides 'an opportunity to address some of the structural limitations of the current system of tax administration.'[45] As an OECD adviser put it, 'in future taxation will be increasingly embedded in everyday processes. Already for business, transactions can be automatically captured through automated cash registers, online accounting systems and payment systems. When tax rules are integrated into these systems, tax returns can be to a large extent automatically generated.'[46]

Finally, in our brief canter through the professions, we turn to architecture. Here, new technologies continued to encroach upon tasks that historically required the creativity of human beings: there has been growing use of systems, for instance, that generate efficient floorplans, design attractive buildings, test the profitability of potential development sites, and compose housing development plans, among other everyday tasks.[47] The Elbphilharmonie, more dramatically, the beautiful new concert hall in Hamburg, was designed algorithmically, without relying on the refined aesthetic sensibility of a human designer as might have been expected.[48] Online libraries of simple, fixed, digital designs were complemented with more sophisticated inventories of algorithms for designing a variety of sophisticated structures.[49] Technologies have moved from prototype to product: Autodesk's generative design system, for instance, at the time of this book's first publication, designed stable chairs and lightweight bike-frames. This has since been made commercially available to design pretty much anything. New technologies that emerged in the intervening years have been adapted for professional use: Fologram and Twinbuild, for example, were developed to allow architects to use Microsoft's augmented-reality headset Hololens to view virtual buildings and objects imposed in physical space.[50]

Longstanding concerns about the nature of traditional architectural education intensified: Sir Anthony Seldon, the Vice Chancellor of Buckingham University and mental-health campaigner, spoke of the 'added burdens' faced by architecture students, issuing an urgent call to 'rethink the courses so they align with the architectural education needs of the future rather than the dictates of the architectural big cheeses of the past'.[51] Given that architects spend much of their time designing physical spaces, the pandemic—which decimated demand for those spaces—hit the profession particularly hard: in the United States, a survey by the American Institute for Architects found that 8 in 10 firms were forced to apply for financial support from the government;[52] in the United Kingdom, a survey by the Royal Institute of British Architects found that almost half of architects had lost income and a quarter were 'struggling mentally'.[53] This experience has prompted a renewed focus on the future of the profession. At recent conferences for architects we have been encouraged by enthusiasm for those in the profession to become more involved in the design of *virtual* spaces, an attractive possibility as virtual reality is likely to become a core part of the human experience.

Taking all these developments together, despite countless clear technological advances across these professions that were our original objects of study, we have yet to find any unambiguous game-changers in mainstream professional service. There has been no Amazon, Uber, or eBay in the professions. This does not surprise us. We are clear in the main body of this book that change in the professions is more likely to be incremental transformation than overnight revolution—there are formidable regulatory and cultural barriers that stand in the way of radical and pervasive institutional change.

To be clear, we do not dismiss out of hand the possibility of new systems revolutionizing individual professions but we doubt that this drastic change can come from within. We have seen little sign of self-disruption within major professional businesses and organizations. If there were to be revolutionary upheaval, it would most likely be wrought by start-ups or by big tech companies that turn their attentions to professional work—no matter how improbable this might seem to today's professionals, especially those who are currently enjoying success in their chosen fields.

Since writing the first edition of this book, we have also been monitoring the world of finance as it has wrestled with and embraced technology. Here, the shift has continued relentlessly over the past few years. In 2016, 'quant funds'—whose investment decisions are made by machines rather than human beings—became the largest source of institutional trading activity in the US stockmarket.[54] Personal finance apps for ordinary consumers took off, with companies like Wealthify, Nutmeg, Monzo, and Revolut becoming household names and displacing traditional advisers. Regulatory institutions started to turn to technology: the UK Financial Conduct Authority, for example, used systems to scan adverts and determine whether they might mislead consumers; while the US credit rating agency, Fitch, took a substantial stake in an AI company, Sigma Ratings, to help it more swiftly identify cases of bank misconduct.[55] And financial reporting changed, too: today, about a third of the content published on Bloomberg.com, for example, is generated by automated systems rather than by traditional journalists; MorningStar, a prominent provider of investment research, automated the rating and reporting on almost 39,000 traded funds for savings and retirement (the 130 human analysts at the firm are left to focus their efforts on covering a comparatively modest 4,284 funds).[56] In broad terms, our expectation is that other professions, like finance, will also be increasingly and profoundly changed by technology.

Technological Advance

Note too that underpinning technologies have also moved on significantly since our original publication. This is reflected in the cluster of examples above. Indeed, one of the frustrations of writing a book about technology is that new case studies inevitably appear soon after the final manuscript is submitted.

Across the board, there has been dramatic progress in technology in the last few years. Google researchers claimed 'quantum supremacy' for the first time, using a quantum computer to solve a problem that, they argued, was out of reach for the finest classical computers (and Chinese researchers swiftly followed with a similar declaration the following year).[57] Blockchain found new applications and cryptocurrencies found new users. The adoption of systems that monitor human emotions in classrooms (are students paying attention?) and remote work environments (are employees working?) drew more attention to the neglected but fascinating field of 'affective computing'.[58] A variety of technologies were developed in response to Covid-19: advances in testing capabilities, track-and-trace capabilities, and vaccines themselves—a process of technological discovery and deployment that would normally take more than a decade was reduced to less than a year.[59]

And, of course, there have been countless advances in AI as well. Half of all AI patents were registered in the period from 2013 to 2018, even though the field dates to the 1950s. The number of US undergraduates majoring in computer science more than doubled from 2013 to 2017, resulting in a reported demand 'far outstripping the supply of professors' to teach them properly.[60]

The total attendance at the largest AI academic conferences more than doubled from 2015 to 2018, as more and more researchers turned their attention to the field.[61] And from 2015 to 2019, disclosed investments in AI soared: one study suggests more than doubling in Germany, almost tripling in the United States and the United Kingdom, more than tripling in Singapore and France, almost quadrupling in India, quadrupling too in Canada, increasing eleven-fold in Japan, and twelve-fold in Israel.[62]

Alongside these general trends, there have been particular moments of remarkable advance. The triumph of AlphaGo, a system developed by Google DeepMind, was one. This system plays Go, a board game so complex that there are said to be more possible moves than there are atoms in the universe. In March 2016, AlphaGo beat the world's best player in a five-game series. This was a remarkable achievement, in part because most AI researchers thought we were at least a decade away from such a result. But the match was significant for another reason. In talking with professionals about the limits of machines, they often say their jobs require creativity, a capacity that machines cannot exhibit. Alan Turing, one of the greatest computer pioneers of the twentieth century, called this the 'Lady Lovelace objection', in so doing criticizing the mathematician Ada Lovelace, who argued that a machine could never 'originate' or do anything new. Turing suggested that this in fact meant a machine could never 'take us by surprise'. And yet, one particular move by AlphaGo led to exclamations from commentators and was described as 'beautiful' by a past Go champion—precisely because it caught them off-balance. Contrary to widespread belief, machines are now capable of generating novel outcomes, entirely beyond the contemplation of their original human designers.

A similarly remarkable event was the release of the GPT-3 language model in 2020, developed by OpenAI. This is a system that, trained on 200-billion words of text, can read and write in a vast variety of formats, on any topic in the world.[63] Its older cousin GPT-2, developed in 2019, was never properly released because of 'concerns about malicious applications of the technology'—the creators worried about what such a powerful system might do in the wrong hands. Yet GPT-3 was more powerful still: 175 billion parameters, for instance, rather than the 1.5bn of GPT-2. And it startled because it could perform tasks that most thought only human beings could take on—it could write stories, compose poems, devise screenplays, take part in flowing conversation. The standard was extraordinarily high: in the original research paper, for instance, human beings were found to be able to identify articles written by GPT-3 just 52 percent of the time—no better than random chance. Once the technology was released to a select group of developers, a flood of alternative commercial uses began to emerge.[64] Critics at the time argued the system was not really 'intelligent', that it did not really 'think' like a human being, it did not have a 'mind' and was not 'conscious'—and they were right. But they also missed the bigger point—this is a powerful example of what we call in this book an increasingly capable *non-thinking* machine. It may not function like us, but it can still outperform us. And in thinking about the future of work, as we argue in Chapter 7, these capabilities are far more important.

Note too that there continues to be no apparent finishing line in technological advance. Remarkable though the above developments might be, the pace of technological change is accelerating so that we remain of the view that our economic and social lives, and certainly our professional lives, will be transformed during this decade by techniques and technologies that have not yet been invented.

Bringing together our update on the professions' uptake of technology and on technological progress, we have four observations to make. The first is that, even though our systems and machines are continuing, relentlessly, to become increasingly capable, the pace of uptake of new technologies by the professions is notably less explosive. Second, most of the technologies that have been embraced so far by the professions have systematized past practices rather than fundamentally changed the way that professionals or their businesses operate. Third, most experts anticipate that the 20s will be the decade during which technological transformation in the professions will begin in earnest (albeit incrementally).

Finally, in our appraisal of the period from 2015 to 2020, we should add that our own thinking has developed and we have each published relevant books separately—*A World without Work* (by Daniel)[65] and *Online Courts and the Future of Justice* (by Richard).[66] These books build on the thinking of this book, the former in providing a more detailed economic analysis of the impact of technology on work and the latter in delving into one particular profession's adoption of technology.

Covid-19

Some technological developments during Covid-19 are noted above. But, more generally, what impact has the virus had on the work of the professions over the last year and more, and how will it shape the longer-term future of the landscape of professional work?

Early in the first lockdown in the United Kingdom, on 26 March 2020, we wrote a short note for those who follow our work, arguing that the professions would recover from Covid-19 in five phases, as shown in Figure 0.1.[67]

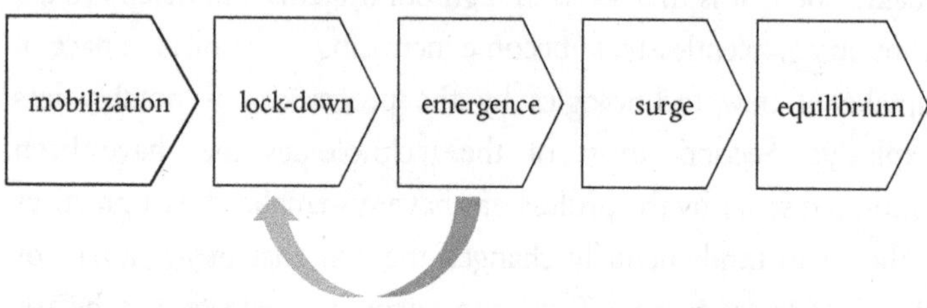

0.1. Five stages of recovery

We projected that most professional firms would progress through five stages in recovering from the crisis. We accepted that the time scales were unclear, of course, but we felt that the direction of travel could be mapped out tentatively.

The first stage we hypothesized was that of mobilization, involving the rapid move from office to remote working. Few were fully prepared for this—in terms of their operations, technology, and culture. For many, the focus at the time was on near-term survival. During this phase, we said that the finest firms would be those who cared for their people and helped their clients as well as themselves. Long-term relationships and reputations, we said, would be won and lost during mobilization. By and large, the shift to remote working went well across the professions. Most of the enabling technologies were already in place.

In our second stage, the great majority of professionals would be locked down, essentially working from home, physically disconnected as never before but using various technologies that enabled good and sometimes excellent online communication and collaboration. As firms re-orientated themselves as best they could in the time available, we expected that much would be lost. But at the same time, there would be new efficiencies and new operating practices established. In many markets, demand would fall significantly.

In most countries, from March 2020 and through that year, most professionals operated in these two stages. Generally, although there will be many exceptions, most firms with whom we have spoken say that, in terms of their financial performance, their figures have been considerably better than they had feared at the start of the crisis. Remarkably, many firms enjoyed growth in both turnover and profit during 2020. The impact on mental health of staff and the long-term strategic health of these firms is much less clear.

As we write, in the United Kingdom and many other countries, through a combination of vaccination and lockdowns, we are at our third stage of recovery, namely, emergence—when restrictions on movement are being planned or relaxed with a view to a return to offices and ordinary life. We said in March 2020 that the details of this would be the hardest to predict. On one view, an optimistic take, we said there might be a relatively swift move from lockdown to emergence. On another view, we noted that Covid-19 might start to spread again, leading to a reversion to lockdown. In the latter event, we expected repeated loops between lockdown and emergence. And so it has been. During the emergence phase, we predicted a novel schism in society—between those who have recovered and are at large and those whose lives are still heavily limited. This could mean, for a while at least, that two markets will need to be served (clients who have emerged and those who have not) and a divided workforce too. This schism is currently being hotly debated in policy and strategy discussions about domestic vaccination passports and return-to-office plans.

Our fourth and fifth stages are still ahead of us (looking at humanity generally). When the great majority of people have fully emerged, we believe there will be a surge in economic activity and in market confidence. This will be the fourth phase. Much lost ground will be regained in the economy, with deals and projects being conducted in compressed time frames. During this surge, industry and business will regenerate and flourish, and there will be great demand for professional services. Many unemployed or furloughed professionals will be re-engaged. Those who looked after their clients in the early phases will now find that loyalty rewarded.

In due course, after the initial surge, a new equilibrium will be established. But in this fifth phase, there will not be a reversion to professional life of late 2019. Many of the technologies and techniques that have been forged in the heat of mobilization and lockdown will be regarded as preferable to the traditional ways. Clients will have seen the great inefficiencies of conventional working practices, been exposed to a variety of impressive digital alternatives, and insist that some of these are maintained.

Even techno-sceptics in the professions are now saying they will never go back, that the virus has accelerated their uptake of technology. Doctors are routinely seeing patients by video, pupils are studying online, accountants are serving their clients without seeing them in person, and many court hearings are virtual—all to an extent that would have seemed absurd if proposed in early 2020. Certainly, in our original research when we canvassed these possibilities, they were invariably and roundly rejected by mainstream professionals. But does this pandemic-induced shift mean that these and other professions have irreversibly succumbed to technological advance?

The leap has surely been extraordinary but there is a danger here of over-claim for the short term. We should not mistake the ad hoc systems that have been cobbled together in haste—putting physicians, teachers, lawyers, and others on Zoom—with what will be needed to industrialize these early achievements. To put in place secure and sustainable systems at scale will require considerable further investment. To begin with, the move to robust, long-term remote working will require different organizational structures, new types of compliance with health and safety regulations, improved domestic connectivity, and of course extra equipment for the millions who may soon be operating largely at home. For some, of course, their environment at home may not be sufficiently adaptable. As a permanent set-up, remote working will not suit all.

It is noteworthy too that most of the recent analysis and discussion on probable post-Covid-19 working practice has been put forward by providers rather than clients, users, patients, and students. The market has scarcely expressed its view. For instance, it may seem likely that the recipients of professional services will prefer in the future to use videoconferencing than to meet face to-ace but this cannot be taken for granted, and preferences might change as the possibility of emergence returns.

At the same time, the winds of conservatism gust briskly through the professions. It may be out of fashion to take this position publicly, but our recent exchanges with a wide range of professionals suggests that some if not many are unobtrusively hankering after the working practices of 2019 and hunkering down until the hurricane passes.

We suggest that Covid-19 can be regarded as a massive unscheduled experiment, a great pilot in the deployment of a range of technologies that have kept many of our key services in action. Often, we have seen proofs of concept. But if this is indeed an experiment, we should be as exacting and methodical in assessing its outcomes as our medical experts have been in their search for vaccines and treatments. We should be gathering data about the impact of specific technologies and applications, the changes in different volumes, the views of managers, employees, and users, the impacts both positive and negative. So far, in the understandable commotion of keeping organizations afloat, the gathering of data about the impact of the technologies has been uneven at best.

Over the last few months, we have collected an inexhaustible supply of anecdotes but we still know comparatively little about what is actually working well and what is not in our remote offices, our virtual surgeries, our online schools and universities, and in our remote courts. If we succeed in capturing and analysing sufficient data about successes and failings, then we can then use these insights—rather than speculation or intuition—as the basis of reliable decisions about what should be maintained after the pandemic fades away and when we should go back to our time-honoured practices, if at all. In this way, our decisions with respect to fundamental change in professional services can be—in some instances for the first time—evidence-based.

More, as much as possible, we must make this data available and intelligible to our social entrepreneurs, who will then have the chance to flourish. And goodness knows, we need some new, creative thinking in the professions. Long before the virus, as we say in this book, our health, education, and justice systems were creaking—unaffordable, often antiquated, and invariably unintelligible to ordinary people. The status quo, how our professions currently operate, is not an option that we intentionally chose based on the available evidence. It is simply what we have inherited. It was unsatisfactory before we locked down and has not been equal to the crisis.

The virus has created the sense of urgency that is the necessary first step to transformation. It has opened many minds and changed some too. It has confirmed that best practice may well be the enemy of good practice and that we cannot always afford the alleged gold-standard—one-to-one, face-to-face service. Covid-19 has made us see that good enough is frequently good enough and invariably better than nothing at all.

Looking longer term, working from the kitchen table is not in fact a much-vaunted shift in paradigm in the delivery of professional services. Video meetings have not disrupted the conventional business models of firms. True, we have seen a rapid uptake of some technologies, but most of those that have been rushed into place have shored up our conventional ways of sharing knowledge through in-person engagement. In the terminology of Chapter 3, Covid-19 has accelerated *automation*. It has sped up the execution of plans that most firms already had in place—to increase remote working and use technology more to collaborate with clients. But this is not the fundamental transformation that is waiting in the wings, foreshadowed by some of the examples given earlier, which is when many of the activities of human professionals are themselves replaced by increasingly capable systems; and health, justice, education, and business guidance become more widely available and affordable across the world. For most professions, AI has been put on hold, while we have secured, as a matter of urgency, better ways of working with clients when unable to meet physically. Again in the language of Chapter 3, we have therefore seen a deceleration in *innovation* during the Covid-19 period. Understandably, firms have focused on survival and have reduced their R&D activity and pursuit of thoroughgoing transformations.

In the post-pandemic world, however, dominated by the inevitable need to deliver more for less, we expect the most prosperous firms to move beyond grafting technologies onto current operating practices. They will turn again to the development of systems that will replace rather than systematize their old ways of working. Which leads us to conclude that we do not expect Covid-19 to alter the long-term course for the professions that is laid out in this book. When the pandemic is behind us, professional work, once more, will be challenged by increasingly capable machines.

How will the professions respond to the return of this technological challenge? In light of the pandemic, the answer may well be 'much more energetically than in the past'. After all, the barriers to the use of technology in the professions are not simply technical (what is feasible?) or economic (will it be profitable?) but *cultural*—what tasks do professionals feel comfortable in ceding to technology? And one legacy of the pandemic, and the technological experimentation that has accompanied it, may be to weaken any bias towards the technological status quo, to soften the forces for technological conservatism, and to create a culture that is more receptive to the use of technology than in the past. Put differently, participation in the pandemic-induced pilot scheme will have desensitized many professionals to technological change; in years to come, they are likely to take in their stride all sorts of developments that they might once have regarded as radical.

We have one final observation that relates to Covid-19. Since we began working together on this book, almost a decade ago, health workers have insisted to us that medical treatment is irreducibly inter-personal, necessarily requiring face-to-face interaction. The virus casts a different light on this claim, or at least some additional light. In the worst health crisis of our lives, it is notable that those who have been fortunate not to suffer from Covid-19 have not in fact wanted doctors. They have not been looking for interpersonal counsel. Instead they have wanted vaccinations. Consistent with our model in chapter 5, that maps the evolution of professional service and points to the gradual commoditization of professional knowledge, the Covid-19 vaccines represent a remarkable exemplar of commoditization. They are the distillation of countless years of expert medical and scientific knowledge, *not* into a face-to-face consultative service, but into a liquid that is injected into a muscle. To be sure, we all want to have confidence in the developers and manufacturers—this equates with the 'quasi-trust' we discuss in Section 6.1. But the demand for vaccines highlights a bigger theme—our preference for prevention over cure, for a problem avoided altogether than a problem solved. Here we see a stark illustration of the shift noted in Chapter 3, from reactive to proactive service.

Recurrent Questions

Returning now to the prospect of systems that might replace professionals in certain activities, we have been confronted since the book was first published with a recurrent set of questions and concerns that are worth rehearsing here. What about privacy and security, and the dark side of the Web? What careers should our children pursue? Do we really think there will be no need for trusted human advisers? And how should governments respond?

Regarding privacy and criminal uses of the Web, we did expressly exclude these issues from the book. In future editions, this would be one of the most obvious gaps to fill. For now, we want to stress, first, that we consider these matters to be of great significance. Their lack of treatment here should not be seen as a dismissal of their impact. Secondly, it has become clear from our conversations that an important role is missing from our list of future roles—the digital security guard. This guard ensures that data privacy is protected, systems are defended from cyber-attack, data is cleansed of bias, and algorithms are subjected to audit. It is clear that many professional firms are blind to the dangers of failing to engage such a protector.

Perhaps our most agitated readers and listeners are parents who fear for the employability of their children. Our brief advice for students embarking upon their college studies is that they should embrace one of two possible career strategies, for now. The first is to look for jobs that are likely to favour human capabilities over artificial intelligence, jobs that depend less on having great swathes of technical knowledge than on having creativity and strong interpersonal skills, such as the ability to empathize. The second career strategy is to aim to be directly involved in the development and delivery of these increasingly capable systems, for example as a systems engineer, a data scientist, or a knowledge engineer (as discussed in Chapter 6 of this book).

In summary, students should plan either to compete with machines or to build the machines. In this context, we remain deeply concerned that our schools, colleges, universities, and professional institutions are continuing to generate twentieth-century professionals rather than graduates who are equipped for the new millennium. It is troubling that current educational systems around the world continue to focus on teaching our students to undertake many tasks for which machines are already better suited.

As for trusted advisers, do we honestly believe that their days are numbered? Surely, we are regularly invited to concede, human beings will always hanker after the reassurance that a warm and empathetic person can afford a fellow human being. We do not deny for a second that great comfort can be given from one person to another. Indeed, we identify the 'empathizer' as an important future role. However, our experience suggests that many of the recipients of professional service are in fact seeking a trustworthy solution (such as an effective vaccine) or particular outcome (immunity from a virus) rather than a trusted adviser *per se*. Looking ahead, when the standard of the output of, say, an online service is very high and its branding is unimpeachable, this will offer its own level of comfort and reassurance. In many circumstances, that will be sufficient for users and invariably more affordable than the warm adviser. Recipients of professional service, in summary, may be more focused on securing desired outcomes than on loyalty to traditional working methods. And practitioners should be careful not to conflate the traditional way of solving a particular problem with the problems themselves.

What about governments? How should they be responding to the claims of this book? Since our book came out, we have had various interactions with politicians, officials, advisers, and researchers. Once again, there is no unanimity of view. Those who have the time to take a long view tend to join us in recognizing that there are unprecedented issues at stake here, concerning, for instance, the ability of workers to adapt to the advent of increasingly capable machines, the possibility of deepening inequalities if these systems are concentrated in the hands of a few, and the moral limitations we might impose on the use of certain technologies. They share our conviction, as advocated in these pages, that we must explore such questions in public discussion. But, in general, we are not convinced that enough public decision-makers are engaged by the prospects of what might unfold in the long run. The electoral systems of most countries do not encourage politicians to think many years ahead—but we must.

Innovation in Professional Firms

As external advisers to the professions, our closest associations since the publication of the first edition of this book in 2015 have been with professional firms populated by lawyers, accountants, architects, and consultants rather than, for example, schools, hospitals, newspaper publishers, or places of worship. In the past few years, the term 'innovation' in these firms has dominated their conversations about strategy and marketing. It has become commonplace, for instance, for firms to point to their work on AI as evidence of their commitment to innovation. In truth, as we have travelled the world, the great majority of firms who claim to have taken innovation seriously are still what we call 'first-generation innovators' rather than 'second-generation innovators', the distinction between which is captured and analysed in more detail in Figure 0.2. In summary, although first-generation innovators talk of their projects with great fanfare, their focus very often turns out to be on efficiency gains. In contrast, the second generation is achieving radical change.

Looking at each element in turn, on careful scrutiny, the innovation work of most professional firms, first of all, is much more about improving current working processes and practices than introducing genuinely novel business models. First-generation innovators concentrate on optimizing the traditional one-to-one consultative advisory model of professional service, whereas second-generation innovators are in search of credible, promising alternatives to the sale of the time of expert humans.

The reality of first-generation innovation is often concealed by the marketing noise that emanates from professional firms that

First generation	Second generation
• process improvements	• new business models
• marketing noise	• substantive progress
• automation	• innovation
• pilots	• fully operational systems
• little impact on figures	• significant revenue and profit
• argument-based	• evidence-based
• minority of partners involved	• majority of partners involved
• intellectual grasp	• emotional commitment
• avoiding competitive disadvantage	• seeking competitive advantage
• short-term, tactical	• long-term, strategic

0.2. First- and second-generation innovation

have decided to hold themselves out as pioneers and disruptors. Amongst these innovation tyros, we commonly find innovation-by-press-release as well as overstatements in conference presentations and in pitches to clients. The second generation proclaim less and deliver more. They prefer substantive, demonstrable progress. They value reality over perception. The first generation claim they are funny, while the second tell jokes.

As for technology, first-generation firms embrace automation—the systematization or computerization of conventional ways of working. They layer technology onto today's processes, whereas second-generation professional businesses use technology genuinely to innovate, to enable them to undertake tasks and deliver products and services that were not possible without technology. More, the first generation tend to deliver pilots, prototypes, samplers, and demonstrators, while the second generation ship fully operational systems. There is a world of difference between a proof of concept and a technological solution that is put to serious daily service.

This difference between a pilot and a finished product is clearly visible in their relative financial performance. First-generation innovators in professional firms, with their prototypes and marketing puff, tend to have little impact on the figures. In contrast, one of the hallmarks of the more mature, second generation is that their innovations yield significant turnover and profit, a return on investment that extends beyond reputational impact to measurable improvements that can be seen clearly in their financial statements.

The second generation usually has an advantage over the first by having concrete evidence of the tangible benefits that their innovations have yielded. They can point to initiatives that have flourished. Success begets further success and provides practical, home-grown case studies. In absence of concrete evidence, the first generation rely on argument, such as theories about disruption and allegations about melting icebergs. These often fail to impress hard-nosed professionals. This is why in first-generation firms, there tends to be only a few partners who are convinced of the worth of innovation—these are the enthusiasts, believers, and evangelists for whom the theory and argument are sufficient. In second-generation firms, where there is an abundance of evidence of the business benefits of innovating, most partners are engaged and supportive. It is not that partners in first-generation firms do not understand the arguments in favour of innovation and technological transformation. They have heard the arguments and, intellectually, they grasp what is afoot. But they do not feel it in their hearts. They are not emotionally committed. In contrast, second-generation partners live and breathe its promise and potency.

Strategically, first-generation firms are more concerned about not being left behind than stealing a march on their competitors. They are engaged in defensive innovation—preoccupied with avoiding competitive disadvantage. Second-generation firms look at the opportunity of innovation rather than the threats it poses. They innovate proactively, in pursuit of sustainable competitive advantage. These strategic positions are polar opposites, and clients can detect the difference more readily than professional firms suspect.

Finally, and in many ways in summary, first-generation innovators are short-term thinkers, tactical players who are preoccupied with early wins and the appearance of change. In contrast, the second generation, and there are much fewer of them, are taking a long view, integrating fundamental change into all aspects of their strategic planning, while recognizing that they are still at the foothills.

In truth, then, progress with innovation in most professional firms is less impressive than might be thought at first glance. In our experience, the same is true of 'transformation' in firms. The majority that we encounter have some kind of transformation programme on the go. However, most transformation projects, like innovation initiatives, end up as efficiency projects—everyone starts off with lofty ambitions of bringing radical change, but in the end they default to streamlining and improving what is already in place.

It is much easier to talk about transformation than to come up with transformational ideas and then put them into service. Most professionals find it much simpler and more comfortable to move forward from the current state than to envisage entirely different end states and think backwards from what might feel like a remote and distant scenario.

More than this, genuine transformation is disruptive if not destructive of current business practices and business models. It is far from clear, as noted earlier, whether successful firms are able to self-disrupt; they will certainly steer clear of self-destruction. So far, we have not yet found any substantial professional firm that has comprehensively transformed and so self-destructed. Learning from other industries sectors, it is easier to imagine disruption coming from new players such as up-start start-ups in professional markets than at the instigation of the incumbents.

A Framework for Thinking about Innovation

In counselling professional firms in their move from first to second generation, we have recently been using an improved version of a tool that we developed together in 2010.[68] It has been especially useful with action-oriented leaders who may well have the resolve to effect change but lack a clear framework within which to plan and act. Our purpose in the remainder of this preface is to introduce the tool and to show how it can help leaders to analyse and categorize the markets in which they work.

As with all the tools and techniques that appear later in this book, we advance them along with some cautionary words. Our framework is not intended to be a sufficiently detailed model of reality that would satisfy the purist or the scholar. Rather, it is a simplification of the complex world of professional service. It is a modest technique to help professionals understand and plan.

We propose that one way of understanding the tensions and challenges of the professional marketplace is through the grid presented in Figure 0.3. The broad aim here is to be able to plot professional work onto this grid and so to improve understanding of different business models, working methods, and pricing mechanisms. The term 'professional work' is used widely here and can include: general categories of professional work; particular engagements; the services of practice areas within firms; and individual tasks that constitute client projects.

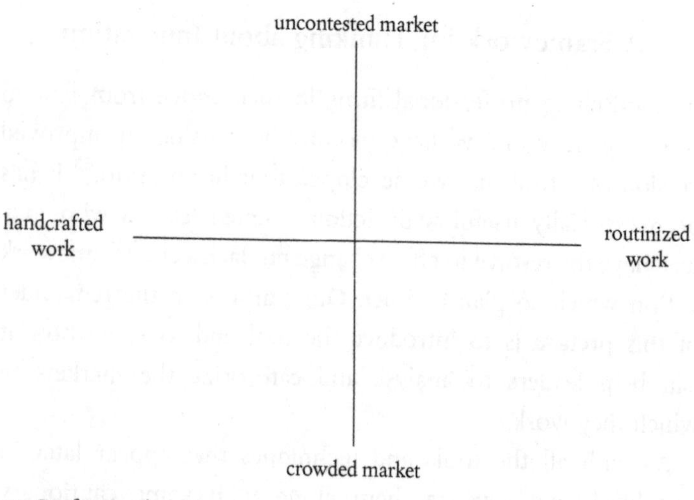

0.3. Professional market

Two dimensions of the professional market are reflected on the grid: on the one hand, on the vertical axis, there is a spectrum between 'uncontested market' at the north end and 'crowded market' in the south. When a market is uncontested, there is no or little competition; when it is crowded there are many alternative suppliers in play. On the horizontal axis, consistent with discussion in Chapters 3 and 5, is the continuum between 'handcrafted' work and work that has been 'routinized'. Handcrafted work is handled in a bespoke fashion. In contrast, when work has been routinized, professional practice and substantive knowledge have been standardized (essentially, an advanced form of knowledge management), systematized (most notably, using AI techniques), or externalized (made available online). (Standardization, systematization, externalized are central concepts of the book and discussed in more detail in Chapter 5.)

Categories of professional work can be plotted onto the four quadrants of the grid that are created by the intersection of its axes. As a starting point, it is helpful to look at the grid from the supply side of the market, that is, from the perspective of firms providing services to their clients. From this point of view, at the top of the grid, where there is little competition, there are, accordingly, very few firms that can undertake work that might be plotted here. In contrast, at the bottom of the grid, where the market is crowded, many firms are able to deliver the service in question. Where the work is located towards the left-hand side of the diagram, it is often considered to be complex. This work will tend to be handled in the traditional handcrafted, consultative, advisory manner; whereas, towards the right-hand side, the work can be routinized—by standardization, systematization, and externalization.

Most commercially ambitious professional firms of today will still prefer to secure work that is positioned in the top-left of the grid (marked 'x' on Figure 0.4). These firms will want to say to their clients for any given engagement, first, that the work required is complex and so must indeed be handcrafted (and so it sits to the left side) and, second, that they are one of a very few firms that are capable of taking it on (and so it is positioned towards the top of the grid). In contrast, most clients will hope or want to argue that any given piece of work can be positioned in the bottom-right quadrant of the grid (marked 'xx' on Figure 0.4) because here there are many firms that can undertake the work and that surely the work is truly of a routine nature. Generally, the work in this quadrant can be undertaken quickly and at low cost (because it can be routinized and there is a plentiful supply of providers), whereas, in the top-left, the work will more likely take longer and cost clients more (because it is complex and there are far fewer suppliers).

Figure 0.4 captures the fundamental tension between professional firms and clients of today, indicating that the preferred coordinates for each are diametrically opposed. More, this figure depicts the pervasive pull of the marketplace—clients, wherever possible, in these difficult economic times, are encouraging or requiring not only that work be standardized, systematized, or externalized wherever possible but also that many firms, and not just a few, should build the capability to undertake the work.

Broad characterizations of the types of providers in the market can be appended as labels to each quadrant of the grid, as is

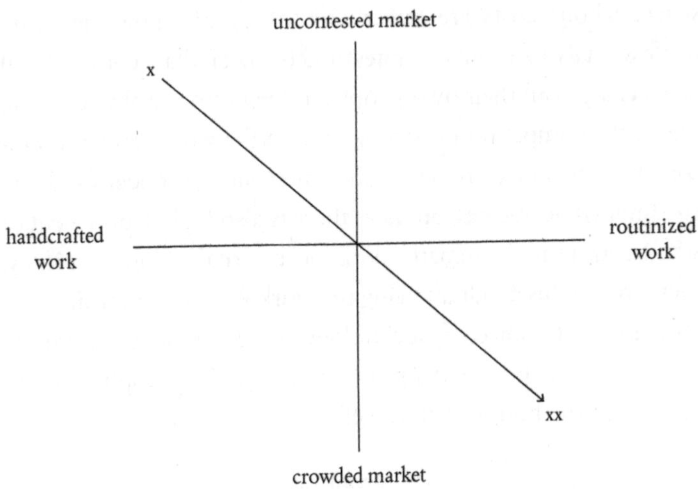

0.4. Firms and clients

shown in Figure 0.5. In the top-left, where the work is complex and the competition is weak, we will tend to find the conventional firm, delivering advisory service in the time-honoured, one-to-one, consultative manner. Moving down to the bottom-left quadrant, where the competition becomes stiffer, and yet the work is still being handled in a relatively bespoke manner because of its apparent complexity, this service remains advisory in nature but the business that delivers it needs to become more streamlined and tightly managed. As competition intensifies, the prices fall, and so profitability is prejudiced unless the cost (to the provider) of delivering the service is reduced. In this quadrant, we are increasingly finding work being off-shored to firms' lower-cost locations; or even sub-contracted to lower-cost providers (usually where labour costs are lower); or to organizations that lease professionals to clients at rates much lower than conventional firms charge out their own people. In the bottom-right quadrant, where the competition is strong and yet the work can be routinized, here again we are seeing the emergence of modernized and streamlined businesses, but here there is also high deployment of standardization, systematization, or externalization. Typically, then, we see this quadrant being the workplace of paraprofessionals who are supported by technology and the presence of process outsourcers, although many of these also have aspirations to move into the bottom-left as well.

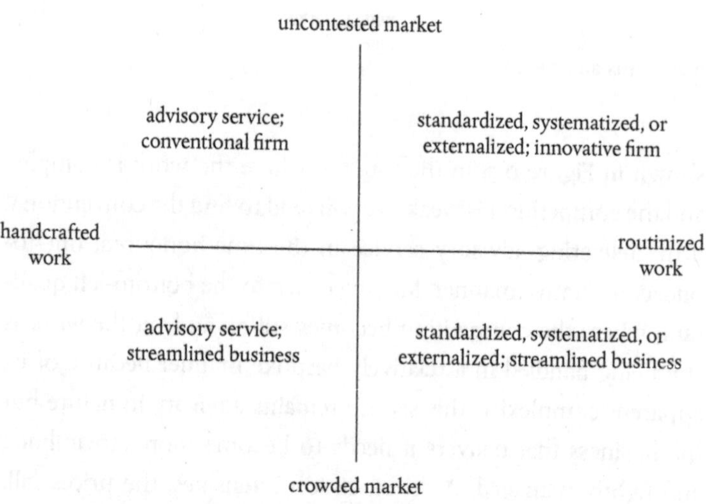

0.5. Professional providers

Finally, in the top-right, where there are few competitors, and yet the work can be routinized, there will be innovative firms that have chosen to standardize, systematize, and externalize. While their competitors still treat this work as complex and so in need of handcrafting, these innovators create new approaches that render complex activity into (largely) routine process. Many years ago, as detailed in Chapter 2, we saw an early example of this move from top-left to top-right in the evolution of the tax compliance work of Deloitte in the United Kingdom. Complex tax work that once required handcrafting was in this case systematized and externalized and here Deloitte emerged as a market leader, with little competition in delivering compliance services to clients at relatively low cost.[69]

In the broadest of terms, we have found that most first-generation innovators are operating in the bottom-left quadrant, focusing on efficiency gains, whereas the second generation occupy the top right. The latter are the disruptive innovators who are committed to radical change; indeed to the introduction of new business models. These disrupters boldly take work that mainstream professionals insist on handcrafting and they routinize that work. Again, they do so either by standardizing, systematizing, or externalizing. Their message to the market is clear—we have the experience or the technology that allows us to undertake work that the rest of our profession is handling as though we were still in the twentieth century. More, if they get their pricing right, they can deliver their products and solutions (rather than advisory service) more profitably for them and at substantial savings. The business model is entirely new—the shift toward products and solutions enables the providers to make money while they sleep rather than charge for the time of their staff.

We sometimes speak of professional firms being bold. But in relation to individual professionals, it is worth noting in passing that one of the characteristics of the very best is that they have the confidence to simplify. We have found this in great practitioners and in thought leaders—many if not most of the world's leading specialists are able to explain their disciplines and issues arising within their disciplines in lucid, straightforward ordinary language. Having the self-assurance to communicate clearly in simple terms and concepts may indeed be the hallmark of truly great experts. It is also the hallmark of providers in the top-right of our grid.

Figure 0.6 plots the path of followers in the professional services sector. These are firms that cling onto the bespoke handcrafted ways of working, even when the competition intensifies. On the first part of this trajectory to the bottom-left, work that was once highly profitable becomes service that many firms can deliver. Worse, in the second sweep, as the competition intensifies, it is clear that to have any chance of securing work, firms must standardize, systematize, or externalize and so move from the bottom-left to the bottom-right.

In contrast, Figure 0.6 also indicates the pattern of leaders amongst firms. These are professionals who drive their services from the top-left to the top-right quadrant, as Deloitte did with their tax compliance work. Similarly, more than twenty years ago, when major City law firms in London automated the production of Eurobond documentation, they made precisely this shift. They recognized, through systemization, that they could leap ahead of their competitors. In consequence, they disrupted their market and only a few competitors were able to follow suit. This

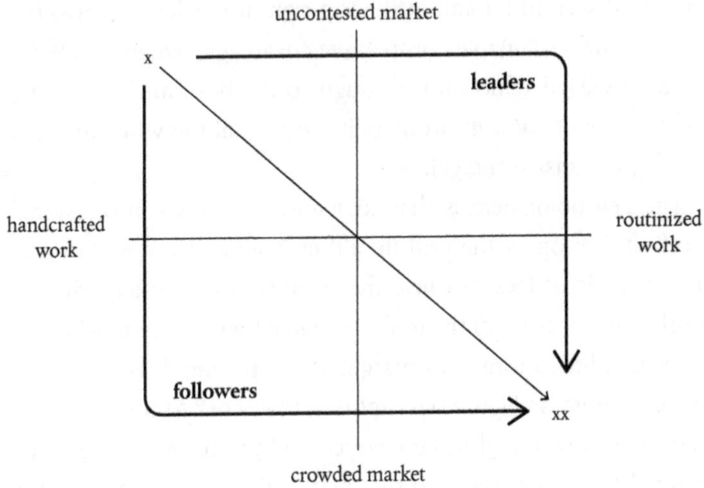

0.6. Followers and leaders

transition from left to right was another early example of second-generation innovation—the leaders remained in a small elite group of firms that were capable of undertaking big-ticket work in the new way. The result was lower fees for clients and more profitable work for the providing firms—fewer hours of effort were required and, although the overall level of fees was reduced, the relative profitability increased.

However, as is the way in competitive markets, in due course, other players will recognize that they too will need to standardize, systematize, and externalize and so, when many firms come to work in the new way, the pioneers begin the descent from the top-right of the quadrant into the bottom-right.

The differences between leaders and followers, on this model, is that leaders enjoy a period of greater profitability and market share and seek to remain in the top-right for as long as possible (by creating sustainable competitive advantage), whereas followers are dragged reluctantly through to the bottom-right having suffered a reduction in profitability (trying all the while to resist competitive disadvantage).

The key point here is that, as Figure 0.7 shows, professional work at the top of the grid (in either quadrant) can attract premium levels of fees (because the competition is weak) whereas work at the bottom of the grid, again in either quadrant, will tend to sustain little more than marginal cost pricing. It is also interesting to note, as Figure 0.6 captures, that work to the left of the vertical axis will tend to be charged and priced on a time-based billing basis, where work to the right of this axis will more often be based on some kind of fixed fee.

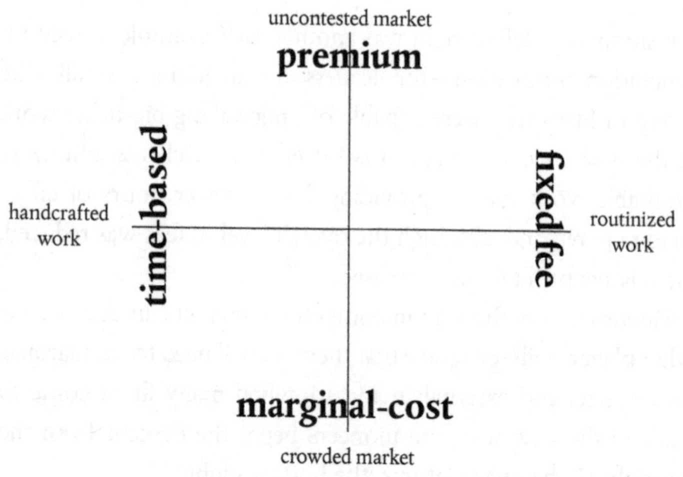

0.7. Pricing

In practice, however, the picture is more complicated than we have so far suggested. Following our arguments in Chapter 3, professional work should not be considered to be indivisible or monolithic packages of work, the entirety of which must be undertaken and charged in one way only. Instead, professional activity can be decomposed, that is, broken down into its constituent tasks, and, as we argue, the market will increasingly require that each task is undertaken in the most efficient way possible (consistent with the level of quality of service that is required).

With this approach in mind, it transpires that one useful and practical way of plotting particular professional engagements onto the grid involves decomposing the work into its constituent tasks and allocating each task to its rightful place on the gird, as illustrated in Figure 0.8. This particular depiction assumes that there are five main tasks involved in the project in question but it can quickly be seen that these are spread across the grid. The implications of this are immediately obvious—consistent with Figure 0.5, the work involved here is likely to be undertaken most efficiently when taken on by several different types of provider working in collaboration; and, doing so, following Figure 0.7, under different charging methods. For example, Task 1, in the top-left, is therefore most appropriately undertaken by a conventional firm, charging by the hour, and at premium rates, while Task 5, in the bottom-right, is better suited perhaps to a process outsourcer on a fixed fee and almost marginal cost basis (noting that the marginal costs for these providers are much lower than those for traditional firms).

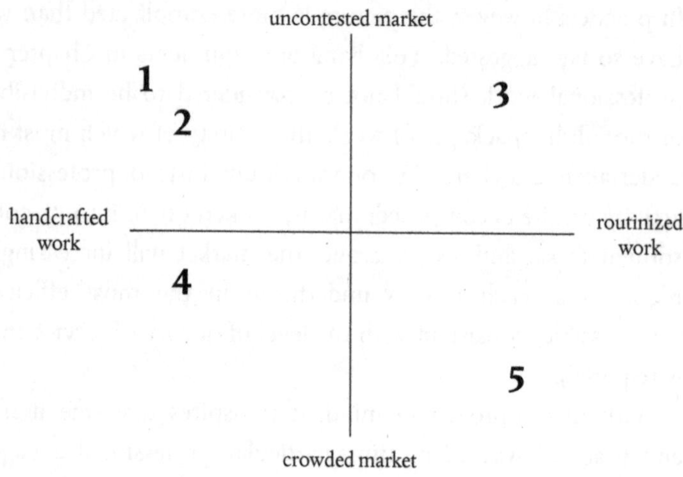

0.8. Tasks

We accept that, in the past, many professional firms sought themselves to carry out all the tasks involved in a particular engagement. In the new world, however, it is likely that no single provider will be able to deliver services across the grid at sufficiently competitive prices.

A final thought

In late 2017, we were invited to address a congress of two thousand neurosurgeons. We were asked to answer the question, 'What is the future of neurosurgery?' and we were also asked to be controversial, to stir things up. Accordingly, we opened by claiming that 'patients do not want neurosurgeons'. There was an audible gasp in the auditorium. We went on to say that 'what patients want is health'. For a particular type of health problem, we acknowledged that neurosurgeons are undoubtedly the best solution we have today. But we went on to predict that this might not always be so, because by, say, 2050, people will probably look back and think it remarkable, indeed primitive, that we used to cut heads and bodies open. We wanted to challenge those present who felt that the future lay only in much-improved or robotic neurosurgery because surgery will surely not be with us in the long run—the health troubles to which neurosurgeons currently devote their energies will in due course be overcome by non-invasive techniques and avoided in the first place by preventative methods.

On reflection, we were being invited to respond to the wrong question. Instead we should have been asked, 'How in the future will we solve the problems to which neurosurgeons are currently our best answer?' To ask, 'What is the future of surgeons?' or indeed, 'What is the future of X?', where X is a professional worker, is to assume X has a future. We do not say this facetiously. Rather, we are challenging what is essentially a leading question. Framed as 'What is the future of X?', this requires 'X' to be central to the answer, which clearly limits the range of possible responses.

A running and related theme of this book is that we do not believe that the most important questions about the future are about, say, the future of doctors, lawyers, or teachers. Instead, our preoccupation is with health, justice, and learning—and how technology can radically promote better access to each.

Richard Susskind
Daniel Susskind
5 November 2021

Introduction

This book is about the professions and the systems and people that will replace them. Our focus is on doctors, lawyers, teachers, accountants, tax advisers, management consultants, architects, journalists, and the clergy (amongst others), on the organizations in which they work, and the institutions that govern their conduct. Our main claim is that we are on the brink of a period of fundamental and irreversible change in the way that the expertise of these specialists is made available in society. Technology will be the main driver of this change. And, in the long run, we will neither need nor want professionals to work in the way that they did in the twentieth century and before.

There is growing evidence that a transformation is already under way. More people signed up for Harvard's online courses in a single year, for example, than have attended the actual university in its 377 years of existence. In the same spirit, there are a greater number of unique visits each month to the WebMD network, a collection of health websites, than to all the doctors working in the United States. In the legal world, three times as many disagreements each year amongst eBay traders are resolved using 'online dispute resolution' than there are lawsuits filed in the entire US court system. On its sixth birthday, the *Huffington Post* had more unique monthly visitors than the website of the *New York Times,* which is almost 164 years of age. The British tax authorities use a fraud-detection system that holds more data than the British Library (which has copies of every book ever published in the UK). In 2014 the US tax authorities received electronic tax returns from almost 48 million people who had used online tax preparation software rather than a tax professional to help them. At Wiki-House, an online community designed a house that could be 'printed' and assembled for less than £50,000 (built successfully in London during September 2014). The architectural firm Gramazio & Kohler used a group of autonomous flying robots to assemble a structure out of 1,500 bricks. The consulting firm Accenture has 750 hospital nurses on its staff, while Deloitte, founded as an audit practice 170 years ago, now has over 200,000 professionals and its own full-scale university set in a 700,000 square-foot campus in Texas. Meanwhile, the Pope has 19.3 million followers on Twitter; the Dalai Lama has a modest 10.4 million.[1]

Our broad argument

We believe that these developments are connected. They are early indicators of a transformation that we have been studying together since 2010, when we started work on this book. At that time, our main preoccupation was with the work of our current professions. However, as our research and thinking progressed, we concluded that a more basic and important question also had to be addressed—*how do we share expertise in society?* In what we term a 'print-based industrial society', the professions have played a central role in the sharing of expertise. They have been the main channel through which individuals and organizations have gained access to certain kinds of knowledge and experience. However, in a 'technology-based Internet society', we predict that increasingly capable machines, operating on their own or with non-specialist users, will take on many of the tasks that have been the historic preserve of the professions. We anticipate an 'incremental transformation' in the way that we produce and distribute expertise in society. This will lead eventually to a dismantling of the traditional professions.

For the current recipients and beneficiaries of the work of the professions, we bring the possibility of good tidings—of a world in which expertise is more accessible and affordable than ever before. For professional providers, although our thesis may seem threatening, we anticipate that a range of new opportunities will emerge. These are our hopes. But we also recognize that the new systems for sharing expertise could be misused, and we are troubled by this possibility. In any event, increasingly capable systems[2] will bring transformations to professional work that will resemble the impact of industrialization on traditional craftsmanship.

To sceptics, who may already be tempted to put the book to one side, consider this: in the mid-1990s, when we predicted (in retrospect, rather unambitiously) that electronic mail would become the dominant way in which clients and lawyers would communicate, senior officials at the Law Society of England and Wales said that we should not be allowed to speak in public, that we failed to understand confidentiality, and that we were bringing the legal profession into disrepute. We recall this anecdote now in order to invite those who feel an intuitive distaste for our arguments to suspend disbelief for a short while and give serious contemplation to the notion that the future may look nothing at all like the past. Although some of the developments we anticipate in this book may seem outlandish today, none is more improbable than the idea of e-mail between lawyers and clients seemed in the mid-1990s.

Professionals play such a central role in our lives that we can barely imagine different ways of tackling the problems that they sort out for us. But the professions are not immutable. They are an artefact that we have built to meet a particular set of needs in a print-based industrial society. As we progress into a technology-based Internet society, however, we claim that the professions in their current form will no longer be the best answer to those needs. To pick out a few of their shortcomings—we cannot afford them, they are often antiquated, the expertise of the best is enjoyed only by a few, and their workings are not transparent. For these and other reasons, we believe today's professions should and will be displaced by feasible alternatives.

The professions as one object of study

Why study the professions as one phenomenon? Although they draw on different bodies of knowledge, their jargon varies, and their working practices can be quite diverse, we suggest that the professions have many features in common. Chief amongst these is that all professions, in analogous ways, are a solution to the same problem—that none of us has sufficient specialist knowledge to cope with all of our daily challenges. Human beings have limited understanding, and so we look to doctors, teachers, lawyers, and other professionals because they have expertise that we need to make progress in life. Professionals have knowledge, experience, skills, and know-how that those they help do not.

There are also practical reasons for considering a collection of professions together in one sweep. First of all, we believe that professions have much to learn from one another. Many have become increasingly introspective, driven into greater specialization, so that practitioners within a given profession often have a limited view of the work and achievements of their own colleagues, still less of the activities and progress in other disciplines. Our discussions with a wide range of professionals suggest that they find it enlightening and exciting to learn of advances in other fields, even if they are not immediate neighbours. They can draw analogies from the work of others and carry lessons learned into their own areas. More than this, professionals frequently see the potential and need for fundamental change in others more clearly than in themselves. Very often, after we give talks on our ideas, we are approached by individuals who argue that what we say applies right across the professions except in one field—their own. Lawyers, for example, tend to be quick to argue for a shake-up in our health and education services, but find it less apparent that legal services would benefit from major overhaul. In tackling a range of professions, our intention is to encourage practitioners from many fields to think more widely and strategically, and to be tolerant of the possibility of change in their own disciplines—a view of widened horizons elsewhere should broaden their perspective at home.

The structure of the book

Although our book is fairly ambitious in scope, there are many important issues that we have placed beyond its remit. We do not, for example, address questions of privacy, confidentiality, security, and liability. Nor do we consider the dark side of the Internet and the many nefarious uses to which, regrettably, our systems are being put. We regard these as vital issues that we hope others can pursue in the context of the professions.

We should also stress that our case studies and experience are largely Anglo-American, and to that extent our theories and predictions may be limited in their reach. That said, informal discussions and client work in India, China, and Australia suggest that our thinking about the future could be applied in most countries with little adaptation.

The book is organized in three main parts. In the first, we explore *change* in the professions. In Chapter 1 we consider the place of professionals in society, the problems with the current set-up, and a variety of theories of the professions. Then we call for a new mindset. Drawing on our own research, in Chapter 2 we bring evidence from the frontiers of striking changes that are already observable across a wide range of professions. In Chapter 3 we capture these changes alongside our experiences from consulting and policy work as a set of patterns and trends across the professions.

In the second part of the book our focus is on *theory*. In systematic and general terms, we try to make sense of the shifts we are seeing and anticipating. In Chapter 4 we show that shifts in the way we store and communicate information have a direct impact on how we share expertise in society, and we anticipate four sets of remarkable developments in technology. We analyse knowledge in economic terms in Chapter 5, which leads us to show how professional work is evolving and to propose six new models for the production and distribution of expertise.

Finally, in the third part, we discuss the *implications* of our research and theoretical work. In Chapter 6 we lay out and respond to a wide range of objections to the future we anticipate. And, in Chapter 7, we address several major topics—the potential and limitations of increasingly capable machines, the impact of technology on employment, and whether emerging models of sharing expertise are in fact feasible. We conclude by asking and answering the question—what future should we want?

PART I

Change

1

The Grand Bargain

There are two possible futures for the professions. The first is reassuringly familiar. It is a more efficient version of what we already have today. On this model, professionals continue working much as they have done since the middle of the nineteenth century, but they heavily standardize and systematize their routine activities. They streamline their old ways of working. The second future is a very different proposition. It involves a transformation in the way that the expertise of professionals is made available in society. The introduction of a wide range of increasingly capable systems will, in various ways, displace much of the work of traditional professionals. In the short and medium terms, these two futures will be realized in parallel. In the long run, the second future will dominate, we will find new and better ways to share expertise in society, and our professions will steadily be dismantled. That is the conclusion to which this book leads.

The first step in our argument involves taking stock of the professions we currently have. We do this, in this opening chapter, to provide a foundation of solid thinking about the professions—about their purpose and common features, their strengths and weaknesses—upon which we build later. We start by sketching an informal portrait of today's professions. We follow this with a more systematic attempt to explain which occupational groups belong to the professions and why. We then discuss the history of the professions and look at the 'grand bargain', the traditional arrangement that grants professionals both their special status and their monopolies over numerous areas of human activity. Next, we reflect on various theoretical accounts of the professions, which leads us to identify a series of fundamental problems with our professions as currently organized. We close with a call for a new mindset, and point to a series of biases that are likely to inhibit professionals from thinking freely about their future.

1.1. Everyday conceptions

To set off at an easy pace, we begin with a set of non-theoretical, everyday views about the professions. On reflection, most people would say that the professions are at the heart of our social and working lives. Their practitioners save our lives and keep us in good health, they educate our children, counsel and enlighten us spiritually, advise us on our legal entitlements, manage our money, assist us in running our businesses, help us complete our tax returns, design our homes, and much more. When we are in need of expert guidance on issues that matter to us, we turn naturally to the professions and draw on their members' knowledge and experience.

The professions are of great economic significance. Some are vast. In the United States, for example, almost $3 trillion was spent on healthcare in 2013.[1] This is more than the GDP of all but three other countries in the world. The professions provide employment for hundreds of millions of people. In the United Kingdom, for instance, healthcare and education each employ more people than any other sector, apart from retail.[2] Some professional firms are giants. The 'Big 4' accountancy firms have combined annual global revenue of more than $120 billion. This means that these four businesses alone have a turnover greater than the GDP of the sixtieth-richest country in the world. Certain professions are more important in some countries than others. The legal services market in the United Kingdom, for example, is the largest in Europe, and is responsible for over one-quarter of the total value of the European market.[3]

Beyond their social and economic significance, being a professional, for many practitioners, is seen to be a labour of love and not simply labour for a wage. It is considerably more than holding down a job. Many of the most fulfilled professionals refer to their daily activities as a calling or vocation: not so much a job as a way of life. For the country vet, the village teacher, the local doctor, and the rural lawyer, to pick a few parochial illustrations, the overriding aim and ethos is commonly thought to be that of helping fellow citizens. This work is often accompanied by a steady income, even if most professionals have not, traditionally, been the most highly remunerated in society. The professions promise job security and steady career progression. This stability has contributed to the sense of solidity that continues to encourage recipients of professional help to feel they have placed themselves and their problems in the safest of hands.

We want to trust professionals, to see them as upright people whose motives often seem noble, and for them to be the embodiments of honesty, probity, and integrity. We expect that they will act in good faith, and put the interests of those they help ahead of their own. We recognize there are exceptions, of course, so that some professionals are felons rather than paragons, but, by and large, we imagine that the professions are populated by people of good standing.

Our reliance on the professions and the respect that we afford them leads, no doubt, to the considerable status and prestige that their practitioners frequently enjoy. Parents are typically proud of their children when they enter or belong to the professions. This is well illustrated by the joke about the elderly Jewish mother at the seaside with her grown-up son who is struggling in the water; she seeks help by shouting: 'My son, the doctor, is drowning!'

The status and respect seem to incline many non-professional workers to want to be reclassified as belonging to the professions. This is a sentiment that offends many in mainstream professions who enjoy their exclusivity. There can therefore be some snobbery here too, notably amongst higher-handed professionals who expect deference from those they help. There is a more general issue of class here—members of the professions disproportionately belong to the same socio-economic groups and share similar educational backgrounds. In the United Kingdom, for example, 75 per cent of senior judges and 43 per cent of barristers went to independent or fee-paying schools (which educate only 7 per cent of schoolchildren).[4] Almost half of newspaper columnists went to Oxford or Cambridge.[5] In 2011, among undergraduates accepted for medical school, 57 per cent were from the highest three socio-economic groups, and 7 per cent were from the lowest three.[6] In a sense, the professions are like a club, admittance to which is permitted only to a select few. Within the club, however, it seems there are various tiers of membership. Surgeons, for example, appear to be part of an elite within the community, while, say, chartered surveyors, if they will forgive us for saying so, are skilled professionals but do not enjoy the same status.

Even those whose occupation cannot formally be said to be one of the professions may nonetheless want to belong to the professions by claiming, for example, that their work is 'professionally' conducted or that their service is 'professionally' delivered. Many people in manual trades, such as plumbing and carpentry, will advertise and assure a 'professional' job done, conveying thereby a sense of proficiency and reliability.

At one time, and especially in the world of sport, the great significance of being professional lay in its stark contrast with that of amateurism. Professionals were paid for their services, but amateurs were not. In some sports, in a different era with a different mindset, it was the amateur who was regarded as an altogether superior specimen. Thus, in the Oscar-winning movie *Chariots of Fire*, when the soon-to-be Olympic gold-medallist Harold Abrahams is being accused by the Master of Trinity College, Cambridge, of having 'adopted a professional attitude' in his training as a sprinter, he responds, 'Perhaps you would rather I played the gentleman and lost?' To this, the Master replies, 'To playing the tradesman, yes.'[7] In that world, for a gentleman (and invariably the inhabitants were male) to submit to professionalism was somehow to concede defeat, to exhibit an insufficiency of the talent required to prevail while holding down a day job. And so Bobby Jones, one of the finest golfers of all time, and of the same vintage as Abrahams, strongly resisted turning professional and yet managed to win the world's major tournaments, both of amateurs and professionals. Notably, when he retired from competition, aged 28, he became a professional of a different kind—a lawyer.

Over time, with the fact of remuneration came an assumption and a reality of superior performance. Professionals, after all, could devote all their waking hours to their sport, while amateurs, even if they had indulgent employers, squeezed their training and practice into their daily working schedules. So too with our professions: now, in critical times, we do not wish to rely on hobbyists or dilettantes. The common conception of the professions has changed radically.

That said, the professions are not free from criticism from the recipients of their work. They are commonly charged with being elitist, they are frequently regarded as unaffordable, and cynics cite their use of jargon as one of many illustrations of how they mystify and ring-fence their disciplines, so that only professionals are able to serve.

This, then, is the everyday conception of the professions. They weave their way—pervasively, invaluably, indispensably—through society, even if they are sometimes regarded with scepticism. And we see these stereotypes reinforced in our literature, art, cinema, theatre, in our media, and in everyday conversation. On this view, the main challenge facing the professions, it is commonly thought, is to streamline, polish, and modernize an institution that is in place for the duration.

Our position is different. We contend that the professions are on the brink of transformation. As currently constituted, they face problems that they seem unable to solve. Before we identify these problems (section 1.7) and unpack the evidence of change (in Chapter 2), some deeper analysis is required—to help us grasp, more formally, the chief characteristics of the professions, how they came to be, and why they enjoy a privileged arrangement in society.

1.2. The scope of the professions

How do we identify professionals and empower them? In the previous section we outline everyday conceptions of the professions and professionalism. But what do experts on the professions think? Over the past eighty years or so, a formidable academic literature on the professions has built up. Alongside practitioners from within the professions, great armies of theorists have become fascinated with the subject—sociologists, economists, historians, philosophers, psychologists, and many more. Given that one of our main claims is that the days of the traditional professions are numbered, we should be very clear about the nature of the people and institutions that are in our crosshairs.

The first fact to note is that the experts who have written on the subject disagree amongst themselves over what a profession is. While no one can sensibly question that doctors, lawyers, and accountants belong to the professions, there can be heated discussion, for example, over whether, say, journalists merit the same honorific. In the course of our research, we interviewed several of the world's most senior management consultants, and they shared the view that management consulting is not a profession, largely because anyone can set up a business and trade as a consultant (we return shortly to this underlying question of exclusivity). Similarly, an eminent professor from one of the world's most prestigious universities said that he did not consider that he or his academic colleagues belonged to a profession, even though the professoriate was one of the first recognizable professional groupings.

In 2009, in a report for the British government, it was said that there were more than '130 different professional sectors' in the United Kingdom.[8] In the course of our research, when we mentioned this statistic it was often met with deep concern, not least by members of the longer-established professions. Can it really be, for example, as that document maintained, that 'local government' is a profession? And if not, why not? This, as hinted earlier, is the problem of scope—it is not at all clear where the boundaries of the professions lie, nor in accordance with what criteria they can be delimited. So long as they are safely in the professional camp, these sceptics of a liberal interpretation of 'professions' may well feel inclined to draw the limits quite tightly.

There is clearly a definitional or conceptual problem here. According to Eliot Freidson, an eminent sociologist writing in 1986, effort expended in defining the professions 'has plagued the field for over half a century'.[9] Nor does any consensus seem to have emerged since then. Indeed, some thinkers doubt whether a tight definition of the professions is even possible.[10] One authority has discarded the exercise of defining professionals as 'futile',[11] while another has claimed that 'a firm definition of profession is both unnecessary and dangerous'.[12] We have immersed ourselves in a wide range of writings, and conclude that the organizational groups that are—or have been, or aspire to become—professions are so diverse, both in substance and in style, that they defy any highly precise single specification. And it is surely to dance on pinheads to quibble over whether one set of necessary and sufficient conditions is superior to another.[13] We do not, therefore, attempt a pat definition of 'the professions'. Nor do we provide an exhaustive list of those groups that we believe deserve the title and those that, in our estimation, do not make the cut. Whether prostitution, for example, can sensibly be called the oldest profession[14] or management consulting the 'newest profession'[15] is an issue we do not debate (at least, not in these pages).

However, because this book looks ahead to a post-professional society,[16] we nonetheless think it is important to isolate the broad features of today's professions and of the people working within these occupations.[17] To do this, we follow Ludwig Wittgenstein's concept of 'family resemblances'.[18] This is the idea that some phenomena appear related not because they have some unique characteristic in common, but instead because they share a range of 'overlapping and crisscrossing' similarities. Four siblings, for instance, may look alike not because they have a particular feature in common but because they share, to different degrees, an overlapping set of similarities.

By analogy, we suggest that members of today's professions, to varying degrees, share four overlapping similarities: (1) they have specialist knowledge; (2) their admission depends on credentials; (3) their activities are regulated; and (4) they are bound by a common set of values. (One qualification should be noted: although the terms 'professionals' and 'the professions' appear alongside one another, they should not be regarded as interchangeable. 'Professionals' are human specialists, while 'the professions' refers to the occupational groups and institutions to which professionals currently belong.) As with family resemblances, sometimes these features are strong, other times they are not, but the loose network of similarities still holds them together.

First, and above all, professionals have knowledge that lay people[19] do not. Doctors, accountants, lawyers, and architects, for example, have technical knowledge of their disciplines that lay people do not have in their heads or at their fingertips. Relative to lay people, professionals are generally regarded as 'expert', although this term is also used within the professions to mark out and recognize those, even amongst specialists, whose knowledge is deepest. In part, the knowledge of professionals is the formal knowledge that can be found in published books, journals, and increasingly online. But the knowledge of professionals, as distinct from that of theorists or academics, extends also to practical knowledge. This travels under many names, but can be looked upon as applied knowledge or know-how, and is a close relative of what are often spoken of as 'professional skills'. To be a professional practitioner, therefore, is not simply to know a lot and to have an intimate grasp of the substantive teachings of a discipline. It also requires the ability and the wherewithal to apply this knowledge to help patients, clients, or students, as the case may be. Yet it is not enough that professionals have knowledge and skills. More than this, it is also expected that their knowledge is current, that is, that they have the latest insights and techniques at their disposal. Further, they have the responsibility for extending the boundaries of their disciplines, for generating new ideas and methods, and this is a role often assumed by the academic branches of the professions. It is the role of professionals to curate the knowledge over which they have mastery, on behalf of their professions and the recipients of their services.

A second feature of the professions is that admission tends to depend on credentials. Being knowledgeable or even expert is not sufficient to allow aspirants into the club. Before they are recognized as fully-fledged practitioners who can work independently, professionals are generally required to undergo extensive education, training, and indenture, and be able to demonstrate that they gained sufficient knowledge and practical experience along the way; and that they received adequate supervision. Historically, in some professions, a working apprenticeship and sometimes journeyman experience were enough to qualify for admission. Today, success in written or practical examinations can be required and some formal, scholarly teaching is expected. As well as being robustly credentialed, aspiring professionals tend also to be asked for evidence of their character—of their fitness to serve others, and of their moral fibre, whatever that might be. The written reference of professionals of standing is usually satisfactory evidence.

Thirdly, the activities of the professions are usually regulated—in two broad ways. On the one hand, most professions are granted exclusivity over certain activities. For many commentators, this is their distinguishing feature. Professionals are licensed to undertake particular categories of work. This effective monopoly is granted by law and is generally justified by reference to the protection it affords members of the public. Only doctors can prescribe certain medicines, so that patients can be assured the drugs they consume are not dangerous. Only auditors are authorized to assure the accuracy of the financial statements of public companies, so that shareholders can confidently make investment decisions. Alongside the restricted competition that the state sanctions, the law frequently confers substantial independence or autonomy on individual professions, so that many professions are permitted or even required to regulate themselves. This leads to the second aspect of regulation for the professions—that their work should comply with clearly stated standards of conduct and ethical codes. These regulations cover issues as diverse as confidentiality, insurance, duties of good faith, conflicts of interest, service levels, pricing, complaints, and much more besides. While some professions are indeed self-regulating, others are regulated by independent bodies, and still others are hybrids of these two approaches. Increasingly, lay people sit on regulatory bodies. In any event, professionals invariably belong to professional associations or societies, membership of which requires compliance with their regulations. Sometimes these organizations are themselves the regulators, but often they are not. That the professions are independent and sometimes self-regulated does not mean that they are not publicly accountable. On the contrary, they are subject, for instance, and most notably, to the law of negligence, and the field of professional negligence, it should be noted, is a thriving branch of litigation in many jurisdictions.

The final feature of the professions is that their exponents are ordinarily thought to be bound by a common set of values over and above any formal regulations that apply to them.[20] We would expect all professionals to confirm, for example, that honesty, trustworthiness, and commitment to serving and reassuring others are at the heart of their work. Others, but not all, would go further and maintain that serving the public good, fulfilling certain social responsibilities, ensuring access to their services, and even some degree of altruism are indispensable components of the professional ethic. Still others want to say that a job in the professions should be 'a career of human significance... in terms of human welfare and advancement'.[21] There is debate over remuneration—some expect only reasonable rewards, while others regard their professional service as no more than one type of business service, so that profit-seeking is not just possible but central to their work. It is less debatable that many people are attracted to the professions and are proud to remain practitioners because their work is regarded as the province of people of good standing, they are held in high esteem by the public, and their endeavours do and should confer status and prestige.

These four sets of similarities give a broad sense of the scope of our current professions. The occupations we discuss in this book share a sufficient number of these similarities to allow us to refer to them all as belonging to the professions. These are the people, practices, and institutions that we claim will largely be replaced in a post-professional society.

1.3. Historical context

However we might choose to characterize or define the professions, profound questions arise from their existence. While, as we note, a diverse collection of scholars and theorists have made the professions their object of study, the literature of the past century and a half is dominated by the work of sociologists and other social scientists. Talcott Parsons, one of the best-regarded of these, puts it this way: 'Comparative study of the social structures of the most important civilizations shows that the professions occupy a position of importance in our society which is, in any comparable degree of development, unique in history'.[22]

Much can be said about this sociological literature. Some of it is rigorous and scholarly, but—if we are honest—much is turgid and tedious. There are not many laugh-out-loud moments. What is certainly not a chortling matter is that the *recipients* of professional service make relatively few appearances in the sociological works—the patient, client, student, and other users of the professions have received little sociological scrutiny. (There is a contrast here with the management literature on the professions, which is more client-oriented. Much of this work focuses on the professional 'firm', as a dominant mechanism for organizing and delivering professional services.[23])

As we say, this sociological literature is also characterized by deep disagreement (more of this in section 1.5). We immediately encounter this when we try to pin down the origins of the professions. On one view, '[t]he professions . . . have existed from time immemorial . . .'.[24] Others disagree, and insist that the professions owe their birth in large part to the craft guilds, and flourished notably when the Church declined after the Reformation.[25] There are those who instead maintain that the professions were a product of the Industrial Revolution.[26] However, no one seems to be suggesting that human experts are a recent phenomenon. We only need remind ourselves of various well-known names to conclude that specialists have been walking the earth for centuries: Hippocrates, the physician of ancient Greece (fifth century BC); Cicero, the Roman lawyer (first century BC); Maimonides, the Spanish rabbi and physician (twelfth century AD); and Christopher Wren, the celebrated English architect of the Enlightenment (seventeenth century AD). Yet none of these remarkable individuals belonged to professions and to professional bodies of the sort we have in place in the twenty-first century.

According to Andrew Abbott, a leading theorist of the professions, '[t]he nineteenth century saw the first development of professions as we know them today. In England the merging of the apothecaries with surgeons and physicians, the rise of the lower branch of the legal profession, and the appearance of the surveyors, architects, and accountants signaled the change.'[27] We agree with this assessment, but it is also helpful to turn the clock back further and consider the emergence of law, medicine, and divinity as well-settled disciplines and communities in fifteenth-century Europe; and to look even further back to the twelfth century, to the appearance of architects in the form of master-masons[28] and the establishment of professoriats in various universities. Determining these historical roots of the modern professions is instructive because many of the attitudes and behaviours that underpin what we call the 'grand bargain' (section 1.4) can be traced, in particular, to the era of the guilds, from the late eleventh century onwards. These medieval guilds (mainly merchant guilds and craft guilds) were associations of specialists and artisans involved with the same trade or craft—they came together to set standards, control competition, to look after the interests of their members and families, and to enjoy the prestige of being part of a group of recognized experts. Here, amongst cobblers, bakers, carpenters, and many others, we find early signs of the self-regulation, monopoly, and the hankering after status that continues to prevail in many modern professions.

In the City of London, members of particular guilds could be distinguished from one another by their livery (ceremonial dress), which led to these guilds becoming known as livery companies. It is telling that new livery companies continue to be set up and flourish. For example, the 100th livery company, the Worshipful Company of Information Technologists, was granted livery status in 1992, while the Worshipful Company of Management Consultants became the City's 105th livery company in 2004. This is an illustration of the tendency of some occupations to 'professionalize', that is, to move towards embracing and exhibiting the characteristics of mainstream professions.[29]

If the pun will be forgiven, the Information Technologists and Management Consultants are in good company. Consider the Company of Barber-Surgeons, founded in 1540. This represented a merger, if you will, of the Guild of Surgeons, which was formed in 1368, and the Barbers' Guild, which was granted Royal Charter in 1462. The new Company of Barber-Surgeons stipulated for the first time who was exclusively permitted to undertake certain categories of work (there were some contested areas of overlap, such as the manipulation of necks and, more importantly, the lancing of boils).[30] From these modest origins came perhaps the most prestigious current professional of all—contemporary surgeons.

In summary, we think it both correct and enlightening to look to the guilds of the late Middle Ages as the forerunners of many of the modern professions that have thrived since the nineteenth century. Today, as we note in section 1.1, our professions are regarded as pervasive, invaluable, and indispensable. We now have some sense of their origins. The next step is to consider why and how they enjoy their privileged position in society.

1.4. The bargain explained

What is the nature of the arrangement under which our modern professions are entitled, often to the exclusion of all others, to provide certain services to the public? What, in other words, is the broad deal between the professions and society? And what do citizens receive in return?

Commentators have variously described the arrangement as a licence,[31] a regulative bargain,[32] and a mandate and claim.[33] Alongside others, we prefer to call it 'the grand bargain'.[34] One version of this bargain, useful as a starting-point, is provided by the philosopher Donald Schön, in the following terms:

> In return for access to their extraordinary knowledge in matters of great human importance, society has granted them [professionals] a mandate for social control in their fields of specialization, a high degree of autonomy in their practice, and a license to determine who shall assume the mantle of professional authority.[35]

For physicians and surgeons, Atul Gawande, a surgeon and a writer, captures the bargain more memorably:

> The public has granted us extraordinary and exclusive dispensation to administer drugs to people, even to the point of unconsciousness, to cut them open, to do what would otherwise be considered assault, because we do so on their behalf—to save their lives and provide them comfort.[36]

Everett Hughes, a sociologist, puts it similarly, when he speaks of 'the license of the doctor to cut and dose, of the priest to play with men's salvation';[37] as did Adam Smith, the great political economist and philosopher, in the late eighteenth century, when he wrote that '[w]e trust our health to the physician; our fortune and sometimes our life and reputation to the lawyer and attorney'.[38] For the legal profession, we have captured the heart of the bargain in more prosaic language:

> the principles underlying the exclusivity of lawyers are similar in most jurisdictions; and the pivotal justification is that it is in clients' interests that those who advise them on the law are suitably trained and experienced. Just as we would not want any Joe performing brain surgery on us, then, similarly, we should not wish that same Joe representing us in the courtroom.[39]

By analogy, across other professions, the broad idea stated here is clear enough. Life is complex and demanding, and people often need reassuring and trustworthy guidance when their general, everyday knowledge and experience is insufficient to sort out their problems. More than this, people need protection, primarily from quacks, charlatans, and sometimes from themselves. This leads us to our own, general rendition of the grand bargain:

> *In acknowledgement of and in return for their expertise, experience, and judgement, which they are expected to apply in delivering affordable, accessible, up-to-date, reassuring, and reliable services, and on the understanding that they will curate and update their knowledge and methods, train their members, set and enforce standards for the quality of their work, and that they will only admit appropriately qualified individuals into their*

ranks, and that they will always act honestly, in good faith, putting the interests of clients ahead of their own, we (society) place our trust in the professions in granting them exclusivity over a wide range of socially significant services and activities, by paying them a fair wage, by conferring upon them independence, autonomy, rights of self-determination, and by according them respect and status.

We accept that this is a bit of a mouthful, but an analysis of the work of the professions and a study of the literature suggests that this is essentially the deal that has been struck. Clearly, it is an oversimplification and does not apply equally to all professions, but it captures the highlights of the arrangement and sets the stage for much of the rest of this book.

In the language of political theory, the grand bargain is a type of 'social contract'. This means that it is not in fact a traditional contract, drafted by lawyers. The grand bargain has never formally been reduced to writing and signed, its terms have never been unambiguously and exhaustively articulated, and no one has actually consented expressly to the full set of rights and obligations that it seems to lay down. That said, the bargain can be looked upon as shorthand for the full set of legislative and regulatory provisions which empower a wide range of occupational groups. Or it can be regarded as a metaphor, suggesting that the arrangement in place between the professions and society is so firmly established, well understood, and widely adhered to that it is as though its terms and conditions were enshrined in a binding contractual document. Either way, the grand bargain, in practice, positions the professions as the gatekeepers of huge swathes of knowledge, experience, and expertise that are fundamental to the social and economic lives of all of us. It is a bargain of manifest significance. It is a deal upon which society places great dependence. It is a costly set-up too—consider, for example, the combined costs of a country's health services, educational systems, revenue authorities, and courts.

In our view, one of the most important questions of our time is whether the terms of the grand bargain should be revised or whether indeed the agreement should be terminated altogether. Before we can answer that question, we need to dig even deeper and consider how various theorists have tried to make sense of the professions and of their dominance in many walks of life.

1.5. Theories of the professions

On the opening page of *The System of Professions*, one of the finest books on the subject, Andrew Abbott poses what many take to be the fundamental question in the theoretical study of the professions: '[w]hy should there be occupational groups controlling the acquisition and application of various kinds of knowledge?'[40]

A casual observer might wonder what all the fuss is about. Is it not glaringly clear that professionals know stuff and can do things that ordinary people cannot, and that we pay them accordingly? On this view, the professions are simply a pragmatic fix, reflecting the fact that human beings cannot know or do everything themselves. If our car breaks down or we have a gas leak, we call a specialist. Likewise, we call our doctor, lawyer, or accountant not because we are compelled by statute, but because circumstances and our ignorance are such that we want to tap into the knowledge of specialists. This seems to be a sensible explanation, but there are many alternative theories. (Readers who are not theoretically inclined should skip to section 1.6.)

Alternative theories

In various early writings on the professions this imbalance, or 'asymmetry', of knowledge was a prime interest. The focus was on how the professions resolve an uneven distribution of knowledge in society.[41] However, other early theorists were concerned less with the imbalance of knowledge, and instead with other important roles that they thought the professions performed. Some argued that the professions strengthened the moral character of society. The professions, their argument went, protect and nurture admirable values and worthy motivations not found elsewhere. For example, they show a concern for 'the welfare of the client' rather than 'self-interest' alone,[42] provide a 'personal service' rather than an 'impersonal service',[43] share a 'collectivity-orientation' instead of a 'self-orientation',[44] show a 'pride in service given' rather than an 'interest in opportunity for personal profit',[45] and encourage a 'functional' society rather than an 'acquisitive' society.[46] The hope was that these values and motivations might spill over from the professions, into the wider community. These ideas closely resemble themes in the work of Émile Durkheim, an earlier, classical social theorist:

> What we particularly see in the professional grouping is a moral force capable of curbing individual egoism, nurturing among workers a more envigorated [*sic*] feeling of their common solidarity, and preventing the law of the strongest from being applied too brutally in industrial and commercial relationships.[47]

Other theorists thought the professions might promote social order and political stability. Talcott Parsons wrote that the professions were 'mechanisms of social control'—they '"socialise"... bring them [the young] *back* into accord when they have deviated'.[48] In 1933 Alexander Carr-Saunders and Paul Wilson maintained that the professions were the 'stable elements in society', that:

> The old formula presses upon them; they inherit, preserve, and hand on a tradition. They know that nothing is to be achieved in their own sphere by destruction or revolution, and they assume the same applies in other spheres. Professional associations are stabilizing elements in society. They engender modes of life, habits of thought, and standards of judgment which render them centres of resistance to crude forces which threaten steady and peaceful evolution.[49]

Again, there are similarities with Durkheim, who writes that, by strengthening the 'professional group or corporation' in society, 'the whole length of the social fabric, the threads of which have become so loose, will be drawn together and strengthened'.[50]

These theorists, concerned with the different functions for the professions—whether correcting an imbalance of knowledge, strengthening the moral character of society, or maintaining social order—are known as the 'functionalists'. It is commonly said by sociologists that the functionalists saw a similarity between the role of the professions in society and the role that our organs play in our bodies—each plays a particular function, each contributes to the health of the whole, and each is critical in different ways.

A second cluster of theorists was more concerned with the distinctive features of the professions than their particular functions. Like zoologists trying to identify and classify different types of animal or plant, these sociologists focused on carefully documenting the traits of the professions, drawing up exhaustive checklists of their important characteristics and defining features, and organizing these specimens into taxonomies. These theorists are collectively known as 'the traitists'. Yet, though their thinking influenced a great deal of work on the professions—competing lists of critical traits are scattered through the literature—their collective efforts are, at the very best, inconclusive. The problem is that there is almost no agreement on what the defining traits are. Terence Johnson, a sociologist, reflecting on their efforts in the early 1970s (when the enthusiasm for collecting traits was nearing a peak), wryly noted that 'the result [of their work] has been a confusion so profound that there is even disagreement about the existence of the confusion'.[51] Geoffrey Millerson, a contemporary of Johnson and also a sociologist, studied the work of twenty-one theorists at the time and found twenty-three distinct features of the professions mentioned—yet not a single one was agreed upon by all the authors.[52]

Exclusivity and conspiracy

For the majority of sociologists who have placed the professions under scrutiny, however, there has been something more valuable to be studied than their functions or traits. Instead, and from a variety of perspectives, the exclusivity of the professions has been a principal preoccupation. Their unifying fascination is with why and how the professions have been able to isolate and ring-fence great expanses of knowledge and related services so that all others (non-professionals) are excluded from becoming involved other than as recipients. In truth, this feature of the grand bargain is more than a fascination. There are traces of indignation here too. Donald Schön, in claiming that 'the bargain is coming unstuck', demands to know 'why should we continue to grant them [the professions] extraordinary rights and privileges?'[53] Keith MacDonald, a sociologist, asks '[h]ow do such occupations manage to persuade society to grant them a privileged position?'[54]

These writers find themselves echoing the ideas of another classical social theorist, Max Weber, and his idea of social 'closure'. Weber offered an early and influential account of how and why certain groups came together to 'establish a legal order that limits competition through formal monopolies'.[55] In our specific context, he pithily observed that, '[e]very bureaucracy seeks to increase the superiority of the professionally informed by keeping their knowledge and intentions secret'.[56]

Theorists have put forward many explanations for this exclusivity. Some claim it is a consequence of the class system, of elitism, or of a collective instinct for self-preservation. Others have seen it as a natural consequence of economic progress. William Goode, a sociologist and one-time president of the American Sociological Association, declared that 'an industrializing society is a professionalizing society'.[57] On this sort of account, there is an inevitable tendency towards 'professionalization'.[58]

Yet other theorists saw the rise of this exclusivity as a more pernicious trend. The most extended contemporary treatment of exclusivity, *The Rise of Professionalism*, by the arch-monopolist Magali Larson, is written in this spirit.[59] On her account, professions not only enjoy a monopoly over economic activity, what Larson calls a 'market monopoly', but they also enjoy a monopoly over status and prestige, a 'social monopoly'.[60] In fact, Larson argues, the professions do not just enjoy status and prestige but, in celebrating their own work, they also actively manipulate our ideas of status and prestige to reflect their activities. This idea that the power of the professions extends beyond the market is widely held among sociologists. Everett Hughes made a similar point some years before Larson:

> Professions, perhaps more than any other kinds of occupation, also claim a broad legal, moral, and intellectual mandate. Not only do the practitioners, by virtue of gaining admission to the charmed circle of the profession, individually exercise a license to do things others do not do, but collectively they presume to tell society what is good and right for it in a broad and crucial aspect of life.[61]

Some are even more extreme in their analysis of this exclusivity. Very loosely, this group can be called the 'conspiracy theorists', and are able to boast of George Bernard Shaw, the playwright and critic, as their most illustrious ambassador. Shaw's dictum—that the professions 'are conspiracies against the laity'—has become their rallying-call.[62] For these thinkers and activists, the vice-like hold that the professions have over knowledge represents more than a crude hunger for power, wealth, prestige, class superiority, exclusivity, or self-preservation. Instead, there is a more insidious and concerted programme of deceit here—a conscious and systematic effort to mystify and conceal, and in so doing to maintain what has been dubbed the 'tyranny' of the experts.[63] As Stanley Fish, the legal and literary theorist, puts it:

> professionalism wears a darker face, the face of manipulation and self-aggrandizement... and stands for an activity in which a small and self-selected group conspires against the laity by claiming a superiority that is based

finally on nothing more than an obfuscating jargon and the seized control of the machinery of production and distribution.[64]

Perhaps the most passionate of those who find pervasive conspiracy in the professions is the political and social philosopher Ivan Illich, who regards the professions as 'disabling' and speaks of a widespread '[s]ocial acceptance of the illusion of professional omniscience and omnicompetence'.[65] For Illich, '[p]rofessionals assert secret knowledge about human nature, knowledge which only they have the right to dispense'.[66] He goes on to suggest that '[i]n any area where a human need can be imagined these new professions, dominant, authoritative, monopolistic, legalized—and, at the same time, debilitating and effectively disabling the individual—have become exclusive experts of the public good'.[67]

While it is hard not to sense a whiff of paranoia amongst the conspiracists, they do challenge us, as many of the other theorists do, to ask whether the professions acting as gatekeepers do so as benevolent custodians of the knowledge over which they have mastery, or whether they are, in effect, jealous guards of that knowledge. The language of the theorists may be arcane, but from all those interested in exclusivity, we are left in no doubt as to the very great influence and dominance of the professions.

The influence of Karl Marx

A great deal of this theorizing about the professions is shrouded in the language and ideas of Karl Marx and Marxist thinking.

We regard this feature of the analysis as forming, if not a fourth school of thought, then at least a very noteworthy pattern. Perhaps it betrays the political prejudices of these scholars. But in any event, a clear enthusiasm for Marxism has shaped the general themes that theorists have chosen to explore. There is, for example, a recurring and critical interest in the impact of 'capitalism' on the professions. Scholars have written, dolefully, of a decline in the self-employed, independent professional of the nineteenth century and a rise of the salaried employee. Using Marxist terminology, they call this the 'proletarianization' of professional occupations.[68] A further harmful consequence of the rise of capitalism, these theorists argue, is that profit has become a dominant motivation for professional organizations. The traditional values and motivations, of the sort noted before, have been eroded. Elliot Krause, a sociologist, pinpoints the key features of this particular shift:

> professional work can be profitable if it is organized in capitalistic forms, forms that no longer place the person who needs the services as the first priority. This trend seems to be leading to a redefinition of what professions are, from something special to just another way to make a living.[69]

Later, Krause bemoans:

> the surrender of positive guild values—of collegiality, of concern for the group, of a higher professional ethic beyond mere profit—that has eroded the distinction between professions and any other occupation and thus left them together as the middle-level employees of capitalism.[70]

It is important, though, not to be dismissive of this work. Putting aside the Marxist obfuscations, the task of exploring how motivations in the professions might have changed over time is a significant one. A fly on the wall in a leading accountancy, law, or consulting firm would find a huge emphasis on strong financial performance. Discussions of conflicts of interest, for instance, often betray a keener interest in profitable work than in delivering genuinely independent advice to clients.[71] Many partners in professional firms invariably now insist that they are running businesses, that profit per partner is the main index of success, and that the number of hours charged should be the basis of reward for employees. When profits trump clients, when the incentives and reward systems of professional businesses favour cash over culture, and when ethics entails minimal compliance by boxticking, then the grand bargain looks outmoded.[72]

In 1939 the sociologist T. H. Marshall wrote: '[t]he professional man, it has been said, does not work in order to be paid: he is paid in order that he may work.'[73] That many of today's professionals need to reread this sentence several times to grasp its sense and sentiment shows how far they have strayed from early professional ideals. We turn to the question of changing values and motivations again in Chapter 6.

Returning to the grand bargain

The above, then, are the various theories of the professions, and in this book we are influenced by many of them. While we disagree with much that they say, and offer alternative views in the pages that follow, we do join them in asking why we tolerate the professions at all—why, in other words, we remain committed to the grand bargain. For us, the most compelling answer is not particularly complex. It comes in two parts. First, the professions do not themselves generally want to change, and so resist reform or revolution. Second, until now there has been no credible alternative to what they have on offer, no competing set-up to the status quo.[74] For Andrew Abbott, this second response relates to a more fundamental question: '[h]ow do we structure and control expertise in society?'[75] In his view:

> Professionalism has been the main way of institutionalizing expertise in industrialized societies. There are, as we sometimes forget, many alternatives: the generalized expertise of the imperial civil services, the lay practitioners of certain religious groups, the popular diffusion of expertise characteristic of microcomputing... expertise is also institutionalized in commodities and organizations. To ask why societies incorporate their knowledge in the professions is thus not only to ask why societies have specialized, life-time experts, but also why they place expertise in people rather than things or rules.[76]

For us, this is a vital passage. It positions expertise at the heart of the professions, and it emphasizes that the professions are not the only way of making expertise available in society. Crucially, Abbott senses the potential of 'microcomputing' as one alternative. But he was unusual amongst theorists of the professions in acknowledging the likely relevance of IT. In the work of his contemporaries, it is remarkable that barely a mention was made of the role that technology might play in transforming the professions.[77] It would have taken no leap of imagination in the 1980s—when auditors and management consultants were already using 'microcomputers', and substantial work was being undertaken on decision-support systems and expert systems in tax and law—to predict that professionals' work might be transformed through technology. Likewise, in the early 1990s, when the World Wide Web was born, social scientists working on the professions should have had some sense that this emerging technology was likely to be relevant. This disregard of technology is a fundamental shortcoming of the academic literature. One aim of this book is to correct this defect.

1.6. Four central questions

In any event, it is time now to shift our focus from the past and to ask whether the grand bargain is a deal that still makes sense in the twenty-first century. Drawing on the theoretical writings that we discuss earlier in this chapter, and building also on our work over the years in the legal profession, we suggest that there are four questions that must be asked and answered.

First of all, might there be entirely new ways of organizing professional work, ways that are more affordable, more accessible, and perhaps more conducive to an increase in quality than the traditional approach? We believe that, in a technology-based Internet society, there must be scope for making at least some of the knowledge and experience of experts available on a different basis. And much of this book is devoted to introducing alternatives to the current set-up.

Second, even if we concede, at least for now, that human beings are indispensable in professional work, does it follow that *all* the work that our professionals currently do can *only* be undertaken by licensed experts? If we break down professional work into more basic tasks, it becomes apparent that much that goes on today under the umbrella of professional service is in fact routine and repetitive. It is hard to see why we only permit experts to undertake this work. We develop this thinking in various parts of the book (especially in Chapters 3 and 5), and suggest that a new division of labour can and should emerge.

The third question follows from the first two, and there is no diplomatic way to put it. Bluntly, then, to what extent do we actually trust professionals to admit that their services could be delivered differently, or that some of their work could responsibly be passed along to non-professionals? If we leave it to professionals themselves to reinvent their workplace, are we asking the rabbits to guard the lettuce? Popular suspicion is fuelled here by the fact that professionals often regulate themselves, and it seems that only they can bring about reform or transformation in their work. Aristotle puts it wonderfully in observing that '[t]he guest will judge better of a feast than the cook'.[78] The future of the professions is too important to be left in the hands of its members. Others, not least recipients of professional services, have a stake and should be entitled to contribute to discussions of the future.

Fourthly, is the grand bargain actually working? Are our professions fit for purpose? Are they serving our societies well? We devote the next section to answering this fourth question.

1.7. Disconcerting problems

Looking back to section 1.1 and to our everyday conception of the professions, they appear, on the face of it, to be well-intentioned, relatively stable, and generally effective institutions. But if we peel away a layer or two and look beneath the surface, it transpires, rather disconcertingly, that our professions are failing in six ways: economically, technologically, psychologically, morally, qualitatively, and in terms of their inscrutability. In combination, over time, these defects will become increasingly problematic. They will and should lead to a renegotiation of the grand bargain; a rebalancing of the relationship between the professions, the state, and society.

We turn first to the economic problem. This can be simply stated: most people and organizations cannot afford the services of first-rate professionals; and most economies are struggling to sustain most of their professional services, including schools, court systems, and health services. This is not simply a consequence of the recent global recession. For some time, the harsh reality, broadly speaking, has been that only the rich or robustly insured can engage many top-flight professionals, such as doctors, lawyers, accountants, and management consultants. The expertise of a very few is being bestowed upon a few. We seem to have a Rolls-Royce service for the well-heeled minority, while everyone else is walking. In many professions, cuts in public funding have deepened this problem. It might be thought unrealistic to hope that all citizens should benefit from the knowledge and experience of leading experts. This expertise, it is popularly supposed, is a scarce resource. On closer scrutiny, however, it is clear that it is not the expertise itself that is in short supply; it is experts who are thin on the ground. The limitation here is in our current method of organizing and delivering professional work, which often requires in-person, face-to-face interaction. We return to this idea frequently in this book.

Even if we settle for a lower standard of professional service that does not depend on the involvement of leading experts, the problem of affordability remains. In most developed economies health service costs are spiralling, schools are lamentably under-resourced, and middle-of-the-road lawyers are beyond the pockets even of other middle-class professionals. Small businesses are disenfranchised. Their owners do not have the resources to retain management consultants, tax advisers, or accountants. Meanwhile, in the world's largest organizations, we also find that professional services are regarded as prohibitively costly. Many CEOs and CFOs are insisting that expenditure on professional services (particularly law, tax, accounting, and consulting) be radically cut. There are serious doubts about whether value for money is being secured, whether the competition for professional services is sufficiently intense, and whether shareholders' interests are well served by fuelling the profits of firms owned and run by exceptionally well-remunerated partners. Clients are calling for new operating models in professional firms. This is not driven by an abstract interest in strategy, but rather by the view that many professional services are inefficient, too costly, and have yet to be subject to the overhaul that the great majority of other industries have endured.

The economic problem, then, is not primarily a concern over the quality of the services delivered by our professions. It is an issue of reach, in that relatively few people can afford to secure the services on offer. Professional expertise is unequally distributed. And this is an inequality of a special kind: in contrast with many other forms of social exclusion, where we witness relatively small groups of people who are hard to reach, it is the overwhelming majority who are cut out when it comes to much professional service. We have built glorious citadels of human expertise to which very few are allowed admittance. To adapt the old judicial aphorism—the services of the professions, like the Ritz, are 'open' to all.

Our second objection to the professions under the grand bargain is that, by and large, the arrangement presupposes a model of professional work, especially advisory work, that rests on increasingly antiquated techniques for creating and sharing knowledge. This is also an idea to which we return regularly in this book. For now, consider that in the professions, knowledge resides in the heads of professionals, in books and filing cabinets, and in the standards and systems of their institutions. Yet this is out of step with the ways in which most information and knowledge is shared in a technology-based Internet society. Additionally, the professions' claims to exclusivity and special treatment rest, in part, on assumptions about the recipients of their work being unable to advise themselves because they lack the expertise, skills, know-how, and experience or, crucially on this narrative, they lack the intellectual wherewithal or facilities to acquire this knowledge for themselves. Again, this is out of step with contemporary behaviour. The Internet has revolutionized our information-seeking habits. Our view is that there is nothing so special or unique about professionals' knowledge to suggest that some of it cannot be made easily accessible and understandable on an online basis.

The third shortcoming of the bargain is of a psychological nature. It can often be empowering for human beings to solve their problems by using their own knowledge or with insight that they acquire through research and inquiry. Clearly there are some difficulties that are too complex to leave in the hands of non-experts without expert guidance. When there is need for brain surgery, or an oral submission to an appeal court, or to understand some arcane tax regulations, it is wise to put such problems in experienced and expert hands. But there is satisfaction and self-respect to be gained from grappling with some straightforward problems on one's own, or with the help, say, of some online service. And even if a problem is indeed beyond lay reach, there surely are psychological benefits from striving to engage and understand the nature of a difficulty, from being better informed, and from taking some responsibility for one's problems. Although, as non-experts, we may sometimes find it difficult to keep apace and simpler to transfer our problems to specialists, there is contentment to be gained from trying.

The corollary here is also significant—that excluding people from understanding their problems and from engaging in their resolution can be *dis*empowering. To outsource an important personal issue to another can be diminishing, and conducive to doubts about one's own self-sufficiency. We can feel inadequate, even powerless, when loved ones rely on others exclusively. When professionals discourage the recipients of services from investigating their problems for themselves, they are, consciously or unconsciously, preserving a balance of power (by possessing but not fully sharing knowledge) that reinforces unhelpful feelings. The experience can be humbling or even paralysing. In turn, these feelings can be magnified by the deference that is often expected and by the dependence that can be formed. In short, our professions, as presently organized, often discourage self-help, self-discovery, and self-reliance; and they can unnecessarily inhibit or even alienate individuals who, once equipped with better insight, would benefit from engaging and participating more directly in their problems.

Our fourth criticism is a moral one. The professions are responsible for many of the most important functions and services in society. Yet affordable access to their work is woefully low. We argue, most fully in Chapter 5, that in a technology-based Internet society there will be a wide range of new ways to create and share knowledge that are more affordable and accessible, and that the benefits of embracing these different methods will greatly outweigh the disadvantages. If this is so, then we ought to adopt them. The nature of the obligation here is explained eloquently by the philosopher Anthony Kenny. Technology, writes Kenny, gives us 'power', but it also 'corrupts':

> not just by giving us power to do evil (for instance, to destroy the world with nuclear weapons), but by giving us the power to do good (for instance, the power to put clean water within the reach of the entire human race). It puts sins of omission as immediately and inevitably within our power as it puts sins of commission.[79]

To fail to introduce these feasible alternatives to today's professions, therefore, would be to commit what Kenny describes as a 'sin of omission'. To express this more positively, if we have the technological means to spread expertise in society far more widely at much lower cost, we believe we should strive to make this happen.

The fifth problem with the professions is that they underperform. This is not to suggest that the professions invariably achieve low levels of attainment. Rather, we maintain that in most situations in which professional help is called for, what is made available may be adequate, good, or even great, but rarely is it world-class. Given the way in which professionals are organized, the work and experience of the very best, as we say earlier, can only be enjoyed by a privileged or lucky few. The finest experts are a very scarce resource. Leading professional firms often say that they strive to bring the best of their knowledge and experience to all of their clients. In practice, this is rarely achieved. Patients are not often treated by the best surgeons and doctors, students are infrequently taught by the most inspiring teachers, congregations are rarely given the finest spiritual guidance, and clients are rarely advised by leading lawyers, accountants, or management consultants. Given the conventional model for carrying out professional work, this is necessarily so—if professionals are only able to share their experience and knowledge by advising on a face-to-face basis, then there can be few beneficiaries of the genuinely outstanding.

Finally, we believe the professions are unacceptably inscrutable. Recipients of professional services, often by the nature of the arrangement, are able neither to evaluate the substance of the guidance they receive nor to judge whether a given profession is best placed to undertake the work. Sometimes, of course, the problem being solved or the work being undertaken is so complex that no lay person could hope to grasp what is going on. But there are occasions, no doubt, when there is intentional obfuscation, to justify high fees, perhaps, or for straightforward self-aggrandizement. Where there is opacity and mystification, there will be mistrust and a lack of accountability. Moreover, it is hard to debate reform or transformation when the phenomenon at issue is poorly understood, inadequately described, or concealed from measured scrutiny.

1.8. A new mindset

When confronted with the criticisms and challenges of this chapter, a common response of professionals (and their representative bodies) is to address each alleged shortcoming in turn and to suggest small modifications. The mindset here is to repair the traditional way of working. But that will not be sufficient. Consider again what we are suggesting—that, by and large, our professions are unaffordable, under-exploiting technology, disempowering, ethically challengeable, underperforming, and inscrutable. This is not a trivial charge-list. In the pages that follow we suggest ways for the professions to resolve these problems. But we also go further. We argue that there are alternatives to the professions. Thinking about these alternatives requires a very different mindset.

Let us start work on this new mindset by considering one of our favourite stories. It is said that one of the world's leading manufacturers of power tools puts their newly recruited executives on an induction course, at the opening session of which a slide of a gleaming power drill is presented. They then ask the assembled executives to confirm that what is on the slide is what they sell. The executives look rather surprised, but gradually buck up the collective courage to agree that this indeed is what their company sells. The trainers, with some satisfaction, contradict this and flick to a new slide, which depicts a hole neatly drilled in a wall. They then suggest that this is in fact what they sell, because this is what their customers actually want; and that it is the job of new executives to find ever more creative, competitive, and imaginative ways of giving their customers what they want. There is a powerful lesson here for the professions, because most professionals, when thinking about their future, tend to be of power drill mentality. They are inclined to ask themselves what it is that they do today—usually some form of one-to-one consultative advisory service, often on an hourly billing basis—and how they might make that service a bit quicker, cheaper, or better. Not often enough do professionals ask themselves the more fundamental question—what is the 'hole in the wall' for the professions?

One promising answer to this 'hole in the wall' query has been provided (although not directly) by KPMG, the global accountancy and consulting firm. At one time their mission statement, or at least part of it, ran as follows: 'We exist to turn our knowledge into value for the benefit of our clients.'[80] This is useful as a starting-point. In a wide variety of disciplines, professionals have knowledge, expertise, experience, insight, and know-how that they apply in the particular circumstances of their clients, patients, and other recipients of their services. On this account, the hole in the wall is the *knowledge* to which clients want access; or, more precisely, the application of that knowledge to their particular circumstances. The KPMG rendition is not, of course, articulated in the following way: 'we exist to provide one-to-one consultative advisory service, delivered in vast reports or at lengthy meetings, on an hourly billing basis.' The mission statement does not confuse the way in which the professionals' knowledge is currently deployed with the actual value afforded. However, the statement is silent as to the nature of this 'value'. Across the professions this value can come in a variety of forms: problem-solving or problem-avoidance; reassurance or insurance; health or relief; edification or enlightenment.

The benefits that the professions bring are diverse. This, however, is not the principal lesson we derive from the 'hole in the wall' thought experiment. The main lesson is that *knowledge,* in ways we discuss shortly, lies at the heart of professional work. Two questions follow. First, how well do professionals capture, nurture, share, and recycle their collective knowledge for the benefit of those they help? In truth, professionals are not generally very good at sharing and reusing their experience and knowledge, and much that is said in this book is intended to point to ways of overcoming this shortcoming. For now, though, our focus is on a second, and more fundamental, question—what if we could put in place altogether different ways of allowing people to access specialist knowledge?

This is where the shift in mindset is needed. In thinking about the future, as is said earlier, most observers take our current professions as their starting-point. Instead, inspired by the story of power drills and holes, we should take a step back and ask a prior question, as follows: *to what problem are the professions our solution?*

Stripped to its basics, whenever human beings seek the help of the professions, they do so because professionals know things that they do not. There is, of course, a natural imbalance, or asymmetry, in society that arises from the fact that some people know more than others about certain matters.[81] But the professions have institutionalized and deepened this imbalance in particular fields of knowledge. This imbalance characterizes all professional relationships, whether between doctor and patient, lawyer and client, teacher and pupil, minister and congregant, management consultant and business-person, tax adviser and tax payer, and so forth. In different ways, the recipients of these services all wish to benefit from the knowledge of the provider. Some insight and understanding is often passed along in the process (and, in teaching, this is the essence of the service), but by and large the role of professionals is to draw upon, interpret, and apply their knowledge, as the particular circumstances of the recipient require.

We can go a little further in trying to pin down what the professions do and why—by thinking about what actually leads people to professionals in the first place. The fundamental need for professional help, in the language of the legal philosopher Herbert Hart, stems from a 'truism' about 'human nature'—that human beings have '*limited understanding*'.[82] No one can know everything. In our daily lives we rely on outside input to help us live and work comfortably. We have invented and constructed our traditional professions to help people overcome their limited understanding. The professions help citizens and organizations to handle certain types of problems and complexities that require knowledge that they do not have. In practice, this places professionals as the interface between uninitiated lay people and great bodies of expertise.

All other dimensions of professional service—such as trust, reassurance, quality, status, training, regulation, and so forth—are secondary factors. Were it not for recipients' limited understanding and corresponding need for knowledge, there would be no trust required, no reassurance desired, no quality to control, no training to deliver, no services or behaviours to regulate. This is elemental. So much commentary on the professions, both academic and popular, is premised on arguments such as 'trust is paramount in the professional relationship' or 'ongoing training of professionals is of overriding importance'. Instead, it is surely people's need for knowledge that is actually the indispensable condition—the *sine qua non* of professional service. Without this ingredient, other factors, such as trust and training, are of no relevance in and of themselves. This point has driven our search for alternatives to traditional professional service. This search is for new and different ways of making knowledge available. These alternatives need not be premised on the asymmetry of knowledge that defines our current professions, and so may not require the same suite of secondary factors.

However, if 'knowledge' is to lie at the foundation of our arguments in this book, there is more work to be done in clarifying this concept. On its own, 'knowledge' is neither precise nor rich enough for our purposes. Our starting-point in refining the concept is our experience of what informed recipients of professional service seem to want. For starters, it is clear that recipients want more than the abstract substantive knowledge that is found in textbooks or published articles by theorists and academics. Few clients or patients would be content, for example, if a professional responded to their problems by handing them a textbook to read. This formally published knowledge is necessary, but a long way short of sufficient.

What else is needed? First of all, recipients of service expect their professionals not just to have substantive knowledge ('know-that') at their fingertips but also to have appropriate 'know-how' at their disposal.[83] When practitioners say, 'well, that's all very well in theory but in practice...', they are often bringing to bear their know-how. This is insight into how and when it is best to apply textbook knowledge. Sometimes this know-how is 'tacit',[84] that is, it is not consciously invoked and has not been formally articulated. Often it is procedural and informal—'tricks of the trade'. Frequently it seems to be based on judgement, gut reaction, rules of thumb, or intuition. This kind of know-how is sometimes captured in what are known as 'heuristics'.[85] Secondly, informed recipients of service also want the knowledge and know-how of the professionals to be deep and longestablished. In short, they prefer their providers to be 'expert', and not just 'knowledgeable'. More than this, they seek reassurance that the expertise has been repeatedly applied in the past with considerable success. This track record in the field distinguishes the practitioner from the scholar. Third, there is an applied dimension that requires the providers to have the necessary skills, techniques, and methods to apply their expertise and experience effectively. In this book we refer to this complex combination of formal knowledge, know-how, expertise, experience, and skills as 'practical expertise'.[86]

A critic might immediately say that it is not possible to use one term, 'practical expertise', in respect of all professions. Although the professions have much in common—generally, professionals have specialist knowledge that those who use their services do not—it is true that there are notable differences amongst them. For example, some professions require manual dexterity, such as medicine, architecture, veterinary science, surgery, and dentistry, whereas others, such as law, tax, accounting, and consulting, do not. Another set of distinctions flows from the nature of the knowledge that underpins our many and various professions. For instance, medicine and dentistry have their roots in knowledge drawn from the natural sciences, whereas in law, tax, and audit the foundations of the expertise are legislation and regulation. In divinity, by contrast, the nature of the knowledge is scriptural and based, according to some, on divine authority. These basic types of knowledge might seem so diverse as to have nothing in common.

Yet, in practice, human professionals in all disciplines handle their respective source materials in much the same manner. Although they rely on different methods, they all have to *interpret* these underpinning sources and *apply* the resultant knowledge in everyday circumstances. Professionals in all fields recast their sources into manageable chunks, which they hold in their heads, publish in books, make available on websites, distil into working (sometimes manual) procedures, summarize in practice notes, and so forth.[87] Accordingly, it makes sense to use the same term to refer to the knowledge, know-how, and experience which all professionals create and upon which they all rely on a daily basis.

A crucial argument of this book, however, is that there are various technologies that can also, in effect, undertake the interpretation and application of source materials, even though we have come to assume that these are the exclusive realm of intelligent human beings. This suggests that we should broaden our concept of 'practical expertise' to include not only the formal knowledge, know-how, expertise, experience, and skills of traditional professionals, but also the relevant output of various machines and systems. In addition, various technologies are now enabling lay people to share the knowledge and experience that they accumulate from solving problems themselves, or from being past recipients of professional service. Alongside the knowledge, know-how, expertise, and experience derived from human professionals and machines, we also characterize this lay knowledge and experience as practical expertise.

We can now provide a better answer to an earlier question—to what problem are the professions our solution? We have constructed our traditional professions to help people overcome their limited understanding, and they act as gatekeepers who maintain, interpret, and apply the *practical expertise* from which we wish to benefit. However, as we claim in this chapter, this construct is no longer fit for purpose. In response, we call for a shift in mindset, away from the conviction that the only or best way to solve the problem of limited understanding is through the professions as currently constituted, towards contemplating that there might be quite different solutions to the problem, ones that are entirely unlike what we have put in place. We ask people to look beyond the professions and to be open to alternative and better ways of handling this limited understanding of human beings. And from the recipient's perspective, crudely, if we can find more affordable, less forbidding, higher-quality, and more transparent and empowering ways of helping people, then we should expect these to be warmly welcomed.

However, it should not be supposed that the transition from what we have today to these alternatives is straightforward. The traditional professions are entrenched in our everyday lives, and firmly held beliefs and practices will need to be abandoned. This becomes apparent when we inquire in great depth into the work currently undertaken by professionals. Many of the problems that they tackle are in fact defined by the solutions that the professions themselves have developed. So when we say, for example, that a client has a tax or accounting problem or that a patient has a dental or surgical concern, these very characterizations of the concerns are framed in terms of the categorizations and capabilities of professional providers. As Abraham Maslow, a leading psychologist, has noted: 'I suppose it is tempting, if the only tool you have is a hammer, to treat every problem as if it were a nail.'[88] However, real-life problems do not always arise neatly labelled as the province of one professional or another. Everyday problems are messier than this—the life events that incline people to seek professional help might, ideally, call for the input of many experts, and not just one. Physics Nobel Laureate Richard Feynman makes an analogous point, relating to the way we chunk up the world around us:

> if we look at a glass of wine closely enough we see the entire universe. . . . If our small minds, for some convenience, divide this glass of wine, this universe, into parts—physics, biology, geology, astronomy, psychology, and so on—remember that nature does not know it![89]

Not only are the professions themselves a human construct, therefore, but so too is the organization of the knowledge that they dispense—knowledge is generally structured and presented in libraries, in textbooks, and on websites, for research and learning purposes rather than for dissemination to end users. We have built these resources and systems to support, and so to sustain, the professions. And before the Internet, for example, it was hard to conceive how we might have done otherwise. These constructs are so embedded in the way we think about the world that when we contemplate change and improvement, we tend to explore better execution of the methods and approaches that we already have in place. Although our professions are failing in significant ways, they are not incentivized to work differently.

1.9. Some common biases

Some professionals are likely to reject our thinking and conclusions. Often this response will be rooted in important anxieties and concerns. We address these in Chapters 6 and 7. But much of this resistance will flow from common biases that inhibit professionals from thinking freely about their future. We turn to these now.

The first is a strong 'status quo bias'—a preference for continuing to do things as they are done today. This bias manifests itself in various ways. One is the special pleading in which many professionals engage. They accept that the professions in general are in need of change, but they maintain that their own particular fields are immune. Exploiting the asymmetry of knowledge, we are told that, 'you don't understand'. This claim tends to be followed by a list of characteristics of their work that make change inappropriate. Often this is bluster. We ought to be suspicious when a professional claims that all professions are dispensable other than his or her own. But this special pleading is usually supported by a compelling form of argument—the argument from 'hard cases'. A professional will claim that a new system or method cannot solve *x* or *y*, where *x* and *y* are the most difficult of problems in their fields. Rather than conceding that many everyday challenges can indeed be met in new ways, the argument concentrates on the atypical. It disconcerts by focusing on extreme examples rather than everyday activity. This is misleading, and ought to be challenged.

A great deal of this book is concerned with technology. Here we encounter three further biases. The first is what we call 'irrational rejectionism'. We define this as the dogmatic dismissal of a system with which the sceptic has no direct personal experience. Often with arms folded, a professional will reject proposals for systems without seeing them in action or listening carefully to what is on offer. Difficulties are quickly noted and applications are swiftly discarded. A variant of this rejectionism is an old chestnut—the suggestion that the system in question would work well in other disciplines but not in the sceptic's own. Often this bias is rooted in a fear of an unknown. Sometimes it is based on an honest belief in the uniquely bespoke nature of the sceptic's work. But, in any event, an inability to keep an open mind to new technologies is a formidable barrier to progress.

Our second technology-based bias is what we call 'technological myopia'. We characterize this as the tendency to underestimate the potential of tomorrow's applications by evaluating them in terms of today's enabling technologies. In other words, this is the inability of a sceptic, because of the shortcomings of current technology, to concede that future systems may be radically more powerful than those of today. Thus, senior doctors and lawyers might reject the idea of conducting a consultation by video-conference because of, say, a poor recent experience of a Skype call with a grandchild. A variation of this myopia is the inability to imagine that a modest user base of today might extend from a small group of early adopters to mainstream use. Technological myopia is a cousin of the phenomenon of 'retrospective modernism', as identified by Frederick Maitland, the legal historian.[90] He was referring to the limitations of viewing and evaluating historical events through the lens of today. Past events are best understood in the context of the time of their occurrence. It is poor scholarship, for example, to judge past decisions by reference to what we have learned since, that is, with the advantage of hindsight. Likewise, although we do not have the benefit of foresight, we should not let present-centredness eclipse our vision of what is likely to come.

We write at a time when there is renewed interest in artificial intelligence (AI). With this has come a third technology-related bias that we call the 'AI fallacy'. This is the mistaken supposition that the only way to develop systems that perform tasks at the level of experts or higher is to replicate the thinking processes of human specialists. This anthropocentric view of 'intelligent' systems is limiting. It emboldens both professionals and commentators, for example, to leap from the observation that computers cannot 'think' to the unwarranted conclusion that systems cannot undertake tasks at a higher standard than human beings. As we show in this book, however, systems of today are increasingly out-performing human experts, not by copying high-performing people but by exploiting the distinctive capabilities of new technologies, such as massive data-storage capacity and brute-force processing.

This final thought about new technologies leads us to express one of our driving principles. In an era of increasingly capable systems, the professions, or elements of them, should survive and prosper because they bring value and benefits that no system or tool can; not because we regulate competitors out of the market, nor because we cannot imagine a world without the professions, nor again out of nostalgic impulse for a fading way of life.

When the arguments and predictions of this book are brought together, especially those relating to the rapid advances of technology and ongoing economic pressures, it seems to us that the *least* likely future of all is that nothing much will change. And yet this is frequently the assumption of practitioners and policymakers—the strategic plans of many professional bodies and firms anticipate little more than some streamlining of twentieth century working practices. We regard this as out of step with mounting evidence, as our next chapter shows.

2

From the Vanguard

In this chapter we change pace. We run through a group of different professions and offer a glimpse of the many ways in which they are changing, largely because of technology. The picture we present, although wide-ranging and varied, is not held out as comprehensive. It reflects activity only in particular parts of the world, predominantly the Anglo-American region, and at just one point in time—the middle of the second decade of the twenty-first century. In years to come, when we look back on the pages that follow, we will no doubt see, with the acuity of hindsight, that we missed some great case studies, that we included some which might better have been omitted, and that some of our exemplars no longer exist. This is to be expected. It would require many more volumes to carry out an exhaustive survey of technological change across the professions, and it would demand supernatural prescience to isolate the eventual winners.

But to dwell on any particular case—success, failure, or omission—would be to misunderstand what we are trying to achieve in this chapter and through much of the book. To paraphrase the literary critic Harold Bloom, we are seeking to look beyond any particular ripple on the surface and, with a broad sweep through our chosen professions, to capture the deeper current of change that we sense is flowing below.[1]

2.1. Health

In *The Patient Will See You Now*, Eric Topol, cardiologist and professor of genomics, anticipates that '[w]e are embarking on a time when each individual will have all their own medical data and the computing power to process it…from womb to tomb… even to prevent an illness before it happens'.[2] There are many other commentators who are making predictions in this spirit. And the contrast with the current and long-established practice of medicine by doctors could not be starker.

Traditionally, when people suspect something might be amiss with their health they book an appointment, they show up in person, they sit in one or more face-to-face interactions with individual experts, who in turn prescribe courses of action, often to be implemented by the patients once they leave. One of the many difficulties with this well-settled approach is that it no longer seems to be affordable. In part, this is as a result of past successes in healthcare, which mean that people are living longer, with expensive long-term care conditions than can be treated but not always cured. In England, for example, long-term care needs for illnesses like cancer, diabetes, and dementia make up 70 per cent of health and social spending.[3]

Within medical communities there has for long been recognition that practitioners can work more efficiently by learning from one another. Thus, as we discuss below, the publication of medical research takes place on a vast scale, enabling physicians to build on the insights of others. While standard protocols and procedures are also invoked daily, the medical profession, as Atul Gawande has shown, expresses considerable ambivalence towards the use of simple checklists, even if their efficacy is well established.[4]

With the advent of the Internet, patients themselves now have access to far more health information. Platforms like NHS Choices and the WebMD network provide extensive guidance on symptoms and treatment—there are a greater number of unique visits (190 million) each month to the latter than to all the doctors working in the United States.[5] Specialized search engines, like BetterDoctor, ZocDoc, and Doctor on Demand, allow people to sift databases of more than 1 million doctors, in some cases assigned an Amazon-style experience-based rating. In 2014, for the first time, all patients in England were able to access thirty-seven different types of data on their GP practices, and were alerted to any particular risks (called 'GP intelligent monitoring'[6]). Basic symptom-checkers are available online at no cost to users, and provide diagnoses instantly, without any outside human intervention.

Offline, there are more powerful computerized diagnostic systems. The Elizabeth Wende Breast Clinic in New York, for example, found that using algorithms to scan mammograms reduced false negatives for breast cancer by 39 per cent.[7] IBM's AI system, known as Watson (see section 4.6), is being used to support cancer diagnoses and recommend treatment plans.[8]

It is also being used to help devise treatments for people with PTSD.[9] Consider that if only 2 per cent of the new medical literature published daily in 2014 were relevant for a doctor, it would have taken a human at least twenty-one hours each day, every day, to read this. A new paper is published, on average, every forty-one seconds.[10] The hope is that Watson can scan such volumes of material swiftly, and is able stay on top of the flow of new publications. At the moment, 49 per cent of readers of the *British Medical Journal* think that evidence-based medicine is 'malfunctioning'—these new systems might be one way to restore confidence.[11] There are good reasons to think this—delayed, missed, and incorrect diagnoses are said to occur from 10 to 20 per cent of the time.[12]

Computerized systems appear elsewhere, too. At Medtronic the design of insulin delivery-pumps is moving in the same direction as their pacemakers—towards dosing of insulin that is automatic and based on sensor data, rather than on the deliberation and manual intervention of an expert (on which, not long ago, the pacemaker depended). The University of California at San Francisco has a pharmacy staffed by a single robot, which has now completed more than 2 million prescriptions without error—on a conservative estimate, US human pharmacists make a wrong prescription about 1 per cent of the time (equivalent to 37 million mistakes each year).[13] The autonomous TUG robot, used in around 140 hospitals, directs itself through corridors and delivers many items, from linen to medicine—at the moment the robots make 50,000 deliveries a week, taking them out of nurses' and porters' hands.[14] Half of US doctors use the app known as Epocrates, a digital drug-reference resource that computerizes the task of finding out how different drugs interact. This task was once a time-consuming, often inconclusive piece of excavation from a 2,500-page drug-reference manual, known as the *Physicians' Desk Reference*.[15]

The conduct of medical research is also subject to computerization. IBM and the Bayor College of Medicine have developed a system, KnIT ('Knowledge Integration Toolkit'), that scans existing medical literature and generates new hypotheses for particular research problems. For example, they estimate it would take a new researcher up to thirty-eight years to digest the 70,000 medical articles written on a tumor-suppressing protein called 'p53'.[16] KnIT scanned these articles, alongside millions of others,[17] and found six possible new chemical 'switches' that would turn this p53 protein on and get it working—until now, only thirty-three others had been discovered.[18] Similar computerized hypothesis-generation software has been used to generate leads in research on hormones and migraines.[19]

On one vision for systems like Watson, patients will not generally be seen by doctors, but instead by nurses, suitably equipped with diagnostic and treatment-planning tools. In this way, vast bodies of deep medical expertise will be at the disposal of the nurses. On another view, these systems might be used with patients by 'physician associates', a new class of health practitioner under the NHS, trained in medicine but not as extensively as traditional physicians.[20] Although there is some controversy surrounding these associates,[21] the conventional occupational boundaries in medicine are no longer sacrosanct, so that nurses, for example, are also now permitted to perform minor operations and have extended prescribing powers.[22]

The practice of 'telemedicine' (or 'telehealth' or 'e-health') uses video links across the Internet to carry out medical tasks at a distance. In teleradiology and teledermatology, experts who are not in traditional medical centres can conduct urgent image processing around the clock. Using telestroke platforms, cardiac specialists can make emergency diagnoses and provide swift advice without being at a patient's side. In telesurgery, supported by advanced robotics, a team of surgeons in the United States was able to remove the gall bladder of a woman in France, over 6,000 kilometres away across the Atlantic (the so-called 'Operation Lindbergh').[23]

Techniques like this are supported by 'remote monitoring' and 'remote diagnosis' devices. The Medtronic Carelink Network, for example, allows cardiac patients to send data reports from their heart devices to their doctor, each report equivalent to an in-person visit. The US Department of Veterans Affairs has a dedicated Office of Telehealth, and used the technology to provide healthcare to over 690,000 veterans in 2014—a particularly disparate group, 55 per cent of whom live in rural areas with limited access to traditional health services.[24] In the United Kingdom, the National Health Service in Airedale, West Yorkshire, uses telepresence to provide several hundred care-homes with nurse support and, in a trial, to avoid hospital admissions for 50 per cent of prison inmates.[25] Sometimes the devices take an unexpected form—Google, for example, has joined forces with the European drug-maker Novartis to develop a 'smart contact lens' to monitor blood-sugar levels, rather than pricking a finger for blood (the traditional way to test for, and manage, diabetes).[26]

There is a growing 'mobile health', or 'mHealth', market of tens of thousands of devices, systems, and apps that build on existing mobile technology—basic phones, smartphones, and mobile networks. Devices and systems are of varying sophistication. The BlueStar system, for example, turns a smartphone into an FDA-approved diabetes-management system, providing patients with personalized treatment advice and doctors with a real-time data stream.[27] The EyeNetra smartphone clip-on costs a few dollars to produce, and provides a mobile eye-testing unit that functions like a traditional autorefractor that costs many thousands of dollars (and, it is claimed, there is no loss in accuracy).[28] The US Food and Drug Agency has suggested that half a billion people with smartphones will have a medical app installed by 2015, and more than triple that by 2018.[29]

There are simpler uses of mHealth. Consider that patients tend to forget between 40 and 80 per cent of the medical information a doctor provides, incorrectly recall half of what they actually do recall,[30] and then as many as half do not remember to take their prescribed medication (at a cost of $100 billion in avoidable hospitalizations each year in the United States).[31] Given this parlous state of affairs, simple text-message reminders to patients (and to health-workers, too) significantly improve health outcomes—for example, in treating HIV[32] and malaria.[33] This also explains the success of devices like the GlowCap medicine vial cap—through a wireless chip it monitors drug use and sends alerts to forgetful drug-takers (it flashes, beeps, then sends a text), data to doctors about adherence, and a notice to pharmacists when a top-up is needed.[34]

The increasing use of digital devices in healthcare generates large volumes of data that, with advanced systems, can yield remarkable insights. The Mayo Clinic, for example, has developed a set of algorithms, called 'sniffers', that run through live-streams of patient data to anticipate and flag potential medical problems. Often, the scale of the data flow demands Big Data techniques (see section 4.6). The Emory University Hospital in Atlanta, for example, has worked with IBM to develop bedside monitors in their Intensive Care Unit that collect and analyse over 100,000 data points for each patient each second.[35]

The commercial availability of many of these devices and systems has also stirred a cultural movement of 'self-monitoring', or 'self-tracking'. Called 'Quantified Self', the many tens of thousands who are involved use devices like Jawbone, Fitbit, and MyFitnessPal to collect large volumes of data about themselves—from pulse rates to digestive behaviour, from sleep patterns to happiness levels—and to analyse it with a sophistication that rivals many clinicians. These devices, designed also with the aesthete in mind, are often called 'wearables'. Proteus Digital Health is developing a range of 'ingestibles'—small, pill-shaped monitors, swallowed by the patient, with no battery (powered instead by stomach acid[36]), that provide internal monitoring.

Large communities have emerged online. At PatientsLikeMe, 300,000 people connect with other people who share their conditions (at the moment, around 2,300 conditions), and swap experiences and treatments.[37] It is reported that Facebook is planning to develop online 'support communities' in this spirit.[38] One-third of doctors in the United States use the network known as Sermo to distribute research, post clinical cases, and talk amongst each other.[39] The same proportion use a network known as QuantiaMD, with similar functionality.[40] More than half of the doctors in the United States are members of Doximity, another doctor-specific networking tool.[41]

Medicine is also making use of crowdsourcing, where large numbers of individuals are drawn upon for their collective ideas and support. At CrowdMed, people post their symptoms and crowdsource diagnoses from an online community of 2,000 doctors—so-called 'Medical Detectives'.[42] At InnoCentive, medical institutions crowdsource ideas by offering large online rewards for those who solve their medical 'challenges'.[43] At Watsi, people in need of medical care, but unable to afford it themselves, can use their online crowdfunding platform to raise finance from donors.[44]

3-D printing techniques enable many medical objects, from casts to prosthetics to dentist's caps and crowns, to be personalized and then printed on demand. Surgeons scan patient parts and print models of them, to practice on before operating in earnest.[45] Nor is the output necessarily inorganic. At the Wake Forest Institute for Regenerative Medicine, progress has been made in constructing a machine to 'print' human cells directly onto burn victims. Researchers are creeping towards printing entire organs.[46] This matters—on average, twenty-one people a day die in the United States, and just under three in the United Kingdom, waiting for spare organs.[47]

Increasing computational power has meant that certain fields, previously conceivable in theory but impossible in practice, are now thriving. Genomics, the science of scanning a patient's DNA to personalize medical treatment and anticipate future disease, is one example. In 2007 it would have cost around $10 million to read a human genome. Now it costs a few thousand dollars.[48] Companies like 23andMe, Navigenics, and deCODE offer commercial testing services from $99.[49] In the field of 'genome editing', scientists search for problematic genes and actively intervene to change or remove them. Nanomedicine, the use of nanotechnology in a medical setting, is another field. Nobel Laureate Richard Feynman's seventy-year-old prediction that we might one day 'swallow the surgeon'[50] has come true—there are already small nanobots that are able to swim through our bodies, relaying images, delivering targeted drugs, and attacking particular cells with a precision that makes even the finest of surgeons' blades look blunt. (At Google X, one of Google's research facilities, they are said to be developing a version of this.[51])

Non-humans are also playing a role. Engineers are developing a large number of sophisticated robotic systems that support patients (sometimes called 'assistive robotics').[52] There are, for example, robotics that help paraplegics to walk, and prosthetics, controlled by patients, to replace lost limbs.[53] Some systems also help practitioners. The 'Hybrid Assisted Limb', for example, built by Cyberdyne, is a mechanical suit that acts as an exoskeleton and costs less than $2,000, allowing nurses to lift and carry far heavier loads than they could on their own.[54] Robotics are also used for social, rather than physical, tasks (often called 'socially assistive robotics').[55] Paro is a therapeutic robotic seal built in Japan, which stimulates and comforts people with dementia and Alzheimer's disease—it is currently being trialed in parts of the NHS.[56] Kaspar, designed by researchers at the University of Hertfordshire, is used to help children with autism—one of many such robots.[57] In the field of 'affective computing' (see section 4.6), scientists and engineers are developing systems that can simulate a sympathetic bedside manner. In one private hospital in Japan, most rooms have their own robot nurses, there not just to undertake the heavy lifting but also to offer company for each patient.[58] These techniques are not limited to robots, but are also used to support online platforms, like AI Therapy—a system that tailors a virtual treatment program for people with social anxiety, without external human intervention.[59]

2.2. Education

Our basic methods of educating have not changed much for centuries. A small number of students assemble in a single physical space and a teacher delivers live broadcasts, each roughly the same length and pace, from a fairly rigid curriculum. The teacher is the 'sage on the stage'. One size has to fit all, and what is not understood in class must be explored in independent study, or not at all. Those who understand, and want to move on, often must wait.

When institutions are well resourced, with a wealth of talented teachers and the brightest of students, this traditional model can deliver outstanding results. However, an excellent outcome is enjoyed only by a fortunate few. In general, in many developed countries we fail to provide a sufficiency of affordable, good-quality education. Internally, countries worry about their uneven distribution of educational outcomes and, particularly in the West, that their systems as a whole are falling behind those of other countries, such as China.

In the past, the deployment of technology in education was modest—perhaps a solitary computer at the rear of the classroom, an electronic whiteboard at the front, and periodic use of the Internet for research. In contrast, at 'hybrid' or 'blended' learning schools, technology is central. At Rocketship Education, a network of nine charter schools in California, students spend three-quarters of their day with a teacher in a classroom, and the remaining quarter using an online platform in a 'Learning Lab'.[60] In this Lab, software draws on individual performance data to tailor what is taught—the content, the approach, and the pace—to the particular needs and abilities of each student. If one individual requires particular attention, the system sends an alert to the teacher. A similar approach is used in New Classroom schools in New York,[61] Matchbook Learning schools in Detroit,[62] and Ednovate schools in Los Angeles.[63]

These schools use what are known as 'adaptive' or 'personalized' learning systems. At least seventy companies now provide these systems: Knewton, Reasoning Mind, and DreamBox are some of the better-known platforms.[64] They challenge the traditional 'one-size fits all' approach. By tailoring what is taught to each particular student, they seek to replicate the personal attention involved in the desirable, but unaffordable, system of intensive one-to-one tutoring. They are also known as 'intelligent tutoring systems'. They try to solve the thirty-year-old 'two sigma problem'—that an average student who receives one-to-one tuition will tend to outperform 98 per cent of ordinary students in a traditional classroom (they are around 'two standard deviations', or 'two sigmas', ahead of the average classroom student).[65] This one-to-one model is, essentially, the tutorial system that has worked so effectively at the universities of Oxford and Cambridge since the nineteenth century.

Online, there are various types of education networks. There are social networks like Edmodo, the so-called 'Facebook for schools', with 48 million users.[66] These are specifically tailored to support communities of teachers, students, and parents. There are media platforms, like Edudemic, Edutopia, and ShareMyLesson, where people share material (blogs, videos, and lesson plans) on what works in the classroom.[67] There are 'learning management systems' and 'virtual learning environments', like Moodle, with 65 million users, and BrightSpace, with over 15 million users, that help teachers organize their teaching, distribute materials, and interact with students outside the classroom.[68]

Other online platforms provide educational content. Khan Academy, for example, is a free online collection of 5,500 instructional videos (watched 450 million times), providing 100,000 practice problems (solved 2 billion times).[69] With 10 million unique visitors each month in 2014—a seventyfold increase since 2010[70]—it has a higher effective attendance than the total primary- and secondary-school population of England.[71] TED, a collection of online talks (eighteen minutes, more or less, in length) on a wide range of topics by thoughtful people, reached its one-billionth view in late 2012, while TED-Ed is a platform that helps build lessons that are based on their videos.[72] YouTube EDU, a part of the video-hosting platform that is allocated for education content alone, hosts over 700,000 'high quality' educational videos—a small fraction of the less-polished, but by no means less-useful, videos elsewhere on the site.[73]

These online platforms are deployed in different ways. Students often use the platforms to catch up and sharpen up outside the classroom. Some teachers draw on them for classroom material, and teach in the traditional way.[74] Why not, they ask, have leading world experts speak to the pupils? Others use the materials to teach in different ways, 'flipping' the classroom, for example, so that students watch routine lectures on these platforms at home, and instead do homework in class.[75] Parents use them for 'home-schooling', where children are educated at home rather than at a traditional school, a practice that has risen sharply in the United States, a doubling in the percentage of the overall school-age population between 1999 and 2012.[76]

These other platforms rely on the clarity of charismatic individuals like Salman Khan (the creator of Khan Academy) personally to handcraft each video from scratch. However, existing institutions that already hold large bodies of expertise are sharing this on similar platforms. In 2011, for example, more than three-quarters of US university presidents said that they offered online courses.[77]

In the past few years the nature and scale of these courses has changed. A range of 'Massive Open Online Courses' (MOOCs) has been set up—online courses, open to all, often free or for a small fee, and rarely with a limit on class size (an enrolment of 300,000 is the largest to date[78]). On online platforms like Coursera, founded by two Stanford University professors, and EdX, founded by Harvard University and MIT, the world's greatest scholars gather from several hundred institutions to compose and deliver thousands of MOOCs, to several million students.[79] For example, more people signed up for Harvard's MOOCs in a single year than have attended the actual university in its 377 years of existence.[80]

At platforms like Udemy and Udacity, any expert, not only academics, can host and run a MOOC.[81] These platforms have also been reused to support smaller classes taking traditional courses, known as 'Small Private Online Courses' (SPOCS), a return to the sort of 'blended learning' noted before.

There is also experimentation with online tools to conduct different forms of assessment and accreditation. For instance, for those running a MOOC, marking the work of many thousands of students in the traditional way is not feasible (teachers already spend, on average, around nine hours a week marking for traditional classes).[82] Some systems use a 'peer-grading' approach, where students mark each other's work, and others use a 'machine-grading' approach, where algorithms computerize the marking process entirely. Platforms like Degreed and Accredible score and certify achievements in this way for work that takes place outside the classroom.[83]

Many of these platforms and systems are used on portable devices. Here they are complemented by education apps. At the start of 2015, education apps were the second most popular category (second only to 'games') on Apple's online App Store.[84] John Doerr, an American venture capitalist, (correctly) predicted that 750 million education apps would be installed on devices around the world in 2014.[85] The apps themselves come in various forms, from self-updating e-textbooks and test material for students, to tools like ClassDojo that help teachers manage unruly students and keep in touch with parents.[86]

As more learning takes place on digital platforms, data plays a larger role. In *Learning with Big Data: The Future of Education*, Viktor Mayer-Schönberger and Kenneth Cukier describe how the handful of data points traditionally used in education—test scores, report cards, attendance records, and so on—are likely to be dwarfed by far larger, and far more diverse, data sets. A rich range of data is captured, from where students click on the screen to how long they take to answer a question. And the data can be collected and stored in respect of hundreds of thousands of students. A new discipline, 'learning analytics', tries to make sense of what is gathered. The aim is to provide better feedback to students and teachers, and refine the individualized approach used in 'personalized' or 'adaptive' learning.[87]

A wealth of platforms also provide open access to collections of knowledge and research. Some are so commonplace that we can forget just how radical they are. Each month at Wikipedia, for example, almost half a billion people dip into a corpus of 35 million articles, content created and updated by around 69,000 main online contributors, provided in more than 280 languages, at no cost at all to these users.[88] The traditional encyclopedia, out of date as soon as it is printed, and costing as much as £1,000 for a multi-volume and undeniably handsome set, now looks quaint and antiquated. There are over 10,000 open-access online academic journals, containing more than 1.7 million articles, which are generally peer-reviewed but available at no charge, online, to read, copy, or distribute.[89] As of 2017, the Gates Foundation (which spends $900 million a year on research) will only fund scholars who publish in a way that is free for the public to read.[90] The traditional subscription approach is expensive—Harvard University, with the largest academic endowment in the world, announced in 2012 that its libraries could no longer afford to pay for traditional journals.[91]

Various business and charging models support these services. Some are free, others rely on paywalls, some are off-the-shelf, and others are open-source. Duolingo, a free online language-learning system, uses a unique model—it asks students to translate bits of foreign text that are lifted from larger bodies of text that companies, for a fee, have asked Duolingo to translate (both CNN and *BuzzFeed* use it to translate some of their news stories). The platform acts, then, as both a free online language-learning tool and as a fee-based translation crowdsourcing service.[92]

In all of these illustrations the historical monopoly of traditional teachers, tutors, and lecturers is challenged. There is less need for the 'sage on the stage' and more of a job for the 'guide on the side'—those who help students navigate through alternative sources of expertise. There are new roles and new disciplines, like education software designers who build the 'adaptive' learning systems, the content curators who compile and manage online content, and the data scientists who collect large data sets and develop 'learning analytics' to interpret them. It is not surprising, therefore, that Larry Summers, former chair of the White House Council of Economic Advisers and past President of Harvard, has said that 'the next quarter century will see more change in higher education than the last three combined',[93] and that Sir Michael Barber, a former Downing Street adviser, anticipates transformations in education in his aptly named report, *An Avalanche is Coming.*[94]

2.3. Divinity

The profession of the clergy is also in turmoil as a result of technology. Like other professionals, they stand as gatekeepers.

They are the interface between worshippers and their scriptural texts. Depending on the faith, they may also be the intermediary between worshippers and their God. Most sacred texts, if not all, are now online. In the past, many worshippers would have considered this depth of access to be blasphemous. The Lollards, for example, an English group trying to reform Christianity from the fourteenth century, were met by thunderous opposition from the clergy (and with violence by others) when they tried to translate the Bible into English (at the time only available in Latin), so that more people could read it. The resistance was so frenzied, as the historian Jonathan Rose notes, in large part 'because a vernacular Bible threatened to break a clerical monopoly on knowledge, and throw scriptural interpretation open to artisans'.[95] Clerics worried about the future of their jobs in the event that their communities became self-enlightened.

This six-centuries-old reaction may seem archaic. Yet, in the past few years a similar spirit divided the Nichiren Buddhists, a form of the religion founded and based in Japan. The conflict focused on *gohonzon*, the beautifully ornate scrolls and tablets of calligraphic script used by Nichiren Buddhists in prayer. The most sacred is the *dai gohonzon*, or the 'great' *gohonzon*, reputedly 850 years old. In 1989 the high priest, Abe Nikken, raised both the admittance fee to worship the *dai gohonzon* and the price of 'official copies' for home use. Many Buddhists were outraged, and left the old religious institutions to practise their religion independently. When the Internet arrived, these independent practitioners put it to service as a way of distributing digital copies of the *gohonzon* among themselves. Members of the old institutions condemned this behaviour as 'sacrilegious' and even 'obscene', rejecting these

pujas, small acts of prayer, using a basic interactive animation.[105] In Second Life, IslamOnline.net have re-created a virtual Mecca, and help people to make *Hajj*, the pilgrimage to Mecca, in this online world (running classes in the lead-up on the history and rituals involved).[106]

There are religious apps that turn mobile devices into 'Psalm Pilots'.[107] For prayer, there are apps that provide prayer times and point people towards Mecca or Jerusalem. For dietary needs, there are apps that use Global Positioning Systems to lead people toward the nearest Kosher or Halal shops and restaurants. For scripture, there are apps like the digital Bible built by YouVersion, available in 679 languages and downloaded by more than 150 million people. For monitoring spiritual heath, SoulPulse asks users simple questions every day for two weeks, and provides a personalized report on their wellbeing at the end.[108] The Vatican, in 2011, granted the first digital 'imprimatur'—the official licence, issued by the Catholic Church, for printing religious texts—to an app called 'Confession', which helps people prepare for confession.[109] This app includes tools for tracking sin and drop-down panels of options for contrition. Sikhs, until recently, were only able to carry around small parts of their bulky sacred text, the *Guru Granth Sahib*—now a digital version of all 1,430 pages can fit in their pockets.[110]

People are no longer passive recipients of the ideas of a few traditional religious figures. They have access to vast quantities of text-based religious knowledge and analysis. They can handpick and download 'Godcasts', religious sermons and lectures, from large online repositories.[111] They can put questions to competing religious experts—AskMoses.com is an online platform that hosts a pool of Jewish scholars and Rabbis ('webbe rebbes') waiting to field questions,[112] while many Imams provide *fatwas*, opinions on questions of Islamic law, over the Web (so called *e-fatwas*). They can use online religious dating sites, like Christian-Mingle, JDate, and Muslima, rather than rely on the historical monopoly that religious figures have had on matchmaking.[113]

Technology is also changing religious scholarship. The Cairo Geniza, for example, is a set of ancient Jewish manuscripts, among the 'oldest records of Jewish life', that were found tattered and torn into 300,000 fragments in the attic of an old Cairo synagogue a few centuries ago.[114] Subsequently they have been scattered across more than seventy collections around the world. In the past researchers have tried, manually, to piece the fragments together as if they were working on a big jigsaw—in almost two centuries of effort they made a few thousand successful 'joins'. In 2010 Lior Wolf, a computer scientist at Tel Aviv University, worked with colleagues to computerize this process—running an algorithm over digital images of tens of thousands of the fragments. Using technology borrowed from facial-recognition software, they swiftly found 1,000 new joins.[115] They have used the same technology to piece together fragments of Tibetan manuscripts[116] and the Dead Sea Scrolls.[117] Nachum Dershowitz, also a computer scientist at Tel Aviv University, used technology in a different way. For centuries, Bible scholars have argued furiously about who wrote different parts of the Bible. Using advances in 'computational linguistics', Nachum Dershowitz found that he could predict with 'over 90 percent accuracy' the scholarly consensus on the authorship of different parts of the texts.[118]

Many online religious communities exist, often functioning without any external direction from traditional religious authorities. Platforms like Beliefnet (5 million unique monthly visitors[119]) and Patheos (6 million unique monthly visitors[120]) host content and support debates on questions of faith, without leaning toward any particular religion. Other platforms do specialize. For Sikhs, networks of these sites have been called a 'virtual *sangat*,'[121] for Buddhists they have been called a '*cybersangha*'[122] (*sangat*, a Sikh term, is related to the word *sangha*, a Sanskrit word, meaning company or fellowship).[123] They can be widely used. Jesus Daily, a group on Facebook, began in 2009, and within two years it had more likes, comments, and shared content than any other page on the social network.[124]

These platforms and systems can strengthen people's existing religious beliefs and can also support entirely new internet-based faiths.[125] Sometimes, though, the services encourage people to question their inherited religions. In 2013 the *New York Times* reported on a quiet crisis in the Mormon Church, where members are struggling to reconcile their religious doctrine with historical fact as found online.[126] The BBC reported that, as early as 1994, the Church of Scientology had tried to shape and censor online content in an attempt to avoid a similar fate.[127] The traditional Abrahamic religions are also experiencing an intensifying scrutiny. Almost two-fifths of young practising Christians in the United States use the Internet to fact-check the statements that their religious leaders make.[128] Many Islamic countries heavily censor the Internet.[129] Some orthodox Jews can only use 'kosher' smartphones with limited browsing capability and a smaller accompanying app store.[130]

2.4. Law

In *Tomorrow's Lawyers*, we predict that the legal world will change 'more radically over the next two decades' than 'over the last two centuries'.[131] Numerous commentators have echoed this view of a legal profession on the brink of unprecedented upheaval.[132] In truth, the working practices of lawyers and judges have not changed much since the time of Charles Dickens. The set-up that has endured is fairly similar around the world, whether in support of resolving disputes, advising on transactions, or in counselling clients on their rights and duties. Legal advice is handcrafted by lawyers in partnership, delivered on a one-to-one basis, the output is documentation (often voluminous), and since the mid-1970s charging has generally been on an hourly-billing basis. To sort out their disputes, parties congregate before an impartial arbiter in a purpose-built courtroom where the procedure is formal, the process is steeped in tradition, and the language is largely arcane. Non-lawyers struggle to follow what is going on.

The greatest current pressure on this traditional approach is cost. Dickens himself may have overstated the problem when he referred to legal papers as 'mountains of costly nonsense',[133] but most legal and court services have indeed become unaffordable to their users, from consumers to global businesses.

In some countries, such as England and Australia, the legal market has been liberalized, so lawyers no longer have a monopoly over legal work. Non-lawyers can own and run legal businesses, while law firms can float on public stock-exchanges or take in external funding, such as private equity.[134] This is shaking up the consumer market, where research suggests that almost two-thirds of individuals would prefer to receive legal help from high-street brands than from conventional law firms.[135] The Co-Op Bank in England has said that it will offer legal services from around 350 of its bank branches, while other well-known non-legal businesses, like BT, the telecommunications company, and the AA, the motoring association, have also committed to providing a range of everyday legal services.[136] The solo lawyer is under threat.

In business law, new providers have entered the fray—legal process outsourcers like Integreon and Novus Law,[137] legal publishers such as Thomson Reuters,[138] and a rash of 'alternative business structures'. The last group, authorized in England and Wales under the Legal Services Act 2007, is well exemplified by Riverview Law, who are able to employ and deploy qualified lawyers at fixed fees and at lower cost than conventional firms.[139] Another growing line of legal trade is networks of freelance lawyers. Axiom led the way here, launching in 2000.[140] Since then, various law firms have followed suit, offering access, largely to their alumni, on a contract basis—for example, Berwin Leighton Paisner's 'Lawyers on Demand' and Pinsent Masons' 'Vario'.[141]

More generally, larger firms are responding to cost pressure by establishing a new division of labour. Lawyers are breaking down legal work into more basic tasks, and finding alternative ways of sourcing the more routine and repetitive work, such as document review in litigation, due diligence work, routine contract drafting, and rudimentary legal research. Legal tasks in this way are now being outsourced, offshored, passed along to paralegals, subcontracted, and sold to clients on a fixed-price basis. Some leading firms are setting up their own low-cost service facilities.[142]

There are moves also towards a new discipline—legal risk management—where the spirit is dispute avoidance rather than dispute resolution, and towards multi-disciplinary practice, where lawyers work alongside accountants, consultants, and tax specialists in providing an integrated professional service.[143]

Technology is playing a central role in the transformation of the legal profession. Aside from heavily used back-office systems (especially e-mail, accounting, and word processing), and well-established legal research tools (such as Westlaw and Lexis-Nexis),[144] a variety of emerging systems are systematizing and sometimes changing the way that lawyers work.[145]

One key category of system computerizes the production of legal documents. These 'document assembly systems'—built using tools like ContractExpress and Exari[146]—can generate high-quality documents after straightforward interactive consultations with users. Originally these were used only to help lawyers. Now similar systems are becoming available online for lay users.[147] Other document services are also available—for example, Docracy, which holds an open collection of legal agreements,[148] and Shake, an app that helps create legal contracts on hand-held devices.[149]

Legal help is also available online. Legislation and case law can be accessed at no cost in many jurisdictions (thanks in large part to the pioneering work of the Australasian Legal Information Institute),[150] although non-lawyers usually find it more helpful to dip into the huge range of state-provided and charity-led websites that offer practical, jargon-free guidance on numerous areas of law. Commercially available online legal services, such as

LegalZoom and Rocket Lawyer, are also taking hold,[151] while there are a few more sophisticated diagnostic expert systems, which tackle highly complex, multi-jurisdictional legal questions and can outperform the best specialists—the international law firm Allen & Overy has a suite of these services,[152] while much newer legal businesses, such as Neota Logic, are delivering systems that model complex rules and reasoning processes.[153]

Online deal rooms and case rooms are increasingly shared between law firms and their clients. These are Internet-based platforms for collaboration, where the documents relating to deals and disputes can easily be stored and retrieved.[154]

In preparation for litigation, intelligent search systems can now outperform junior lawyers and paralegals in reviewing large sets of documents and selecting the most relevant,[155] while Big Data techniques are underpinning systems that are better than expert litigators in predicting the results of court decisions, from patent disputes (the Lex Machina service[156]) to the US Supreme Court.[157] Similar technologies, such as Kira and eBrevia, are being used by corporate lawyers for due diligence work.[158]

Fundamental challenges to the courts are also being launched. Legal technologists are asking whether court is a service or a place; whether people and organizations in dispute really need to congregate in physical courtrooms to settle their differences. One alternative is the virtual court.[159] Already used for vulnerable witnesses to give evidence or for preliminary hearings in criminal cases, this is a conventional courtroom set-up in which participation—by lawyers, parties, or witnesses—is via some kind of video link. Another alternative is online dispute resolution (ODR), recent proposals for which in England and Wales were welcomed by the Master of the Rolls, the top civil judge, as 'an exciting milestone in the history of our civil justice system'.[160] Here, the process of resolving a dispute, especially the formulation of the solution, is conducted across the Internet—from quarrels amongst citizens to conflicts between individuals and the state. One example is 'e-adjudication', one of various ODR techniques that are used to sort out a staggering 60 million disagreements that arise amongst traders each year amongst eBay users (more than three times the total number of lawsuits filed in the entire US court system).[161] This is based on a widely available platform for ODR, known as Modria.[162] Another is Cybersettle, a web-based 'e-negotiation' system that handled over 200,000 personal-injury and insurance claims of a combined value of almost $2 billion.[163] Yet another is Resolver, a free web service that helps UK consumers pursue their grievances with over 2,000 organizations.[164]

Online legal communities are emerging. Legal OnRamp[165] originally led the way here for major law firms and their clients, while non-lawyers too are beginning to contribute, sharing their practical experiences of resolving legal problems in what we call 'communities of legal experience'.[166]

In another direction, interest is developing in embedding legal requirements into our social and working lives, so that, for example, automatic compliance with health-and-safety regulations can be integrated into the design of buildings that can identify and respond when temperature levels are above some statutory level. In this way, human beings do not need to know the law and make a conscious decision to comply, and consequently, lawyers' direct involvement is not needed.

Even when lawyers are being used, their selection is no longer by word of mouth. Instead, there are online reputation systems where clients can pass along their views on particular practitioners or firms (Avvo, for example, has reviews of almost 200,000 US attorneys),[167] price-comparison systems (for both hourly rates and on a project basis),[168] and web services, such as Priori Legal, which locate suitable lawyers for users.[169] Online auctions for the selection of legal advisers have been in operation for over a decade.[170]

Looking to the longer term, then, the future of legal services is unlikely to look like John Grisham or Rumpole of the Bailey. More probably, our research suggests that traditional lawyers will in large part be 'replaced by advanced systems, or by less costly workers supported by technology or standard processes, or by lay people armed with online self-help tools'.[171]

2.5. Journalism

Since the early 1800s the print newspaper has for many people been their main window on the outside world, beyond the chatter of close friends, co-workers, and family. Today, in many places, it is in decline. Consider the US daily papers, often regarded as a harbinger for the rest of the traditional print-based industry.[172] In the words of Robert W. McChesney and John Nichols, in *The Death and Life of American Journalism*, they are in 'free-fall collapse'.[173] In the ten years leading up to 2014, per capita daily newspaper circulation fell by 32 per cent.[174] In the same period, the number of print journalists fell by one-third.[175] Advertising revenue is now at the same level as when records began in 1953 (adjusting for inflation).[176] When the editors of the British newspapers the *Guardian* and the *Sunday Times* were asked recently whether they would stop printing their papers, they replied that 'they thought their papers had bought their last printing presses'.[177]

At the same time, online platforms are ascendant. In 2008, for the first time, more people in the United States said the Internet was their main source of news (40 per cent) rather than newspapers (35 per cent).[178] In 2013 this figure had risen further to 50 per cent.[179] In the United Kingdom, over the past seven years the proportion of people who access news and magazines online has more than doubled (from 20 per cent to 55 per cent).[180] In Iceland the figure is almost 90 per cent (and as high elsewhere in Northern Europe).[181] Among younger people, those who will become tomorrow's journalists as well as tomorrow's readers, use of the Internet for news (and disuse of newspapers) is even greater.[182] Eric Alterman estimated in the *New Yorker* that the average age of a traditional US newspaper reader 'was fifty-five, and rising'.[183] That was in 2008.

While the contrasting fortunes of print newspapers and online platforms are, of course, related, they do also reflect a deeper, long-standing, dissatisfaction with the old print-based model. The amount of time that people spend reading newspapers has plummeted over the past thirty years (falling by around a half). Yet most of this decline took place before 2000 and the spread of the Internet.[184] In part, this is a consequence of television's historical growth in popularity as a source of news, though this too is changing. In the United States, in 2013, the Internet superseded the television as the main source of news for all those under 50, although for younger people this watershed was reached several years before.[185]

As a result, the traditional newspaper business model is in crisis. It relied primarily on print advertising fees, which were topped up by paper sales (particularly at local newspapers). But advertising expenditure has drifted to online platforms, where messages can be better targeted at wider audiences. As print circulation falls, sales revenue is under pressure.[186] Yet most traditional news organizations have continued to pursue the print market. They have consolidated existing operations, launched new papers, and experimented with their format and pricing.[187]

Most have also built new digital platforms and moved existing print content online. Broadcasters have responded in similar vein. These platforms are well used, and make up most of the twenty-five most visited news sites in the United States.[188] There is, though, no definite relationship between success in print and success online. The *Guardian* newspaper has the second *lowest* print circulation among the eleven daily papers in the United Kingdom, but the second *highest* number of unique website visitors among all English-language newspapers in the world (overtaking the *New York Times* in September 2014).[189] Nor is there yet a clear alternative to the old business model. Digital advertising remains a small fraction of total revenue for newspapers (around 9 per cent in the United States in 2013).[190] And though a number of innovative payment mechanisms have been explored, from paywalls (where subscription is required to access certain content) to micropayments (where a small payment is made for each article), still only about one in ten people paid for online news in 2013.[191] News delivered via tablet devices promises much, but is far from a foolproof way to make a profit—when Rupert Murdoch launched the *Daily* in 2011, an iPad-only newspaper, it collapsed in less than two years.

At the heart of online news are social media platforms like Facebook (used by over 1.39 billion people[192]), Twitter (284 million users[193]), and YouTube (over 1 billion users[194]). Of those who use these networks, half use them to share news stories, images, and videos with each other.[195] Pervasive mobile devices let people use these networks in any place and at any time they are connected. For example, during the London Olympics in 2012 between 30 and 50 per cent of the visits the BBC website received were from mobile devices.[196] More than half the visitors to the *New York Times* site at the end of 2014 were from mobile devices—a figure that 'increases with each passing month'.[197] Half of YouTube views are from mobile devices,[198] and over 85 per cent of Facebook's monthly users are mobile users.[199]

Traditional news organizations use these platforms to distribute their existing material. On Twitter, in 2010, three-quarters of the links that people shared with each other were for 'mainstream' news sites.[200] Many individual journalists have far more followers than the print newspapers for which they write.[201] The profile for *BBC Breaking News* alone has more followers (13.9 million) than the entire British print daily-paper circulation (7.5 million).[202] Whether a news site is promoted or ignored by these platforms is critical. When Facebook, for example, adjusted the algorithm used to determine what news their users receive, the traffic to the *Guardian* and the *Washington Post*—which had until then received 'eye-popping traffic'—fell significantly.[203]

The traditional institutions are only a small part of the picture. Networks of individuals (freelancers, activists, and ordinary people) also use these systems (Facebook, Twitter, YouTube, and so on) to produce and share their own original reporting and commentary. This so called 'citizen' or 'participatory' or 'do-it-yourself' journalism, and the blogs that support it, adds a deafening crowd of voices to the once solitary narrative of the established institutions. *Bleacher Report*, a blog written by 2,000 sports fans, now has 22 million unique users each month, enough to rival Yahoo and CNN sports.[204] Global Voices, an online network of 1,200 writers and editors, who are largely volunteers, scrape through the Internet to find, curate, and translate pieces (into thirty languages) that are written outside the mainstream press (what they call the 'citizen and social web'). Scott Gant captures this new spirit in the title of his book, *We're All Journalists Now.*[205]

New 'digital-only' institutions have also emerged, often with non-traditional business models. The *Huffington Post* is a for-profit online news platform on which anyone can submit an article, alongside paid writers. Set up in 2005, within six years it had overtaken the *New York Times* website in unique monthly visitors.[206] *ProPublica* is an independent, not-for-profit online newsroom, financed by the charitable Sandler Foundation, which only conducts investigative journalism. Set up in 2007, it has won two Pulitzer Prizes and a Peabody award. *Wikileaks* is a not-for-profit organization, financed by donations, that provides an online platform to publish private, secret, and classified material. When it released 251,287 confidential US diplomatic cables on 28 November 2010, the *New York Review of Books* noted that it would have taken journalists 'a couple of centuries to wheedle out this volume of information by traditional methods'.[207] For many of these online platforms, success depends upon social media. *Buzzfeed* is a for-profit online news platform, financed by digital advertising (and venture capital), which in 2013 had more unique monthly visitors than the *New York Times*.[208] It receives three and a half times more traffic from Facebook than from Google.[209]

Several platforms are experimenting with different modes of journalism—'explanatory' journalism at *Vox*, 'public-interest' journalism at *The Marshall Project*, 'news-aggregation' at *Real Clear Politics*, 'data-journalism' at *FiveThirtyEight*.[210] In fact, data is important not only in what is reported but how it is reported. At the *Huffington Post* editors simultaneously test alternative headlines for given articles on different readers to see which draw the greatest audience (so called 'A/B testing'). Chartbeat, an online system, provides media sites with real-time data, displayed on a simple dashboard, showing, for example, the site's top pages, where traffic has come from, what devices it is being viewed on, and so on.[211] There is, across platforms, a notable rise in the use of video alongside the printed word. This is sensible—over one-third of US adults watched news videos online in 2013.[212]

In 1995 the futurist Nicholas Negroponte was considered radical for predicting that the newspaper of the future would be a 'DailyMe', an 'electronic' paper where the headlines and content would reflect readers' particular interests—as if the 'newspaper company were willing to put its entire staff at your beck and call for one edition'.[213] Yet only two decades later this kind of personalized news provision is commonplace. Flipboard is an online platform (used by 90 million people) that produces a 'personal magazine', where the news is tailored to readers' interests, as derived from their social networks.[214] Facebook newsfeeds and Twitter streams are filled with content filtered through users' friends or those who are followed. This is not without controversy. The algorithm that determines what news appears on users' Facebook newsfeeds, for example, is in effect a computerized editor—and its editorial stance is unclear.[215]

As a result of these changes, some of the tasks that fall to traditional journalists, and the way they undertake those tasks, are very different. Journalists can manually sift through social media looking for breaking news or popular stories, or use computerized systems like Storyful.[216] They can secure help with their copy-editing from apps like Grammarly, and with note-taking from Evernote.[217] And, as noted, some tasks are no longer undertaken by people at all. In 2014 *Associated Press* started to use algorithms developed by Automated Insights to computerize the production of several hundred formerly handcrafted earnings reports, producing fifteen times as many as before.[218] *Forbes* now provides similarly for earnings reports and sport, using algorithms developed by Narrative Science.[219] The *Los Angeles Times* uses an algorithm called 'Quakebot' (which is currently followed by 95,600 people on Twitter) to monitor the US Geological Survey for earthquake alerts, and automatically to compose articles if an event takes place.[220] Users can struggle to tell the difference.[221]

2.6. Management consulting

In 2013 Clayton Christensen claimed, in a *Harvard Business Review* article, 'Consulting on the Cusp of Disruption', that change was 'inevitable' in consulting, and that those who had traditionally helped others in management difficulties were themselves 'being upended'.[222] Duff McDonald concluded his book *The Firm* with the observation that consulting was more 'hotly contested than it has ever been'.[223] Lucy Kellaway suggested in the *Financial Times* that, 'fifty years hence, McKinsey won't exist'.[224] Christopher McKenna called the industry 'the world's newest profession', whose status as a profession is ambiguous, and whose future remains uncertain.[225]

As Christensen notes, the consulting business model has changed little in the past 100 years. A smart outsider or team of external specialists is sent into an organization for a limited period of time and asked (at least on the face of it) to provide possible answers to the clients' most important questions. Over the years, consulting firms have sought to differentiate themselves in various ways—by claiming, for example, that their people are brighter, more rigorous, or with greater experience of particular industries or sectors than the competition. Some consultancies have also developed proprietary tools to mark themselves out as superior. Andersen Consulting (later Accenture) were leading exponents of this in the 1980s—their system development and project management 'methodologies' were like large recipe books, extending to many volumes. They laid out, step-by-step, how to undertake complex processes. Consulting knowledge, in this way, was reduced to a set of standard procedures.

Another source of differentiation in the past for some consulting firms was that they had access to data and information that others did not. Well-stocked research libraries and heavily staffed internal research departments gave consultants an edge. Some strategy consultants with whom we spoke estimated that, in the past, their firms spent up to 80 per cent of their time gathering data in this way. With the coming of the Internet, much of this data and information is now freely available. Where it is not readily available online, clients can turn instead to traditional 'research-only' organizations like Gartner, Forrester Research, and IDC. Digitizing processes mean that clients can collect basic internal data themselves, rather than hire consultants to spend time manually counting heads, monitoring inventories, and manipulating spreadsheets and databases. Customer data can be collected directly from online 'data exhausts' (the flows of information from retailers, for example, about what we buy and where we click), offline innovations like loyalty cards (16.5 million people use Tesco's loyalty card, for instance[226]), or mined from other unstructured sources of data, rather than through bespoke surveys and face-to-face interviews. Reflecting on these changes, one consultant noted to us that the 'heart was ripped out of their business model'. Data and information work fell to less than 30 per cent of the services provided by strategy consulting firms.

The availability of basic analytical tools, and more sophisticated systems as well, enables people outside traditional consultancies also to process data and to tease out the sort of insights over which consultants once held a monopoly. It is far harder for consultants to create the 'million-dollar slide'—what Bain & Co. once called the 'single image' containing information so insightful for a client that it alone was worth $1 million in consulting fees.[227]

As a result, traditional strategy consulting firms now offshore a great deal of their routine research. Bain and McKinsey, for example, have teams of researchers, mainly in India, who support their mainstream consultants (Bain Capability Centers and McKinsey Knowledge Centers, respectively). IT consultancies have acted similarly, transferring much of their routine work to bases in countries with lower labour- and operating-costs. Around one-third of Accenture and Cap Gemini's employees, for example, are based in India.[228] Most have also invested in more sophisticated analytic capabilities, particularly in Big Data, to try to reclaim and retain the analytical upper hand.

Some consultancies have taken their new-found expertise in data analysis and packaged it into a range of different off-the-shelf products. Their clients can choose from a pre-prepared bundle of software and tools, rather than the consultants crafting an entirely new set from scratch. McKinsey, for example, offers sixteen distinct products, called McKinsey Solutions.[229] Deloitte offers nine distinct products, called Deloitte Managed Analytics.[230] Once installed at a client, these packages provide a computerized stream of insights rather than the traditional one-off transfer of expertise in a presentation or final report.

For the old strategy institutions, there is less conventional strategy work (described by one seasoned campaigner as 'drawing curves')—now only 20 per cent of what they do, compared to 60 to 70 per cent three decades ago.[231] Many consultants have been forced to specialize in particular regions or sectors, and only the largest firms have maintained generalist, or 'systems level', capabilities. There has been a rise in IT consulting, but here too there are lower cost providers competing for their work. There is a definitional issue here—some firms do not consider system development work to fall under the heading of 'consulting', while for others it is at the heart of their consulting businesses.

The largest three strategy consultancies have built distinct 'thought-leadership' practices to develop and spread expertise that is gathered outside of typical consulting assignments (bcg. perspectives, Bain Insights, and McKinsey Insights, respectively). New consulting disciplines have emerged. There is 'digital' consulting, from organizations like BCG Digital Ventures and Deloitte Digital, and 'behavioural' consulting, applying insights from social psychology, from organizations like the Behavioural Insights Team (once part of the British Government, now part of NESTA).[232]

Beyond the traditional consulting organizations is a growing number of individual consultants, small boutique consultancies, and specialized research or data analytics firms, all actively competing for work. Hal Varian, Google's chief economist, calls these set-ups 'micro-nationals', made possible by the Internet providing 'communication capabilities that only the largest multinationals could afford 15 years ago'.[233]

The Internet also supports network-based organizations that draw on pools of experts and consultants to provide on-demand services. The Gerson Lehrman Group and Guidepoint Global put clients in touch with their large online networks of experts, of 400,000 and 200,000 people respectively.[234] Eden McCallum, Business Talent Group, and Cast Professionals are able to build more formal, ad hoc teams for clients from online networks of vetted freelance consultants.[235] At 10 EQS, the teams are 'digital-only', and clients interact with them using a dedicated online platform.[236] Expert 360, Skillbridge, and Vumero act more like online marketplaces that help clients sift through and choose individual consultants when required.[237] The Corporate Executive

Board, a membership-only consulting business, uses its online member network of 16,000 executives to identify and spread best practice.[238]

Recently, crowdsourcing platforms for consulting services have been built. Open IDEO is an online platform built by the design consultancy IDEO. Problems, predominantly social, are posted online, and anyone who signs up can log on to the Open IDEO platform and help to solve them collaboratively. Wikistrat is an online network of around 1,000 experts with backgrounds in politics, the military, government, and academia.[239] Clients set questions for a select crowd of these experts, who then assemble on the Wikistrat platform to work through the problem together. Kaggle is an online platform where clients supply their data, set a clear question about it, and a network of statisticians from across 100 countries compete to answer it with the greatest insight.[240] In the Cabinet Office of the British Government, the Open Policy Making Team uses a range of online platforms (blogs, social media, crowdsourcing) to try to break the 'monopoly' that traditional civil servants have on policymaking.

There are systems that require less human input. Platforms like Ayasdi and BeyondCore profess to provide 'automated' data analysis—rather than waiting to be set an initial question by a human being, these systems are said to dig through data sets for correlations and draw out interesting relationships for further analysis, or point out additional data that might be needed.[241] IBM's Watson has been recalibrated to act as a 'c-suite adviser'—it scans strategy documents, listens to and digests conversations at meetings, and, when asked, provides analytical advice based on its insights—for example, on possible companies for investment.[242]

Kensho, a system in which Goldman Sachs has invested, provides computerized answers to financial questions asked in plain English (for example, what happens to technology stocks when there is a privacy scare?). This would otherwise require extensive human research.[243]

Traditional consultants have noticed a change in their clients' behaviour: they are more cautious about using external support; they are more willing to decompose it (break it down into separate work packages) when they do; and they are happier to use different people and systems rather than relying on single suppliers. One consultant spoke of an 'emperor's new clothes moment'—a realization by their clients that some of their stock techniques, from 'activity based costing' to 'value based management', were not as sophisticated as they had thought.

Some traditional consultants consider *in-house* consultants as their main competitor. The rise of in-house teams is attributable partly to the availability of data and analytical tools on the Internet and partly to the large numbers of alumni from traditional consulting firms who are able to run these teams (around 50,000 of these alumni from the main three firms).[244] It is also to some extent because the classic qualification of the consultant, the MBA, is far more widely held. As the best business schools begin to open up their MBA programmes, this will accelerate. Since 2014, Harvard's historically exclusive, two-year MBA, costing $90,000, has been complemented by an online learning platform, HBX. This offers a shorter online qualification, CORe, lasting nine weeks and at a fee of $1,500 (described as 'a primer on the fundamentals of business'), and a range of specialized individual business courses. Building this platform was not without controversy—Michael Porter and Clayton Christensen, two of Harvard Business School's best-known professors, disagreed publicly about whether it was the right approach to take.[245]

For entrepreneurs and small businesses, the Internet supports a growing 'do-it-yourself' culture. Offline, there are 11,000 business books published each year in the United States, excluding self-published books.[246] Online, networks of writers, practitioners, academics, and lay people share their expertise and experience across a wide range of platforms and communities. Intellectual frameworks for thinking through problems have been standardized—Barbara Minto's 'Pyramid Principle', for example, is a tool widely used by leading consultants to analyse and tackle a problem in a logical way. Once the province only of McKinsey, this tool is now available online in text-based instruction, video lectures, online courses, and a mobile app called 'Minto'.[247]

Tellingly, the Big Four accounting firms (PwC, EY, KPMG, and Deloitte) now do more consulting than the big three consulting firms (McKinsey, Bain, BCG).[248] For the Big Four, it is a return to an old role—before the collapse of Enron, all these firms had large consulting practices. After the Sarbanes-Oxley Act was introduced, three of the Big Four divested themselves of their consulting businesses (only Deloitte held on to theirs). In the past few years, however, they have rebuilt their consulting capabilities, acquiring several small consulting firms, and some larger ones too. PwC bought Booz & Co. (renaming it Strategy&), while Deloitte bought Monitor (renaming it Monitor Deloitte). Revenue from consulting services at the Big Four is now growing far faster than revenue from audit services.[249] At Deloitte, for example, if consulting and audit continue to grow at their 2013 rate, consulting revenue will overtake audit revenue within five years.[250]

Management consulting is not a regulated profession. Anyone can start up a business and call it a consulting firm. This does not mean that the major consulting firms have no interest in professional values. On the contrary, it is clear, for instance, that professionalism was a passion of McKinsey in the 1960s (when it was mandatory for their consultants to wear bowler hats as evidence of their professionalism[251]), while it remains a preoccupation of Accenture today. But the lack of formal boundaries does perhaps allow the large consulting businesses to diversify more radically than other professions might be inclined. Accenture, for example, now employs 750 hospital nurses, and more than 10 per cent of its fee income is currently derived from advice on 'digital marketing', even though this may more intuitively be thought to be the role of the advertising and marketing communities. Accenture is not alone in being known as a consulting business, and yet one with traditional management consulting work that represents a small percentage of its current portfolio of services.

2.7. Tax and audit

Tax and audit work is largely undertaken by the accounting profession. The two disciplines have much in common—they are heavily regulated, they involve regular interaction with the state, and the raw material upon which they operate is financial data. Although famously the butt of Monty Python's biting wit,[252] accountants have played a central role in advanced economies. There are signs, however, that much that they do will be challenged by technology. This is not news—in the 1970s some groundbreaking work on artificial intelligence identified tax accounting as fertile ground for development work, while in the 1980s spreadsheet software and microcomputers (as they were then known) were warmly embraced by most leading accounting firms.

Turning first to tax, taxpayers in the past had two options when filing their tax returns. They could either labour at the task themselves, or they could pay a human expert, familiar with the relevant law and practice, to analyse their figures and complete the forms on their behalf. The latter was a tempting option. Tax regulations in most jurisdictions have piled up over time, extending often to several thousand pages, written in abstruse language and frequently changed. In the United States in recent years, for example, tax regulations have been updated, on average, once a day.[253] But the human expert option has proven to be expensive. Historically, tax advice was handcrafted for each client, and the advice was bespoke. In the 1970s, for instance, tax computations were completed manually after lengthy consultation with fat ledgers and paper accounts.

In recent years, however, a third option has emerged for the personal taxpayer—online computerized tax preparation software. Some well-known systems in the United States are TurboTax, H&R Block at Home, and TaxAct.[254] Using these applications, individuals answer a set of simple questions about their financial affairs and, in response, the software automatically compiles their returns. There is no need for a human expert. In the United States, in 2014, almost 48 million people prepared their own returns online, without a tax professional, using tax preparation software—either commercial systems, like those mentioned above, or free software provided by the tax authority (from basic forms that help with calculations, to more sophisticated systems).[255] Most of the software providers also host accompanying online services. Here, taxpayers and tax professionals can share their experience and any advice or guidance received. TurboTax's AnswerXchange and H&R Block's The Community are two illustrations of this.[256]

In the past, individuals and small businesses likewise needed accountants to help monitor their cash-flow, handle invoices, record expenses, and so forth. Now a growing range of online accounting software is available to computerize many of these tasks. Some of the better-known systems are QuickBooks, Xero, and Kashflow.[257] Thanks to a partnership with the UK tax authority, Kashflow also computerizes VAT returns, so that businesses that use its system to track their finances can, at the end of the year, use in-built routines to compile complete tax returns automatically and then file them swiftly online. It is a small step for other online systems to do the same. In March 2015, in the United Kingdom, the Chancellor of the Exchequer announced the 'end of the tax return' and the launch in 2016 of the 'digital tax account'.[258]

For large organizations, with more complex tax affairs than those of individuals and small businesses, there is a large and growing collection of tax technologies to assist them complete their tax returns. There are systems, for example, to capture the data needed for a tax return; to calculate how much tax is owed; to submit the final returns; to compose formal accounts and reports; and to forecast and test the effect of different tax strategies.[259] Some tax systems are highly ambitious. At Deloitte, in the United Kingdom, for instance, the collective expertise of around 250 of their tax specialists was distilled into a system to help major clients directly prepare and submit their corporate tax returns. This system was being used by more than 70 per cent of FTSE 100 companies when it was sold in 2009 to Thomson Reuters, the global information provider. Also at Deloitte, the task of recovering foreign VAT payments is no longer done by human experts, but by a system, Revatic Smart. This scans clients' documents using optical character-recognition software, and automatically files the correct forms, with little human input.[260] In most cases, these tax platforms computerize tasks that would have once been done manually by a human being. But the firm also employs more than 10,000 people in India to undertake routine tax work.

With regard to national tax authorities and their operations, many still rely on taxpayers, from individuals to the largest multinationals, to self-assess. The standard process is for a human being to log on to some system, truthfully answer a set of questions, and submit a return in the prescribed form at a designated time. Brazil has recently eliminated much of this sort of self-assessment. Their businesses are no longer required to file tax returns at all. Instead, they submit their original accounting records electronically to the tax authority. Under this system, called the Public System of Digital Bookkeeping (SPED), the tax authorities, not the taxpayers, analyse the data submitted and determine how much tax must be paid.

Computer-based systems like this are also used to tackle tax evasion and fraud. In Latin America, for instance, a popular evasion tactic is to file fraudulent invoices, using these fictional transactions to help reduce the amount of tax due. In Chile, Mexico, Argentina, and other countries, tax authorities are replacing traditional, easy-to-fake, paper-based invoices with mandatory online 'e-invoices' that must be submitted to tax authorities as soon as transactions take place.[261] Again, as in Brazil, tax authorities then hold the raw data. Meanwhile, in Italy, tax authorities use the 'redditometro' system, which trawls available data and estimates what a specific taxpayer might spend in any particular year—if their estimate is more than 20 per cent greater than that declared by the taxpayer on their tax return, then they ask for an explanation.[262] In the United States, various states use Risk Solutions by LexisNexis, a set of algorithms that run through data to spot when tax fraudsters are using fake identities to claim illegitimate tax refunds. They promise a 200 per cent return on the cost of the software.[263] The volumes of data involved here are vast. For example, the system used by the British tax authorities to detect fraud, called 'Connect', sifts through over a billion pieces of data.[264] It is said that it holds more data than the British Library, no mean feat, given that the library holds a copy of every book ever published in the United Kingdom.[265]

As many tax tasks become computerized, the daily work of tax professionals is changing. Recall the case of Brazil, where original accounts (and not completed tax returns) are submitted. This has reframed what leading Brazilian tax advisers now do. They no longer help clients prepare tax returns, but instead help clients prepare their original accounts. In doing so, they use software that is similar to that which the tax authority will eventually use to calculate the tax due. The advisers then test what tax will be due for a given set of original accounts, and make appropriate changes to the accounts where possible.

For more traditional tax practices, competition is coming from different directions. In-house tax teams, management consultancies, software developers, and business information providers are all increasingly interested in conducting tax work. In response, traditional tax practices are focusing less on tax compliance work (preparing and submitting returns) and undertaking more tax planning work (for example, where to locate an HQ, or where to be domiciled, to reduce tax liability) and tax transaction work (for instance, advising on the tax implications of mergers and acquisitions). The advice is increasingly proactive rather than reactive. Deloitte, for instance, provides expats abroad with computerized advice on where they can and cannot travel to minimize their tax burden, based on GPS data from their mobiles.

The tax profession is said to be at particular risk from technology. Carl Benedikt Frey and Michael Osborne, authors of 'The Future of Employment', estimate that only 1 per cent of 'tax preparation' work is safe from computerization. Of the 700 occupations they review, this is among the ten 'most at risk'.[266] There is therefore great scope for change—6.1 billion hours are spent filing taxes every year, equivalent to 3 million people working full-time.[267]

In the spirit of the special pleading lamented in Chapter 1, tax professionals who are expert in planning and transaction work are often quick to concede that it is the work of their compliance colleagues that is terminally threatened. However, these planners and transaction advisers are themselves also vulnerable. As early as the 1980s it was recognized, for example, that tax planning and tax compliance were, technologically speaking, two sides of the same coin. They both operate on the same complex bodies of regulations and practice. The only difference between the two, in information processing terms, is that tax compliance involves progressing forwards through the rules driven by the facts and the law, while planning entails reasoning backwards through the rules in search of legal and factual premises that can justify a target tax liability.[268] This underlying similarity is echoed by thought leaders in the world of tax who say that much tax planning work will also soon be conducted by machines. As for those who advise on tax deals, accounting firms at the leading edge are looking (as are progressive corporate lawyers) at the computerization of the due diligence work and the standardization of much of the documentation. The transformation of tax is well under way.

Leading auditors also say they are on the brink of fundamental change, but they observe that their transformation is not coming as quickly as in tax. This is often attributed to the conservatism of the regulators, who are alleged to resist new ways of working. But market forces may be at play here as well—the audit of the world's largest corporations is dominated by the 'Big Four' (Deloitte, KPMG, EY, and PwC). In 2013 in the United Kingdom, for example, these four firms audited 98 per cent of the FTSE 100, 96 per cent of the FTSE 250, and 78.8 per cent of the entire UK market.[269] None of the Big Four has yet tried to disrupt the others by undertaking audit in radically new ways. Perhaps there has been no obvious incentive for these incumbents to rush and replace the status quo.

Auditors play a pivotal role in the corporate world. Like tax professionals, they review and master financial information. But their job is quite different. In compliance work, tax specialists generally serve those who manage businesses, and they review financial statements to calculate and (broadly speaking) minimize the tax payable. In contrast, statutory auditors are tasked with reviewing financial statements to assure that they are an accurate, complete, and fair reflection of a company's actual trading activity. Simply put, auditors confirm (or not) that a company is telling the truth in its published accounts. For the audit, the end user is the investor whose decisions are influenced by audit opinions. Auditors therefore can boost confidence in individual businesses as well as in markets more widely.

Audit is big business. The global market leader, PwC, undertakes the audit work of 30 per cent of the world's listed companies, with around 70,000 of its people devoted to this on a full-time basis, scattered across 157 countries, delivering fees of around $10 billion.

Pivotal though auditors may be, it is clear that much of the conduct of a financial audit is heavily process-driven. For decades it has been supported by standard checklists and, in larger firms, by sophisticated audit methodologies, such as KPMG's KAM and EY's GAM.[270] These provide step-by-step guidance on how to go about the fundamental audit activities—planning, risk assessment, evaluation of controls, testing of transactions and accounts, reporting, and so forth.

The amenability of financial statement auditing to technology is long established. In the 1980s auditors were early adopters, as noted, of spreadsheet and microcomputer technology, and there was much talk about the great potential of 'audit automation'. It was during that era too that the discipline of computer audit came of age—auditors had to have the skills to review and interrogate computer-based accounting systems, as well as paper-based materials.

Since then, 'computer-assisted audit techniques' (CAAT) have evolved in several waves. Today, the largest firms have developed and deploy their own proprietary software—for example, PwC's system, Aura.[271] These are designed to help carry out complex audits across large corporations with businesses in many different countries. These systems help standardize the audit process, capture and analyse the relevant data, support project management, and document the audit itself. Meanwhile, smaller practices use highly functional off-the-shelf packages, and are served by an active audit software industry, some of whose products are developed by the major firms themselves.

Despite the apparent sophistication of the audit profession, there are frequent and loud calls for its reform. In part, these follow from concerns about the dominance of the Big Four, and from their involvement in the delivery of non-audit services. In part, the demand for reforms also stems from a disappointment with auditors' past performance. Observers and sceptics want to know, as John C. Coffee, Jr. asks in his book *Gatekeepers*, why 'did the watchdogs not bark' when, for example, auditing Enron and WorldCom,[272] and why they have continued not to bark in more recent financial scandals.[273] Another driver for reform, frankly acknowledged by leading auditors, is the inadequacy of current CAAT to handle the sheer volume of transactions now involved in large audits.

Ideally, on an annual basis, auditors should be able to scrutinize every individual transaction record and then check for any discrepancies in the accounts. In practice, this is not possible. In large audits there are too many transactions to review. There are too many data, whether handled manually or with the support of current CAAT. Accordingly, sophisticated techniques have been developed so that auditors actually review a relatively small number of carefully selected transactions. This small fraction of the available data is known as a 'sample'. In selecting samples, auditors have been heavily guided by the notion of 'materiality' (crudely, financial information is material if its misstatement or exclusion might influence investor's decision-making). And they have also traditionally relied on 'heuristics', simple rules of thumb to help them find the common errors and typical omissions that take place in sets of accounts. From this small sample, and with these heuristics, auditors are able to draw broader conclusions about the reliability of financial statements. They try to complement this analysis with other activities—face-to-face discussions at client sites, walking the floor, kicking the metaphorical tyres—to get a feel for the business under scrutiny. But, in the end, auditors have to concede the inevitable shortcoming in their approach—extrapolating from a limited sample is risky (even if statistically valid), and their heuristics are often misleading (as, for example, the field of 'behavioral auditing' shows[274]).

As time has passed, however, auditors have had to handle far larger volumes of data—many billions, if not trillions, of data over a year for a client (creeping towards a billion transactions each week for the largest clients). This is due partly to the great size that audited companies have become. It is also because more activities are captured and recorded in electronic form. The traditional approach, set out above, was to take a small sample and extrapolate. New systems attempt to handle larger samples. In some cases—and this is a major shift—they are now attempting to handle *all* the data, getting rid of the need to take samples at all. This is the spirit of HALO, PwC's latest audit software. It is designed to run algorithms through entire data sets (that is, all recorded transactions), and computerize the search for outliers and inconsistencies. This is also the spirit of the prediction made by KPMG's James P. Liddy, that the future of audit was 'the capacity to examine 100 percent of a client's transactions'.[275]

This ambition of '100 per-cent testing'—using all available data, and not just a representative sample—is a particular case of a more general ambition very much in vogue in statistics, as discussed by Viktor Mayer-Schönberger and Kenneth Cukier in their book *Big Data.* One of the general features of Big Data, the authors argue, is precisely this move from taking small samples of data to using all the data instead (as they put it, 'from some to all').[276]

The next step on from 100 per cent testing is a phenomenon referred to by auditors at the vanguard as 'continuous auditing'. Combining ongoing review of transactions and traditional financial accounts with platforms that can draw on more varied data sources, the aim is real-time insight into a company's financial health. Again, this is a reflection of a general ambition in Big Data—to use data derived from many different sources, in different formats, and with less formal structure (not, for example, data that are carefully presented in a spreadsheet). In short, the aspiration is to use data that is 'messy'.[277] It may well transpire that remarkable insights into a company's financial state might be gained, for example, by comparing its messier data with vast data sets of similarly messy data collected from comparable businesses.

An analogy of this approach is the Billion Dollars Prices Project, a novel method to measure US inflation. Currently, the US Bureau of Labor Statistics sends a small team of researchers to a carefully selected sample of businesses to record individual price changes for specific products over a given period of time and in a standard format to be published at fixed intervals. This is much like the 'sample and extrapolate' process used in a classic audit. This traditional approach costs $250 million a year. Eduardo Cavallo and Roberto Rigobon, the MIT economics professors who run the Billion Dollars Prices Project, instead use software to trawl the Internet and draw out and analyse about half a million individual pieces of price data a day, in different formats and from different places, to generate a more frequent—and far less costly—measure of inflation.[278]

This broader conception of audit (testing all financial data and non-financial data too) may align with the wider notion of 'assurance' to which many accountants are now referring. When people make business and investment decisions, they often seek assurance in relation to factors that are outside the scope of the financial audit (for example, variables that are specific to particular industries). Leading audit firms are now extending their audit practices to include assurance (and risk-management) services. Their selling proposition is that the assurance given is by trustworthy and expert specialists, in whom clients have confidence.

In less complex audits, crowdsourcing has been used. For example, in 2009 the British Government published, online, 700,000 individual documents that related to the expenses of British MPs. In response, the *Guardian* newspaper built an online platform to host these documents, and asked readers collectively to sift through them, a task too large for one person alone, and flag those that might be of interest, adding analysis if need be.

A community of over 20,000 individuals engaged in what was, in effect, a public audit.[279]

In both audit and tax, experts predict that all financial data will come to be represented in some globally accepted standard form ('xbrl' is currently a strong candidate here[280]), and that their work will largely then involve running ever more powerful algorithms, searches, agents, and routines across the data. While the traditional auditor may claim that this will never replace the 'judgement' of the auditor (for example, as to whether the client is handling provisions appropriately), the market leaders are now looking very seriously at how artificial intelligence can also help here.

2.8. Architecture

In the past, architecture was considered as a sort of pastime for a 'gentleman'.[281] Today, it has not fully shaken that reputation. Courses remain prohibitively long and expensive. In the United Kingdom, for example, the average time taken from beginning architectural studies to qualifying as an architect is nine and a half years.[282] For an individual, it can cost more to qualify than in any other profession—on graduating, student debt might be in the region of £100,000, compared to £50,000 in law and £70,000 in medicine.[283] The training has changed little since the 1960s.[284] Nor are the fruits of these toils spread particularly widely—in the United States, for example, the proportion of buildings whose design directly involved architects is said by some to be as low as 5 per cent.[285] Phillip Johnson, an eminent US architect, once quipped that 'the first rule of architecture is to be born rich, the second rule is, failing that, to marry wealthy'.[286]

Not many decades ago, architects started each project afresh with a blank sheet of paper and, using a set of hand-tools (compasses, T-squares, pencils, and so on), crafted bespoke designs and plans for each client. The arrival of 'computer aided design' (CAD) changed this process. Desktop design software like AutoCAD, Revit, and CATIA has replaced the traditional tools, and digital designs have substituted hand-drawn designs. They led, as David Ross Scheer put it, to 'The Death of Drawing'.[287]

Nonetheless, a great deal of architectural work remains bespoke, albeit in a digital setting—for example, architects manually click, drag, and drop each newly created part of their design into place on a screen. Used in this way, CAD simply streamlines the old approach, with digital designs becoming more detailed, more easily corrected, and more readily shared and reused than the hand-drawn alternative. The new technologies also give rise to new possibilities: three-dimensional simulations can be walked through and explored, deconstructed and put back together, turned upside-down and zoomed in on, and there can be endless experimentation with different shapes and structures. The available systems offer much greater flexibility for draughtsmen than was possible in the past.

There are more complex uses of CAD systems, known collectively as 'computational design'. These approaches are responsible for the curves and bubbles—the 'blobitecture'—seen in some contemporary buildings; for example, the Beijing National Stadium ('The Nest'), or City Hall in London ('The Egg'). In one sub-field, 'parametric design', architects no longer manually craft a single building, but instead use CAD to model a family of possible buildings through a set of adjustable 'parameters' or variables. When these parameters are tweaked, the model generates a new version of each building. More radical yet is 'algorithmic design'—architects set out their design criteria for a building (for example, its structural strength or its environmental performance) and algorithms sift through all possible values of the parameters to generate a building that best fits the criteria.[288] Autodesk, a company that builds CAD software, is seeking to go further with its 'Dreamcatcher Project'—software that can generate many possible digital designs from a set of design criteria alone (for the moment, they have used it to design stable chairs and lightweight bike-frames).[289]

In a similar way, the arrival of 'computer aided engineering' (CAE) has transformed the work of structural engineers. Physical prototypes of a possible structure are replaced by computer simulations, and are tested with far greater rigour and precision than in the past. Advances in computational power mean that more complex, and so more computationally challenging, problems can be solved, and so more adventurous construction projects undertaken. The best structural engineers borrow from neighbouring fields like aeronautics, and use their computational techniques to solve their own problems (using, for example, their understanding of how air might flow over a sportscar to understand how it might flow round a building).

For non-specialists, there are simpler, but still powerful, CAD systems. Most are available online, often at no cost, like SketchUp, Chief Architect, and MatterMachine.[290] These systems allow people to build virtual models and designs, from small products to entire homes, and to turn them into formal plans. There are other CAD systems that solve very particular design problems. Ply Gem's Designed Exterior, for example, is a free platform that helps users to plan the exterior of a house (the windows, the siding, the guttering, and so on). TimberTech's Deck Designer is a free platform that helps people to plan their outdoor decking. There are innumerable others, from kitchen builders through bathroom planners to bookshelf sketchers. Collectively, these systems make it more likely, as Steven Kurutz wrote in the *New York Times*, that people 'skip the architect altogether'.[291]

Other online platforms challenge the traditional architect–client relationship. At the website WeBuildHomes, anyone can build a virtual model of a home from a set of fixed 'building blocks' provided by the site, and submit it online. People can sift through the final designs, look for those that match their budget and taste, and if they find one that is suitable WeBuildHomes will construct it for them.[292] At Arcbazar people submit design projects (ranging from simple renovations to large-scale construction), set a deadline, and post a reward. Anyone who thinks they can meet the brief can then submit a proposal (on average, nine people do so for each project) and compete to win the bid.[293] At WikiHouse an open community of designers worked together, online, to draw up designs for a house capable of being printed and assembled with no training, and for less than £50,000 (an early version, WikiHouse 4.0, was built in London during September 2014, and assembled in eight days by eight volunteers).[294] At Paperhouses, established architectural practices submit their blueprints online, in an open source format, available for others to download and build upon.[295] And at the Open

Architecture Network, people post design problems, and an online community of over 47,000 designers works together to solve it.[296]

Online services are used not only to source ideas for projects but also to raise finance. The Prodigy Network, for example, used their online platform to crowdfund more than $200 million from 4,200 people for a sixty-six-storey skyscraper, BD Bacatá, in Bogotá, Colombia (the tallest in the country).[297] On a smaller scale, the Dutch city of Rotterdam has partly crowdfunded a 39-metre wooden bridge, called the Luchtsingel, where individuals pay for particular planks and parts.[298] The WikiHouse project is also funded in this way.

As tasks have become digitized and easier to share out, building projects increasingly draw on a more disparate network of people—architects, structural engineers, mechanical and electrical consultants, designers, contractors and suppliers, ordinary people, and computerized systems—each of whom have their own models, collect their own data, and focus on different aspects of the building. This is a move away from the architect at the helm of the project, responsible for every task. To coordinate their efforts, new online platforms called 'Building Information Modeling' systems (BIM), have been developed. Instead of relying on a set of hand-drawings or a CAD sketch, these online BIM platforms pool all the disparate efforts of the different people involved in the project into one, often very large, shared, virtual model. This makes outsourcing of particular tasks even easier—it is alleged that in India, for example, on average one new engineering college is founded every day.[299]

Many of the machines and tools used to construct buildings are now computerized. Rather than being operated by hand, they are directed by a computer system that follows a digital design—known as 'digital fabrication', or 'computer numerical control' (CNC). Traditionally, these machines were subtractive—the final object was milled out of a larger object, or cut from a large sheet of material. New 3-D printing techniques, a widely discussed technology, instead are additive—they print multiple thin layers of material on top of one another, gradually building up final objects (hence its other name, 'additive manufacturing'). Their significance is that they can, as a result, create more sophisticated or more one-off objects on demand (sometimes referred to as 'mass customization'). 3-D printers were first used to create small models and 'rapidly prototype' initial concepts. Now they are put to service in the fabrication and construction of the final buildings themselves. At the start of 2014 a Dutch firm, DUS Architects, began to assemble a house made entirely of printed parts, using a machine that is able to print objects 3.5 metres tall.[300] A few weeks later a Chinese firm, the WinSun Decoration Design Engineering Co., announced that over the course of a day they had printed ten houses, using a machine that was 32 metres long, 10 metres wide, and 7 metres tall.[301] At the end of 2014, NASA sent a 3-D printer to the International Space Station to test whether tools and spare parts (and even food) could be customized and printed on demand.[302]

As the cost of these tools falls, they spring up in some unconventional settings. Andrey Rudenko, for example, an engineer from Minnesota, assembled his own concrete printer, and designed and printed a modest castle for his back garden.[303] More and more community workshops are stocked with these tools, so-called 'Makerspaces' or 'Fab Labs'. Chris Anderson, in his book *Makers: The New Industrial Revolution*, argues that 'we are all designers now'.[304]

Certainly, any firm distinction between designing and building seems to be blurred by emerging technologies. Robots have been equipped with 'almost every conceivable tool' to help put buildings together.[305] Many of these are the 'robot arms' (known formally as 'six axis' robots, since they have six separate axes or 'joints') that are found in other industrial settings. Some of these are used to fabricate materials by drilling, cutting, or milling. The United Kingdom's 'Seed Cathedral', for instance, the top pavilion at the 2010 World Expo in Shanghai (a fair at which every country in the world has a stand) and the most visited UK tourist attraction that year (beating the traditional victor, the British Museum), could not have been built without robotics—the building, 15 metres wide and 10 metres tall, was covered with 60,000 acrylic spikes, each 7.5 metres long, and each requiring its own precision-drilled hole, looking, in the end, like a sort of giant iridescent hedgehog.[306] There are other robots that transport materials, and put them together. For example, ROB Technologies' BrickDesign software directs a robotic arm to stack brickwork, based on digital designs, in patterns and shapes that even the most skilled human beings would struggle to replicate.[307] Gramazio & Kohler's Mesh-Mould uses a robotic arm, equipped with a small 3-D printing nozzle, to print 'formwork' for concrete buildings—the traditionally handcrafted moulds into which concrete is poured, that take up 60 per cent of the cost of building with concrete.[308] There are other robots adapted to paint, pour, polish, weld, and so on.

In more radical illustrations, individual robots are replaced by a swarm of multiple robots. In 2012, Gramazio & Kohler used a group of autonomous flying robots to build a structure out of 1,500 bricks and, in a separate test, to weave, and knot ropes in mid-air[309] (called 'flight assembled architecture', or 'collective construction'[310]). In 2014, Harvard engineers built a swarm of one thousand robots that could self-organize, without human intervention, to form several complex two-dimensional structures out of themselves (similar to a shoal of fish or an army of fire ants[311]). Neri Oxman, a professor at the MIT Media Lab, has developed methods of 'swarm printing'—a group of autonomous robots, each armed with a 3-D printing nozzle, that fly and print objects as they go.[312]

Substantial online communities support most of these different systems and tools. For those using basic CAD software, for example, there are large online digital repositories where people store and share each other's designs—the SketchUp 3D Warehouse, for example, contains several million designs, while GrabCAD holds more than 660,000 designs that can be borrowed and reused.[313] For those who use more sophisticated software, there are communities like the one allied to the CAD software called Grasshopper, where developers share code and help resolve each other's errors and bugs.[314] More formal online communities like Archinect enable architects and engineers to share their expertise, and less formal, searchable archives like Architizer and virtual scrapbooks like Pinterest are open to anyone to share their favourite designs and styles.[315] There are various flourishing architecture blogs, like ArchDaily, which is visited by around 2.6 million unique users a month.[316]

In architecture, then, as across all the professions, we are seeing remarkable early instances of technology bringing great change. The Canadian science-fiction writer William Gibson could well have been speaking of technology in the professions when he said: '[t]he future has already arrived. It's just not evenly distributed yet.'[317]

3

Patterns across the Professions

In the previous chapter we describe a wide range of developments across a diverse group of professions. One of our aims in this book is to make sense of the change that is taking place. We tackle this job in various ways. In Part II of the book we offer theoretical accounts of the flux. Before that, our project in this chapter is more practical—to identify patterns and trends that are shared across the professions.

In teasing out these patterns and trends, we extend our analysis beyond the largely technological focus of the previous chapter. While we do address the broad implications of these technological advances, we also explore more general movements in professional work. We rely here on insights drawn from our interviews, research, and consulting work. From the last, we gained a sense of the daily preoccupations of the leaders of a sub-set of professional providers (most notably auditors, lawyers, tax advisers, and consultants), who organize themselves in 'firms'. Some of the trends that we initially identify—relating, for example, to bespoke service, routinization, and decomposition—are given more rigorous treatment in Part II, where we develop a fuller theoretical account of the future of the professions. Accordingly, this chapter should be regarded as a bridge between our findings in the previous chapter and the theory in Part II.

In Box 3.1 we summarize the eight broad patterns that we have observed and, for each of these, we pinpoint clusters of more granular trends. Some of these trends overlap and interrelate. We are not offering a taxonomy. At this stage we are instead trying to capture the main features of the flux.

Although we advance these patterns and trends in respect of most professions, no individual profession currently displays the full set. Roughly speaking, each of the professions we studied seems to exhibit around half of the trends. It is our hypothesis that over the next decade or two each is likely to take on most of the rest. For those who are trying to understand possible future directions for their own profession, we suggest that one promising line of inquiry is to identify those trends that already apply and to anticipate that most if not all of the remainder will take hold, sooner or later.

Many of the patterns and trends that are noted in this chapter challenge mainstream thinking about professional work and professional service. Consider, for example, the words of David Maister, one of the leading writers on the professions. In the introduction to his best-selling book *Managing the Professional Service Firm*, he focuses on two characteristics of professional work that present particular challenges for firms. The first is that 'professional services involve a high degree of customization' by human beings, and the second is that 'most professional services have a strong component of face-to-face interaction with the client'.[1]

Box 3.1. Patterns and trends

The end of an era

- *the move from bespoke service*
- *the bypassed gatekeepers*
- *shift from reactive to proactive*
- *the more-for-less challenge*

Transformation by technology

- *automation*
- *innovation*

Emerging skills and competences

- *different ways of communicating*
- *mastery of data*
- *new relationships with technology*
- *diversification*

Professional work reconfigured

- *routinization*
- *disintermediation and reintermediation*
- *decomposition*

New labour models

- *labour arbitrage*
- *para-professionalization and delegation*
- *flexible self-employment*
- *new specialists*
- *users*
- *machines*

More options for recipients

- *online selection*
- *online self-help*
- *personalization and mass customization*
- *embedded knowledge*
- *online collaboration*
- *realization of latent demand*

Preoccupations of professional firms

- *liberalization*
- *globalization*
- *specialization*
- *new business models*
- *fewer partnerships and consolidation*

Demystification

Maister takes these characteristics to be axiomatic; and they certainly appeared to be so a decade ago. Today, however, with the emergence of a very different kind of customization, 'mass customization' (where there is no need for human beings, see section 3.7), and of 'telepresence' (where there is no need to meet in person, see section 3.3), neither can now be taken for granted. We choose these two examples to highlight a larger point—that the changes sweeping through the professions should urge us to rethink the nature and relevance of this group of occupations whose stability we have long taken for granted.

3.1. An early challenge

Before discussing the patterns and trends that are emerging, we should confront one important initial objection to the narrative that is unfolding. The challenge is that while the case studies and illustrations of the previous chapter might suggest fundamental shifts are afoot, in fact they are exceptional, peripheral, and not indicative of any likely future for the professions. This argument travels in various guises, but at its heart is the claim that the developments we identify will prove to be passing hi-tech fads, mere temporary blips, rather than informative signals of deeper change. The professions have always had to adapt to prevailing economic and technological pressures, the argument runs, and once again the order of the day will be sober, common-sense adjustments to current practice rather than anything as radical as transformation.

Our premise here is different. We believe that the professions are in the throes of an important shift—Chapter 2 provides a scattering of early examples of these alternative systems and practices. Many of these bear little resemblance to professional service of today. And yet, within one or two decades, they will be middle-of-the-road. It may also be argued that those we interviewed, and those we advise, are already converts; a self-selecting group of agitators who will naturally foresee a brave and barely recognizable new world. However, in our research we deliberately went beyond these pioneers and also spoke (amongst many others) with the existing market leaders for whom new ways of working can be deeply threatening. And the news is that these leaders also anticipate major shifts. In fact, the main difference that we found between the disruptors and the incumbents is over the *pace* of change. New providers expect upheaval in the short and medium term, whereas the well-established providers anticipate a more leisurely and civilized transition. Whether inclined towards imminent revolution or longer-term evolution, there are very few professionals or providers who have thought deeply about the future and concluded that the professions will carry on indefinitely as they have for the past fifty years.

3.2. The end of an era

We start with a helicopter view. We have spoken with those who are at the forefront of change across the professions. We have immersed ourselves in books and papers about the future of professional work. And, on a daily basis, we work with leaders in various professions who are engaged in long-term thinking. There is a strong sense that the professions, as currently organized, are approaching the end of an era—in the work that they do, in the identities of the providers of service, and in the nature of the service that is delivered. We are advancing into a post-professional society.[2]

In the late 1990s, when dotcom fervour was rife, it was often said that one 'internet year' was like seven ordinary years, such was the speed and atmosphere of the apparent revolution. In the professions, we believe that a similar pace of change is picking up. We are struck also by how pervasive this change is likely to be—across the professions and across the globe (although this book has an Anglo-American focus, our exposure to other countries suggests that the trends we note will be global).

This state of flux presents some challenges for the various participants in the professional world. Many professionals who are at the closing reaches of their careers hope they can last out and keep transformation at bay until they hang up their boots. At the other end, prospective entrants to the professions are having second thoughts about committing. Their parents and careers advisers speak mainly of the professions of the twentieth century, but this talk bears little relation to the post-professional possibilities being sketched out by those who take an interest in the decades ahead. Educators are unsure what they are training the next generation of professionals to become. Regulators are hesitant about what it is that they may soon be regulating and, by and large, they are steadfastly discouraging change. Insurers have little grip on the new risks that are emerging from radically different working practices. The leading strategists within the professions are also now engaged. Some are exploring 'blue oceans',[3] while others are 'disrupting'[4] their current ways of working. To be sure, nobody wants to be dubbed a late adopter in the post-professional society, and so the laggards are now pleased to say (or rationalize) that they prefer to be a 'fast second'.[5]

The end of the professional era is characterized by four trends: the move from bespoke service; the bypassing of traditional gatekeepers; a shift from a reactive to a proactive approach to professional work; and the more-for-less challenge.

The move from bespoke service

For centuries, much professional work has been handled in the manner of a craft. Individual experts and specialists—people who know more than others—have offered an essentially bespoke service. In the language of the tailor, their product has been 'made-to-measure' rather than 'off-the-peg'. For each recipient the service has been disposable (used once only), handcrafted ordinarily by a solitary scribe or sole trusted adviser, often in the spirit of an artist who starts each project afresh with a blank canvas.

Our research strongly suggests that bespoke professional work in this vein looks set to fade from prominence, as other crafts (like tailoring and tallow chandlering) have done over the centuries. Chapter 2 indicates why. Significant elements of professional work are being routinized: in checklists, standard form materials, and in various sorts of systems, many of which are available online. Meanwhile, the work that remains for human beings to handle conventionally is often not conducted by individual craftspeople, but collaboratively in teams, sometimes collocated, but more often virtually. And, with the advance of increasingly capable machines, some work may not be conducted by human beings at all.

Just as we witnessed the 'death of gentlemanly capitalism' in the banks in the 1980s,[6] we seem to be observing a similar decline in bespoke professionalism.

The bypassed gatekeepers

In the past, when in need of expert guidance we turned to the professions. Their members knew things that others did not, and we drew on their knowledge and experience to solve our problems. Each profession acted as a 'gatekeeper' of its own, distinct body of practical expertise. Today this set-up is under threat.

We are already seeing some work being wrested from the hands of traditional professions. Some of the competition is coming from within. We observe professionals from different professions doing each other's work. They even speak of 'eating one another's lunch'. Accountants and consultants, for example, are particularly effective at encroaching on the business of lawyers and actuaries. We also see intra-professional friction, when, for example, nurses take on work that used to be exclusive to doctors, or paralegals are engaged to perform tasks that formerly were the province of lawyers.

But the competition is also advancing from outside the traditional boundaries of the professions—from new people and different institutions. In Chapter 2 we see a recurring need to draw on people with very different skills, talents, and ways of working. Practising doctors, priests, teachers, and auditors did not, for example, develop the software that supports the systems that we describe. Stepping forward instead are data scientists, process analysts, knowledge engineers, systems engineers, and many more (see Chapter 6). Today, professionals still provide much of the content, but in time they may find themselves down-staged by these new specialists. We also see a diverse set of institutions entering the fray—business process outsourcers, retail brands, Internet companies, major software and service vendors, to name a few. What these providers have in common is that they look nothing like twentieth-century doctors, accountants, architects, and the rest.

More than this, human experts in the professions are no longer the only source of practical expertise. In Chapter 2 there are illustrations of practical expertise being made available by *recipients* of professional work—in effect, sidestepping the gatekeepers. On various platforms, typically online, people share their past experience and help others to resolve similar problems. These 'communities of experience', as we call them, are springing up across many professions (for example, PatientsLikeMe and the WebMD communities in medicine). We say more about them in a moment. More radical still are systems and machines that themselves generate practical expertise. These are underpinned by a variety of advanced techniques, such as Big Data and artificial intelligence (see section 4.6). These platforms and systems tend not to be owned and run by the traditional professions. Whether those who do so will in turn become 'new gatekeepers' is a subject of some concern (see the Conclusion).

In this emerging world, where the boundaries of the professions are being redrawn and different types of people and institutions are creating new sources of practical expertise, the 'grand bargain' that we set out in Chapter 1 makes less sense. The keys to the kingdom are changing. Or, if not changing, they are at least being shared with others.

Shift from reactive to proactive

Traditional professional work is reactive in nature. The recipient of the service tends to initiate the engagement and then the professional responds. There is a paradox here, in that the burden of recognizing that professional help is needed lies in the hands of the inexpert. Sometimes the trigger can be obvious—for instance, an unbearable pain, an eviction notice, receipt of a threatening letter from a tax authority, or a meltdown over homework—but often recipients do not know if, or at least when, they should best seek advice. When they are eventually (and unhelpfully) told that it would have been better if they had sought help many weeks earlier, we see the paradox in action. It seems you need to be an expert to know if and when to consult an expert. The concern here is that problems have often escalated unnecessarily by the time a professional is called upon.

To tackle this problem, professional work is becoming increasingly proactive. We have witnessed this phenomenon for some years in health, for example, in the shift towards preventative medicine and health promotion. People are encouraged to opt for exercise and sensible eating rather than heart surgery, or to limit their exposure to the sun rather than have chemotherapy for melanoma. People generally prefer problem-avoidance and problem-containment to problem-solving. In short, they prefer a fence at the top of the cliff to an ambulance at the bottom. And yet, traditional, reactive providers, in their quest for greater efficiency, are often preoccupied with equipping the ambulance better than rivals or ensuring its arrival at the scene of the problem sooner than competitors.

There is evidence that this is changing in sophisticated ways. In medicine, for example, remote monitoring systems track patients' vital signs, and can prompt an intervention before the patient realizes something might be wrong. In education, personalized learning systems track students' progress, and can provide advance warning of particular difficulties in understanding. In some professions, this shift to proactivity is expressed as a growing focus on risk management. Another dimension to this issue, as we explain later in this chapter (section 3.7), is that proactivity can be achieved by 'embedding' practical expertise in our machines, working practices, and regular daily activities.

The more-for-less challenge

A more prosaic driver of change is the intense cost pressure that we find across the professions. All recipients of professional service, from major corporations to individual consumers, seem to be short of money. More than this, though, managers in businesses complain not only of shrinking budgets but also that they have more need of professional help. Industry and commerce are becoming increasingly complex, which means that there are more calls for professional help from lawyers, consultants, accountants, tax advisers, amongst others. Similarly, hospitals and schools, especially those that are publicly funded, are also strained, always balancing smaller purses with growing demand. We call this problem the 'more-for-less' challenge. How can we find ways of delivering more professional service at less cost? Most individuals and organizations are struggling to respond.

It might be thought that the more-for-less challenge is a child of the global economic downturn. However, in our research and consulting work in 2004 and 2005, prior to the crisis, we were already hearing from the clients of professional firms that cost pressures were building. The recession, we suggest, was an accelerator of a trend that began to take shape a few years before. The challenge will continue after the recovery.

In broad terms, we observe two responses to the challenge—what we have called the 'efficiency strategy' and the 'collaboration strategy'.[7] The former involves finding ways of cutting the costs of professional work, while the latter requires that users of the professions should come together and share the costs of the service. Both strategies tend to rely on technology.

3.3. Transformation by technology

Technology lies at the core of most of the changes that we are encountering in the professions. Traditionally, practical expertise has been held in people's heads, textbooks, and filing cabinets. Increasingly, this expertise is being stored and represented, in digital form, in a variety of machines, systems, and tools. As a result, it is being handled, shared, used, and reused in very different ways.

No matter how complex the underlying systems, we suggest that the impact of any technology on the professions can be categorized under two broad headings—*automation* and *innovation*.[8] This marks a break from our recent writing,[9] where we relied on Clayton Christensen's deservedly influential distinction between 'sustaining' and 'disruptive' technologies.[10] Broadly speaking, according to Christensen, sustaining technologies are those that support and enhance traditional ways of operating in an organization or an industry, whereas disruptive technologies are those that fundamentally challenge and change working practices. When we speak in this book of 'automation', this generally means much the same as when Christensen refers to a technology as 'sustaining'.

However, we are less comfortable now with Christensen's second term—'disruptive'. While the language of disruption is widespread in contemporary business writing, we worry that it might mislead as to what and who is being disrupted. In the professions, when disruption and disruptive technologies are discussed,[11] this generally refers to overhaul of the conventional professional providers (lawyers, teachers, doctors, and so forth). This can sometimes conceal the corollary—that the disruption of the traditional professions may be empowering for the recipients of professional work who might benefit from, say, a more accessible and affordable service. While we can see that many of the changes charted in this book do indeed disrupt the professions, this is only part of the picture. To emphasize disruption introduces a negative undertone that we are anxious not to overemphasize. We accept that the changes brought by technology might be disruptive for the current professions. But when we take into account recipients and alternative providers, we regard these changes as socially constructive, and not disruptive (still less 'destructive'[12]). More, we have found that many of the so-called 'disruptors' that we interviewed do not themselves regard their efforts as disruptive. They view them as liberating. Accordingly, in this book, we generally prefer 'innovation' (as defined shortly) to the more emotive and one-sided idea of 'disruption'.

Automation

Automation is what most professionals have in mind when they think of the relevance of technology for their disciplines. They think of how they work today, they identify some inefficient activities, and then they imagine computerizing them. Their focus is often on streamlining manual or administrative work.

Old ways of operating are not discarded. Instead, a drive for efficiencies and cost-savings leads to an optimization of traditional professional work. Although adjustment in this spirit could be undertaken by introducing better manual systems, most current streamlining across the professions involves the deployment of technology. This automation therefore complements but does not fundamentally change the central way in which services are delivered. Many illustrations of automation are found in Chapter 2. Automation is the comfort zone of technological change for most professionals. They recognize great scope for technology in support of their current ways of working.

Much of the focus of automation is on routine work, on the drudgery, so that professionals might be released to get on with their traditional jobs with the support of a more efficient machine. Yet automation can also be transformative. Take the idea of what can be called 'teleprofessionalism'—rather than meeting face-to-face, consultations between professionals and their clients, patients, or students can be conducted by video link across the Internet. In a fairly primitive way, this is already happening via Skype. Doctors, for example, use telemedicine to consult with their patients, employing traditional methods but from a distance; while religious leaders use online platforms to preach and proselytize without meeting their congregants and possible converts in person. In Chapter 2 there are many other illustrations. Future systems, using 'telepresence' techniques (for example, high definition desktop-to-desktop video-conferencing), will provide an experience for both provider and recipient that is greatly superior to current video-conferencing systems. We think of telepresence as 'Skype on steroids'. Notice, however, that teleprofessionalism is not a fundamental departure from traditional ways of working. The interaction is still real-time and face-to-face (just about). Of course, teleprofessionalism may not work when, for example, a physical examination is required, as might happen in medicine; and it may not be suitable when matters of great emotional or commercial sensitivity are concerned. But many current interactions fall into neither category, and remote meetings are much less costly than physical get-togethers. More, teleprofessionalism greatly extends the reach of many professions and so enables service to be delivered when physical meetings are not feasible.

In Chapter 2 we present other cases of automation. These technologies do not challenge the traditional approach to professional work, but make it more efficient. It should not be assumed, however, that automation will leave the professions more efficient but unscathed. As automation moves from the back office to the front office, from leaner administration to technology-enabled interactions between professionals and the recipients of their work, this itself could be transformative.

Innovation

Consider now the ATM or cash dispenser. Was it the case, fifty years ago, if customers needed money in the middle of the night, that they went down to their local bank, approached a large hole in a brick wall, peered through, and asked a patiently seated bank-teller for £50? Did a hand stuffed with banknotes then emerge from this hole and hand the money to consumers, thereby concluding the transaction? Was it this manual process that was automated, providing us today with the facility of cash dispensers? Of course not. Cash dispenser technology did not automate some inefficient pre-existing manual banking practice. Rather, technology created an opportunity to deliver a domestic banking service in an entirely new way—one that no longer involves a daytime exchange between a customer and a human teller. And this has transformed the interaction between customers and their banks.

This is an illustration not of automation, but of innovation. We build on this in Chapter 5, where we introduce alternatives to what we call the 'traditional model' of the professions. Whereas automation is the use of technology to support this traditional model, innovation enables ways of making practical expertise available that simply were not possible (or even imaginable) without the systems in question.

It is striking, when we look globally at the use of technology in different sectors—for example, in manufacturing and photography—that the significant technologies in these sectors have invariably been illustrations of what we call 'innovation'. These technologies (such as robotics in factories and digital cameras) have been instrumental in displacing traditional ways of working. We are beginning to see the same for the professions. In the long run, most of the technologies that will transform the professions will be innovative technologies, systems that will make practical expertise available in ways that generally have not been possible without it. In summary, while much of the work of professionals, both administrative and at the coalface, is being streamlined and optimized through automation, a wave of innovative technologies is steadily extending beyond the automation of pre-existing manual, traditional practices and bringing about more fundamental transformation in professional work.

In Chapter 2 we describe many technologies that are innovative in the sense just outlined. Tax preparation software and automatic filing systems displace the traditional way in which tax advice is provided. Adaptive learning software customizes how and what students are taught, in a way that cannot be replicated without one-on-one tuition. Online dispute resolution systems and document assembly software often replace the need for traditional lawyers. Online diagnostic systems enable people to try themselves to resolve their health problems, before they have to see a traditional doctor. CAD or CAE software allows architects to design, and engineers to erect, buildings that would have been unimaginable or unfeasible with a set-square and a slide-rule.

Technological innovation is already benefiting the recipients of professional work in two quite different ways. On the one hand, innovative systems provide services at a lower cost, or to a higher quality, or in a more convenient way, than in the past; so that recipients may come to prefer these new ways of working to the old. Essentially, these systems displace the traditional models of professional work. We accept that this is threatening, but it is not a new story. On the other hand, there is a less threatening and yet—perhaps surprisingly—more impactful type of innovation. This comes into play when innovations provide new and different forms of service, but these do not replace existing people or working practices. Instead, they provide access to practical expertise where it was not affordable or possible to offer help in the past. These innovative systems extend the reach of the professions to people that have previously been deprived of expert help. This is what we call realization of 'latent demand' (which is a trend in itself—see section 3.7).

In education, for example, 'blended learning' may become a preferred way to organize existing classrooms—students spend some of their time online, and the rest in a traditional classroom. This is innovative in the first sense, providing a higher-quality education. But the introduction of online platforms like Khan Academy, or the use of MOOCs by some of the top educational institutions, make it possible to put the expertise of the finest educators and thinkers within the reach of people who would have otherwise been unable to access it—and this at no or low direct cost to the current recipients. This is innovative in the second sense, providing affordable access when there has previously been unmet demand.

3.4. Emerging skills and competences

Chapter 2 indicates that the working environment for professionals is in a state of flux. For today's practitioners to thrive, they will need to be willing to take on new skills and competences. In particular, they will need to learn to communicate differently, to gain mastery of the data in their disciplines, to establish new working relationships with their machines, and to diversify. More generally, there is a catch-all capability that tomorrow's professionals will need to embrace—that of being *flexible*. There will be very few jobs for life, much less security, and very little predictability. There will be an emphasis instead on being able to learn, develop, and adapt rapidly as new roles and tasks arise.

Different ways of communicating

Not many decades ago professionals communicated in three ways—face-to-face, in writing, and by telephone. That was it. Today there are many more options, from e-mail to telepresence, from text messaging to social networking, from real-time chat to online collaboration. Chapter 2 shows that these technologies are already in action. Meanwhile other systems, such as fax and telex, are no longer in play. All of this may seem rather self-evident. But recall from the Introduction that we were condemned in 1996 for suggesting that lawyers would regularly communicate with their clients via e-mail. Similar condemnation is often forthcoming today, when we suggest that professionals will regularly use social networks to engage with those they help.

It is an unavoidable truth that many older professionals find it difficult to embrace the latest tools for communicating. Although there has been substantial take-up of e-mail and texting amongst all generations of professionals, there is palpable resistance to social networking as a way of keeping in touch with, say, clients and patients. This takes us back to our distinction between automation and innovation. Sending e-mails and texts is an automated version of writing letters, whereas social networking is an innovative technology, by which we mean, in this context, that it gives rise to ways of communicating that were not possible in the past. Comparing the two—automation (using e-mail) seems natural, while innovation (using social networks) is threatening.

But successful professionals of tomorrow will need to embrace new methods of communicating, not least if these are the channels that are preferred by the recipients of their service. And as

Chapter 2 establishes, this is what many at the vanguard are currently doing. Those who hold back are in danger of being out of step with those for whom they work. Lawyers and tax advisers who—in 2015—refuse to use e-mail are finding their clients exasperated and then voting with their feet. It is in the context of communicating on social networks that we find professionals displaying the 'irrational rejectionism' that we note in section 1.9. It simply does not make sense to dismiss new technologies without at least trying them out.

Mastery of data

For a long time professionals have found it important to have all sorts of information at their fingertips—in books, technical papers, and case files. But a different need is arising, and this is for professionals to have mastery over massive bodies of data that bear on their disciplines. This need emerges clearly from Chapter 2. Doctors, teachers, tax advisers, consultants, and auditors, for example, are finding that very large data sets, relating to their patients, students, and clients, can yield useful insights. For example, doctors who have access to data sets on past patients (not just their own) can use this data to help anticipate problems for future patients. Likewise, tax advisers, who have completed returns for great numbers of clients, can determine average effective tax rates for companies of a certain size in a given industry. Many leading consulting firms believe their mastery of data—about industries, markets, and sectors—makes them stand out from their competitors. And, as for auditors, as they move from statistical sampling to 100 per cent testing, their capacity to work with great bodies of data lies at the heart of their work. For these professionals and most others, being on top of the data is not an optional add-on in the future.

For most professionals, new tools and techniques are required here, both to gather and then to analyse these large volumes of data. These belong to the hazily defined fields of 'Big Data', 'predictive analytics', 'data mining', 'machine learning', and so on. The precise terms are not as important as recognition that new disciplines are emerging and new skills are needed. Specialist system developers and data analysts are required in each professional sector, technicians who understand the field itself and are expert in capturing and analysing data. At the same time, professionals need to be trained to know how best to interpret and apply the output of the systems that are built. There will be a shift from looking the recipient of professional work in the eye to making sense of the volumes of data that are being processed.

Professionals also have to become skilful in identifying, building, acquiring, and trading in data sets. As a matter of government policy in many countries, large public data sets are now being made freely available.[13] This is a start, but much useful data is actually held, for example, by patients, students, and clients themselves. Just as consumers' buying habits in supermarkets have been captured through loyalty cards and, in turn, yielded insight into consumers' buying habits, then so too in the professions. A major challenge is to find ways, consistent with settled principles of privacy and data protection, of obtaining the data from consumers and businesses. This requires a talent in its own right.

New relationships with technology

In the early days of computers, the assumption made by most professionals was that machines would prove to be handy tools—excellent at crunching numbers, a sensible replacement for the filing cabinet, good at generating documents quickly, a splendid back-office resource. In the event, as Chapter 2 demonstrates, we have developed systems that are far more versatile than originally envisaged. Some are now operating at the coalface of the professions. Rather than knowing their place in the back office, there is a burgeoning range of systems at the vanguard, making practical expertise available in new and different ways. Moreover, as we note in Chapters 4 and 7, there is no finishing-line for technological progress.

At a rudimentary level, Chapter 2 suggests that professionals must become more adept users of technology. Too many over-forties now say, indulgently, that their children know more about technology than they do. But with effort, training, and commitment, anyone can become an advanced user of the latest systems. Many retired octogenarians are now power-users. For professionals to settle for less is to underperform, to fail to take advantage of well-established efficiency tools. More than this, however, professionals should become directly involved in the development of the systems that handle and deliver practical expertise. While it might be tempting to say that online activity is for others, the next generation of leading professionals will be in the thick of projects that lead to systems of the kind discussed in the previous chapter.

There is a deeper level at which professionals will need to revisit their relationship with their technology. To insist that machines should, as it were, know their place, namely, in the back office and not on the front line, is to ignore the signals of change. Instead, two new forms of relationships need to be developed, and each demands new skills and an open mind. The first is the notion that machines and systems will work alongside tomorrow's professionals as partners. The challenge here is to allocate tasks, as between human beings and machines, according to their relative strengths. And, working together, humans and machines will outperform unassisted human experts. This is the position taken by Bryonjolfsson and McAfee in *The Second Machine Age*—they say we need to race 'with the machines', rather than against them.[14] The second relationship is harder to concede. It is based on frank recognition that some systems will soon be manifestly superior at discharging entire bodies of work that today are undertaken by people—machines, in other words, will replace human beings.

The idea that, in some sense, the technology is 'smarter' than us is unnerving. We can accept that machines can move quicker and lift heavier, but we like to think we hold dominion over certain types of tasks, especially those that require our brainpower. We look at this in more detail in Chapter 7. Human professionals will have to come to terms with the need to defer to the superior capabilities of machines. More than this, they must seize this opportunity to encourage the better service that technology can provide. This is the sort of task that occupies those at the vanguard.

Diversification

In Chapter 2 we see at least two ways in which people are diversifying. The first, as discussed above, involves embracing a variety of new technology-related disciplines, so that professionals are directly engaged in making some of their expertise available online. The second way in which people are diversifying has a longer history and involves professionals extending their areas of expertise into new disciplines, often those lying next to the ones over which they already have mastery. This second thread is being pursued by many of the leaders with whom we have met and worked. Though our emphasis below is on professional firms where diversification has perhaps been starkest, we anticipate this as a wider trend extending to other disciplines.

Although multi-disciplinarity in the professions has a chequered history, many recipients of their work, especially clients of professional firms, continue to insist that their problems do not neatly subdivide into individual professional disciplines, and that there are strong attractions in engaging one organization to undertake all of the work required—for example, accountants, lawyers, corporate finance specialists, and consultants on mergers and acquisition work. For too long, clients' problems have been defined and addressed in accordance with the structural boundaries of the traditional professions. The attractions of having a more holistic approach are clear. Everyday problems are less structured than is suggested by the clear boundaries amongst our professions. The circumstances that lead people to seek professional help often call for the contribution of many experts and not just one. We discuss this at greater length in section 1.8.

Although multi-disciplinary practice in various professions was set back very considerably in the early 2000s, with the fall of Arthur Andersen and the avalanche of law and regulations that followed,[15] these developments did not and do not negate the fundamental benefits for clients of having one provider looking after many or all of their professional interests. Although conflicts can and do arise when professionals from different fields collaborate under the one roof, many of these can be managed, and represent a lesser burden than the hassle and transaction costs incurred by maintaining several teams of competing advisers.

As the boundaries of the professions blur and service becomes more focused on meeting clients' overall needs, it is probable that multi-disciplinary practices will be formed and re-establish themselves as commercially viable. At the same time, firms that do not choose to merge may instead choose to diversify. In the mid-1980s, Ernst & Whinney (a predecessor firm of Ernst & Young, the 'Big 4' practice now known as 'EY') ran an advertisement campaign with a slogan that ran as follows: 'We don't just add up. We also help you multiply.'[16] Consistent with their major competitors of the time, this signified their evolution from being accountants to more general business advisers. It foreshadowed their very substantial move into management consulting and computer services, and the great expansion of their tax and corporate advisory services. Today, EY's strap-line is 'Building a better working world',[17] indicating even greater ambitions. It is likely, several decades on, that other professions will similarly diversify, if not perhaps on the same scale as the largest of what we still call the 'accounting firms'.

3.5. Professional work reconfigured

The long-standing view of many human experts is that their work is a sort of craft and not reducible to, say, checklists or pre-articulated procedures. However, our research suggests that this view is mistaken, and that much of what professionals do can indeed be expressed as standard process. Three core trends reflect this move from handcrafting to process: routinization; disintermediation and reintermediation; and decomposition.

Routinization

Traditionally, professional work was handcrafted and bespoke, as we note at the start of this chapter. However, as we see in Chapter 2, innovative providers of professional help are now striving to routinize their work—both the substantive content of the work, and the process of delivering their services. We use the term 'routinize' fairly generically to refer to the reduction of professional tasks to standard operating procedures or pre-articulated and settled processes, which may or may not be executed by computer systems. This accords with common usage of professionals, who often say of some parts of their work that they are 'routine'. By this they mean there is a regular and repeatable way of doing that work. This routinization helps professionals avoid reinventing the wheel and duplicating effort. Routinization also brings greater efficiency and consistency of work, whether through the use of checklists, protocols, standard-form documents, algorithms, online services, or the like.

Routinizing is not just possible and desirable in some disciplines, it is necessary. According to author and surgeon Atul Gawande, '[s]ubstantial parts of what…lawyers, and most certainly clinicians do are now too complex for them to carry out reliably from memory alone'.[18] He advocates the much wider use of checklists, especially for 'routine matters that are easily overlooked under the strain of more pressing events'. Checklists, which are a form of routinization, 'remind us of the minimum necessary steps and make them explicit'.[19]

Accordingly, we are seeing versions of routinization in all professions. An unhelpful distinction is often drawn, however, between work that is regarded within disciplines as definitively routine or non-routine. This is unhelpful, because it leads to assumptions about what can or cannot be handled differently in the future. What may appear to be non-routine today may in fact be *routinizable* in the future, that is, capable of being reduced to some routine form, if only enough effort is expended or sufficiently 'smart' technology is applied. Whether professional tasks or activities are routinizable is an interesting and important question. It is also a running theme of those at the vanguard (and indeed of this book) that much professional work of today, although considered by practitioners as irreducibly non-routine, is indeed routinizable. Note, however, that just because a professional task is non-routinizable, this does not mean that it cannot be performed by a machine—another theme of this book is that machines can undertake some non-routine tasks *not* by rendering them routine but by tackling them in entirely different ways (for example, using statistics rather than the reasoning that is characteristic of human beings).

The most ambitious form of routinization is found when practical expertise is made available through systems of the sort that are described in Chapter 2. Insight and guidance that once could only be delivered directly by professionals are routinized and then represented in, say, an online service. Some of these systems may have complex models of practical expertise embodied within them, even though this may not be apparent because the interactive platforms have been simplified with lay users in mind.

Another distinction can be found in Chapter 2—between internal and external routinization. The former occurs where tasks are reduced to paper checklists, standard documents, or computer systems for use by the professional themselves. This leads to a reuse of knowledge and expertise, enabling human experts to deliver the same service again and again to a wide range of recipients. Here the reuse is internal, and takes place on the supply side, within the professions. Professionals enhance their own productivity by reducing the time taken to deliver some service, and the service itself is built once and delivered many times for many users. In contrast, when guidance and advice is made available online and recipients can access practical expertise directly, then the use and reuse jumps to the demand side. This is external routinization. A service is built and delivered once for many users. On this latter approach, the recipients rather than the providers are the main beneficiaries of the recycling. We see both of these possibilities in operation in Chapter 2.

Disintermediation and reintermediation

Across society we find many intermediaries, variously referred to as agents, brokers, and middlemen. Frequently these intermediaries serve the interests of lay people, generally by simplifying some process or service. Travel agents, for example, act as intermediaries between holidaymakers and holiday providers, while insurance brokers try to secure cover for their clients from insurers who provide the most favourable terms. Professionals as gatekeepers are also intermediaries, supplying their practical expertise when the recipients of their work do not have sufficient experience, skills, or understanding to handle circumstances themselves.

Since the advent of the Internet, the work of many intermediaries has come under threat. The main challenge they have faced is whether or not the human service that they have traditionally provided is more valuable than can be delivered, crudely, by some online service. If it is not more valuable, then intermediaries will, in due course, be disintermediated, which means they will be removed from the supply chain in which they work. Just as it is now commonplace for travel arrangements to be made and insurance policies purchased without the involvement of human agents, then so too with professionals—if recipients of their services can secure a more affordable, higher-quality, or more convenient service online, then professionals will face the prospect of being disintermediated.

For example, to some extent at least, tax advisers are already being disintermediated by online tax preparation software, lawyers by document assembly systems, doctors by diagnostic apps, teachers by MOOCs, architects by online CAD systems, and journalists by bloggers.

In response, some innovative professionals are seeking to reintermediate themselves, that is, to insert themselves in new places in the supply chain. They are helping in new ways. This might take the form of involvement, for instance, in the development of new online systems that are of direct help to users, often in situations where guidance would otherwise not be available at all. In tax, when advisers move from compliance work to tax planning they are engaged in reintermediation, as are teachers who, in blended learning, shift from working as a 'sage on the stage' to becoming a 'guide on the side'.

Decomposition

Historically, in most professions, certainly until recently, professional work has often been allocated in a haphazard way. Frequently, senior professionals are involved in activities for which they are alarmingly overqualified. At the same time, many professionals complain that they are bogged down by administrative chores, and that others, less qualified, could very competently perform these tasks instead. Many other industries and sectors addressed these same issues decades or even centuries ago. Consider, for example, the manufacturing sector. If we think of our laptops, for instance, we are not surprised when we are told that their various components—screens, keyboards, motherboards, batteries—are manufactured by different companies, invariably in different countries. And, within these factories, we would imagine a strict division of labour, with tasks allocated to appropriate individuals with appropriate levels of experience. We know that the disciplines of supply-chain management and logistics support the bringing together of diverse activities into a seamless single offering for the purchaser.

Likewise, we see a move towards what we call decomposing and multisourcing across the professions. Professional work is no longer regarded as a monolithic, indivisible lump of activity, but instead is being decomposed (some say 'disaggregated')—that is, broken down into constituent tasks and allocated to other people and systems who are best placed to discharge the work at as low a cost as possible, consistent with the quality and the nature of the service required. And so we are finding evidence of professional service being sourced by individuals and organizations of greatly differing experience, often in quite different locations. This is multi-sourcing. As we note in the next section in our discussion of labour arbitrage, outsourcing, offshoring, near-shoring, co-sourcing, and many other alternative methods of sourcing are becoming the order of the day. This is not a call for the establishment of professional sweatshops; it is a recognition that we do not need to treat professional work as an indivisible whole. (At this stage we are painting only part of the picture. In section 5.6 we place the concept of decomposition in the broader context of a theory of the evolution of professional work.)

There are many illustrations of decomposition and multi-sourcing across the professions. In architecture, 'Building Information Modeling' (BIM) systems allow the work of architects and engineers to be broken down into different types of task, and carried out by a diverse network of different specialists. In consulting, traditional clients turn to specialized firms for particular tasks (such as research) or to looser networks of individuals for discrete and irregular projects. Within large consulting firms, they rely on an internal division of labour—their routine tasks, like polishing slides or basic research, are done elsewhere. In journalism, institutions are starting to specialize in narrow sets of tasks: *ProPublica* focuses only on investigative journalism; software such as Storyful performs aggregation; and there are platforms that host the disparate efforts of a range of contributors, from simple blogs to formal platforms like the *Huffington Post*. In education, students and teachers draw on materials put together by a wide range of different people, and use tools and systems not built by traditional teachers. In litigation, it is established practice in many large firms to carve out the document review work and pass it along to legal process oursourcers.

3.6. New labour models

At the heart of traditional professional service has been a distinctive approach to organizing labour: human beings work as specialists in particular disciplines, are highly credentialed, tightly regulated, and, it is often said, bound by some common set of values. A variety of phenomena—labour arbitrage, para-professionalization and delegation, flexible self-employment, new specialists, user participation, and machines—appears to be changing and supplementing this approach.

Labour arbitrage

One common shift in the division of labour within professional services is the allocation of work to individuals and organizations in locations where labour costs, operating costs, and property costs are lower. This is not the same as delegating tasks to less-expert providers. Instead, what we have here is the relocation of jobs and tasks to similarly qualified (or even better credentialed) individuals who undertake work at lower cost than traditional professionals, employed in expensive buildings, in expensive cities, in countries where wages are high. In our research, we were told, for instance, of architects in Kenya who draw up plans for international clients, and of teachers in India who provide tutorials to British students by Skype—at far lower rates than in the United Kingdom and United States.

There are two broad approaches here. The first is 'offshoring', when an organization transfers work packages to one of its lower-cost centres, for example, in Malaysia. On this model, the work is still undertaken within the boundaries of the organization, but is done in places where overheads, and especially wages, are lower. The spirit here is akin to purpose-built, low-cost call service centres. Similarly, consulting firms organize some of their research facilities with teams of researchers based abroad. The other approach is 'outsourcing'. Here the idea is that the work is transferred out of an organization and undertaken by an independent third party, whose operations, once again, are in locations where costs are lower. For example, tax firms do this with some of their routine compliance work, and hospitals act similarly by inviting radiologists to review scans from another part of the world.

Whether the preferred model is offshoring or outsourcing, what is happening here is a form of labour arbitrage, in that work moves to countries where the wages are lower. And as different countries step forward offering yet further reductions in labour costs, then the work is likely to be reallocated there so long as the required level of quality can be maintained.

Para-professionalization and delegation

When professional work is decomposed, constituent tasks tend to be allocated to the least costly sources consistent with the quality and nature of the work involved. Professionals across all disciplines are now recognizing that traditional modes of working have often involved senior people undertaking work that could quite properly and reliably be delegated to less-experienced professionals. One of the jobs of what we call the 'process analyst' (section 6.8) is to identify the level of person best suited for the range of decomposed tasks. On analysis, it is frequently becoming apparent in various disciplines that para-professionals who are sufficiently trained, knowledgeable, and equipped can undertake tasks that previously were taken on by senior professionals. This passing of work to para-professionals and responsible delegation more generally is coming about in three broad situations.

The first is when a task, frankly, does not require the time and attention of a fully-fledged expert professional. In this situation, the experience and knowledge of the para-professional or less senior professional is sufficient for the decomposed task. Sceptical experts should spend just one day analysing their work, and may be disconcerted to find how little of their time is genuinely needed, that is, how many of the tasks they undertake could be delegated or sourced differently. Secondly, less senior professionals and para-professionals are being invited to undertake more specialist and complex work, reliably and to a high quality, when supported by clearly articulated procedures, standards, and processes, often supplemented by supervision from a more seasoned professional. The third role for less senior professionals and para-professionals is emerging when they are equipped with technologies that assist them in undertaking advanced work to a necessary standard.

In all three instances, the deployment of less senior professional and para-professionals is, essentially, a form of delegation. Historically, delegation has not been an overwhelming success in many professions, often because work has been delegated without providing appropriate tools to help the junior professionals to work reliably and confidently. Culturally there have also been challenges—experts are frequently nervous about losing control, and are distrustful of work being done by less-experienced and less-qualified individuals. There have also been process problems here. Those organizations that are systematically decomposing their work using techniques of process analysis (see section 6.8) have found it easier to pinpoint those tasks that are well suited to delegation. But most have not worked in this fashion, and so have not felt confident to parcel out tasks in new ways. Nor have they understood how best to manage delegated work.

One further point should be made about passing work to more junior professionals. The features of tasks in the workplace that make them amenable to delegation and para-professionalization—that they are well bounded and can, in part, be captured in standard processes—are precisely those features that render them strong candidates in due course for the application of technology (both automation and innovation). There are cost implications here—while there may be savings secured by passing work from professionals to para-professionals, the savings gained from full-scale use of technology can be much greater.

Flexible self-employment

Across the professions, we find professionals (and para-professionals) operating as contractors rather than employees, working remotely, often from home. This is frequently being made possible by online platforms that allow professionals to promote themselves and enable those who are seeking their services to find and select the most suitable provider. Various online collaboration tools make it easier for those who are hired to interact—with each other if working in a team, and with the recipients of their work—increasingly without meeting face-to-face. Chapter 2 provides numerous illustrations of this, such as Axiom in law, 10 EQS in consulting, and Doctor on Demand.

This pattern is likely to continue. In part this is being driven by a sense of the superfluousness of gathering in large, costly buildings in which the recipients of the services never have cause to appear. But it is often a conscious lifestyle preference of the professionals themselves, who are attracted to the flexibility, the autonomy, and the possibility of achieving a more favourable work/life balance than employment often affords. Sometimes this new army of independent professionals work on a solo basis. Often they find work through a new breed of agency that matches professionals either directly with clients or sometimes with large professional providers who require some part-time workers. However they operate, the self-employed practitioners do pay a price for this flexibility. They forego the stability of full-time employment, they no longer enjoy a steady income, and they are not part of an organization with clear opportunities for progression. Still less do they have the chance to spend an entire career in one institution. Instead, they have to build their own portfolios, made up of capabilities and competencies—being proficient at a range of particular tasks rather than at a specific job. This is the 'flexibility' we discuss in section 3.4.

As for professional firms, they find it appealing to reduce their full-time head-count and draw on a contractual fringe of independent professionals. This enables them to cope comfortably with the peaks while reducing the risk of an under-utilized workforce in times of trough.

New specialists

As we note in our discussion about the bypassed gatekeepers, a new cadre of specialists is emerging, and they are indispensable in providing access to practical expertise. Online services, whatever their content, cannot be developed and delivered without the involvement of graphic designers and systems engineers. When what is on offer is professional content, the talents of knowledge engineers and process analysts are also required. And if the systems are technically ambitious, data scientists, amongst others, are called upon. (These roles are discussed in section 6.8.)

Traditional professionals do not generally have the wherewithal to develop systems themselves. Some hobbyists may have a go, but the results of their endeavours are often disappointing. Online medical diagnostic systems, computerized document drafting applications, and web-based tax compliance systems are best not developed by doctors, lawyers, or tax advisers who aspire to being systems engineers in their spare time.

Instead, professionals (the subject matter experts) have to join forces with the new specialists. This is a new division of labour, and traditional professionals sometimes struggle here because they are no longer in the driving-seat.

Users

In the conventional model of professional service, the provider of the knowledge and experience is invariably a trained human expert. In contrast, and to the likely scepticism of traditional professionals, one emerging source of guidance is the experience of the *recipients* of past professional service. In the spirit of the open source movement and what is known as 'user generated content', we are finding 'online collaboration' playing a growing role as a way of producing and distributing practical expertise.[20] Just as Internet users have come together, on a shared basis, and with varying motivations, to build, for example, Wikipedia and Linux, so too an analogous production process is giving rise to the creation and maintenance of large repositories of useful knowledge and experience. These resources are being built up by users for users. Although this type of practical expertise is not provided directly by human experts working in the professions, it is useful nonetheless. It offers easy access to know-how and knowledge that has worked in practice.

At this stage, all that need be noted is that non-professional lay people are emerging as a new source of practical expertise. Later in this chapter we identify the other side of this coin—that online communities constitute another option available to the recipients of professional work.

Machines

We speak earlier of the need for professionals to develop new relationships with machines. In terms of the conduct of work, this shift can be expressed differently—a different allocation of work is taking hold, as between human beings and machines. In the past, machines have taken on the grunt work, releasing professionals to focus on tasks that require their brains or dexterity. Machines have been consigned, actually and metaphorically, to the basement, leaving human professionals to interact directly with the recipients of their services. However, as Chapter 2 shows, there is a new generation of machine in action now, and these are systems (much more of which in Chapter 4) that can replace parts of, and sometimes all of, certain kinds of professional work.

3.7. More options for recipients

Traditionally, most professional work has been delivered on a face-to-face basis, from human expert to lay person. This is how practical expertise has been distributed in most print-based industrial societies. However, different options are emerging. The most significant of these are online selection, online self-help, personalization and mass customization, embedded knowledge, and online collaboration. In turn, these options are satisfying 'latent demand'.

Online selection

The way in which professionals are identified and selected is changing. Conventionally, professionals have been chosen on the strength of word-of-mouth recommendations, past positive experience, reputation on the street, published capabilities and credentials, and so forth. There are all sorts of hitches with this approach, not least that the prospective lay recipient does not generally know enough to gauge a person's suitability nor to judge whether a fee proposed is reasonable. This asymmetry, between buyer and seller of professional work, is being removed in large part through a variety of online facilities, early versions of which are already up and unsettling the traditional approach.

First there are online reputation systems, which enable recipients to share their views, online, on the performance and levels of service of their professional advisers, just like customers of restaurants and hotels, using systems like TripAdvisor.[21] Next are price-comparison systems, which put the respective prices and rates of different providers online, alongside the likely costs of particular types of work. Third are online professional auctions, not unlike eBay in concept, but especially well suited to professional tasks that are routine and repetitive. For professionals who used to benefit from their recipients not knowing what alternatives were open to them, these technologies are unhelpful. For the consumer, in contrast, these web services are empowering. Today, as documented in Chapter 2, these systems are in their early versions—for example, BetterDoctor and ZocDoc in medicine, WeBuildHomes in architecture, Avvo in law, and Expert360 and Vumero in consulting.

Online self-help

Given that it is second nature for many people to turn to the Internet when seeking information or guidance on most topics (there are now almost 3 billion Internet users), it is to be expected that people will come to regard online services as an everyday and sensible source of access to practical expertise.

This is so, even though it is still considered natural for many, especially the long-standing amongst us, to ask for advice on a face-to-face basis from other human beings. In this way, problem-solving and advice-seeking are increasingly being undertaken on a do-it-yourself basis. This professional self-help can be swift, inexpensive, and reliable; and over time, as online assistance becomes more sophisticated, so the depth, the range of cover, and the quality of guidance will be greatly improved. Some of these self-help resources are already being built by traditional professionals, and others by new providers. Still others are being set up as online communities—case studies of success and failure, made available by past recipients of professional advice. The main attraction here is not that these online services will soon outperform the finest of human experts (although, over time, they may well do), but that these facilities provide guidance when previously this was unaffordable or inaccessible in the traditional way. This is what we call liberalizing 'latent demand' (see the discussion later in this section). It also seems that recipients of traditional professional service who belong to the Internet generation are migrating to online self-help because it is more convenient, less costly, and more readily understandable.

In the longer term, though, just as we are coming to terms with the idea of driverless cars, so too we will feel comfortable with the concept of teacherless students, doctorless patients, lawyerless clients, consultantless businesses, clergyless parishioners, and so forth.[22]

Personalization and mass customization

One of the fears of professionals is that the routinization and digitization of professional work really means the imposition of inflexible, standardized answers on a wide range of problems. Professionals say, with some justification, that the circumstances of the recipients of their work are always unique, so that individual solutions must be customized for each. We broadly agree with the premise here, about the uniqueness of situations of recipients' circumstances, but we do not accept the conclusion, that human professionals are always needed to deliver the service. Rather, the digitization of practical expertise has led to what has been called 'mass customization'—the use of systems and processes that do indeed meet the specific needs of individual recipients of service, and yet are implemented with a level of efficiency that is analogous to mass production. By embracing some of the many technologies discussed in this book, it is possible to combine the low production costs of mass production with the handcrafted effects of individual customization.

In law and tax, for example, a computerized document assembly system is one that asks its users a series of questions and, on the basis of the responses given, is able to select and delete appropriate words, sentences, and paragraphs, and then generate a polished document that represents one among many millions of possible permutations. This is not a system that simply prints out a standard document. Here mass-production techniques are being used to create and deliver a high level of personalization. This is also the spirit of 'adaptive' learning systems in education, 'personalized' news platforms that tailor news and stories to the particular interests of each reader, and a wide spread of technologies in medicine—from 3-D printing to genomics—that promise medical interventions far more carefully tuned to the specific needs of each patient.

There is a more profound point here—that the conventional working methods of many professionals, deploying limited doses of standardization and technology, have ironically led today to a type of service that is in fact fairly generic. Contrary to the intuitions of sceptics, new technologies are enabling greater personalization of professional service than has been possible in the past. Far from homogenizing service, these systems are accommodating the uniqueness of individual recipients.

Embedded knowledge

When most people, lay and professional alike, think of the application of expertise to everyday problems, they tend to assume that human beings need to be directly involved. For example, if there is a medical, legal, or tax issue to be sorted out, then, in one way or another, a flesh-and-blood adviser is required to do the thinking and then provide guidance. The work of the professions, on this account, entails some kind of human interpretive process—after consideration and evaluation, specialists apply some body of knowledge to the circumstances (the symptoms or evidence, for example) as they are presented to them.

We are seeing signs of the emergence of a radically different approach to the application of knowledge to problems; one which does not directly involve human beings. This is when practical expertise becomes embedded in our machines, systems, processes, working practices, and regular daily activities.

Consider the electronic card game Solitaire, which many years ago was conducted with playing-cards made up of atoms. We called it 'Patience'. When playing that game with physical cards it was easy to cheat, even if it was not entirely obvious why anyone would want to be dishonest in a solitary pursuit. The cheating could involve placing, say, a red 9 beneath a red 10. It was physically possible to arrange the cards thus. In contrast, with the electronic version it is entirely impossible to bend the rules in this way. An attempt to place a red 9 beneath a red 10, as suggested, leads immediately to the rejection of the move by the system and the return of the card to its original position. What is happening here is that the rules are embedded in the system. In the world of bits and bytes, failure to comply is simply not an option: it is neither meaningful nor possible.

We record early illustrations of embedding in Chapter 2. In medicine, for example, insulin delivery-pumps are evolving towards automatic dosing based on sensor data, and so without the manual intervention of a medical expert. In journalism, rather than calling upon a traditional editor, online systems tailor news and stories to match the preferences of readers (based on their online activity). In the world of religion, smartphones are being re-programmed to have limited web-browsing capability, so observant Jews do not need to worry about visiting 'non-kosher' websites.

This shift toward embedded expertise will change the way in which we call upon and share practical expertise. On the traditional model, we invoke practical expertise, generally, in a rather reactive way. The burden is usually on the potential recipient of the service to recognize situations in which expertise is needed or would be beneficial; and then, in one of many ways, having decided on the best source of professional help, to engage or instruct a professional human being. Much rests here on the ability of the recipient to know if, and when, advice is needed. In contrast, when professional expertise is embedded in our everyday lives, it is automatically invoked and applied. This will often help bring about the shift from reactive to proactive service, as discussed earlier in this chapter.

Online collaboration

Three broad types of 'online collaboration' are taking hold in the professions. First of all, in many professions we observe the emergence of what we call 'communities of experience'. These are online communities, packed with content provided by users and, in particular, with their experiences of both successes and failures, drawn from their direct involvement in situations requiring practical expertise. In the same way that Internet users can obtain guidance from others when they have problems with their computers, the practical expertise held on these online 'communities of experience' can provide similar assistance in a wide range of settings. We see these communities across the professions: for instance, PatientsLikeMe in healthcare, and Beliefnet and Patheos in religious practice.

The second type of online collaboration is taking place in 'communities of practice'.[23] Whereas communities of experience are generally created and maintained by lay people, communities of practice are populated by experts. For instance, on platforms like QuantiaMD in healthcare and ShareMyLesson in education, doctors and teachers respectively share their experience and insights with each other. Of course, these two types of communities overlap. In Chapter 2 we observed cases where experts and lay people collaborate with each other, with the former, for example, reviewing, editing, or supplementing the user-generated content.

A third type of online collaboration is crowdsourcing. Here large numbers of people—experts or non-specialists—are invited to contribute to a well-defined project or problem that is so large that it requires many hands, or is so difficult that it might benefit from the 'wisdom of crowds',[24] or so obscure that an answer is most likely to be found if the net of inquiry is spread widely enough. WikiHouse and Arcbazar in architecture, and Open Ideo and WikiStrat in consulting, have run crowdsourcing projects in this manner.

Realization of latent demand

One of the attractions of the new approaches to professional work and, in particular, of various online services, is that practical expertise is steadily becoming more affordable and accessible. From the evidence we have gathered, we can observe the early realization of what we call 'latent demand'. We are referring here to the occasions on which people would benefit from the insight of professionals, but to obtain this today in the traditional form is too costly, confusing, and forbidding. Unmet professional need should be a concern to all of us—whether as citizens, professionals, or policymakers—not least when what is at stake is so important (better health, education, and legal services, for example).

The early signs are that user-friendly, low- or no-cost systems are already offering help, guidance, and insight that is more affordable and convenient than conventional professional service. While some of the online services mentioned in Chapter 2 automate and enhance the conventional work of professionals, most bypass these gatekeepers. More than this, they often seem to be more easily accessible than the services of conventional professional providers. We regard this greater reach as a 'liberation' of practical expertise—knowledge and experience to which professionals have historically been the gatekeepers is now directly available and usable by lay people. This is a fundamental issue to which we return in Chapters 5 and 7.

3.8. Preoccupations of professional firms

A sub-set of professional providers—most notably, lawyers, auditors, tax advisers, and consultants—have come to organize themselves in 'firms'. These firms are run as commercial businesses, and in their various forms have been the object of substantial study by management theorists.[25] It is clear, both from our consulting work and from our interviews with market leaders, that these professions are preoccupied with a further set of issues, over and above the other patterns and trends that are laid out in this chapter. In conversation with, say, managing partners of these firms, mention is made repeatedly of liberalization, globalization, specialization, new business models, the inappropriateness of the partnership model, and consolidation. No account of the future of the professions would be complete without consideration of each of these.

Liberalization

Liberalization has some pedigree. For a long time, consumer activists have lined up with sociologists and social reformers in claiming that the professions are monopolies—unjustifiably restrictive and patently anti-competitive. These closed communities of specialists, the argument goes, do not offer sufficient choice for their users. Accordingly, many critics have campaigned for a relaxation of the laws and regulations that govern who can offer professional services and from what types of organizations and businesses. This is a call for liberalization, and it flows naturally from decomposition. When professional work comes to be broken down and, in consequence, many component tasks are recognized as routinizable, pressure is brought to bear on practitioners to acknowledge that some of the decomposed tasks no longer need to be the exclusive province of professionals. This pressure is now coming from the market and from regulators. The latter are concerned with fair competition and choice—where there is no apparent justification for monopoly (and self-interest does not count as a plausible justification), the professions, individually and collectively, are finding it harder to claim that their exclusivity is in the interests of those they serve, which, after all, is one of the main reasons for granting exclusivity in the first place. Some of the reallocation of work may involve granting permission to less-qualified professionals and to para-professionals to undertake certain tasks. (We are seeing this across the professions, and not only in firms—for example, nurses are formally allowed to conduct minor surgery in some countries.)

The terms 'liberalization' and 'deregulation' are often confused. In fact, they are far from synonymous. Most supporters of liberalization still want professionals to be regulated; more than this, they generally want new categories of professional service providers to be regulated as well. Few advocates of a more open market are suggesting a free-for-all. Instead, the call is usually for more proportionate regulation—granting exclusivity only where it is manifestly in the interests of recipients, requiring regulation of alternative providers who are delivering commercially and socially significant services, and leaving tasks and activities unregulated where it belies common sense to wrap them in barbed wire. As a result, they anticipate greater choice and lower prices for consumers, even if this gives rise to a more competitive market for providers. And so, for instance, if para-professionals are granted permission to perform certain tasks in particular disciplines, it does not follow that they will be unregulated and unconstrained in the conduct of their work. On the contrary, where the service involved is of high value, or of social significance, it makes sense that individuals who are less experienced and less knowledgeable will be subject to appropriate standards and rules. Inevitably, however, as some tasks are undertaken on a do-it-yourself basis (section 3.7), this means that lay people are involved, and it is hard to see how they might be regulated in the same way as professionals or para-professionals.

Globalization

The term 'globalization' is rarely off the lips of leaders of large professional firms. In the middle of the nineteenth century, when the modern professions were born (see section 1.3), service was dispensed largely on a face-to-face basis, and international travel was a relative rarity. Communication and transport technologies have brought enormous changes, facilitating remarkable flows of people, goods, and information around the world. As our social and economic worlds have globalized, so too have our professions. But it is early days, and we hear frequently that several factors are now accelerating globalization. In the first instance, most sizeable clients operate internationally and so look for professional help across their global estate. In the business world especially, professionals are expected to fly to wherever their clients may ask. Equally, e-mail and video-conferencing make it easy, subject to time-zones, to communicate with clients across the world as though they were in the same building. With the advent of telepresence, this new form of real-time, synchronous communication across continents is becoming natural and commonplace. Changes in regulation have also accelerated globalization, in that many professionals are now encouraged to practise in a variety of geographies. In the past, lawyers, doctors, and others were more firmly rooted in the jurisdictions in which they qualified. Another enabler of globalization are various forms of alternative sourcing of professional tasks, not least labour arbitrage (section 3.6), which encourages professional businesses to build or pay labour forces in countries where the costs of employment, operations, and property are lower.

Specialization

Turning to specialization, this trend extends beyond professionals in firms to many other professions, most notably in medicine. While specialization may sound like good news to the lay person, professionals in many disciplines complain that their fields today have become too specialized. They say that the most highly-rated and talented individuals work intensely in ever smaller corners of their disciplines, with poor communication with neighbouring specialists, and almost non-existent engagement with exponents in more distant fields. The concern here is that professionals miss the larger picture and that they fail to think in holistic terms. Increasing specialization also discourages multi-disciplinary collaboration—for example, if lawyers and consultants struggle to cooperate with their own colleagues, they are even less likely to team up with professionals from other disciplines.

This turn towards specialization pre-existed many of the other trends noted in this chapter. As disciplines evolve and become increasingly populated, professionals seem driven or attracted to ever more esoteric and often arcane corners of their world. It is probable, in response to some of the trends noted in this chapter, such as decomposition, that many traditional professionals default defensively towards conventional bespoke service. In other words, they incline towards specialization. This is a well-established comfort zone for today's professionals. However, this move to yet further specialization, combined with a reluctance to work differently, may destine experts to the role of subcontractor. Deeply entangled in their own branches of knowledge, these undeniably expert professionals may tend to be confined to labouring over discrete modules of complex work. It will be down to others (for example, a new breed of project manager—see section 6.8), to integrate expert output with, say, that of para-professionals or online services. The contribution of specialist experts will continue to be indispensable, but they may be a diminishing community, more in the mould of the back-office technician than front-office service provider.

New business models

At the heart of the current business model of most professional businesses is the notion that the time of professional providers is of central value. The time of professionals is the scarce resource for which recipients pay. This is reflected in the practice of most professional firms, whose dominant way of charging for their services is on an hourly billing basis. More than this, this method of billing has come to dictate the way in which many professionals actually think about the value of their work. Although this charging model can reward the indolent and the inefficient while penalizing the speedy and the productive, it has proven remarkably resilient since the mid-1970s. More recently, however, client dissatisfaction with hourly billing has mounted steadily. As cost pressures have descended upon the professions and clients have had greater bargaining power, charging by the hour has begun to diminish in significance. Clients of the future will be inclined to pay for output rather than input, for the value delivered rather than the effort expended. And when professional service comes to be routinized, often made available online, it will no longer make sense to charge for six-minute units of effort (the common practice of lawyers—10 units per hour).

There is a vast literature on alternative pricing models, but our research suggests—and this is not a great shock—that time-based billing is most likely to be displaced across the professions by charging on a fixed-fee basis or on the basis of the value of the performance or outcome delivered. In both cases, professionals are better incentivized to meet the likely financial needs of clients than when charging for their time. However, there is a view amongst the more innovative leaders in professional firms that to fixate on pricing models is to miss a bigger point—that the real drive will not be to change the way traditional professionals charge for their work, but to source the work of professionals in new ways. There will be a move from pricing differently to working differently (for example, by para-professionalization or online services).

There are also strong signs of a shift away from the traditional pyramidic structure of profitability, in accordance with which the owners of professional firms (equity partners) employ younger professionals and pay them less than they charge them out to clients. On this model, the more young professionals engaged, the broader the base of the pyramid, and so the greater the leverage or gearing of the business. Pile them high, reward them well enough, dangle the carrots of promotion and partnership, and equity partners secured a healthy flow of profit. This approach worked a treat from the early 1980s until the crash of 2007. Since then, clients have been less willing to support this model. Many, indeed, have objected quite vocally to paying high (often hourly) rates for junior professionals to undertake routine work, and to subsidize their training at the same time. Most clients no longer want to fund professionals at the bottom of the pyramid. Instead, they are attracted to new approaches, such as the greater use of para-professionals or increasing deployment of technology-based solutions.

Fewer partnerships and consolidation

Changes in charging, profitability, and scope of service are likely to be accompanied by another phenomenon—a decline in the prevalence of the partnership as the dominant legal structure for professional firms. For many decades this was thought to be the most appropriate type of firm for many professionals. It aptly captured the commercial reality of a group of skilled persons who were carrying on their business together with a view to profit, and who should not be able to escape liability through setting up some corporate structure. However, as partnerships have grown, now extending to many thousands in individual firms, the original notion of a small group of collaborating professionals, lunching daily around one table, now seems inapt. If it is accepted that large international clients require correspondingly large international firms of professional advisers, managed in a businesslike way and at the heart of high-value commerce, it is not clear, for example, why these firms should not be afforded the protection of limited liability that is enjoyed by their clients. As various interviewees and clients tell us, there is something bizarre about professionals (and their families) being jointly and severally liable for the activities of colleagues whom they may never have met, working in countries they may never have visited. And if we do release huge professional firms from unlimited liability, it would be equally bizarre, as professional bodies are quick to observe, to maintain a higher level of responsibility for smaller firms and sole practitioners.

In any event, the partnership model has innumerable shortcomings as a business vehicle. Most notably, it fosters a confusion between equity interest and management, it nurtures the paralysis that flows naturally from communal decision-making, and it is a poor mechanism for attracting and raising capital. More fundamentally, when professional work comes to be decomposed and sourced in new ways, especially by non-professional providers, the tasks involved will not require the spirit and methods of traditional professionals who have historically clustered in partnerships. Alternatively sourced tasks will be delivered through quite different entities—from start-ups in industrial parks to online, collaborative communities.

Although many of the world's highest-profile professional organizations are very large concerns (for example, Accenture employs in excess of 300,000 staff, while Deloitte has over 200,000), a great number of professionals still work today in relatively small outfits and even as sole practitioners. The smaller concerns that have not yet embraced technology and other modern management techniques are the cottage industry of the professional services world. Increasingly, they will find it hard to compete on price and harder still to keep pace with technological developments in their fields. As a result, in order to survive many smaller professional providers will merge and, in this way, will be able to achieve economies of scale that were previously beyond their reach. In the professions, as elsewhere, the corner shop will be displaced by the supermarket, bringing savings and efficiencies, but often also a loss of personal interaction. For professional workers who prefer working alone, they may well opt instead to join the ranks of self-employed contract workers, as described in section 3.6.

Consolidation has not been restricted to solo and small practices. Much larger professional firms are also merging, not least in the worlds of lawyers and actuaries. It is unlikely that any other single sector will end up like the world of accountants—that is, dominated by less than a handful of suppliers—but we will see the emergence of many more very large global professional businesses.

Merger may also give birth to an increase in the number of multidisciplinary professional firms, both small and large. In this connection, one very major shift is looming in the wings—the possible disengagement of the audit practices from the multidisciplinary firms in which they sit. Since the collapse of Enron, a steady flow of legislation and regulation has imposed limits on the extent to which auditors are permitted to provide non-audit services to their clients.[26] A prominent recent addition to this corpus is the European Directive that amends the Statutory Audit Directive of 2006.[27] Broadly speaking, these rules inhibit firms that undertake audits from providing any other services where a conflict might arise. There is a particular aversion to auditors benefiting commercially from the special insight they gain into the businesses they scrutinize. In the 1980s, in contrast, the management letter that was written to company boards at the end of an audit was considered a standard and proper platform from which to offer additional services that would happily overcome problems recognized during the audit.

After the collapse of Enron and Andersen, the casualties of the tighter regulations were the legal and consulting practices that had been flourishing in the leading accounting firms. But the odd man out here is really the audit function. It is the auditor's work that causes the greatest potential conflicts with consultants, lawyers, and tax professionals. And so it is at least possible that the audit practices might be severed from the main body of the large accounting firms in years to come. This would open the door to fascinating merger opportunities—for example, international law firms with global tax businesses. We sketch this as a possibility rather than a likelihood.

3.9. Demystification

A final pattern that forms the backdrop to much else that is noted in this chapter is a steady demystification of the professions and professionals. Herbert Hart, the legal philosopher, fluently sets the scene in his analysis of mystification and demystification:

> The central idea that these words are used to express is that unjust, anachronistic, inefficient or otherwise harmful social institutions, including laws, are frequently protected from criticism by a veil of mystery thrown over them. This conceals their true nature and effects, perplexes and intimidates the would-be reformer, and so prolongs the life of bad institutions. The forms of mystery...include not only glorification by open eulogy and pomp and ceremony; not only the use of archaic dress and diction unintelligible to the layman, but also, and more importantly, mystification consists in the propagation of a *belief*: the belief that legal or other institutions of society are infinitely complex and difficult to understand, and that this is an invincible fact of nature, so that long-standing institutions cannot be changed without risk of the collapse of society.[28]

On this account, a shroud of mystery is thrown over certain institutions, protecting them from challenge and change. And those who mystify use language, custom, clothing, and rhetoric as the tools of their trade. In a similar vein, Harold Laski, the political theorist and left-wing activist of the first half of the last century, described how '[t]he expert, to-day, is accustomed to a veneration not very different from that of the priest in primitive societies; for the plain man he, like the priest, exercises a mystery into which the uninitiated cannot enter.'[29]

When we look at the particular case of the professions, you do not need to share Hart's legal philosophy or Laski's political radicalism to recognize that these writers are on to something. The use of specialist language within the professions is illustrative. Recipients of their work are daily bamboozled, distracted, and even diminished by medical terminology, legalese and journalese, consulting jargon, tax technicalities, and the rest. Often this may be legitimate shorthand, even if it is plainly unhelpful for the recipient of their work. But sometimes it is intentional mystification, designed to exclude recipients and to protect providers. In the language of sociologists, this is a form of 'social closure', designed to maintain the monopolies that professionals enjoy (section 1.5). (Sociologists, incidentally, do not seem to be alive to the irony of their use—even by our standards—of obfuscating jargon in criticizing the obfuscating jargon in the professions.)

Many of the patterns and trends discussed in this chapter suggest that mystification of the professions will no longer be possible in coming years. When professional work is broken down into more basic component tasks (section 3.5), then the activity involved will be far more widely understood. No longer will the service of professionals be some kind of black box, whose inputs (the circumstances of the recipient) and outputs (the guidance of the professional) are the only elements that are transparent to non-professionals. Instead, the contents of the box itself will have been the subject of what we call 'process analysis' (see section 6.8), and the substance of the professional work will be much more readily apparent. In this way, mystery and mystique will no longer be characteristic of professional work. Nor will it be possible, by claiming complexity beyond the lay person's reach, to elevate the knowledge and expertise involved to some kind of supernatural or mystical level. Equally, when non-specialist tasks are carved out and handed over to lay people to undertake for themselves, here again the recipient of the service will have far greater insight into what is involved.

Where real talent, proactivity, creativity, strategic insight, or deep experience is genuinely required, this will be apparent, because this work will have been consciously and expressly identified as requiring craftsmanship and traditional bespoke handling. The conduct of this work will surely attract respect and admiration, but perhaps not the excessive deference that was characteristic of mystified professional work in the past.

PART II

Theory

4

Information and Technology

In Part I of this book, by reporting on our own research and reflecting on the writings of others, we offer evidence of the changes that the professions are facing. In these opening chapters, however, we do not provide an explanation of why this transformation is taking place. That is our purpose now, in Part II of the book. Our aim is to provide a more general and systematic account of what is going on. We advance a variety of theories and models that explain the evidence we have uncovered and suggest how these may help us predict what is yet to unfold.

Our initial focus in this chapter is on what we call the 'information substructure' of society, and how this influences the way that human beings have shared practical expertise in the past and are likely to do so in the future. Then we turn to technology, and talk about the worth of making predictions. Our conclusions here help us to identify what we regard as the four most important sets of future developments in technology. In concluding this chapter, we present a fifty-year overview of the changing impact of technology on the professions. This then sets us up for Chapter 5, where we discuss the nature of knowledge, the evolution of professional work, and the models for the production and distribution of practical expertise that will displace the traditional working practices of professionals.

4.1. Information substructure

In everyday conversation, people often now use the terms 'technology' or 'tech' more often than 'information technology' and 'IT'. This emphasis on the technical angle is understandable, because the technological accomplishments that underpin our everyday devices are remarkable. The technology can be mesmerizing, both in its power and design, and we justifiably marvel at the genius and ingenuity of those who contribute to its development. But to focus exclusively on the 'T' rather than on the 'I', to neglect the 'information' in our wonder at the 'technology', runs the risk of failing to grasp the role and value of *information*—in our world generally, and especially in the professions.

We suggest that one way of making sense of the changes we are seeing and anticipating in the professions is by reference to what we term the 'information substructure' in society.[1] By this term we mean the dominant means by which information is stored and communicated. We use the word 'information' fairly generically here, embracing a wide variety of related phenomena—from raw data at one end of a spectrum through to knowledge and expertise at the other. Using as a starting-point the insights of Walter Ong, in *Orality and Literacy*,[2] we propose a four-phase model of the development of the information substructure in human society. According to this, we say that societies have been dependent, respectively, on periods dominated by orality, script, print, and information technology.[3]

The important issue for us is the extent to which a society's information substructure affects what practical expertise is available, how it is created and shared, and who is able to access and understand it. Our hypothesis is that the way in which practical expertise is created and shared is strongly influenced by the systems that are available for its storage and communication. More precisely, the information substructure, in ways that have not yet been fully explored and understood, determines the quantity of practical expertise, its complexity, its sources, its availability, the frequency with which it changes, and the human beings or other systems that can reliably apply it to human affairs. The literature on the history and development of information and communication systems, as well as from anthropology and sociology, appears to confirm this idea.[4] In short, then, we are suggesting that the information substructure strongly influences the way in which practical expertise is produced and distributed.

We go further, however, and suggest that when we examine the impact of the information substructure across all four stages—of orality, script, print, and information technology—then we can make predictions about likely future developments in the professions and beyond. When most professionals are invited to give thought to the shift in society from, say, a 'script-based world' to a 'print-based world', they quickly and instinctively recognize that the way that knowledge was organized changed considerably through that transition. Yet professionals of today seem less inclined to acknowledge that similar change is likely when we move from a print-based society to a society with great dependence on information technology and the Internet (this disinclination is a manifestation of some of the biases discussed in section 1.9). To understand this change, it helps to consider one stage at a time.

4.2. Pre-print and print-based communities

As we hunch at our laptops and poke at our tablets, it is not at all easy to imagine what a society would have been like in the absence of script, print, and information technology, that is, in the era of orality. Ong makes the point memorably:

> Fully literate persons can only with great difficulty imagine what a primary oral culture is like, that is, a culture with no knowledge whatsoever of writing or even of the possibility of writing. Try to imagine a culture where no one has ever 'looked up' anything. In a primary oral culture, the expression 'to look up something' is an empty phrase: it would have no conceivable meaning. Without writing, words as such have no visual presence, even when the objects they represent are visual. They are sounds.[5]

Today, in an era when our information-seeking habits have been profoundly affected by the availability of the Internet, it is hard to conceive of a way of life in which information is not at our fingertips. In the spirit of Ong, it is difficult to imagine a world in which 'to Google' would be an 'empty phrase'. However, if we pause to reflect on a community capable only of oral interaction and communication, we can easily see that this environment would exert strict limitations on the availability of expertise. While it is likely that some human beings exercised their memories more strenuously and were perhaps therefore more retentive,[6] it was surely not feasible, in any field, for vast quantities of detailed knowledge to be held in the heads of anyone. No one could have recalled even a small fraction of the bodies of knowledge upon which the professions depend today.

Expertise that was readily available at that time was much less voluminous, complex, and detailed than today. There are always difficulties, well known to anthropologists and historians, in assessing societies and their capabilities of the past in terms of the ideas and views of today.[7] Nonetheless, from our twenty-first century armchairs, we can suppose that, in the age of orality, mastery of what we now regard as individual areas of expertise would be given only to a few—senior elders of communities, of almost mystical status, who attained these positions precisely because of their ability to draw easily upon their recollections of past experiences, and from insights passed along from previous generations; insights that they too would have handed to their successors. In the age of orality there were no formal professions, no organized bodies of recorded knowledge, no techniques for disseminating expertise widely across society, nor institutions under whose roofs these senior elders would gather.

Moving forward now to consider the era during which script was the dominant information substructure, Ong once again is alerting:

> Writing... was a very late development in human history. *Homo sapiens* has been on earth perhaps some 50,000 years... The first script, or true writing, that we know, was developed among the Sumerians in Mesopotamia only around the year 3500 BC.[8]

And again:

> Indeed, language is so overwhelmingly oral that of all the many thousands of languages—possibly tens of thousands—spoken in the course of human history only around 106 have ever been committed to writing to a degree sufficient to have produced literature, and most have never been written at all.[9]

In early societies, with the advent of script, it then became possible to augment the capacity of human memories with writing and other pictorial representations. As James Gleick describes, in his book *The Information*, '[t]he power of this artificial memory was incalculable'.[10] In turn, this meant that the quantity of knowledge and expertise in communities could increase and yet remain manageable. As it became possible to articulate and record knowledge and experience, more precise and rigorous expressions of expertise were to hand and passed around within communities. A new layer of complexity was also added here, when specialists chose to record their thinking in the jargon and shorthand of fellow specialists, rather than in the language of lay people.

In the era of script, although knowledge could be captured and revised, its widespread dissemination was inhibited by the limitations of manual transcription, the only method then available for reproduction. This was both error-prone and time-consuming, and so limited the ease with which knowledge could be spread and the frequency with which it could be altered. But it was necessary for lay people to have access to specialists, those who had a grasp of evolving bodies of experience, concepts, and jargon. These early gatekeepers were both advisers and problem-solvers, identifiably expert but not yet organized within professions. This does not mean there were no identifiable professionals. As we note in section 1.3, by reference to Hippocrates the physician, Cicero the lawyer, and Maimonides the rabbi, experts were very much in action in the era of script, but they were not educated in the manner of contemporary professionals; nor did they operate alongside others under the umbrella of identifiable professional associations, of the sort we have today.

The earliest signs of professions and professional associations can be found in the guilds, associations that were the focal point for particular trades. The flourishing of many of these guilds coincided with the emergence of print. In the middle of the fifteenth century Johannes Gutenberg invented the printing-press and a moveable type system that revolutionized the way in which human beings educated one another and practised their religions (the Gutenberg Bible was the first major printed book in the Western world). Print also transformed the way in which knowledge and expertise could be produced, stored, and shared in society, so that, over time, scholars and researchers could share their findings and insights, emerging thinking could be captured and stored in a fixed form for consultation, and printed papers and books could easily be distributed. In turn, this gave rise to an explosion in the quantity and complexity of recorded information.

In what became a print-based society, it might have been thought at first blush that knowledge would therefore be at the fingertips of all. On the contrary, it transpired that intermediaries were needed to help make sense of, manage, and apply the volumes of materials that were produced. There emerged, especially after the industrial revolution in the nineteenth century, a pressing need for specialists who were expert in the handling of large bodies of information and knowledge that were subject to regular change. Identifiable groups of specialists, belonging to groupings that we now generally regard as the professions, thrived in this environment.

4.3. Technology-based Internet society

Information technology and the Internet have combined to transform the information-creating, information-seeking, and information-dissemination habits of human beings. While print brought great change, the process of printing itself for centuries remained a specialist activity, requiring heavy-duty equipment and skilled human beings. Although we think little today of using word processing software and laser printers to produce high-quality documentation, these facilities were rare as recently as the 1980s and only came into widespread usage in the 1990s. Most people today, at work and home, have immediate access to a set of technologies that can support the production of high-quality printed material. A succession of technological innovations, such as large-volume photocopiers, transferable word processing files, high-capacity printers, and Internet-based file transfer, have changed the way we produce and distribute documents. We used to call some of this 'desktop publishing', but so pervasive have the facilities become that we no longer distinguish them with their own label.

However, an improved capacity to create and share polished documents has not led us to a world in which knowledge and expertise are easily accessible and straightforwardly understood by all. There can be little doubt that the Internet enables easy access to large quantities of content, but it is also the case that websites, social networks, and online publishing have generated more source material than we had before, most of which, once again, is impenetrable to the non-specialist. While lay users can undertake basic searches online—in medicine, law, architecture, accounting, and elsewhere—the fruits of this work tend to be collections of potentially relevant but technically complex documents or web pages rather than answers to problems or distilled advice. An online encyclopedia, for example, may educate and orientate, but it does not generally advise, counsel, or tell users what next steps to take with the challenges before them. What is more, it is not easy for most users to know when online resources in complex areas are authoritative and reliable.

This analysis leads some sceptics to conclude that the Web and social media has a damaging effect on society, creating mountains of information that increase rather than decrease the need for specialists who can reliably interpret and apply this information in particular circumstances. This conclusion, however, mistakenly assumes that we have fully transitioned from the print-based industrial society into what we call the technology-based Internet society (note that the 'technology' here is largely 'information technology'). We argue instead, as we did in 1996, that we are still in a long transitional phase between these two eras, and that so-called 'information overload' is one of the many unfortunate but temporary consequences of being in this interim state of flux. We accept that, during this transitional phase, traditional professionals working in conventional institutions will still be needed as the main interface between the lay person and the bodies of knowledge to which they might now have access but not yet the wherewithal to interpret. However, once we have fully progressed into the technology-based Internet society, the quantity and complexity of materials will be hidden from users, new technologies themselves will help with their interpretation, and so traditional professionals will no longer be this dominant interface between lay people and the practical expertise that they need to apply to their own particular circumstances and problems.

Central to this thesis is a concept we first articulated in 1996, known as 'the Technology Lag'. At that time we wrote as follows:

> our ability to use computer technology to capture, store, retrieve, and reproduce data, wildly surpasses our ability to use technology to help analyse, refine, and render more manageable the mass of data which data processing has spawned. We are great at getting information in, but not so good at extracting the information that we want.[11]

The Technology Lag described the delay between what technologists then called 'data processing' and 'knowledge processing'. And we went on to argue that we would not have progressed to a mature technology-based Internet society until the lag was eliminated and knowledge processing became equal to the task of extricating us from the information management dilemmas left by its ancestor, data processing.

In other words, we were saying that technologies such as photocopiers, scanners, word processors, and e-mail were giving rise in the 1990s to the information overload for which we had not yet invented the technological ripostes. Thus, in the professions, the rapidly growing bodies of source materials were like a fire-hose of information blasting at the laity; and, far from removing the need for expert advice, we seemed, in the mid-1990s, to require professionals more than ever before. Yet we predicted that:

> we are now refining our techniques in the field of knowledge processing and gradually developing systems which will help us analyze and manage the vast bodies of information which we created for ourselves. And these systems will themselves help us pinpoint *all but only* the material relevant to our particular purposes as users.[12]

This prediction was met with great scepticism at the time. However, we only need to reflect on the capabilities of search facilities like Google, the success of data science initiatives (for example, in the field of Big Data), and the emergence of a new wave of artificial intelligence systems such as Watson, to realize that the Technology Lag is now closing steadily. Our prediction then, 'that advances in knowledge processing will be stunning in the coming twenty-five years, thus easing us from this transitional period' into what we now call the 'technology-based Internet society', will prove, we think, to be fairly accurate.[13]

In relation to the professions, with these technologies in place, the quantity, complexity, and changeability of source materials becomes less of a challenge for lay people, because the systems will far more accurately pinpoint relevant materials for them. More than that, our increasingly capable systems (see section 4.6) will come to solve problems and offer advice, rather than simply retrieve and present potentially relevant documents. More ambitious still, the systems will anticipate our needs and offer guidance and forewarning, even before we know that a problem or opportunity has arisen.

Just as our demand for specialist guidance from expert human beings has changed over time, as the information substructure of society has shifted from orality to script and then to print, so we must expect a further shift as we progress into a world that is underpinned by processing power and communication capabilities that are much greater than in the past. The professions are knowledge-based (see section 5.2), so that if the dominant means by which we store and communicate knowledge changes radically, then it is not a great leap to suppose that the way in which we store and communicate professional knowledge will similarly be transformed.

This is not simply a question of our current professions failing to exploit new technologies, and so missing the opportunity to be more efficient. The shift in information substructure is more fundamental than this. It determines how we organize and make available our collective knowledge and expertise in society.

We expect, as we move from a print-based industrial society into a technology-based Internet society, that the changes in the ways in which we share expertise will be as far-reaching as when we moved from the age of script to the era of print.

This is not a shift that is waiting for politicians or professionals to initiate. We have already seen the power of social networking in overthrowing political regimes. We should not suppose that almost 3 billion people connected to one another will be any less motivated to bring about change in the way that expertise is shared when it becomes apparent to them that the means comprehensively to improve their quality of life and standard of living is already to hand. When it becomes clear to people that, for example, better health, education, and legal protection can be secured through online service, then these systems are likely to be embraced, whether or not policymakers and professional practitioners are actively in support.

4.4. Future impact

Much of what we say in this book is in anticipation of the emergence of new and improved technologies. Although we take this to be all but inevitable, it is often said to be naive to speak about long-term trends in technology, because great advances are so unpredictable. 'The only thing we know about the future', according to the management guru Peter Drucker, and innumerable others, 'is that it will be different.'[14] We strongly disagree—not that the future will be different, but with the proposition that this is the only thing we know.

We do recognize, though, that in support of the position that the future is unpredictable, its advocates often give good examples: that the PC, launched by IBM in 1981, had not been widely anticipated a decade earlier; that the birth of the Web also came as a shock in the early 1990s; and, likewise, that the emergence of social media was not predicted by experts, even though their uptake has since been widespread. Because we did not (and, some say, could not) predict these important developments, then, similarly, there is an argument that there is little point in trying to look five to ten years hence. We are bound to get it wrong. We will miss the next major leap.

In contrast, we believe there are three ways in which it is worthwhile to attempt to predict the future of technology. First of all, even if there are no advances in technology in the next decade as fundamental as the PC, the Web, and social media, if we follow existing and emerging technologies to their probable and much greater exploitation, this alone takes us into a very different world. The mistake here is to presume that because we cannot foresee any revolutionary changes, then we should not extrapolate from what we already have. If we work within our current frame of reference and in the context of technologies that seem steadily to be taking hold, then we are more likely to have a sense of where we are going than if we choose to ignore the future altogether. We may well miss the next revolution, but at least we will keep pace with the evolution of current technologies.

Secondly, we think that it is important to seek to identify overall direction and general trends in technology. We may not be able to pinpoint, with any precision, the next wave of specific applications of technology, but if we reflect on probable patterns and trends, both in human behaviour and in emerging systems, then this can provide a useful context when discussing the future. The least likely future for technology is that our systems will stay as they are today. And yet those who dismiss attempts to predict the future often fall into the trap of assuming there will be no change. An unwillingness to try to determine overall interaction is akin to driving a car at night with no headlights. Making qualified predictions of the kind we have in mind is like having the headlights on. We accept, of course, that there is much that we still cannot see. More than this, we expect that many of the Internet-based systems that will change our lives over, say, the next twenty years have not yet been invented.

The third sort of prediction that is worth making, in the context of this book, is about technologies that can easily be imagined as

Box 4.1. **Four main developments in information technology**

Exponential growth in information technology
Increasingly capable machines
Increasingly pervasive devices
Increasingly connected humans

widespread in the *professions* specifically. In anticipating such systems, we are not engaging in speculation about issues of high theory, concerning, say, 'computability' or 'post-silicon processors'. Instead, we are simply noting systems that have succeeded in some professions but not in others; and are suggesting that they are likely to be adopted more widely.

In the next sections of this chapter, especially with the first two of these kinds of prediction in mind, we identify and discuss four major, and to some extent overlapping, developments in information technology. These are summarized in Box 4.1. In our view, these are the most significant developments relating to the growth and development of IT and Internet-based systems.

In combination, this set of changes will transform the way our professions function and how we make practical expertise available in society.

4.5. Exponential growth in information technology

As users of tablets, social networks, video-conferencing, online games, streamed TV shows, and innumerable other systems, few of us give much thought to what is going on technically, deep in the bowels of our machines. Certainly, it is hard to think of these everyday facilities in terms of ones and zeros. Most of us, though, do have some inkling of some technical concerns—when our systems are slow, we might hazard an untutored guess that we could do with a faster processor, or more memory, or greater bandwidth. The good news is that in research laboratories around the world there is considerable effort being put into providing all of this and more. The advances are staggering. Along with many other observers, our starting-point in trying to convey the scale of the progress in information technology is the 'exponential' growth in processing power,[15] and more particularly, what is known as Moore's Law. In 1965, three years before he co-founded Intel, Gordon Moore predicted, approximately, that every two years we would be able to double the number of transistors we could put on a chip (an integrated circuit).[16] Put more generally, he was projecting that the processing power of computers would double every two years or so; or, as technologists often put it, 'price/performance' would double in a twenty-four-month period. Sceptics at the time said that Moore's Law would hold for a couple of years. But it is still going strong. Indeed, some say that processing power is doubling every eighteen months now. And material scientists, computer scientists, and industry analysts go further, and suggest that Moore's Law will hold for decades yet. Strictly, there are physical limits to the number of transistors that can be packed onto a chip, but when people talk of Moore's Law continuing, they are loosely predicting a doubling in processing power even if this is achieved through techniques quite unlike the silicon-based integrated circuits that Moore had in mind.[17]

To appreciate the power of exponential growth, consider the following thought experiment. Start by imagining an ordinary sheet of paper of unremarkable weight.[18] Now imagine repeatedly folding this sheet in half. After four folds, it will be as thick as a credit card. This is not particularly spectacular. If it could be folded eleven times, it would then be as tall as a can of Diet Coke. This is still not remarkable. After ten more folds, however, it would be taller than Big Ben. After a further ten folds, it would reach into outer space. After twelve more folds, it would reach the moon. And, if you could fold this single piece of paper 100 times, it would create a wad over 8 billion light years in thickness. Growth, that accelerates so quickly, and stretches to these sorts of scale, is very difficult to imagine. But this is what is happening as processing power continues to double. While mathematicians call this 'exponential growth', professionals might simply think of it as explosive growth.

This growth in processing power has already had profound effects. Michael Spence, a Nobel Laureate in economics, notes that Moore's Law resulted in 'roughly a 10-billion-times' reduction in the cost of processing power in the first fifty years of the 'computer age' (which, he thinks, began roughly in 1950). Ray Kurzweil, in his books *The Singularity is Near* and *How to Create a Mind*, stresses that this will continue. According to Kurzweil, the 'fundamental measures of information technology follow predictable and exponential trajectories'.[19] In explaining exponential growth, he says that:

the pace of change for our human-created technology is accelerating and its powers are expanding at an exponential pace. Exponential growth is deceptive. It starts out almost imperceptibly and then explodes with unexpected fury—unexpected, that is, if one does not take care to follow its trajectory.[20]

To give a sense of what this means in everyday life, consider Kurzweil's claim that, by 2020, an average desktop machine (costing $1,000 or so) will have roughly the same processing power as a single human brain (conservatively, he says, capable of undertaking 10^{16} calculations per second).[21] More mind-boggling still, consider his claim that, by 2050, following the curve of exponential growth, 'one thousand dollars of computing will exceed the processing power of all human brains on Earth'.[22] Readers may call us radical, but if we can foresee a day when the average laptop has more processing power than all of humanity combined, then it might be time for professionals to revisit some of their current working practices.

Notice too that this exponential growth is not confined to processing power. Other technologies—including hard-disk capacity, Internet traffic, bandwidth, magnetic data storage, and random access memory—are also growing at similar rates.[23] Memory cards provide a compelling illustration. In 2014, 128gb cards were commonplace. In 2005, ten years earlier, the equivalent was a 128mb card. This represents a (slightly more than) one thousandfold increase in capacity in ten years. This is a doubling every year, a steeper exponential growth than in processing power. In the same vein is Metcalfe's Law, which states (broadly speaking) that the value of a network to its users is proportional to the square of the number of the users connected to it. This is sometimes referred to as the 'network effect', and it means that a network's utility increases non-linearly with the number of new users who join.[24] Yet another illustration is Koomey's Law—that the electrical efficiency of computation will double roughly every eighteen months, as it has done for the last six decades.[25]

We accept that Kurzweil's theories do not command universal assent.[26] However, other experts and commentators draw similar conclusions on the question of the exponential growth in processing power.[27] We also acknowledge that exponential growth in information technologies need not always lead to an explosive increase in the speed and scale of adoption of new systems. But if the exponentialists are anywhere near the mark in their predictions and extrapolations, then it does seem that we are about to live through a time of unprecedented technological progress.[28] Our message here for professionals is that, although we have already seen remarkable growth in the impact of a wide array of systems, we are still at the foothills, at the opening phase of an acceleration in the capabilities of various information technologies. Within the lifetimes of most readers, our personal and working lives will be overhauled by spectacular brute-force processing power, a 'cloud' that offers seemingly limitless storage capacity, lightning quick communications, ever-greater miniaturization, and rapid decline in the cost of components.[29] This is not next year's iPhone. This is a transformation in the power of the tools available to professionals and those they help.

In the terminology of the remainder of this chapter, this exponential growth will directly enable increasingly capable machines, increasingly pervasive devices, and increasingly connected humans.

4.6. Increasingly capable machines

We turn now to what we believe is the most significant characteristic of technology for the professions. We capture this in one proposition: *our systems and machines are becoming increasingly capable*. If readers leave this book with just one message about technology, it should be this. When it comes to the future capabilities of our machines, the overall trajectory of technological advance is clear and of great importance for the professions—more and more tasks that once required human beings are being performed more productively, cheaply, easily, quickly, and to a higher standard by a range of systems. And there is no apparent finishing-line. New capabilities are emerging on an apparently daily basis.

Some professionals doubt the pace and scale of technological change. Often they suffer from the 'technological myopia' that we mention in section 1.9. By this we mean the tendency to underestimate the potential of tomorrow's applications by evaluating them in terms of today's technologies. When we speak of machines taking on new human tasks, the sceptical professional will express doubt because current systems are not up to the job. This is short-sighted. Recall Chapter 2, where we discuss a variety of technological innovations across the professions. What is striking about most of these systems is they could not have been delivered five years ago. We did not have the technological wherewithal—the mobile platforms, the bandwidth, the software, and more.

An important sub-theme here is that our machines are no longer confined to the grunt work—the basic administration in the office and the cookie-cutting in the modern factory. Again,

Chapter 2 should make us pause for reflection. Many of the systems noted there invite us to revise the popularly held view that our machines and systems do 'routine' work, while human beings focus on activities that require dexterity and intelligence. The boundaries are being pushed back as our machines become more capable.

There are many ways of characterizing these new, increasingly capable machines and systems. Some refer to 'smart machines',[30] while others have fastened onto 'superintelligence.[31] Others favour 'artificial intelligence' or, more commonly, 'AI'.[32] Our own preference is also for the language of AI, but we regard the emerging systems as constituting a 'second wave' of AI (section 4.9). Although we speak of emerging systems, in truth we do not and cannot know what particular systems will bring the most significant change. As we say earlier, some of the life-changing technologies of the next two decades, we predict with confidence, have not yet been invented.

To give a flavour of the progress being made, we turn our attention now to four developments that demonstrate the ways in which our machines are becoming increasingly capable. The first is that machines can now delve into our reserves of past experience and discern patterns, identify trends, and make accurate predictions (Big Data). Second, there are systems that can perform tasks that we would normally think requires human intelligence (IBM's Watson). Next, there are machines that can interact with apparent manual skill and dexterity in the physical world (robotics). Finally, there are systems that can detect and express emotions (affective computing). Volumes have already been written on each of these four subjects. We try to give an overview rather than make an academic assessment. We are not suggesting, incidentally, that these are the only important developments. We could also have added the 'semantic web', 'search algorithms', and 'intelligent agents'.[33] But to debate which technologies are primary distracts from the bigger point—that, exploiting various technologies, our machines will continue to become increasingly capable, and able to discharge more and more tasks that we used to think were the distinctive province of human beings.

Big Data

In 1988, foreshadowing much that is now claimed in the field of 'Big Data', Harvard's Soshana Zuboff made the following claim in her ground-breaking book *In the Age of the Smart Machine*: 'Information technology not only produces action but also produces a voice that symbolically renders events, objects, and processes so that they become visible, knowable, and shareable in a new way.'[34] In more homely terms, she was referring to the value of the great streams of information that are generated as a by-product of computerization. For example, early stock-control systems yielded useful information about customers' buying habits. Zuboff termed this the 'informating power of intelligent technology'.[35] Although the term 'informating' did not catch on, her main insight is now received wisdom—that analysis of large bodies of data generated by our technologies can provide us with valuable new insights, and can help us make more responsible predictions in many fields. The discipline that has emerged to specialize in this capture and analysis of information is now popularly referred to as 'Big Data'. When this term was first used, it was confined to techniques for the handling of vast bodies of data—for example, the masses of data recorded by the Large Hadron Collider. Now, Big Data is also used to refer to the use of technology to analyse much smaller bodies of information. Some speak instead of 'data analytics', 'data science', and 'predictive analytics', all of which seem to mean roughly the same thing.[36] Specialists in the area, whatever label is preferred, are often called 'data scientists'.

There has been no shortage of hype about Big Data. There are commentators who argue, with some justification, that its claims are too extravagant and that its methodology is underdeveloped.[37] What is hard to deny is the volume of data that are swilling around. In 2010, Google's Chairman, Eric Schmidt, claimed that we create as much information every two days as was created between the dawn of civilization until 2003.[38] Following available figures, by 2020 that quantity of information will be generated every couple of hours.[39] This leap can be attributed in part to the quantities of video, images, and audio content that are pouring onto the Web, and in part to the rapid growth of inexpensive sensors. In relation to the latter, on one view, the 'proportion of the world's data that comes from such sensors is expected to increase from 11 percent in 2005 to 42 percent in 2020'.[40]

The upshot of all of this is that great volumes of data are now at large, and the broad aim of data scientists is to develop methods for collecting, analysing, and exploiting these data. Case studies of success in Big Data abound. One (not entirely uncontroversial) illustration is Google Flu Trends, a system that can identify outbreaks of flu earlier than was possible in the past, by identifying geographical clustering of users whose search requests are made up of similar symptoms. Another is provided by Walmart, which analysed the buying habits of its customers prior to hurricanes and found not just that flashlights were in greater demand but so too were Pop-Tarts; and this insight enabled them to stock up accordingly when the next storm came round. Natural language translation systems and self-driving cars are also said to operate on the back of Big Data techniques.[41] While there are many ways in which Big Data is valuable,[42] most specialists in the field would agree with Mayer-Schönberger and Cukier that, '[a]t its core, big data is about predictions...it's about applying math to huge quantities of data in order to infer probabilities...these systems perform well because they are fed with lots of data on which to base their predictions'.[43] More extravagantly, Eric Siegel, a computer scientist, goes further when he speaks of 'computers automatically developing new knowledge and capabilities by furiously feeding on modern society's greatest and most potent *unnatural* resource: data'.[44]

If we combine these views of Big Data, we can see its promise for the professions—as a way of making predictions and as a way of generating new knowledge. To pin this down further, we have to identify the data sources that might be used here. We have in mind the data that are created by professionals in the course of their work. This includes the information they gather and the guidance they provide—in medical records, legal files, financial accounts, tax returns, architectural drawings, consulting reports, and so forth. In the past, before the Internet was widely used, and even in its early days, most professionals expressed little interest in capturing and analysing these bodies of data. Instead, the focus of most professionals was on the particular job at hand. The data generated (the 'data exhaust', as some would name it) were treated as though they were disposable once the file was closed. To some extent, it was largely left to academics, if to anyone, to gather together and study the data that were created as a by-product of the delivery of professional work in the conventional way. The revelation from the field of Big Data is that if this work product is captured, it may well yield patterns, correlations, and insights not previously recognized by professionals. This could be new practical expertise of a sort, and might form the basis of valuable predictions. This is not the equivalent of a professional informally saying, 'we have seen this before and it is likely that...', although it would be useful to have this formalized. Rather, the use of Big Data should identify trends and unearth knowledge that professionals simply had not noted or known of in the past. In this way, data can be regarded as 'a priceless collection of experience from which to learn'.[45] Already there is analysis of large data sets that link symptoms to diagnoses in medicine, fact patterns to judicial decisions in law, and performance to teaching methods in education. And as techniques become more sophisticated, these data could produce medical diagnoses, legal predictions, and educational insights that human practitioners could not. We provide examples of these in Chapter 2.

The new knowledge that flows from Big Data techniques falls into our category of 'practical expertise'. In section 1.8 we define this concept widely, not just to include the knowledge that professionals themselves produce and apply, but also the knowledge that is generated by systems and machines. Whether this is practical expertise or not does not depend on its origins—either a human mind or data and software—but whether it can be used to solve a particular set of problems. Our expectation is that systems based on Big Data techniques will often draw conclusions, offer advice, and provide guidance at the standard of human experts or higher.

It is important to stress that these high-performing systems will not simulate or model the way that human beings work. A system that makes a diagnosis on the basis of a comparison between a particular patient's symptoms and a database of 10 million past patients is not carrying out a differential diagnosis like a regular human doctor. Nor does a system that predicts the decision of a court by comparing the facts of a case with a database of hundreds of thousands of past cases operate like a normal practising lawyer. Big Data techniques do not and will not, in the language of section 3.3, *automate* professionals' working practices. Instead, by capturing and reusing huge bodies of past experience, this technology provides an approach to professional work that simply was not possible in the past. In the words of Patrick Winston, a leading voice for decades in the world of artificial intelligence, 'there are lots of ways of being smart that aren't smart like us'.[46]

IBM's Watson

In the same spirit, IBM's system Watson, which we regard as a landmark development in artificial intelligence, was not designed to solve problems in the way that human beings do.[47] Watson was developed in part to demonstrate that machines could indeed attain exceptional levels of apparently intelligent performance. Named after the founder of IBM, the system was developed to compete on *Jeopardy!*—a TV quiz show in the United States. This represented IBM's latest contribution to the branch of AI that in the 1980s was called 'game-playing'. Previously, IBM had developed Deep Blue, a computer system that beat the world chess champion Garry Kasparov in 1997. In the early 1980s such a system had seemed beyond our reach. It was clear to most researchers who were working on chess-playing systems that the very best players in the world seemed to make creative, intuitive, and strategic leaps which were beyond the understanding of the players themselves, never mind that of those who were trying to develop systems. In the end, of course, brute-force computing, fuelled by the exponential growth in processing power, delivered a system that could outperform the best human players, largely by being able to look many more moves ahead—and so not by playing in the same way as humans. While there is some merit in the claim that chess-playing machines are not really engaging in the same pursuit as human chess players, to diminish the systems excessively on this ground is to commit a version of our AI fallacy (section 1.9)—the mistaken view that the only way to develop systems that perform tasks at the level of experts or higher is somehow to replicate the thinking processes of human specialists. This error is also found in much of the critical commentary on Watson.

The development of Watson, of course, was a different order of challenge. To compete well on *Jeopardy!* requires contestants to have deep and wide-ranging knowledge, which is precisely what AI critics said in the 1980s was beyond the scope of computers. As is now well known, on 14 January 2011, on a live TV broadcast of *Jeopardy!*, Watson beat the two best-ever human contestants.

This was a truly remarkable achievement. This is a computer system, effectively, answering questions on any topic under the sun, and doing so more accurately and quickly than the best human beings at this task. It is hard to overstate how impressive this is. For us, it represents the coming of the second wave of AI (section 4.9). Here is a system that undoubtedly performs tasks that we would normally think require human intelligence.

The version of Watson that competed on *Jeopardy!* holds over 200 million pages of documents and implements a wide range of AI tools and techniques, including natural language processing, machine learning, speech synthesis, game-playing, information retrieval, intelligent search, knowledge processing and reasoning, and much more. This type of AI, we stress again, is radically different from the first wave of rule-based expert systems of the 1980s (see section 4.9). It is interesting to note, harking back again to the exponential growth of information technology, that the hardware on which Watson ran in 2011 was said to be about the size of the average bedroom. Today, we are told, it runs on a machine that is the size of three pizza boxes, and by the early 2020s Watson will sit comfortably in a smartphone.

The leap we ask of readers is to contemplate the impact of Watson-like technology when it is applied across the professions. It is a leap that IBM have themselves made. On their website they expressly say that 'Watson has been learning the language of the professions and is trained by experts to work across many different industries'.[48] IBM speak of the 'Watson Ecosystem', a community or organizations that are developing Watson-based applications. Lawyers, doctors, bankers, insurers, and educationalists are already involved. While the commercial opportunities are considerable, in early 2014 it was reported that IBM also intends to invest $100 million in a ten-year initiative to use Watson to help with healthcare and education in Africa.[49]

It is notable that one of IBM's main applications of Watson is in the field of healthcare. Already Watson-based systems can perform diagnoses, prepare treatment plans, and conduct research to a high standard. Although IBM and the medical experts working with them are cagey on this point, for some tasks it appears that Watson is already outperforming human beings. Before long, we expect, many more tasks will be executed by Watson. We conclude, from our own study of Watson, that the technologies already exist to support the development of powerful systems in other professions. The day will come, for most professional problems, when users will be able to describe their difficulties in natural language to a computer system on the Internet, and receive a reasoned response, useful advice, and polished supporting documents, all to the standard of an expert professional practitioner.

Robotics

In 1495, in Italy, Leonardo da Vinci designed and perhaps even constructed the first 'humanoid robot' in the Western world.[50] The word 'robot', derived from the Czech word *robota*, meaning 'drudgery' or 'servitude', is of more recent origin, first used in 1921, in a play, *R.U.R.*, by the Czech author Karel Čapek.[51] Since then, human beings have been captivated by the notion of artificial human beings (whether cyborgs, androids, or humanoids), and they have played a prominent role in Western literature and theatre.[52] Generally, the term 'robot' is now used to refer to some kind of software-driven, electro-mechanical machine. Sometimes, but not always, these robots are autonomous, which means that they can go about their business without human intervention.

Until recently, though, the direct daily impact of these machines was modest. In the 1980s, for example, in the academic and research worlds, robotics was a moderately low-key branch of AI, while in the commercial world at that time the main take-up was of industrial robots—heavy duty, single-purpose machines, for soldering, welding, bolting, spray-painting, or assembling. These have typically been used in the manufacture of cars.[53]

Progress in robotics during the past decade has been dramatic, as Frank Levy and Richard Murnane would now have to agree. They are US economists and, in 2004, wrote an important book, *The New Division of Labour*, in which they asked what tasks computers could undertake better than people (and vice versa) and what jobs would survive (we address these questions in Chapter 7). They argued that computers had caused 'a major upheaval in the nature of human work', and that they would continue replacing people in 'an ever widening range of tasks… the list becomes longer each year'.[54] But they stopped short of declaring that computers would replace all jobs. One task that they thought was beyond their reach was driving. They said it was 'hard to imagine' that truck-drivers would ever be computerized. Is it not remarkable, therefore, that Google has developed a small fleet of self-driving cars just one decade later? In ten years robots have moved 'from making cars to driving them'.[55] By 2014, Google's vehicles had travelled almost 700,000 miles, with only one incident (said to be caused by a car driven by a human being).

In the United States legislation has been passed in four states and in Washington, DC, allowing driverless cars.[56] By 2020 most major car manufacturers also expect to be selling autonomous vehicles. Our guess is that, in due course, people will look back with incredulity and say, 'it's amazing people actually used to *drive* cars'.

Other illustrations of advanced robotics abound. Every year, in manufacturing, an additional 200,000 industrial robots are installed (adding to an expected total of 1.5 million robots in 2015).[57] In 2014, for example, Amazon had more than 15,000 robots in ten of its warehouses. This army is charged with the task of bringing shelves of goods out of storage and carrying them to human employees.[58] These robots are a safer, cheaper, quicker, and more reliable workforce for the job in question.

Nonetheless, professionals may still be surprised to learn that robotics might have a direct bearing on their work. We suggest that robots are relevant for the professions in three ways. Firstly, for those professional services that require manual skills and dexterity (for example, surgery, dentistry, veterinary work, and architecture), robotics will come to augment, and sometimes replace, today's human activity. The medical and surgical fields have already demonstrated the potential here—from robots that dispense drugs and deliver linen in hospitals (see section 2.1) to tele-surgical operations carried out by surgeons in New York on a patient in France, using Zeus, a surgical robot.[59] Prosthetics also fall under this umbrella. As David Rose, a researcher at the MIT Media Lab puts it, '[p]rosthetics amplify our bodies, the power of all of our senses, and the dexterity of our hands... it internalizes computational power. It becomes a part of us, so much so that it *is* us.'[60] In time, robotic components will seem like natural extensions to our bodies.[61]

The second aspect of robot technology that bears directly on the work of professionals is the sub-field known as 'robotic sensing'. This imbues robots with the capability, for example, to detect physiological states of, and changes in, human beings and animals. As we discuss below, under the heading of 'affective computing', this in turn will enable machines to determine and respond to the emotional states of their users. More than this, robotic sensing gives machines the ability to hear (signal processing), see (image processing), touch (pressure and pattern processing), as well as to identify location, speed, temperature, barometric pressure, light, wind, humidity, and sound. In short, our machines can interact with the physical world.

Third are what can be called 'companions'.[62] These systems were available as early as 2004, when 'Paro' was made commercially available. Paro is a therapeutic robotic baby seal, whose cuteness is intended to have a calming effect on patients. We accept that not everyone will want a robotic seal, but over the last decade analogous systems have been built and refined with a view, in healthcare, to providing some kind of ongoing companionship for patients. One central idea is the use of robotics to take care of the elderly. These are systems that can take on some heavy lifting, pick dropped items off the floor, help with eating and washing, and also provide companionship and even empathy (see section 6.5).[63] Using the sensing devices just mentioned, as well as sensors sewn into patients' clothing (see section 4.7), these robotic companions can interact with those they help. There is a more general point here—that robots are likely to become one standard interface or front-end or delivery vehicle for practical expertise. Rather than sitting in front of a screen and contemplating what to type into Google, it will be commonplace instead to chat with some kind of robotic companion, to ask it questions. Some might regard this as a type of robotic 'trusted adviser'.[64]

In each of these three branches of robotics just noted there have been remarkable recent advances in the technologies that underpin them. Strides have been made away from industrial manufacturing to precision applications of robotics—smaller, cheaper, more flexible, autonomous, mobile, multi-purpose machines that are becoming increasingly dexterous, perceptive, and companionable. And we are just warming up. Global spending on robots is expected to rise from $15 billion in 2010 to $67 billion in 2025.[65]

And yet there is something disconcerting here. Many people are unnerved by the notion of machines that act as empathetic companions that might even be able adapt to their surroundings. We arrive here in what the Japanese roboticist Masahiro Mori, in 1970, termed the 'uncanny valley'.[66] This is the idea that the more human robots appear to be, the more positive our emotional responses to them tend to become. But only up to a point—because when their features and movements are very human-like, we often experience a sense of revulsion. There are shades of Freud in this analysis, but it creeps again towards committing the AI fallacy. We should be open to new ways of engendering the comfort that people enjoy when they feel that others are empathizing with them. This is not far-fetched—it is clear that we are already forming emotional attachments to our machines. As David Rose observes, '[o]ne of the tricks that designers use in creating robots . . . is to play on the human response to neotony—cuteness'.[67] We are suckers for the wide eyes and the endearing giggles. Which leads us into a related field, where machines seem to exhibit emotional behaviour.

Affective computing

In 1997, in her pioneering book *Affective Computing,* Rosalind W. Picard explained that she was making 'a call for a change in computing, a declaration that we have left a key term out of the computer intelligence equation... computers that recognize and express affect'.[68] By this she meant, roughly speaking, that until our systems and machines can handle *emotions,* they are unlikely to engage in activities and perform tasks at the level of intelligent human beings.

Almost twenty years on, the idea of emotional machines has gained momentum. In the *New Yorker,* Raffi Khatchadourian writes that 'computers can now outperform most people in distinguishing social smiles from those triggered by spontaneous joy, and in differentiating between faked pain and genuine pain', and that voice experts have developed software that 'can scan a conversation between a woman and a child and determine if the woman is a mother'. He also talks about smartphones that 'can be configured to detect stress, loneliness, depression, and productivity', and about 'emotion-sensing vending machines'.[69]

While all of this may be reminiscent of Woody Allen ('I have never in my life had good relationships with mechanical objects'),[70] affective computing is now an established discipline. It lies at the interface of computing and psychology, and its remit is the research, study, design, development, and evaluation of systems that can recognize, interpret, respond to, and generate human emotions. This field is not well known and has slipped below the radar of many technologists. Nonetheless, the recently published *Oxford Handbook of Affective Computing* extends to more than 500 pages. As well it might, the first chapter describes the discipline as 'burgeoning'.[71]

At its core, the focus of affective computing is on systems that can detect and express emotions. This is not, therefore, a stand-alone enterprise. It overlaps most notably with certain branches of robotics. The sensors that detect human emotions are often housed in robotic devices, while the systems that express emotions are often robots of some kind.

Many professionals say that their ability to 'read' and respond to their patients, clients, and students is central to their daily work. How on earth could a computer system detect the emotions of human beings? In practice, this is achieved, more or less, through a variety of sensors that automatically recognize a user's emotional state by identifying and assessing physiological indicators and changes in human beings. Emotion is communicated, for example, through facial expressions, which can be analysed by computerized face analysis; body movement that can be measured, for instance, by gyroscopic sensors; posture, detected through pressure-sensing chairs; and skin conductance—electrodes can pick up indicative changes in perspiration or in electrical resistance. It is also possible to infer emotional states from humans' blinking patterns, head tilts and velocity, nods, heart rate, muscle tension, breathing rate, and, as might be expected, by electrical activity in the brain. Numerous sub-specialisms are emerging here, such as vocalics (techniques for analysing voice) and oculesics (study of eye movement), automatic linguistic analysis of natural language, speech-based emotion recognition, and perhaps trickiest of all—humour recognition. The implications of all these innovations are profound for professionals. Imagine, for example, systems that can detect boredom, confusion, or frustration amongst a body of students.

Systems that can express emotions rely on a different tool-kit. One challenge here is to develop 'speech-production systems', also known as 'speech synthesizers' or 'artificial talkers', with voices that express a wide range of emotions. Another is to design machines that can mimic, empathize, or become attuned to the human beings with whom they are interacting. The computational modelling of bodily and facial expressions is one of many techniques used here. More ambitious is the development of 'embodied conversational agents' (ECAs). These are dialogue partners for human users, endowed with human-like communication capabilities. Some are animated virtual humans or robots, capable of social interaction with people through dialogue and non-verbal behaviour, complete with appropriate voices and intonations, facial expressions, postural shifts, and gestures. There is ongoing work devoted to building cultural values and norms into these anthropomorphic agents and robots, so that their emotional behaviour can be extended to include culture-specific variations.

To enable systems to detect and express emotions, they need to have large databases of emotions on which to draw. To meet this need, affective computing and Big Data have also joined forces. This means that very large databases of 'affective data' are being assembled. Some of this data is being taken from existing data sets. And some of it is being gathered using crowdsourcing methods.[72] The data themselves are of various types. Some of them are plain text, but many of them are audio-visual. Importantly, the data are not specific to particular social groups: they aspire to being multicultural and multilingual. Physiological data are being captured too. Interesting projects are also devoted to the development of an 'emotion mark-up language' which would be a standard way of describing data about emotions.[73] In short, vast bodies of data are being gathered and stored, and the more that these are put into service, the better our machines will become at recognizing and generating human emotions.

Work on affective computing is not reaching any kind of plateau. All people involved in the large and sprawling world of technology hanker after systems that are ever more user-friendly. Accordingly, the investment in systems that recognize, respond to, and generate human emotions is mounting. This, then, is another phenomenon that—alongside Big Data, AI, and robotics—encourages us to predict that our machines are becoming increasingly capable.

4.7. Increasingly pervasive devices

Not many decades ago a computing capability was defined, in large part, by the physical space that it occupied. Heavy-duty processing required large machines, located in mightily air-conditioned rooms. Suppliers and advanced users spoke with reverence and awe of 'mainframes', large machines that only substantial organizations could afford to buy and maintain. Today, the processing and storage capabilities of these mainframes can comfortably be accommodated in hand-held devices.

In the 1970s and 1980s, as Moore's Law took hold, mainframes gave way to mini-computers, which in turn stood aside for desktop personal computers. Then, in the early to mid-1980s, came the first wave of portable computers, in the form of laptop machines, considerably chunkier than the streamlined versions that are now commonplace. At the time we called them 'luggables'. They looked like toolboxes and weighed as much. Lighter laptops followed (our first one had a 10mb hard disk; today one of our laptops, at about one-third of the weight, has flash storage of 1 terabyte—100,000 times larger in thirty years).

Much more common now than laptops are hand-held devices, used mainly as mobile phones and for Internet access. There are now more than 6 billion mobile-phone subscriptions around the world. Of these subscribers, there are currently said to be 2 billion people using smartphones with an Internet connection, a figure that is expected to double to just over 4 billion by 2020.[74] More people in our world, in other words, have mobile phones than toothbrushes (which perhaps speaks as much about dental hygiene as 'pervasive computing'). At the same time, as a halfway house between laptops and smartphones, tablets are becoming more popular (though the boundary between small tablets and large mobile phones is becoming more blurred by the day). There will always be some people with no access to the Internet. But as computing becomes more portable and increasingly affordable in this way, this group will steadily diminish. Already in the United Kingdom and United States, for example, most people now have access to the Internet.[75]

This avalanche of hand-helds may seem pervasive in its own right. But when we speak of 'increasingly pervasive devices', we also include the phenomenon known as the 'Internet of Things'.[76] Alternatively referred to as 'ubiquitous' or 'pervasive' computing, the idea here is to embed processors, sensors, and Internet connectivity into physical objects.[77] It is as if we have tiny connected computers planted inside everyday things: an alarm clock that can check train times online and let its owner sleep longer if there are delays; an umbrella that is able to check online weather forecasts and light up at the front door when rain is predicted; electronic books that can update one another; plant-pots that can monitor moisture in soil and refill as appropriate; refrigerators that can detect when the amount of some food-stuffs has fallen below a prescribed level and reorder accordingly; boilers, lights, and thermostats that can be switched on and adjusted remotely.

Computer processing and Internet connectivity can be weaved into clothing and incorporated into other 'wearable' items. Thus, we might have jackets that give their owners small hugs when someone 'likes' their Facebook posts,[78] or shirts that can measure distance, calories, heart rate, and send data to their wearers' hand-held devices.[79] Internet-enabled watches with graphical user interfaces have been launched, while simpler fitness bracelets with sensors to monitor physical activity are commonplace. For the intrepid, there are ski-goggles that not only protect against the elements but come with a built-in 'accelerometer, a gyroscope, GPS, and Bluetooth'.[80] In the same spirit are optical head-mounted displays, embedded in spectacles, such as Google Glass.[81] Why, though, stop at spectacles? Work is afoot on technology that projects directly onto the retina of the eye (the users see objects suspended in the space ahead of them).[82]

Retinal display hints at yet another kind of embeddedness, one that hit home for us at a recent conference. An octogenarian approached us after a lecture and confided with pleasure, 'I am now connected to the Internet'. Initially, we thought he was making the unremarkable claim that he had joined the ranks of the world's almost 3 billion Internet users. He must have sensed our nonchalance, for he then simply patted his chest and told us, with the pride of the owner of a new hi-tech gadget, that 'my pacemaker is connected to a hospital and my heart is being monitored remotely'. This gentleman is an early adopter of the tiny Internet-connected processors that will frequently be implanted into or ingested by human beings. Miniaturized circuits can be introduced into flesh and blood, of humans and animals—measuring, monitoring, dispensing, capturing, and transmitting information to specialists, patients, or to other systems. Similar technologies are being used in the corporate world. For example, GE calls this the 'industrial Internet'—embedding sensors in their machines and sending large bodies of data into the 'cloud', and so bringing together the Internet of Things and Big Data.[83]

This, then, is what we mean by 'increasingly pervasive devices'. In the first instance, there is a surge in the number of tablets and hand-held machines, meaning that more people can be the beneficiaries of online practical expertise. Secondly, and as dramatically, very small processing and communicating components are being embedded in machinery, buildings, people, animals, clothes, and other everyday objects, and this has application in the work of various professionals (certainly for doctors, dentists, vets, opticians, and architects).

It has been estimated that by 2020 there will be 40 to 50 billion devices connected to the Internet.[84] Here again we are witnessing exponential growth. In 1943, Thomas J Watson, a past Chairman of IBM, is said to have announced that 'there is a world market for about five computers'. Six years later a reputable journal, *Popular Mechanics,* predicted that 'computers in the future may weigh no more than 1½ tons'.[85] We have come a long way.

4.8. Increasingly connected humans

When almost 3 billion people are connected to one network, important consequences follow.[86] In Box 4.2 we summarize much of what humans do when they are connected. No doubt they do much else, but we have isolated the uses that have a

Box 4.2. **What connected humans do**

Communicate
Research
Socialize
Share
Build communities
Co-operate
Crowdsource
Compete
Trade

bearing on the work of the professions. Many of these categories overlap with one another. Our purpose here is to give a sense of what happens online, and not present a watertight taxonomy.

In the first instance, human beings who are online are able to *communicate* with one another in new ways and on a larger scale. Leaving voice calls to one side, the current use of e-mail and various other forms of online messaging is remarkable. In 2014, for example, more than 196 billion e-mails were sent each day (in effect, twenty-eight e-mails for each human being).[87] When these methods are considered alongside video calls (for example, by Skype) and telepresence (emerging steadily), it is clear there is an ongoing shift in the way that professionals communicate with those they work with and help. Our modern professions developed in an era that was characterized by letter-writing, face-to-face meetings, and later by fixed-line telephone calls. Communication in the twenty-first century no longer reflects this outmoded trinity. The working practices of professionals are being transformed accordingly.

As radical in impact is the Web, which has become the first port of call for most people whenever they want to *research* any conceivable subject. Google is ubiquitous, and libraries and encyclopedias—the information sources of choice for professionals in the nineteenth and twentieth centuries—have largely been superseded.

However, a bigger revolution is playing out. There is a new generation of users, quite different from their Internet ancestors who were—in the early days, that is, way back in the 1990s—but passive recipients of whatever content website providers chose to make available. Users now contribute and participate directly.

Readers can now be writers. Recipients can be participants. Users generate content and make it available to others through a growing range of systems.

For example, various platforms have been developed which enable users to *socialize* online. These systems—most notably Facebook, with 1.39 billion users (one in six human beings)—play host to people who want to keep in touch with one another, easily and on a regular basis. And they do so with an intensity that bemuses most people who are north of 40. Typically, users provide information about themselves—news, photographs, updates, views, and more—to a network of friends around the world. For hundreds of millions of people, social networking in this way dominates their non-working lives.

Connected humans who socialize online also generally *share* online—photographs, videos, presentation slides, and so on.[88] This is not a peripheral activity. Every minute 300 hours of video are uploaded to YouTube (the repository for online video-clips), and the service currently has over 1 billion users.[89] Internet users share their ideas, thoughts, and experiences—from the trivial to the grave—online. Some do so by blogging. There were around 181 million blogs as early as 2011.[90] On the micro-blogging platform Twitter, around 288 million people share messages of no more than 140 characters in length with each other—on average, 500 million tweets are sent each day.[91]

While much Internet-based interaction is transient and ephemeral, it is increasingly common for users to *build communities* online (as is discussed briefly in section 3.7). Facebook, as already described, is home to many such communities, as is LinkedIn, which is often referred to as 'Facebook for grown-ups'. Orientated towards people in the workplace, this network has over 332 million users.[92] Facebook and LinkedIn are fairly generic platforms accessible to all Internet users. Here and elsewhere, we are seeing the emergence of what we call 'communities of experience'—online gatherings where people with common interests (whether recreational or work-related) come together and share their everyday experiences, insights, successes, failures, hopes, aspirations, and disappointments in remarkably candid ways. On Patients Like Me, for example, recipients of medical service share advice and guidance with each other, based on their own experience. Sometimes this experience of lay people is complemented with the experience of professionals. Khan Academy is a good example, where students learn from each other as well as from the formal instruction of a teacher. Yet other communities have restricted access and are populated by professionals alone—so-called 'communities of practice'. Sermo in medicine and Legal OnRamp in law are good examples. On this model, there are a relatively small number of users because the community itself is not open to the public. This can be an invaluable facility for specialists and experts, disseminating their thinking on arcane or technical fields of interest.

Perhaps the most dramatic result of connected human beings is our ability to *co-operate* online. Consider the concept of a 'wiki'. Named after a Hawaiian word (*wikiwiki*, which means quick), a wiki is a website that users can directly alter and add to. The best known wiki, by some way, is Wikipedia, 'the free encyclopedia that anyone can edit'.[93] As we note in Chapter 2, Wikipedia has been written co-operatively by over 69,000 main contributors, constantly refining and submitting materials, and adding cross-references and citations. This largely voluntary exercise is a case study is what is known as 'mass collaboration'.[94] Wikipedia has amassed around 35 million articles in over 280 languages. It is said to attract almost half a billion users each month. While sceptics in its early days anticipated that it would be a wholly untrustworthy resource, Wikipedia is now widely acclaimed as a notably reliable body of knowledge, built by a self-refereeing community of enthusiasts. The central idea of mass collaboration, then, is that very large numbers of Internet users are drawn together by some common purpose and cooperate on some sizeable project. Other notable illustrations are found in the world of software. Linux, for instance, the most commonly used operating system, is the result of mass collaboration amongst around 10,000 developers. Together they have written more than 17 million lines of code.[95]

Although mass collaboration can lead to the availability of robust, accurate, and up-to-date resources, it is not defined or driven by traditional academic or publishing methods. Often there is little editorial intervention or direction. Instead, large bodies of information and knowledge, reflected in documents and in software, are built up in an evolutionary fashion. The ongoing amendments and supplements of contributors act as a form of real-time peer review.

Co-operation and collaboration amongst connected human beings need not be 'mass'. Online co-operation on a very modest scale is another commonplace in the twenty-first-century workplace. Fifteen years ago, for a professional organization to develop its own online workroom facility could comfortably cost in the region of £1 million. Today this kind of shared online platform can be set up in minutes, using inexpensive off-the-shelf software. In this way, for example, it is easy jointly to co-author complex documents, even if the contributors are in different countries.

A related form of production occurs when online humans *crowdsource* (as is discussed briefly in section 3.7). Ordinarily, this involves large numbers of people being called upon to co-operate on discrete projects whose completion would be beyond the scope of individuals or conventional organizations. A common approach adopted here is to break some large task down into a manageable number of sub-tasks and invite a community of users each to undertake some of them. Crowdsourcing draws on networks of human beings to solve particular problems, to carry out pieces of work, or even to raise finance for given initiatives. Again, this is highly collaborative. A load is shared: a problem, or a piece of work, or a sum of money is subdivided and the burden is distributed across a community. There is an overlap here with mass collaboration, but 'crowdsourcing' tends to be the term used when a given project is well bounded in scope and likely timescale, and there is a clear commission or invitation from an individual or institution for the contributions of others.[96] There are many businesses that specialize in crowdsourcing. At CrowdFlower, for example, it is said that an online workforce of millions of people can be drawn from to put together teams to clean up incomplete and messy bodies of data, while at Mechanical Turk, an Amazon Web Service, requests can be sent out to Internet users to offer support for tasks that computers are currently unable to do. At Watsi, the cost of raising money to pay for healthcare is shared out among donors.

The apparently selfless nature of this socializing, sharing, community-building, and co-operating can be surprising. On the face of it, there is a spirit of co-operation here that defies popular thinking about human nature, which assumes that people are predominately self-regarding, if not selfish. More, it also seems to challenge classical economic thinking, which presumes that people strive to maximize their own self-interest alone, and are not inclined to contribute to others where there is no obvious and direct payoff to themselves. One of the leading academic commentators on the Internet, Yochai Benkler, in his book *The Penguin and the Leviathan*, strives to make sense of this apparent generosity, of the way in which 'co-operation triumphs over self-interest'. As he puts it:

> the Internet has allowed social, nonmarket behaviour to move from the periphery of the industrial economy to the very core of the global, networked information economy. Information and news, knowledge and culture, computer-mediated social and economic interactions form the foundation of everything in all aspects of our lives—from the pursuit of democracy and global justice, to the latest trends in business and media, to the best innovations in the most advanced economies. The Internet has revolutionized how we produce information and the knowledge foundations of our society.[97]

What motivates people to exhibit this 'nonmarket' behaviour? Yochai Benkler's explanation is a useful starting-point: 'people contribute their time and effort, for free, because they think it's the right thing to do, because they think contributing is fair, because it enhances their sense of identity and community and, quite simply, because it's fun.'[98]

Not all networks, however, support cooperation. Instead, some networks enable and encourage people to *compete* with each other. Providers use networks to set out their offerings, to allow themselves to be ranked against their competitors, and to make themselves searchable for recipients. This is what we see with BetterDoctor and ZocDoc in medicine. On other sites, recipients can actively pit competing providers against each other. This is in evidence at Kaggle, for example, where data is supplied to a network of statisticians who vie with one another to provide the best analysis. At InnoCentive, in the spirit also of crowdsourcing, people are invited to compete in the solving of a wide range of difficult problems.

Finally, connected human beings now *trade* extensively online. We are not referring here simply to online retail shopping, although this phenomenon now accounts for 13–15 per cent of retail spending in the United Kingdom.[99] More noteworthy is the scale of trading and exchanging that now goes on directly amongst individuals, with no wholesalers or retailers or other intermediate channels cluttering the supply chain. The prime example of trading in this way is eBay, the online auction and shopping website.[100] Founded in 1995, almost 150 million active traders, casual and accomplished users alike, buy and sell in this electronic marketplace. In the fourth quarter of 2012 alone $19.1 billion worth of goods were traded on eBay.[101] Currently there are more than 700 million items listed on eBay. There are no physical markets with even a fraction of this inventory. eBay is also a good example of a service that has liberated what we call a 'latent demand'. It is not that the trading currently conducted on eBay used to be carried on in a pre-Internet manner and somehow eBay has made it all a bit more convenient. Rather, eBay has created an entirely new market for many of its 150 million users. It has helped to release and satisfy a latent demand for trade that was not in evidence in the past.

Linked closely to online retail and trading systems—indeed, to many online services—are reputation systems that allow customers to rate providers (and sometimes the reverse as well). This is an effective method of encouraging honest practice. In Chapter 2 we note that online reputation systems are in use in various professions now. Likewise, in trade generally and in the professions in particular, online price comparison is enjoying success amongst prospective purchasers. This is the widespread phenomenon of searching the Internet for the lowest possible prices for some goods or service; which, in turn, may lead to an online purchase or perhaps to a more robust negotiation with conventional face-to-face providers.

To sum up, when almost 3 billion people are connected to one network, they communicate and research very differently than in a pre-Internet world; but much more than this, they are also able to socialize, share, build communities, co-operate, crowdsource, compete, and trade in ways and on a scale that has no analogues in the analogue world. Systems and services such as Twitter, Facebook, eBay, and YouTube, all now household names, are leading examples of services that connected human beings have created. None of these existed twenty years ago. Today they are used by billions of people. They have changed, and will continue to change, the way we live and work. Dov Seidman, the author of *How*, is correct when he says that '[w]e will never become *less* connected'.[102] But two simple predictions make it likely that we will become *increasingly* connected. The first is that the number of Internet users will continue to rise. Secondly, and more significantly, most people who are connected will steadily extend their use of the systems discussed in this section and others like them.

4.9. A fifty-year overview

There is one final step to be taken to complete our understanding of 'information and technology' and their impact on the professions. In part this is in response to those who might say, 'we have been here before—in the 1980s—and there is nothing new', and in part it is to help us build a picture of the changing impact of technology on the professions over a fifty-year period.

Let us rewind, first of all, and reflect on the work undertaken in the 1980s in expert systems and AI in a variety of professions. During that decade, we (the authors) were at the heart of the community that was working on AI and the law. This was an exciting time for AI, the heyday of what has since been called the era of GOFAI (good old-fashioned AI). The term 'artificial intelligence' was coined by John McCarthy in 1955, and in the thirty years or so that followed a wide range of systems, techniques, and technologies were brought under its umbrella (the terms used in the mid-1980s are included in parentheses): the processing and translation of natural language (natural language processing); the recognition of the spoken word (speech recognition); the playing of complex games such as chess (game-playing); the recognition of images and objects of the physical world (vision and perception); learning from examples and precedents (machine learning); computer programs that can themselves generate programs (automatic programming); the sophisticated education of human users (intelligent computer-aided instruction); the design and development of machines whose physical movements resembled those of human beings (robotics), and intelligent problem-solving and reasoning (intelligent knowledge-based systems or expert systems).[103]

Our project at the University of Oxford (1983–6) focused on theoretical and philosophical aspects of this last category—expert systems—as applied in the law. We conceptualized these as computer applications that could, at least in principle, solve legal problems and offer legal advice at the standard of a human expert or higher.[104] In 1988 we moved out of the research laboratory and into the marketplace, by co-developing the world's first commercially available expert system in law. This was an electronic legal adviser in a complex area of the law. What was most remarkable, although we say so ourselves, was that we managed to build a legal problem-solver that was in significant respects a better performer than the lawyer (the domain expert) on the basis of whose knowledge it was built.[105] After that project we broadened our interest and worked on expert systems in tax as well as systems that were for use by auditors. Here again, we were heavily involved in the development of systems that could undertake expert tasks at a high level.[106] At the same time, we also kept close to parallel advances in medicine where substantial progress was being made. These early successes generated much excitement.

Then came what is often referred to as the 'AI winter', the period during which AI seemed to stall. In the professions, certainly, thirty years on, there are far fewer operational expert systems of the sort we developed than we had expected. What went wrong? Why have so few expert systems in law, tax, and audit emerged since then? Why was this great early promise not fulfilled?[107] One reason for the lack of uptake was commercial—these systems were very costly to develop (hugely time-consuming for the experts whose knowledge went into the systems), at a time when law and accounting firms were increasingly profitable and saw no reason to embrace innovative technologies that might undermine their winning streak.

However, it is short-sighted to end the story by concluding simply that there was no business case for these systems. We have an alternative explanation that hinges on a particular way of looking at the history of technology and expert decision-making. According to this view, to review and assess the adoption of expert systems in terms of their underpinning technologies is to have too limited a perspective. Consider instead that there are two quite different ways of characterizing expert systems for the professions. The first is what we term 'architectural', which involves classifying systems by reference to particular techniques and technologies. In the 1980s there was, for example, great debate over the relative merits of different approaches to structuring knowledge in a system (some favoured, say, 'logic programming' over 'semantic networks'). When commentators and academics argue that expert systems in law, tax, and audit have failed, they are often saying that, architecturally speaking, few systems that were developed using the techniques of the 1980s have ever left the research labs.[108]

But there is a second way of defining expert systems, and that is 'functionally'. On this view, which is the one we have always preferred, we characterize expert systems not in terms of the technologies they embody, but according to the functions they perform. Our functional definition of expert systems has, since the mid-1980s, run something as follows: 'the use of computer technology to make scarce ... expertise and knowledge more widely available and more easily accessible'.[109] The emphasis here, therefore, is not on what technology is used, but on what the systems actually do. If we accept this functional definition, then progress in the field to date can be regarded more favourably. Consider the many professional services that are already available online, a small selection of which are mentioned in Chapter 2. At their most modest, using techniques such as checklists, flow-charts, and frequently asked questions, complex areas of expertise are now accessible and explained to all web users, often at no cost. These online systems were barely imaginable when we were working on AI and the law in the 1980s, because, of course, the World Wide Web had not yet been invented. While they do not use the techniques with which we were engaged at that time, they nonetheless meet our functional definition of expert systems, in that they use technology to make scarce expertise more widely accessible. We are not saying that these systems are expert systems or illustrations of AI. We are claiming instead that we are currently harnessing IT, in a variety of ways, in the same broad spirit as those of us in the 1980s who were exploring ways of using computers in the professions. And, as the pace of development and uptake speeds up, and as applications are increasingly available on mobile devices, professional content, guidance, and materials will be far more widely available than we could have predicted in the 1980s.

Our view is that the invention of the Web shifted the emphasis of the computers-in-the-professions community away from developing AI and expert systems towards the evolution of systems (a huge range of websites) that work in entirely different ways. It is early days yet, but irrespective of the underpinning technologies, this new wave of systems and services is already proving to be of great help to non-professionals and professionals alike. They may not yet perform at the level of experts, but they are highly useful nonetheless.

Leaving mainstream websites to one side, we can see now that to move from the first wave of AI systems in the professions (the expert systems) to achieve much higher levels of performance requires not just more powerful systems but a different approach. Broadly speaking, workers in the first wave of AI in the professions—from the mid-1950s to the mid-1980s—tried to understand what knowledge and reasoning processes underpinned human intelligence, and sought to replicate these in computer systems. The prevailing method of the 1980s was somehow (through 'knowledge acquisition' or 'knowledge engineering' techniques[110]) to mine the jewels from human experts' heads and hardwire their knowledge and experience into a system, often in the form of complex decision-trees around which users could navigate. The results were fascinating, but of limited commercial or practical application. We believe that the next wave of AI systems will not be premised on the enabling technologies and research of the GOFAI community. We expect far more ambitious applications, but of very different design and conception.

To grasp the likely shift in approach, it is helpful to think that there are two ways of enabling machines to behave in an apparently intelligent fashion in the professions. The first is to codify human knowledge and drop it into a system; and this, as we say, characterized much of the expert systems work in the 1970s and 1980s. The second is for the system itself to be sufficiently capable that it can perform impressively, even though it is processing relatively unstructured data. The second approach is technically much more ambitious—to develop systems that can operate on raw source materials and deliver high performance without having to map out a problem-solving process in advance. These would indeed be much more capable systems, and we expect their steady uptake across the professions. Big Data and Watson are promising examples of this approach.

What we envisage for the professions has happened in the world of AI more generally. Take speech recognition as an illustration. In the 1980s it was thought that for computers to recognize speech they would need, in some sense, to understand the context in which words are spoken, and that this, in turn, would require a general understanding of the world around us. It was thought, for instance, that a computer could only understand the difference between the two spoken phrases, 'she is a tanker' and 'she is at anchor', if it understood the context in which these utterances were made. Because human beings were believed to understand speech by understanding context, the view was that artificial intelligence would in the end be achieved by, essentially, modelling human intelligence and human beings' ways of processing information and of thinking about the world around them. This would require systems that had common sense and general knowledge. However, speech recognition was eventually cracked through brute-force processing, massive data retrieval and storage capability, and statistics. This means, for example, that a good speech recognition system that 'hears' the sentence 'my last visit to the office took two hours too long' can correctly spell the 'to', 'two', and 'too'. It can do this not because it understands the context of the usage of these words as human beings do, but because it can determine, statistically, that 'to' is much more likely immediately to precede 'the office' than 'two' or 'too'. And this probability is established, effectively, by very fast searching and sorting across a huge database of documents. This was an early example of Big Data, and a similar approach was taken in developing machine translation (now commonly used in the form of Google Translate).

Likewise, in many other areas of AI, brute-force processing and massive storage capacity, rather than simulation of human thought processes, are enabling machines to perform tasks that we would traditionally have expected to require some form of intelligence. By analogy, in the professions we predict the evolution of systems powered by brute-force computing that operate over very large bodies of historical data. These systems will provide high-quality advice and guidance, but not by reasoning or working in the same way as skilled specialists; nor by seeking to model human thoughts and reasoning processes; nor again by having common sense or general knowledge. These systems are high-performing but are not intelligent in the way that human beings are (we expand on this in section 7.1).

On this view, we need to reappraise AI. For many commentators, the AI winter was a euphemism for AI's demise. But it transpires that AI has not been expiring. It has instead been hibernating, conserving its energy, as it were, ticking over quietly in the background, waiting for enabling technologies to emerge and catch up with some of the original aspirations of the early AI scientists. In the thaw that has followed the winter, over the past few years, we have seen a series of significant developments—Big Data, Watson, robotics, and affective computing—that we believe point to a second wave of AI.

In summary, the computerization of the work of professionals began in earnest in the late 1970s with information retrieval systems. Then, in the 1980s, there were first-generation AI systems in the professions, whose main focus was expert systems technologies. In the next decade, the 1990s, there was a shift towards the field of knowledge management, when professionals started to store and retrieve not just source materials but know-how and working practices. In the 2000s, Google came to dominate the research habits of many professionals, and grew to become the indispensable tool of practitioners searching for materials, if not for solutions. Our current decade, the 2010s, we expect to be characterized by major progress in Big Data and search. Into the 2020s and beyond, we predict the emergence and adoption of a second wave of AI systems in the professions.

5

Production and Distribution of Knowledge

We arrive now at the theoretical heart of the book. In Chapters 2 and 3 we describe how the professions are changing. In Chapter 4 we explain these changes by reference to the information sub-structure and developments in technology. In this chapter we draw these observations and arguments together. First we develop a model to show how professional work is evolving. Then, building on all we have said and done so far, we step away from the professions and describe the people and systems that will replace them in the future.

In broad terms, our focus in this chapter is on the way that we handle a particular type of 'knowledge' in society. We are, of course, not alone in exploring this concept. All manner of scholars have applied their minds to 'knowledge' over the centuries. Philosophers, for example, who specialize in epistemology ask such fundamental questions as 'what is knowledge?' and 'how can we know anything?', or again, 'of what knowledge can we be certain?' Sociologists study the connections between knowledge and power, culture, and class. Lawyers handle questions about the ownership, protection, and sharing of knowledge. Information theorists consider the relationships between knowledge, information, and data. We are fascinated by each of these perspectives, but for the most part they fall beyond the scope of our work.

Instead, the particular type of knowledge that is our preoccupation is what we introduce in Chapter 1 as 'practical expertise'. Now we explore this concept in greater detail, looking at how we currently create and share it, and how we might handle it differently in the future. We seek to show, in economic terms, that knowledge has special characteristics that make its widespread and low-cost production and distribution both possible, and desirable, in a technology-based Internet society.

5.1. The economic characteristics of knowledge

Practical expertise, or our conception of it, is the knowledge that is required to solve the sort of problems for which the professions, traditionally, were the only solution—the knowledge that is used to sort out a health worry or resolve a tax problem, for example. In the professions this practical expertise is a complex combination of the formal knowledge, know-how, experience, and skills of professionals. But the professions are not the only source of practical expertise. In this book we argue that new sources of practical expertise are emerging—through increasingly capable machines, operating on their own or with non-specialist users. These will enable us to solve many difficult problems *without* the direct involvement of the traditional professions.

Any type of practical expertise, though, whatever its origin, is a form of knowledge. And knowledge is an interesting beast, with its own remarkable features. The ways in which we create and handle knowledge are very different, for example, from the ways in which we create and handle physical goods. One of the great contributions of economists is to have shown that these differences arise out of four special characteristics of knowledge.[1] And it is these that explain why the shift from a print-based industrial society to a technology-based Internet society is particularly transformative for the professions and the work that they do. We turn now to these characteristics.

Most goods are *rival*, which means that if they are consumed, then there is less left for others. If someone takes a bite of a chocolate bar, or uses a car to make a trip, then there is less chocolate left for others to eat, and less fuel in the tank for later drivers. There is what is known as 'rivalry', or 'competitiveness', when people consume these goods.[2] Knowledge, however, is *non-rival*. This is the first distinctive characteristic. If we draw on some knowledge to solve a problem, it does not leave less knowledge for others who want to use it afterwards. A lawyer who drafts a contract for one client is not thereby divested of insight and understanding; he is not more ignorant about the law when he comes to prepare another agreement for a different client. A doctor does not forget a chunk of her medical knowledge each time she makes a diagnosis. A journalist does not become worse at analysing and communicating the more articles he writes. Unlike most goods, knowledge does not run out, or get worn down, each time it is used.

Sceptics might point out that the lawyer or the doctor cannot see more than one client or patient at a time. In that way, they might say, things are not as non-rivalrous as we claim. This is a mistake, but a helpful one. The error is to confuse the knowledge that these professionals draw upon, which is itself non-rivalrous, with the way in which we distribute that knowledge—a one-to-one, face-to-face interaction, which, we agree with our doubters, is frustratingly limited.

Most goods are also *excludable*. This means that it is easy to prevent people from consuming them unless they pay. For example, owners of sweet shops can stop customers from eating their confectionery if they have not paid. They simply refuse to hand over the goods. In contrast, the second distinct characteristic of knowledge is that it has a tendency towards being *non-excludable*. This means that it can be difficult to prevent non-payers from using it. If a lawyer drafts a basic will for a client, and in doing so passes on some of her legal knowledge to that client, it is then hard for that lawyer to stop the client from sharing that knowledge with someone else. Similarly, if a doctor explains to a patient how to treat a simple illness, there is little the doctor can do to prevent the patient from communicating the insight to someone else. A journalist who passes on breaking news to a friend confronts a similar problem. It is hard to contain and, say, make its release conditional on payment. It can therefore be difficult for the lawyer, doctor, or journalist to stop other people from using their knowledge, even though they have not paid for it.

Knowledge is not always non-excludable, though. Consider Coca-Cola's secret recipe—this is knowledge that is held by a select few at the company. And it is knowledge that many people (particularly their competitors) would like to have, but are successfully excluded from finding out. On the whole, despite the examples above, the professions also manage to exclude people from their respective bodies of knowledge. In Chapter 1 we argue that this is largely an element of the grand bargain.[3] But note how the grand bargain, if it is to hold firm, must continually resist this tendency of knowledge to spread without compensation.

The third characteristic of knowledge builds on the first. We noted that knowledge is non-rivalrous, and does not diminish when it is used. But the use and reuse of knowledge to solve problems often makes it *more* valuable, not less. A teacher's knowledge of how to conduct a class, a consultant's knowledge of how to run a business, a doctor's knowledge of how to treat some symptoms, or a journalist's knowledge of how to investigate events and report a story—these bodies of knowledge get larger and richer each time they are brought to bear. Economists call this the 'shoulders of giants effect'[4]—just as Isaac Newton's understanding of the world built on the work of those who came before him ('If I have seen further it is by standing on the shoulder of giants', Newton said, though reputedly in sarcasm rather than earnest), so too with other types of knowledge. Put differently, the use and reuse of existing knowledge can often lead to the generation or production of new knowledge.

The fourth characteristic of knowledge is that often it can be *digitized*. This means that we can convert it into digital form, and process it electronically. More formally, to say we can digitize knowledge is to say that we can represent the knowledge as 'bits', as binary signals made up of ones and zeros, the language of modern electronics. Our capacity to digitize, and our enthusiasm for doing so, is a recent phenomenon. As late as 2000, Cukier and Mayer-Schönberger note, only 25 per cent of the world's stored information was in a digital form. Today that proportion is 98 per cent.[5]

In contrast, physical goods cannot be digitized. We might be able to capture them in an image, or describe them using text, and in turn convert these images and texts into digital form. This is what we do when we take a digital photo of a physical object, or type up a description of a physical object using word processing. But the object itself cannot be digitized; only a representation of it. This leads Hal Varian, Google's Chief Economist, to distinguish between 'information goods', those goods that can be digitized, and 'industrial goods', those that cannot.[6] Using this distinction, knowledge, and in particular our unit of analysis, practical expertise, can clearly be categorized as an information good.

However, for three reasons, we need to be cautious in thinking about this fourth characteristic. First, we are not saying that all types of knowledge can be digitized. As we argue in Chapter 1, some of the practical expertise of the professions is 'tacit'—broadly speaking, this is the sort of knowledge that people struggle to articulate in words, still less turn into a set of zeros and ones. There is some knowledge that professionals use to solve problems that we cannot seem to 'get out of their heads' and put into a digital form.

Secondly, we are also not saying that if some knowledge is digitized, then the technologies that handle it must in some sense 'know' or 'understand' what it is that the zeros and ones express. We address this question of machines and thinking in section 7.1.

Finally, and most importantly, we are not saying that the practical expertise some technology might rely upon in solving a problem is identical to the knowledge that a professional would apply in tackling the same challenge. There are many ways to approach any given professional task. The traditional method of using professionals is not the only option. The practical expertise embodied in and applied by machines might be of a different sort. To think otherwise may be to fall foul of the AI fallacy set out in Chapter 1—to make the error of supposing that the only way to solve a problem currently handled by human experts is to articulate and then re-apply the specific knowledge on which the human expert currently relies. This is an excessively anthropocentric view. As machines become more capable, high performance can be achieved in many different ways.

This final point may be particularly comforting for those who might at this point be worrying that not all the knowledge in the heads of human experts can be digitized. Some of this knowledge, as we note earlier, might be tacit and so hard to articulate. For example, if we asked Tiger Woods to explain how he hits a golf ball so far, he might be able to offer us insight into a few of the thoughts that pass through his mind as he swings the club. He might also perhaps pass on a few hints. But he would struggle, we imagine, to articulate the complex network of accumulated heuristics, intuitions, and hand-to-eye interactions that have contributed to his supremacy as a golfer. Many of these will be unconscious, inculcated through repeated practice and use, and some so deeply embedded that even Tiger himself would be unaware of them. Yet none of this precludes us from building a mechanical swinging arm that could hit the golf ball further and straighter than Tiger—this would be solving the same problem, as it were, but in a different way.

In summary, knowledge has four special characteristics. It is non-rival, in that use of it does not diminish what is left for others. It has a tendency towards non-excludability, in that it is difficult to prevent non-payers from using it. It is cumulative, in that its use and reuse in turn give rise to new knowledge. And it is digitizable, in that we can often turn it into machine-processable bits. Practical expertise, one particular type of knowledge, shares these four special characteristics.

5.2. Knowledge and the professions

Professionals in all disciplines have for long recognized that knowledge lies at the heart of their work. The acquisition of knowledge through education and training has always been a priority, and professionals distinguish themselves by being more knowledgeable than their colleagues. However, when professionals are told—by academics and consultants, for example—that they are in the 'knowledge business', somehow this terminology does not resonate. Similarly, when professionals are informed that they are central to the so-called 'knowledge economy', they are rarely moved.

A simple distinction is also often ignored in thinking about the 'knowledge economy'—between industries, on the one hand, that have come to depend deeply on knowledge and those, on the other, whose very purpose is to provide knowledge itself. In the former camp, for instance, fall the manufacturing and retail sectors, whose operating models have been enhanced through the development and application of innovative ideas, fresh thinking, new working practices, imaginative use of technology, and more systematic management. One business can outperform another on the strength of this sort of knowledge. But there is a major difference between businesses exploiting knowledge to triumph over their competitors, and the professions whose role is actually to produce and distribute knowledge itself. Knowledge, for the professions, is not simply an enabler; it is fundamentally what is on offer. The professions have knowledge that those they help do not, and their role, in large part, is to develop, curate, and provide access to that knowledge.

If knowledge is indeed at the heart of the professions, two questions follow. The first is this—how effective are the professions at producing, capturing, nurturing, and reusing their knowledge within their own organizations? We know from discussing its special characteristics that knowledge can be used and reused, and that new knowledge might be created in doing so (it is non-rival and it is cumulative). The professions ought to take advantage of this. The second question lies at the heart of this book, and is the subject of much of this chapter—might there be different and better ways of producing knowledge and making it available in society, methods that might not directly involve the traditional professions at all?

The first question has been the primary preoccupation for decades of those who work in the field of 'knowledge management'. These are specialists who advise in the professions on the ways that relevant knowledge can be handled more effectively. On the face of it, knowledge management has firmly taken hold across the professions. Doctors have their protocols, lawyers have their precedents, management consultants have their methodologies, auditors have their checklists, tax advisers and accountants have their pre-populated spreadsheets, and so forth. Commentators on knowledge management speak confidently about its use in the professions, and point to various categories of knowledge: know-who (information about who knows most about given subjects within an organization); know-what (substantive technical knowledge, and ideas as well); know-how (procedural knowledge about how to go about some activity); know-where (knowledge of where to go for help, guidance, and expertise on any given topic); know-why (explanations of the rationale behind ideas, activities, processes, and services); and know-when (insight into when best to take action or refrain from acting). The more reflective experts and commentators in the field of knowledge management recognize that there is more to expert performance than formal, published, explicit knowledge. They agonize over an issue we raise in section 1.8—whether knowledge might instead be tacit, and whether the gut reactions and intuitions of professionals might also be formally articulated.

However, deeper scrutiny reveals a profound reluctance amongst many mainstream professionals to share and reuse their knowledge. Put bluntly, professionals tend not to like sharing what they know with other professionals. This leads many knowledge managers, in their darker moments, to confess that their discipline has struggled to flourish in the professions. Instead, in many professions knowledge sharing has been counter-cultural. By training and disposition, professionals enjoy working on their own. Even in the largest professional institutions the workforce is, in reality, a coincidence of sole practitioners who have been assembled under the one roof and brand. Reward systems in most professions, for example, no matter how much HR people protest otherwise, tend to encourage individual achievement rather than team working. More than this, there are uncomfortable questions here about trust and confidence—many experts do not trust their colleagues to work with and reuse their knowledge, while others are nervous about making theirs available, for fear that their efforts might be challenged and so their ignorance exposed. Commercially, too, knowledge management has not made sense in profit-seeking professions, when payment has been on the basis of time spent. Why embrace knowledge management as a tool for avoiding duplication of effort, for reducing hours on the clock, if your competitors are equally and happily inefficient with their clients' money, and these clients are not demanding change?

On balance, the field of knowledge management has not been an unqualified success. It has not satisfactorily answered the first question we set out before, about how effectively the professions create, curate, and recycle their knowledge. Moreover, knowledge management specialists have barely addressed our second question at all—whether there might be better ways of producing knowledge and making it available in society that do not directly involve the professions, as currently constituted. Until recently, knowledge management has been an almost entirely inward-facing enterprise, devoted to building and sharing bodies of knowledge within organizations. In thus confining its attentions, it has failed to recognize that the traditional way of handling knowledge, and the conventional ways of producing and sharing it, might be temporary and interim. In the next section, by looking at the evolution of professional work, we explore what is likely to follow.

5.3. The evolution of professional work

Many practitioners and commentators are already thinking beyond traditional professional practices when they speak today of the 'commoditization' or 'commodification' of professional work. The terminology here is not precise, but the broad idea is clear enough—that routine professional work in most disciplines is being reduced to sets of standard practices, so that tasks that formerly required human experts can now be conducted by less knowledgeable, even lay, people with the support of appropriate processes and systems.

In many discussions about commoditization, this phenomenon is seen as threatening, especially to those professionals who charge by the hour (because activity that used to yield considerable fees may now no longer demand large portions of time, nor indeed be the sole territory of traditional experts). Commoditization is also sometimes regarded as distasteful, as diminishing the worth of a service that can or has been reduced to routine work. It follows, if some professional tasks can be commoditized, then many traditional providers, especially the sceptics and the threatened, downplay the significance of these activities, often dismissing them as no longer worthy of their attention. And yet dismissing commoditized work in this way ignores its value—that, from the perspective of the recipient, client, or customer, it is often a good thing, bringing lower costs, greater accessibility, and higher and more consistent quality of service.

The term 'commoditization' has become rather overused in the literature. Its negative overtones and variety of meanings render it less useful than once it might have been. Some new terminology and, more importantly, some new thinking would be helpful here. This is what we now provide—we introduce and explain a model of the evolution of professional work that is carried out by human experts. The model is illustrated in Figure 5.1. It depicts four main stages in the evolution and delivery of professional work: craft; standardization; systemization; and externalization (this last category is itself subdivided into three).[7]

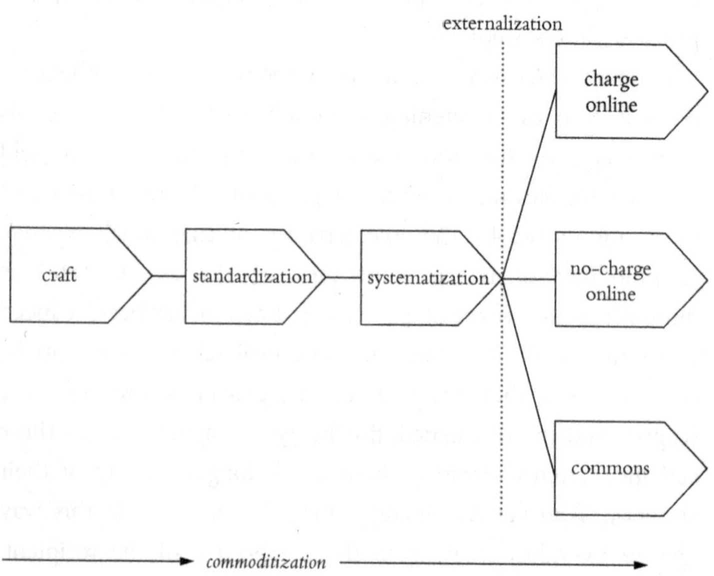

5.1. The evolution of professional work

In the broadest of terms, our claim is that market forces, technological advances, and human ingenuity are combining to drive professional work from left to right on our model, away from being provided as a form of craft by human experts, through various stages of development that will result, in due course, in much practical expertise being available, in a variety of ways, on an online basis. We regard this movement from left to right on our path as capturing and characterizing a fundamental transformation across the professions. In the parlance we find unhelpful, this movement away from craft does indeed represent the 'commoditization' of professional work, but it can be seen at a glance that this is not a single bound from traditional to commoditized. Instead, it is a more complex transition.

Like all models, this evolutionary path is, of course, a simplification of reality. We recognize, for example, that some of the categories overlap with one another; that not all professional work will evolve neatly and linearly through each stage; that some work or parts of work may never evolve beyond one particular stage; and that some work may not evolve from an early stage but may spring to life at a later stage. It is, however, a useful simplification. Despite its limitations, our experience in introducing this model and earlier versions of it across the professions has been encouraging, and seems to capture the substance and direction of change as well as the choices that the professions are facing. Our hope for the model is that it helps professionals explain and predict the developments they are witnessing within their own fields, and that it offers a common vocabulary and conceptual framework for comparative analysis across different professional disciplines.

There is one further characteristic of the model that should be borne in mind from the outset. We are not suggesting, for any particular piece of professional work—for instance, the treatment of a patient, the resolution of a dispute for a legal client, the teaching of a class, the auditing of a company's accounts, the investigation of events or the reporting of a story for a reader—that the challenge for professionals is to determine into which of our boxes their work sits. Rather, our claim is that, for any piece of professional work, it is possible to decompose the work into constituent tasks and allocate each task to the most appropriate of the boxes. We discuss this at greater length later in this chapter, under the heading of 'decomposition' but it is important to bear this point in mind as our argument unfolds.

The first of the four steps on our evolutionary path describes professional work when practised and delivered as a form of 'craft'. This echoes our discussion in section 3.2. For many professionals and observers, this is the quintessential approach to professional work. On this view, professionals are craftspeople. Drawing on their practical expertise, and often with great patience and focus, they will tailor and customize their work each time afresh, honing their provision to the unique circumstances of each of their clients, patients, students, or customers, as the case may be. Characteristically, this approach involves face-to-face (often one-to-one) interaction between professionals and the recipient of their work. The advocate in the courtroom, the surgeon in the operating theatre, the professor in the tutorial, the tax adviser with the chief finance officer, the journalist drafting a leader, the auditor poring through accounts—in each of these illustrations, we have in mind a person of expertise and experience who handcrafts a solution or service from scratch, like an artist working on a blank canvas, or a tailor fashioning a bespoke suit. This is the conception of the professional person to which generations of young people (and their parents) have aspired to become. This is the conception of professional work that is presupposed in much academic writing. And this is the conception of the professional that we find in our literature, theatre, and television—in law, we have the inimitable Rumpole and the unimpeachable Atticus Finch; in medicine, there is the irascible but brilliant diagnostician Gregory House; in education, Mr Holland and John Keating, the inspiring teachers; and even Monty Python's disparaging portrayal of the 'boring' chartered accountant.[8]

Thrilling, romantic, and inspiring though these characters and this conception of the professional may be, we believe that much professional work is not actually delivered as a craft today. More, we submit that it is both probable and desirable that this bespoke approach will continue to diminish as the preferred approach in years to come.

We are not arguing that the craft approach to professional work will disappear entirely. Our claim instead is that a significant number of tasks that used to require handcrafting are already being done very differently. And, as cost pressures build and increasingly capable systems emerge, more and more tasks that used to require the engagement of human experts will be undertaken either by less-qualified people with the support of appropriate systems, or taken out of human hands altogether.

We can draw again here on an analogy from the world of traditional crafts. Some history helps. In the City of London there is a thriving community of 'livery companies'. As we note in section 1.3, these organizations can be traced back to the ancient guilds and, in their early years, their focus was largely on regulating their trades. There are now 110 of these institutions, the longest-standing of which is the Mercers' Company, founded in 1394 and now located in Ironmongers Lane in London. Mercers were traders in fine cloths and silks, but the last of their number to become an apprentice did so in 1888, since when, like many other livery companies, the Mercers have shifted their focus from trade to charity and education. But the fate of the traders known as Mercers is instructive. Improvements in transport and communications, the impact of industrial machinery, the invention of alternative synthetic fibres, the introduction of mass-market retailing, and the rise of an increasingly influential fashion industry—these factors transformed the world of the Mercers, and unsettled the cottage industries and craftsmen of which they were part. The same fate has befallen many other crafts whose names are borne by livery companies—for instance, the Cordwainers (who worked with fine leathers), Tallow Chandlers (who rendered animal fat as candles), and the Wheelwrights (makers of wheels). Their original ways of working, and that of innumerable fellow craftsmen, were similarly revolutionized. Crucially, however, the demand for the products of these trades—cloths, materials, candles, wheels—has not faded. Quite the reverse. Today the output of these historical trades is in even greater demand. However, market forces and technological advances have eliminated these craftsmen from everyday life.

The move away from craft in the professions is not news. Our second step on the path, that of standardization, has already been embraced by many professions, as their exponents have sensibly avoided reinventing the wheel on each new project or initiative:

management consultants have used methodologies (for example, for system development and project management); lawyers have used templates and precedents; doctors have relied on protocols; teachers use last year's notes; while auditors deploy standard checklists, as do tax advisers and actuaries.

When we speak of standardization, we have in mind two broad ways in which practical expertise can be routinized for later reuse: in terms of process, using checklists, procedure manuals, and standard guides; and in terms of substance, using standard form documents with reusable content. Historically, this shift from craft to standardization was not driven solely, or even mainly, by a passion to cut costs. A more fundamental force has been at play here, well captured by the surgeon Atul Gawande, in his book *The Checklist Manifesto*:

> Here, then, is our situation at the start of the 21st century: We have accumulated stupendous know-how. We have put it in the hands of some of the most highly trained, highly skilled, and hard working people in our society. And, with it, they have indeed accomplished extraordinary things. Nonetheless, that know-how is often unmanageable. Avoidable failures are common and persistent, not to mention demoralizing and frustrating, across many fields—from medicine to finance, business to government. And the reason is increasingly evident: the volume and complexity of what we know has exceeded our individual ability to deliver its benefits correctly, safely, or reliably.[9]

He drives the point home by reference to medicine:

> The ninth edition of the World Health Organization's international classification of diseases has grown to distinguish more than thirteen thousand different diseases . . . Clinicians now have at their disposal some six thousand drugs and four thousand medical and surgical procedures . . . It is a lot to get right.[10]

Even the world's leading experts cannot function faultlessly by relying on training and recall alone. With professionals, standardization need not represent what the critics of commoditization fear, namely, a diminishing of the worth or status of the tasks and activities involved. Rather, we standardize to prevent avoidable errors, to ensure consistency across our work, and to prevent duplication of effort. More than this, we often standardize to elevate the quality of our work—when groups of lawyers, doctors, accountants, or teachers collaborate in producing standard processes and materials, the distillation of the experience and knowledge of these experts often gives rise to tools that enable average professionals to outperform leading experts. As a matter of fact, then, standardization is already common within our professions. Remember again that standardization does not replace craft in its entirety. Instead, particular tasks that can be routinized are identified within the bundle of the craftsperson's activities, and these are isolated for more efficient handling.

The move from craft to standardization makes particular use of two of the special characteristics of knowledge that we set out before. First, it takes advantage of the non-rivalrousness of knowledge—a given checklist or standard guide, for example, can be duplicated and used and reused by many professionals without wearing it out or depleting it. Secondly, it takes advantage of the cumulativeness of knowledge—the more a checklist or standard guide is put to use, the more likely it is that any errors or omissions are noticed, the more likely further improvements are conceived and built in, and the more valuable the tool becomes.

Looking forward, as new techniques are developed, it follows that the professions will want to embrace ever more sophisticated methods of standardizing and so magnify the various benefits just noted. Technology has given birth to precisely the kind of tools that can bolster the benefits of standardization. This is our third step, when professional work becomes systematized. We are not referring here to the many technologies that have supported administrative and back-office functions of professional organizations around the world for decades (word processing, databases, e-mail, and so forth). Rather, our focus is on systems that are developed and used to assist human experts, or replace them altogether, in carrying out professional tasks themselves. Whereas standardization involves reducing these tasks to reusable paper-based routines, systematization involves applying more sophisticated technology to these activities. The systematization we have in mind at this stage on the evolutionary path is of the tools and systems that are used internally *within* the professions and their organizations, but are not made available directly to the recipients of the work (this is what is involved in the fourth and final stage).

In some professions these technologies support manual tasks and can enhance the dexterity and precision of human beings. Examples here are robotics in surgery and dentistry and CAD in architecture. In wider use across the professions are systems that computerize the standards and processes that are characteristic of the second step along our evolutionary path. Some of these systems are no more than electronic checklists, as deployed frequently in audit work. Others are more ambitious work-flow tools that computerize the progression of high volume, relatively repetitive professional work. More ambitious still are systems that, in various ways, directly apply practical expertise in discharging particular tasks. In tax practices, such systems enable practitioners to complete online forms and then generate tax returns in formats acceptable by revenue authorities. In law, there are document assembly systems that ask users various questions and on the basis of their responses will generate polished first drafts. In education, personalized learning systems help teachers tailor the material to particular students. In medicine, there are diagnostic tools, and in accounting, there are systems that computerize large parts of audits. The details of these applications are less significant than the way that they operate. They do much more than store standard procedures and documents (the second stage of evolution) for human beings to apply. Instead, in a sense, they actually undertake professional work. After interaction with their users, they generate substantive output.

The move from standardization to systemization takes advantage of three of the special characteristics of knowledge. It exploits the fact that knowledge is non-rival and cumulative—not only can the knowledge in these tools be used and reused without wearing it out, but it becomes more valuable with usage. The more we use the systems, the more likely we are to identify shortcomings and make enhancements. And so, in an iterative way, we uncover their failings and limitations, we come across bugs and errors, and we respond through innovation and improvements. But systemization also relies on a further characteristic of knowledge—that it can be digitized. These tools and systems use practical expertise articulated in a digital form, no longer just stored in the head of particular professionals or in filing cabinets. The practical expertise can be handled—stored, retrieved, modified, applied, and shared—with greater ease than before, no longer slowed down by the bottleneck of face-to-face interaction with the craftsperson. In turn, the digitization of practical expertise sets us up for the fourth step.

5.4. The drive towards externalization

We use the term 'externalization' to refer to the fourth step on our evolutionary path. This is the stage at which the practical expertise of human experts is made available to non-specialists on an online basis. As Figure 5.1 illustrates, we suggest that there are three ways in which externalization can take place—as 'charge online' service, as 'no-charge online' service, or on a 'commons' basis. The distinction between the first two and the third hinges on who owns and controls the externalized materials. While this division itself can rest on some difficult and arcane questions of intellectual property law,[11] the general thrust can be simply stated.

The 'charge online' service is likely to flourish when professionals (or the organizations to which they belong) are attracted to externalizing their practical expertise because it can deliver revenue. Professionals who provide chargeable online services fall into this category. Invariably, these professionals will retain both full ownership and full control of their systems and their content.

When securing some kind of subscription is not the aim, but the professionals want to remain in charge of what is on offer, then the system can be characterized as a 'no-charge online' service. There is no direct cost for users, but these services may be financed by indirect costs (for example, by collecting and commercially exploiting the data of users) or subsidized by other parts of the profession or by other institutions (for example, by governments or charities). Again, the professions will tend to keep full control over the content, but may concede, through licence, some rights of full ownership, for example, in allowing users to reproduce the materials.

Externalization on a 'commons' basis comes about when the content is made available as a resource that is used, reused, and shared, at no cost, with most if not all members of society. In the commons of practical expertise, the motivation is to make this knowledge far more widely accessible. To enable this, the providers permit others to edit, add to, share, and reuse the content where possible. The professions and others largely concede both ownership and control, and the content is held in common for the benefit of all.

Most professionals will be familiar with the concepts of 'charge online' and 'no-charge online' services. They may be less familiar with the notion of the 'commons'. This is the formal name given to a resource that is shared among a group of people. Lawrence Lessig, the Harvard law professor, entertainingly describes several simple cases of commons in *The Future of Ideas.* Many of our local parks and public streets, for example, are commons. No individual can exclude another from taking a stroll. Great ideas, like Albert Einstein's theory of relativity, are available for all of us to understand (or to try to). No individual can exclude another from reading it. We do not have to 'obtain the permission of anyone else' to enjoy these resources. Ownership and control of them is shared out among the group.[12]

In the commons that we have in mind, this shared resource is practical expertise. Managing resources that are shared in this way is difficult. The political economist Elinor Ostrom was awarded a Nobel Prize for her thinking on commons, and their related difficulties, which are (unsurprisingly) called 'commons problems'.[13] We explore these problems and their possible resolutions in section 7.5.

(For the sake of completeness, these three forms of externalization are not the only types of online service that offer access to practical expertise, but they represent the final stage in the evolutionary path along which our traditional professions are travelling. Other examples of online service that do not evolve from today's professions are 'communities of experience', and facilities whose knowledge is machine-generated. We turn to these in a moment.)

Externalization, of any of the three types, can be done in two spirits. The first we call 'opening the vault'. The idea here is that internal systems—that is, those that are used within the professions by today's professionals—are made available to Internet users generally. The gatekeepers, to a greater or lesser extent, stand aside, and at least some of their practical expertise is made accessible. Systems that are already deployed within the professions, for example, can be offered directly to clients, across the Internet, in the form of an online service. In this spirit, some accounting firms, consulting businesses, law firms, and tax practices have put some of their internal knowledge resources online. More advanced internal systems can also be externalized, for instance, when a tax practice provides the tax departments of its clients with the same tools as it uses; or a law firm offers its document assembly tools for direct use by the clients themselves. The systems of tax and law firms and the knowledge held within them are, in this way, packaged online for the convenience of the client in the form, crudely speaking, of a DIY professional service.

Commonly, however, online resources that have been developed and delivered by the professions cannot trace their origins to existing applications or systems within their organizations. Instead, they are 'purpose-built' for direct use online by end-users. This is the second way of externalizing, and this phenomenon is illustrated by e-learning systems in education, personal tax return completion systems, most online legal document assembly systems, health advisory systems, and business diagnostic applications. The externalization here is not of pre-existing systems but of some of the practical expertise of the professions that hitherto was confined to their experts' heads and in standard materials.

Looking more generally now across the evolutionary path, it is clear that the nature of professional work changes as we move from left to right. Work delivered in the manner of craft, at the left-hand end of the spectrum, tends to be provided by a trusted adviser, often a leading expert or thought leader, while practical expertise that is provided online will usually represent the distillation of the collective experience of many individuals. At the same time, different forms of technologies are embraced across the spectrum. Generally, the further right one travels, the more capable and innovative the technologies become. They are innovative, in the sense we introduce in Chapter 3, precisely because they challenge or even displace the traditional working methods of the craftsperson.

Emotionally and psychologically, therefore, the comfort zone of traditional professionals or advisers is towards the left of our path, and progress away from craft to externalization becomes increasingly alien, if not objectionable. Put differently, as one might expect amongst more conservative professionals, the further we progress from craft, the less plausible our narrative becomes. Individual practitioners, from most disciplines, will tend to acknowledge that a major shake-up in all professions is long overdue—other than in their own. So deeply are they entrenched in the traditions of their profession, and so profoundly immersed in working practices of the past, that most professionals find it hard to conceive that their knowledge and experience—their practical expertise—might be made available in entirely different ways. A doctor may well see scope for transformation in law and consulting, an auditor might indeed support calls for overhauling journalism and teaching, but all professions seem to share the bias of finding difficulty in imagining any thoroughgoing re-engineering of their own discipline. This is the special pleading we note in section 1.9, and it is significant because, traditionally at least, change within professions tends to come from within. If professionals struggle to acknowledge the scope for overhaul in their own specialisms, they are unlikely to be champions for change. More obviously, if doctors, lawyers, accountants, and teachers feel threatened by new and different ways of working, then they are rarely found stepping forward with alacrity and zest to demand their own extinction.

There is one clear exception to the general rule that traditional professionals prefer to operate at the left-hand side of the spectrum. This is when some experts (especially, lawyers, accountants, consultants, tax advisers, and others for whom time is equated with money) are called upon to move from working on an hourly billing basis to providing a fixed-fee service. It quickly becomes apparent, for those in a commercial environment, that a move to the right generally brings cost savings and efficiencies that can increase the profitability of their work.

In any event, there are larger forces at play here than the self-sustaining and often self-serving preferences of suppliers. Deferring for now the particular incentives for each of the three forms of externalization (this is addressed in section 7.5), we suggest that there are economic and technological factors that will drive many professions and professional tasks from left to right on our evolutionary road.

The first of these factors is cost. Ordinarily, as we move from left to right, the cost of the conduct of professional work goes down. This is because, by and large, it is less costly to undertake tasks that have been standardized and systematized than it is to handcraft them afresh each time. Once the initial fixed costs that are required to create a standardized or systematized professional process have been sunk, the cost of offering one additional unit of the service—its 'marginal cost'—will tend toward zero. This is because it becomes very easy to reproduce practical expertise once it has been articulated and, especially, digitized. This means that the cost of offering one additional unit of the service becomes very low, if not zero. Consider, for example, how easy it is to copy an electronic document, or a piece of music, or a set of pictures, and send them to a friend. So too for practical expertise, when kept in digital form. There is also a change in the distribution of the fixed costs of handling practical expertise as we move left to right. On the left these costs are concentrated in the professions, and shouldered by them alone—they invest in the buildings and the equipment required to carry out professional work in the manner of the traditional craft. But as we move to the right, these capital costs are shared by the recipients of services (for example, in the cost of each of their computers).

However, while the move from left to right means that the costs of reproducing practical expertise will fall towards zero, and fixed costs might be spread out, it is also unlikely that prices will stay as high as they were on the left. As we move right, if the competition is strong enough, this will drive down the price of professional work towards the cost of producing one new copy, its marginal cost. But because this cost is negligible, as we note, the price of practical expertise will also tend towards zero. Professionals understandably fear the advent of work whose price is zero. Moving left to right, then, is a double-edged sword for the professional provider—costs are likely to fall, but so too might prices. Margins, as a result, are uncertain. Carl Shapiro and Hal Varian, experts on the economics of information, note the two dimensions of this move to the right:

> Because the marginal cost of reproducing information tends to be very low the price of an information product, if left to the market place, will tend to be low as well. What makes information products economically attractive—their low reproduction cost—also makes them economically dangerous.[14]

For a profit-seeking organization, there are two strategic options in moving its work rightwards—one is to seek to limit the competition (for example, by differentiating the offering), which then allows prices to be kept high. The alternative is to secure a higher volume of work at narrower margins. There is another cause for concern here for professionals—that the reduction of professional tasks to mere digital offerings devalues their profession and diminishes the perceived contribution that human professionals can make. This is one common objection to commoditization.

On the other hand, the move away from the crafting of professional tasks towards more cost-efficient methods of delivery can be of immense significance for the recipients, that is, for people who are in need of some service. As we explain in section 1.7, we are living at a time when high-quality professional work is unaffordable. We can be more precise now—most citizens and organizations are struggling to afford the charges of most professional service providers who handcraft in the bespoke tradition. CEOs and CFOs of the world's largest companies complain frequently about the costs of their lawyers, accountants, auditors, management consultants, and tax advisers. This is rarely a denial of the value that these professional advisers can bring, but more usually reflects a conviction that these professionals are inefficient in their working methods and not managed tightly enough. Whether or not this intuition or suspicion is well informed, management boards around the world are demanding substantial reductions of expenditure on professional services, even though their workload is on the increase (not least because of ever growing and changing bodies of regulation). Meanwhile, small- and medium-sized businesses often confess that they undertake much professional work on their own, in a haphazard and untutored way, because they simply cannot afford the fees of external professional advisers or the costs of employing them internally. In these businesses, professional work is undertaken on a shoestring. As for individual consumers, the prohibitive costs of traditional professionals exclude most individuals from taking expert advice. Each profession faces its own variation of this problem. Health services around the world, for example, are failing as costs escalate, and it is widely recognized that there is insufficient funding available to run high-quality schools and universities if teachers and professors operate in the traditional way.

As it becomes possible to reduce the cost of professional work by moving from craft towards externalization, we believe there will naturally be a strong market pull in this direction. The demand here is not just from those who are reluctantly paying for service today. We also expect that externalization will satisfy what we call (in section 3.7) a 'latent demand'. This refers to the large unmet need of those who currently would benefit from professional guidance but cannot afford it.

There is a further attraction to undertaking professional tasks towards the right-hand side of our evolutionary path—that, broadly speaking, the further one moves away from craftsmanship, the more certain the cost of work is likely to be. When professionals handcraft, the process tends to be rather open-ended. Just as it seems inapposite to ask an artist or a musician how long it might take to complete some great work, it has also seemed inappropriate to trouble an expert on the question of time scales when some professional craft is in the process of creation. In truth, it is not easy to put limits on the likely effort required from a professional whose creativity, innovation, and strategic insight are required to tackle a complex and challenging task. But as tasks come to be standardized and systematized, providers can with much greater certainty estimate the effort required to discharge their work. If the standards and systems already exist, for example, their application in practice will be a known quantity, and the more uncertain variable—that of any human contribution—will tend, relatively, to be a less significant proportion of the work.

There is another, less intuitively obvious reason why there is likely to be a market pull from left to right by the recipients of professional work. The gut reaction of many seasoned professionals when exposed to our model is that the quality of work will inevitably diminish the further one moves from craft. Craft is perceived as the most refined and sophisticated professional approach, the apotheosis of the professional class, and, overwhelmingly, the preferred method where it can be afforded. However, it is now apparent that, for some tasks at least, online professional service can outperform, in terms of quality and consistency as well as speed and ease of use, the conventional handcrafted service.

Take, for example, Deloitte's tax system for UK-based corporate tax compliance. This application, as introduced in section 2.7, contains the distilled expertise of more than 250 tax experts and comfortably attains superior performance levels to those of any individual who labours alone. Similarly, a world-class online lecture by a wonderful communicator and leading specialist, delivered onscreen to a class of students, will invariably trump a class taken by a less expert teacher operating in the time-honoured way. Or again, it is clear that, in some situations at least, the treatment planning of IBM's Watson will outstrip many, if not most, traditional physicians consulting with their patients in the traditional manner. As professionals move further to the right, therefore, and they externalize their expertise, the quality of service can rise.

In summary, those who are at the receiving end of professional work have robust reasons for asking their providers to move from left to right: the work will cost them less, the cost will be more certain, and the quality will often increase. The market will, therefore, pull many professionals away from handcrafting. Some will come along grudgingly, whereas more innovative professionals will need little urging.

While there can be little question that embracing technology can often bring new efficiencies, it would be to conceal the full picture to suggest that the use of technology constitutes no more than a response to the stressed market's demands for cost-cutting. Another driver is the cluster of human inclinations—towards curiosity, invention, and improvement—which seem to urge innovators in all professions to challenge old ways of working and explore and introduce technology that either complements conventional practice or replaces human work altogether. This appetite for embracing technology in the professions has grown in recent years amongst the pioneers, even if not all commentators share their optimism.[15]

In contrast, some professionals adopt technologies for more prosaic reasons—they do not want to be left behind or regarded as laggards. Even the most conservative professions evolve gradually, if reluctantly, when their working practices become embarrassingly out of step with the wider adoption of technology in society. And so, even though they were late adopters, the professions did, in due course, eventually embrace the PC, the Web, e-mail, and tablets.

5.5. The liberation of expertise: from craft to commons?

As practical expertise is externalized and made available online, a profound opportunity arises. On the traditional model, whether or not enhanced by standardization and systematization, professionals remain the gatekeepers of the expertise over which they profess mastery. In standardizing and systematizing, this may improve the efficiency of the professions, but the practical expertise that they guard still remains firmly under their lock and key. The professionals, as gatekeepers, maintain their vigil at the interface between people who require access to particular types of practical expertise and the sources of this knowledge.

If some practical expertise can be produced and shared online, however, we can anticipate a great release of knowledge. It will no longer be held solely in the heads of particular professionals, in their publications and standard operating procedures, or in their internal systems and tools. Instead, lay people will have direct access to it. Since it is non-rival, recipients can use and reuse it without wearing it out. Since it is cumulative, recipients can share it and, if able to adjust it and amend it, so the body of online practical expertise will become richer and more valuable with use. It is when practical expertise is externalized in this way that we can fully exploit these special characteristics of knowledge. In a print-based industry society these characteristics lie dormant and largely unrealized. In a technology-based Internet society, when knowledge is digitized, it can be liberated.

As the analysis of this chapter shows, however, there are degrees of liberation involved here. If a professional organization makes its practical expertise available through an online subscription service, this is a rather weak form of liberation. The content is not freely available, and although accessing this content may be more convenient than conventional interaction with a professional, the old gatekeepers are still in place. A stronger form of liberation arises when the expertise can indeed be accessed by users at no cost, but generally these users are no more than passive recipients of the content—the providers are in control of what is available, and of when and whether it can be reused.

The strongest form of liberation comes about when the practical expertise is made available as a commons resource, owned and controlled by those outside the professions, and intended for further development and reuse. This third option represents the fullest and most radical liberation of expertise, bringing an end to an era during which practical expertise was possessed and controlled in turn by human specialists and later, collectively, within the professions. This form of liberation builds on another of the economic characteristics of knowledge—its tendency towards being 'non-excludable', which means that it can be difficult to stop it spreading without payment. If the liberation is strong, there is no need to resist this tendency.

Whether society will choose to favour the third model of full liberation, the second model of partial liberation, or the first model of minimal liberation is a complex question of commerce, politics, and morality. It might well be asked what would incentivize the professions to embrace the third and strongest form of liberation. We ask and answer this question in section 7.5.

5.6. The decomposition of professional work

We should pause now to clarify what we are *not* claiming. We are not suggesting that, in everyday professional activity, the challenge for professionals and those who help manage their workload is to map each individual project, engagement, or service onto one particular step on our evolutionary path. This would not be feasible. Rarely, for example, will the problem of a client or patient be easily categorized as suitable for resolution using, say, standardization alone. The professional work required to solve a problem—consultations, deals, guidance, writing, advice, and so on—is not a monolithic, indivisible block of endeavour. Each piece of work is made up of many different tasks, processes, and activities. The appropriate question, then, by reference to our evolutionary model, is instead this—in any set of circumstances that call for professional input, how can the work be divided up, or broken down, and what is the optimum balance and distribution of those *component parts* across the four steps?

To put this more concretely, we argue that professional work should be *decomposed*, that is, broken down into its constituent 'tasks'—identifiable, distinct, and separable modules of work that make it up. Once decomposed, the challenge then is to identify the most efficient way of executing each type of task, consistent with the quality of work needed, the level of human interaction required, and the ease with which the decomposed tasks can be managed alongside one another and pulled together into one coherent offering. There will be no definitive way of decomposing any particular piece of professional work into constituent tasks. Often the tasks identified will correspond fairly clearly with the conventional life-cycle of the work in question. However, on some occasions the decomposition itself will reveal anomalies and inconsistencies that lead to a reformulation or re-engineering of the work into a structure or approach that bears little resemblance to current practice. We refer to the person who breaks down professional work, dispassionately assessing and structuring the allocation of tasks, as the 'process analyst', one of the future roles for tomorrow's professionals that we discuss in section 6.8.

Proceeding in this way, in terms of component tasks rather than indivisible bodies of work, helps us to think clearly about how any particular piece of professional work can be carried out more effectively. But it also serves a second purpose—it helps us to think clearly about the future of professional work in general. In everyday conversation, when we talk about the work that different people do, we tend to talk about their different jobs. When we speak of professionals, we refer to lawyers, doctors, teachers, journalists, accountants, and so on. However, the notion of a 'job' is not entirely illuminating. It is an unhelpful term, in the same way that the term 'work' is unhelpful. As with any given piece of work, a job is also not a monolithic, indivisible block of endeavour. Again, to contemplate the future of professional work in general, it is instructive to look in depth at what people actually do in their jobs, and to concentrate on the particular types of *task* that make up their jobs.

The deeper issue here is that any changes in the work that people do tend to originate at the level of particular tasks involved, and not with the job in general terms. Consider what happens if we introduce a new technology to computerize some activity of a professional. A doctor, for example, might find that a remote heart monitor reduces the need for in-person check-ups. Clearly, there has been change here. But to suggest, for instance, that the doctor's job has been 'destroyed' would be inaccurate and hyperbolic. Consider further that some new technology might also allow the professional to innovate, to work in new ways, releasing the doctor to spend more time undertaking some kind of research. Once more, there has been change. But we would not say that a new job has been 'created'. To discuss these two changes solely in terms of 'jobs' would be inappropriate.

What we would want to say is that, in some sense, the job that the doctor does has become 'different'. And by thinking about the *tasks* that make up the job, we can do this more coherently. What has actually happened is that the tasks the doctor undertakes have changed. In this case, she has lost a particular type of task (face-to-face heart monitoring) to a new technology. But she also takes on a new type of task or, if she was involved in research before, puts more effort into an old type of task. This is why the term 'job' is too general and sweeping. Thinking in terms of tasks is more revealing.

Of course, if a professional loses *enough* tasks to other people or to new technologies, then it might be true that he loses his job. In that case, it would be reasonable to say that the job has been destroyed. But to think clearly about the future and sustainability of any given job, we should start by thinking about its constituent tasks and move on from there. As the example with the doctor shows, changes in a person's job start from an underlying churn and adjustment in the bundle of *tasks* that make it up. Some tasks are lost (to other people or to machines) and others are gained. This has far-reaching consequences for the future of work, and in sections 7.3 and 7.4 we develop these ideas more fully. There, we use them to provide an answer to pressing questions about 'technological unemployment'—whether, as machines become increasingly capable, there will be any reasonably-paid work left for people to do.

There is a further, practical reason for thinking in this way. If we proceed with a jobs- rather than a task-mindset, we are encouraged to think of professional work in terms of artificial, self-contained compartments. For instance, a legal problem is something necessarily resolved in its entirety by a traditional lawyer, a medical problem by a doctor, and so on. However, clients' and patients' problems often transcend the job-based boundaries that are imposed. A more holistic approach to professional work is promoted by assessing what is needed in terms of tasks rather than jobs. (See also section 1.8.)

The concept of decomposition with a task-based focus on work has pedigree. Many classical social theorists were preoccupied with the subject, although their focus was on manufacturing rather than the professions, and they used the terminology of the 'division of labour'.[16] In the early 2000s an important line of economic thinking developed in economics, led by David Autor, a professor of economics at MIT.[17] From the point of view of legal work, we were thinking along similar lines in the mid-1990s. We first argued for a task-based approach to the analysis of legal work in 1996, in *The Future of Law*, and formalized this a few years later, in 2000, in *Transforming the Law*, where we suggested that legal work ought to be 'decomposed, so that some of the constituent tasks may more cost effectively be delivered by providers other than law firms'.[18] In 2008, in *The End of Lawyers?*, we again used the concept:

> I suggest that any legal job or category of legal work can be decomposed, that is, broken down into constituent tasks, processes, and activities . . . I use

the term 'tasks' fairly generically to include processes and activities as well as tasks. In this sense, tasks are identifiable, relatively distinct, and so separable modules or portions of work.[19]

We embrace the same approach to decomposition in this book.

5.7. Production and distribution of expertise: seven models

Some professionals may decide that they are not comfortable with the idea of making their expertise available online (in whatever format). Some indeed may be reluctant even to standardize or systematize, and prefer to conserve their traditional crafts. But there will be innovative professionals who will find opportunity in the online world, perhaps to build a more profitable business or simply to provide a better service.

Either way, the story of the professions does not end at externalization. In the account set out in Figure 5.1, practical expertise can always be traced back to a human expert. It is an expert, engaged in craftsmanship, whose practical expertise is first standardized, then systematized, and finally externalized. Yet not all practical expertise originates with human experts. Building on the technological developments laid out in the previous chapter, the characteristics of knowledge discussed earlier in this chapter, and the new systems and tools that are already in operation (see Chapters 2 and 3), it is clear that there are other ways of producing and sharing practical expertise. Alongside the professions is a diverse mix of machines, systems, tools, as well as ordinary people and para-professionals, some working alone, others working together in networks or in online communities, but all of whom, in different ways, are trying to solve the sort of problems that traditionally were cracked only by human experts in the professions.

In this mix, we can make out two new and distinct sources of practical expertise. The first is from non-expert people. The second is not from human beings at all, but from new systems and tools. There are, in a sense, two new divisions of labour arising in society, both focused on providing alternatives to the traditional professions: the first is a reallocation of effort away from professionals towards different types of people; the second is away from professionals towards a variety of machines. A complete story of the future of the professions must take into account these new divisions of labour, and should not focus on traditional human experts alone.

In some circumstances these alternative sources of practical expertise will sit neatly outside the traditional boundaries of the professions, entirely distinct from the practical expertise of conventional human experts in the professions. On other occasions, though, there will be bold professionals and institutions that bring these alternatives inside their walls, and use them to complement their human experts. We can already see examples of this: the design consultancy IDEO uses an online community of ordinary people to work with their traditional consultants; Rocketship Education uses a personalized learning system built by computer programmers to support their traditional teachers; and Forbes and Associated Press use software designed by AI specialists to computerize the production of certain types of article alongside their traditional journalists. No longer are professional institutions populated, as they were in the past, exclusively by traditional human experts, such as consultants, teachers, and journalists. Yet it remains the case that we are very far indeed from this hybrid set-up being the dominant state of affairs. On the whole, the professions themselves remain firmly committed to a traditional model that draws on and provides access to the practical expertise of human experts.

Our aim now, however, is to look beyond the traditional professions; beyond the boundaries of practical expertise that the professions tend to own and control. We gather together the many arguments and findings of this book and consider, in broader terms, other possible ways of making practical expertise available in society. In the language of economists, we express the possibilities as seven different models for the production and distribution of practical expertise, as summarized in Box 5.1.

The traditional model represents the dominant way that professionals work today, while the other six are alternative models,

Box 5.1. Models for the production and distribution of practical expertise

The traditional model
The networked experts model
The para-professional model
The knowledge engineering model
The communities of experience model
The embedded knowledge model
The machine-generated model

each now feasible or at least foreseeable because of recent advances in technology. We acknowledge that these models map more neatly onto some professions than others. Certain features, like one-to-one interaction, may only apply to specific professions (to medicine, for example, and not to journalism). Although the details may differ, we expect that all the models will be taken up across the professions, but refined by each to meet their own requirements.

The traditional model

The first model of production and distribution is the traditional model. In broad terms, this involves human professional providers undertaking their work, usually by way of a real-time, face-to-face interaction that is rewarded according to the amount of time spent. This is the model that dominates professional service of today. On this traditional model, the practical expertise that is used is originated by human beings. In any given situation, it may be that the professional involved has sufficient knowledge to undertake the work without further research or separate preparation, but recourse is frequently made to written resources, online materials, or to consultation with colleagues. In other words, the practical expertise is frequently produced on a just-in-time basis, sometimes invented on the spot, but frequently drawing directly on the past experience and training of the individual professional. Often professionals will rely on published resources that are generated by their academic community, while sometimes they may benefit from the knowledge systems developed within their organizations or made available more widely by their peers in their discipline.

The advice, guidance, or service that is offered aspires to being of a customized sort, focused on the particular needs of the particular recipients. Thus, the knowledge is said to be tailored and refined afresh for each particular user. The service is usually delivered through one or more of face-to-face discussions or presentations, written reports (in print or electronically), or consultation by phone or video link. The format tends to be of a one-to-one nature, delivered by one human being to another. The content of the guidance or service is not generally intended for reuse, although insights gained and research undertaken can contribute to later work. The technologies that support the traditional model of professional work, in the language of Chapter 3, are instances of automation rather than innovation. This means that the technologies support and streamline conventional, long-standing working methods and do not challenge or change the status quo. The work itself is labour-intensive, usually requiring individual professional experts, often with the support of more-or-less junior professionals. The traditional model of professional services is reactive, in the sense that instigation of the work is invariably at the discretion of a client, patient, or student, and so its effectiveness can depend on the non-expert recognizing if and when they are in circumstances that would benefit from external professional help. Unless there is explicit agreement to transfer ownership, the intellectual property in the work will tend to be retained by the professionals.

To see this traditional model in action, visit almost any surgery, school, law office, or place of worship.

The networked experts model

The second model of production and distribution is the networked experts model. This also involves human professional providers. Unlike on the traditional model, where experts work alone or in relatively stable organizations and groups, when experts are networked they convene as virtual teams. The practical expertise again is originated by human beings. The aspiration, once more, is that the work is customized to the particular needs of the recipient. Yet it differs significantly from the traditional model in the way that the professionals are mobilized and interact with each other, and in the way that the professionals in turn engage with the recipients of their work.

On this model, professionals cluster, more or less formally, via online networks rather than in physical organizations. Groups of specialists, often self-employed freelancers, use online platforms to communicate and interact with each other, forming transitory affiliations to solve particular problems. The size and composition of the networks varies, from individuals working alone to large teams. The spirit of their interaction with one other also varies. Sometimes it is cooperative, where a team comes together to tackle a shared challenge. Frequently it is more competitive, where individuals in a group compete to offer alternative and better solutions. The professionals need not know one another. Nor need they have worked together previously. Nor, indeed, do they always need to meet in person as they work, although this can happen. These professionals are not traditional white-collar workers. Nor are they blue-collared. Instead, reflecting their ethos, we might refer to them as 'open-collared' workers.

The relationship with the recipients of their service is also different. The work that they undertake varies in scale, complexity, and time. It is likely to be more of an ad hoc service than on the traditional model. The professionals are available 'on tap'[20] or 'on demand'.[21] The transitory nature of the arrangement makes it well suited to short, self-contained packages of work rather than more extended and complex projects. Particular problems are identified by recipients, individual professionals are called upon and gathered together as a team, and then disbanded on completion. Arrangements and relationships are temporary. Online selection plays an important role, with recipients sifting through potential providers using customized search engines, relying on experience-based rankings to discriminate between options, and sometimes calling upon human beings to help put together a team or group. Technology is critical in the delivery of the work. In the terminology of Chapter 3, this is innovation rather than automation. It allows traditional professionals to convene, collaborate, and deliver services in teams and structures that were not possible in the past. It enables combinations of talent and practical expertise that could not have been assembled in the print-based industrial society. Unlike the traditional model, the service is not always provided face-to-face with recipients, or indeed in real time. The work tends to be reactive rather than proactive, initiated by the recipient and not prompted by the provider.

In terms of the intellectual property rights, here again, unless there is agreement to transfer ownership of the work product, the human professionals on the networked experts model will tend to retain the intellectual property rights in the service offered. In contrast, the network on which this model rests (if it is a separate entity from the individual involved) will tend not to be owned or controlled by the professionals who participate.

There are many variations on this model. There are search engines like BetterDoctor and ZocDoc that let people browse virtual listings of doctors; services like 10 EQS and Axiom Law that support ad hoc teams of consultants and lawyers; bands of writers and reporters who use social media to engage with each other, their readers, and traditional news institutions; and online project management systems like BIM in architecture.

The para-professional model

Next is the para-professional model. This is similar to the traditional model, in that service is provided by way of consultation, one human being with another. However, the provider here is not a specialist, but rather is a person of more rudimentary training in a discipline. Such a person could not reliably deliver the full professional service unaided. Instead, the para-professional is equipped with procedures or systems that have generally been produced by experts, and these greatly enhance the para-professional performance. This is not the same as the paralegal or paramedic of today, who work independently on clearly delineated but limited tasks. Instead, this model assumes that para-professionals are boosted by procedures and systems so they can take on work that historically was the province of human experts. The knowledge that is thus brought to bear is a combination of the general skills of the para-professional and the subject matter expertise that has usually been standardized or systematized by the professional specialists. It is a joint effort, enabled by the support tools that have been developed to help them. These support tools are created by seasoned professionals of considerable expertise and experience, who distil this expertise into procedures and systems that assist the para-professionals. These standards are prepared at a sufficient level of generality that enable them to be applied across a wide cross-section of clients and recipients. They will not of themselves offer direct customized solutions for individual recipients, but when combined with the skills of the para-professional they will achieve precisely this.

The format of the service will tend to be on a one-to-one basis. And the service itself will be delivered in person, whether in real time or in a dedicated document or advice. The content of the actual work is not generally intended to be recycled and used by others—the paralegal, supported by appropriate tools, delivers a customized service (although the standards and the systems that the para-professionals use are pitched at a far higher level of generality).

The technologies that support para-professionals are of two kinds. First, there are those that are similar to the systems used on the traditional model, to automate the traditional advisory process. Second, there will be more advanced systems that extend beyond the automation of current process to the provision to para-professionals of systems that to some extent will replicate the performance of human experts. And these systems will become more capable over time. In due course, the knowledge that supports paraprofessionals may well be machine-generated (see our discussion of the final model in this section). The actual delivery of the para-professional service is undertaken by human para-professionals who will tend to be a lower-cost resource than traditional experts. Additionally, the para-professional model requires the effort and investment of expert professionals to prepare the processes and systems. Often para-professional work will be undertaken on a fixed-fee basis and will not be paid according to the time spent on the work. Generally, as with the traditional model, the para-professional service will be reactive rather than proactive.

On the para-professional model, the ownership of the intellectual property generated will, unless negotiated otherwise, be shared between the experts who provide the procedures and systems and the para-professionals who deliver the service.

Nurses working in tandem with Watson provide an example of the para-professional model. As does the junior teacher who is supported by world-class online lectures and personalized learning systems, and so is able to deliver expert-level classes. The freelance blogger who uses standard templates, finds his sources on social media, and then distributes his work on online platforms, is working in this spirit too.

The knowledge engineering model

The fourth model is the knowledge engineering model. Here, practical expertise is represented in a system that is made available to users as an online service. This model can trace its origins to the 1980s, to expert systems work that was regarded then as mainstream AI.

The production process involves two tasks. The first is to identify the formal, well-documented knowledge of a given area of expertise. This is often held in textbooks. And a version of this has to be incorporated into a system. More importantly, the second task is somehow to mine the jewels from expert professionals' heads. In AI, this is known as 'knowledge elicitation'. The expertise captured from human experts is often unstructured and informal—based on experience. It is the practical know-how that underpins expert performance. Sometimes experts say that their knowledge cannot be articulated, that it is 'gut reaction' or 'intuition'. But through introspection and with the support of 'knowledge engineers' (specialists in knowledge elicitation—see section 6.8), they often find that they are able to model their expertise. This knowledge taken from experts' heads is combined with the formal knowledge and represented in systems that are made available to less expert or lay people.

The models of expertise thus represented will be at a sufficient level of generality to enable them to be applied to a wide range of problems within their problem areas. This knowledge is not therefore cast in a form that can of itself be said to be customized. Instead, this expertise is like a large decision tree, around which users navigate, ordinarily through some kind of question-and-answer interaction. In the end, this provides users with specific guidance that is a type of customization that we introduce in section 3.7 as 'mass customization'.

On the knowledge engineering model, practical expertise is delivered and distributed as a form of online self-help. Users are able to tap into practical expertise without consulting directly with human beings. The knowledge engineering model is a one-to-many approach to the delivery of professional service. In this respect, it is a major departure from the traditional and para-professional models. For these latter services, service is delivered each time afresh to individuals (or groups) on a once-and-for-all basis. When the knowledge is engineered, the same corpus is intended to service many users on many occasions. The content itself, as explained, is delivered not by human beings but through some form of online service.

To the extent that the knowledge and expertise is articulated and made available online, this content is a type of shared content. It is intended to be reusable, whereas the knowledge on the traditional and para-professional model tends to be disposable and is rarely recycled. The technologies that underpin the knowledge engineering model are innovative, as described in section 3.3, in that they facilitate access to practical expertise in a way that previously was not possible. It is not, in other words, that these systems directly automate traditional professional service. Instead, the professionals or para-professionals, who might otherwise be involved, are disintermediated—they are removed from the chain and no longer directly involved in the delivery of the service.

Three broad forms of labour are required to develop and deliver versions of the knowledge engineering model: subject matter experts, whose practical expertise is embodied in systems; knowledge engineers, who are specialists at articulating and representing practical expertise; and online service providers, those who put together the systems to which users have access. The individuals involved in the development of these systems will, again, sometimes charge for their services and on other occasions will not. Likewise, some online services will be available at no or very low cost, while others may incur very considerable charges.

Some online systems of this sort provide a reactive service, when, for example, users recognize they have a problem and so consult the service. However, these systems can also, at least in principle, deliver a more proactive service, by offering, for example, online alerts or early-warning facilities.

When the knowledge engineering model is in play, the intellectual property of the represented knowledge is generally owned by those who make the service available (the originators of the expertise, the human professionals, may or may not be owners or partial owners, and may or may not enjoy a cut of the action).

Illustrations of the knowledge engineering model are scattered across Chapter 2: from medical self-diagnostic systems, through DIY tax preparation software, to online contract drafting tools.

The communities of experience model

Fifth is the communities of experience model, in accordance with which evolving bodies of practical expertise are collaboratively sourced—built up through the contributions of past recipients of professional service or of non-experts who have managed to sort out problems for themselves. These are people who are therefore prepared to share the techniques, methods, insights, and knowledge that worked for them. These bodies of experience will be edited, supplemented, and kept current by a group of committed participants, in the spirit, for example, of systems like Wikipedia or Linux. On this model, in a variety of ways, the content of the systems in question is created by human beings, although not directly by those with deep expertise.

Alternatively, where problems or challenges arise, members of communities, often in large numbers, are called upon each to contribute, often modestly, to the resolution of some issue. This is an example of crowdsourcing (see sections 3.7 and 4.8).

The content or know-how that is assembled in this way will be less structured and generalized than on the knowledge engineering model, and not as focused as, for example, with the traditional model. It will tend to be less formal and less tailored than when experts are involved, and yet, because much of the experience will be described in detail, they will often have the feel of customized content.

Here again, traditional advisers are disintermediated. Although the format of this special form of practical expertise will often have its roots in one-to-one service, when it is made available for others to peruse and exploit, it transitions to being a form of many-to-many service. While human beings are at the heart of the community that generates the content, the delivery itself will invariably be on an online basis and not in person. This content itself is a shared resource, to which and from which members of the community will be warmly encouraged to contribute and draw, often on a 'commons' basis (see sections 5.5 and 7.5).

The enabling technologies here belong, broadly, to the world of social networking, empowering non-experts to collaborate and create shared bodies of experience. The result is systems that do not automate the traditional working practices of the professions. Rather, these systems are innovative, enabling entirely new ways of sharing practical expertise that were unimaginable not many years ago.

On the face of it, the labour costs involved with this model are low—generally, the knowledge is produced and distributed by volunteers. However, it may be that some expert moderation and editorial guidance will be appropriate, given the social and economic significance of the contents and the consequences of its use. For the most part, then, contributors to such systems will not expect remuneration. Nor will users expect to pay. While many of these services will be used in response to problems or situations that have arisen, there is clearly an opportunity through these communities of experience to provide guidance of a more proactive sort. Often, the existence of these facilities will become apparent from everyday interactions amongst members of given communities, which may lead to much earlier recognition of the need for help and the availability of assistance.

It is probable, when the practical expertise is collaboratively sourced in communities of experience, that this content will not be owned by the contributors but made available on a shared basis, perhaps using an intellectual property regime akin to Creative Commons.[22]

Once again, Chapter 2 provides illustrations: PatientsLikeMe in medicine; Edmodo in education; BeliefNet in divinity; GlobalVoices in journalism; OpenIDEO in consulting; AnswerXchange in tax; and WikiHouse in architecture.

The embedded knowledge model

The embedded knowledge model, our sixth model, involves the distillation of practical expertise into some form that can be built into machines, systems, processes, working practices, physical objects, or even into human beings and animals. The broad idea is that this knowledge becomes an integral part of the entity or host in which it is housed. This knowledge is not invoked expressly and separately, but is applied automatically. As an example, in the world of religion smartphones are being reprogrammed to have limited web-browsing capability, so observant Jews do not need to worry about visiting 'non-kosher' websites. Another illustration is intelligent buildings that have sensors and systems that test and regulate the temperature in accordance with environmental law, with no intervention of lawyers or compliance specialists. Today, the knowledge in these systems is often produced much in the same way as with the knowledge engineering model—it is originated by human beings, articulated and formulated, using traditional techniques of knowledge elicitation (although, in the future, the knowledge might be generated by machines—see our final model). The distribution model is quite different from that associated with the knowledge engineering model. The expertise is not accessed via some online system but, as said, is embedded more deeply in some environment (although admittedly sometimes the knowledge is stored in objects that are themselves connected to the Internet—see section 4.7 on the 'Internet of Things').

The models of knowledge themselves provide a powerful example of 'mass customization'. Although the knowledge is designed on a fairly generic basis for a wide range of environments, it can be fine-tuned for particular circumstances and, in operation, will apply its embedded expertise in addressing the unique circumstances of its hosts. Because the systems are designed to operate within many hosts, this again is an illustration of a one-to-many offering. This means that the same body of knowledge can be reused on many occasions. The practical expertise, in this event, is delivered neither in person nor on an obviously online basis. Often, indeed, the expertise and its method of delivery will effectively be concealed from those who benefit from its presence.

The knowledge embedded within the system will not be a shared resource, in the sense of being online and widely available. But it will be a resource shared amongst its hosts. The technologies that support embedded knowledge, once again, do not automate or optimize the traditional or para-professional model of professional services. Much of the technology here will be highly innovative, enabling the availability and application of knowledge in ways that were not possible or conceivable prior to their invention.

In terms of the labour required to support this model, in so far as the expertise is originated using knowledge engineering techniques, the content will be derived from subject matter experts, enabled by knowledge engineers, and delivered by technicians and engineers. Given the development costs of these systems are likely to be high, their developers will no doubt expect a return on their investment and so hosts and owners of hosts can expect to pay for embedded knowledge. One of the great advantages of embedding knowledge is that it will be possible to build in early-warning facilities, so that the knowledge can be deployed not just in addressing problems as they arise but in pre-empting problems in the first place or in containing their escalation.

It is likely, on the embedded model, that the ownership of the delivery mechanism, as well as the content generally, will remain in the hands of the distributors.

Further examples of the embedded model can be found in most professions. In medicine, for example, a pacemaker monitors a patient's heart and communicates remotely with a central system. In tax and audit, there are 'agents' that roam through financial systems, flagging exceptions and irregularities without human intervention.[23]

The machine-generated model

Seventh, and last, is the machine-generated model. On this approach, practical expertise is originated by machines and not by human beings. While the production model here is clear, it is less obvious how the content will be distributed. Consistent with our views in this book about the future of technology, increasingly capable machines will, in due course, be capable of generating bodies of practical expertise that can resolve the sort of problems that used to be the sole province of human experts in the professions. Whether this is achieved using Big Data, artificial intelligence, intelligent search, or techniques not yet invented, the machines' ways of working are likely to bear little resemblance to that of human beings.

It is too early to be dogmatic about the likely functionality of machine-generated service. It is conceivable that this machine-generated knowledge might come in the form of fairly generic content of wide potential application, or it may be specific, customized insight for particular and unique circumstances. Machine-generated knowledge might be applied in practice either by human beings or by machines. Again, services based on machine-generated knowledge may operate on a one-to-one or a one-to-many basis. While these systems could generate practical expertise for a human professional or para-professional to deploy, it is as likely that the service they support will be some kind of online service or will provide content for an embedded service. The content itself, depending on who owns the machines, could be made available at a fee or at no cost to recipients.

The underpinning technology here is fundamentally innovative. Although early work on artificial intelligence sought to model and replicate the brains, thinking, and reasoning of human beings, we argue that this category of future systems, increasingly capable as they will be, will not automate the working practices or reasoning patterns of human beings or human professionals. To suppose otherwise runs the risk of committing the AI fallacy (see section 1.9).

In relation to the roles for humans beings, even if they are not called upon at the point of delivery of the service on this model, human beings will be needed to design the machines in the first place. The skills required here will include systems engineering, data science, and subject matter expertise (see section 6.8). As with the embedded model, because the development costs of machines that generate practical expertise are likely to be considerable, some developers are likely to want some return.

As these machines become increasingly capable, it is reasonable to expect that they will operate not just reactively by responding to problems as they arise, but also proactively, extending their impact and knowledge to help users identify when best to seek help and to avoid difficulties arising in the first place.

For the longer term, there are some unanswered questions. Who will own the output of these systems when they generate re-usable content? Will this intellectual property be in the clutches, for example, of an oligarchy of wealthy individuals or corporations, who would therefore become the new gatekeepers, or will it be transferred into a commons? The answers to these questions will to some extent determine whether this content is a chargeable offering or available at no cost to users. We return to these questions in section 7.5.

In terms of the most likely practical applications, we can expect systems that can, more or less autonomously, make diagnoses in medicine, analyse financial information, design buildings, and predict the decisions of courts. Some people are uncomfortable with the idea of machines operating in this way. In the next chapter we address this worry, along with many other concerns that are often expressed by those who are uneasy about a future in which systems conduct some or much of the work of today's professionals.

PART III

Implications

6

Objections and Anxieties

We surface now from our theorizing in Part II to address more practical matters. Roughly speaking, the story so far is this—the professions are our current solution to a pervasive problem, namely, that none of us has sufficient specialist knowledge to allow us to cope with all the challenges that life throws at us. We have limited understanding, and so we turn to doctors, lawyers, teachers, architects, and other professionals because they have 'practical expertise' that we need to bring to bear in our daily lives. In a print-based industrial society, we have interposed the professions, as gatekeepers, between individuals and organizations and the knowledge and experience to which they need access. In the first two parts of the book we describe the changes taking place within the professions, and we develop various theories (largely technological and economic) that lead us to conclude that, in the future—in the fully fledged, technology-based Internet society—increasingly capable machines, autonomously or with non-specialist users, will take on many of the tasks that currently are the exclusive realm of the professions.

While we do not anticipate an overnight, big-bang revolution, equally we do not expect a leisurely evolutionary progression into the post-professional society. Instead, we predict what we call an 'incremental transformation' in the way in which we organize and share expertise in society, a displacement of the traditional professions in a staggered series of steps and bounds. Although the change will come in increments, its eventual impact will be radical and pervasive.

Our personal inclination, articulated at greater length in the Conclusion, is to be strongly sympathetic to this transformation. Our professions are creaking—they are increasingly unaffordable and inaccessible, and suffer from numerous other defects besides, as we describe in section 1.7. Change is long overdue.

In conversation with mainstream professionals, in response to our thinking, two words in juxtaposition are uttered again and again—'yes but . . .'. Sometimes, what then follows is the special pleading that we note in section 1.9—professionals argue that our thinking applies to all professions other than their own. More importantly, many professionals express genuine worries about the implications of the greater use of technology, both when it displaces human beings and when it enables less expert human beings to perform at the level of specialists.

This chapter is devoted to exploring and responding to what we take to be the most important objections and anxieties. Some of these apply to specific professions, and others extend more widely. The emphasis is on concerns or regrets about abandoning aspects of the traditional professions. Many features of our current professions are held dear, and regarded as too important to discard. We try to identify those elements that people particularly value, consider why they value them, and reflect on whether they are indispensable and so worth protecting (at a cost of slowing the pace, or narrowing the scale, of the transformation).

We address eight concerns. The first is about the loss of trustworthy institutions—without the professions, how can we protect ourselves from exploitation by unscrupulous quacks? Second is an anxiety about the loss of the moral character of the professions—if liberalization sweeps away the professions, are we comfortable with the market and market values playing a larger role? The third reflects a worry about losing the old way of doing things—do we want to protect traditional professional crafts and skills? The fourth uneasiness is over the loss of the personal touch—is it important to preserve face-to-face interaction? This relates, fifthly, to concerns over the question of empathy—how can machines ever empathize with those to whom they are offering help? Next, the sixth misgiving concerns the nature of the work that will remain—will meaningful and fulfilling work be possible in the future? Seventh is the objection that the new models we propose will cut our pipeline of experts—how do people learn their trade when machines are undertaking the routine work? The eighth concern is about future roles—what work will tomorrow's professionals do, and what are we training them to become? Finally, we suggest that each of the apprehensions is rooted in three mistakes.

We are conscious that this chapter does not address all possible objections and anxieties to the future we project. We have concentrated on those most commonly raised with us. But there are other, more general, concerns that certainly need to be confronted sooner rather than later. For example, there are questions of privacy, confidentiality, and security that require attention. There are also complexities relating to legal liability that arise, for example, from online professional guidance. Who is responsible when systems get it wrong—the software developers, the subject matter experts, or the Internet service providers? And what is the legal impact of the online disclaimers that commonly stress that any guidance offered is intended to be general and not to be relied on in particular circumstances? On the other hand, when might a professional be held to be liable, say, for *failing* to use or provide an online service? There is a vast literature on these subjects, but they are beyond the scope of our work.[1] Also beyond our remit is the dark side of the Internet. We recognize that there are many online resources that promote and enable a wide range of offences. We do not underestimate their impact or threat, but they stand beyond the reach of this book.[2]

6.1. Trust, reliability, quasi-trust

The first objection is that without the professions we will not have alternative, *trustworthy* institutions that are capable of addressing problems and delivering the services that are currently handled by the professions. This is the *trust objection*. Other people and systems may replace the professions, but there will be no guarantee that the guidance they provide is reliable and safe to act upon. (This objection is often framed by reference to the indispensability of 'professional ethics'. Sometimes the term 'ethics' is used in this connection to refer to conduct that is, from a moral point of view, good or bad. Alternatively, 'ethics' is equated with the regulations governing the conduct of professionals. Our concern in this section is with the former.)

Trust

Recall from section 1.8 that the fundamental problem we wish to solve is that none of us is expert in everything, if indeed in anything at all. We have limited understanding. When we face a problem for which we have no knowledge, we currently rely on the experience of others. Most of us do not know, for example, how to build our own furniture, repair our own plumbing, wire our own electrical systems, and so on, in a similar way, across all fields of human activity. Instead, we rely on the know-how of carpenters, plumbers, electricians, and the countless other groups of people who do have relevant experience. This is how we currently divide up knowledge in society, and it means that none of us needs to be omniscient. Yet when we need access to medical or legal knowledge, for example, it seems different—the knowledge required is usually of greater complexity, the consequences of its misapplication can be more severe, and it is often harder to know what kind of knowledge we require or what the precise impact of its use will be.

The professions have been our traditional resolution to this problem. We trust that the members of these institutions, whose behaviour is shaped both by formal constraints (for example, certification to determine who are members of given professions) and informal constraints (for instance, professional norms of conduct), will not take advantage of what they know and others do not.[3] Just as people find reassurance in the warranty that comes with a second-hand car (so they know the car is not a 'lemon') or the Corgi licence held by a gas engineer (so they have confidence that a repair is not dangerous), so too the reputation and status of the professions carries weight. In effect, membership in the professions is a sort of institutional kitemark, a signal that their members' behaviour is trustworthy and their insight and guidance is safe to act upon.

The *trust objection* follows from this. Without the professions, there will be no alternative people or systems that we can trust to resolve our most difficult problems. There is nothing to stop quacks and their acquaintances taking advantage of us. We were warned eighty years ago in the *Lancet* that '[q]uackery is undoubtedly "big business" and the quack knows how to sell his wares'.[4] To protect ourselves from this exploitation by new and unscrupulous institutions, we ought to preserve the professions and resist any change and transformation.

There are, however, reasons to be cautious with this objection. One is that at the vanguard we see people and systems building trusting relationships without any claim to being part of a profession. In education, students rely on online platforms like Khan Academy, where many of the key contributors are not qualified teachers. In journalism, reputable writers build large and trusting followings on social media (earning, for example, Twitter's 'blue tick' of verification) without joining established newspapers. In tax, people rely on tax preparation software like TurboTax, even though they never sit face-to-face with a chartered accountant to work through their particular tax challenge. This pattern, of new relationships of trust developing beyond the professions, repeats itself across different fields.

Of course, it may be that some of these new institutions betray the trust that is placed in them. That people choose to trust them is no guarantee of protection from the possibility that, in the end, their trust will turn out to be misplaced. But as a cursory search on Google will show, there are many cases in which the traditional professions also betray the trust put in them. The Solicitors Regulation Authority has around 400 full-time staff handling complaints and allegations of professional misconduct. The General Medical Council of England and Wales spends almost £30 million each year determining whether certain registered doctors are 'fit to practise'.[5] These overheads are not atypical. Simply belonging to the professions does not guarantee probity and honesty. Implicit in the *trust objection* is the notion that the professions have some kind of a monopoly over trustworthy behaviour—that they alone are capable of it, and others are not. But in practice there is no clear reason why a division of labour in society should necessarily imply a division of moral behaviour as well. The fault-lines of expertise and good conduct do not lie perfectly on top of one another. It is a mistake to think that only certain groups of people are capable of conducting themselves in a trustworthy way.

Reliability

A further, more substantive reason to challenge the *trust objection* is that trust may often be too demanding a requirement in a technology-based Internet society. Consider that, when we say we can only 'trust' the professions, there are two different senses of 'trust' that we might mean here—that the professions are *trustworthy* on the one hand, or that the professions are *reliable* on the other. The difference, as the philosopher Natalie Gold explains, is important.[6] When we say someone is reliable, we often mean only that he or she performs as expected. Trustworthiness, on the other hand, as Gold notes, can mean far more than this. It can be a 'moral virtue'. Saying someone is trustworthy goes beyond saying he or she is simply reliable. It expresses an additional moral judgement—that there is something good about that person and their motivations. To grasp this distinction in practice, bear in mind how much better it feels if friends call you trustworthy than if they simply call you reliable. The former is richer praise.

In everyday conversation, at different moments, we use the word 'trust' in both ways. Sometimes when we say we trust someone we only mean it in the *weak* sense, to say that the person is reliable. On other occasions we mean trust in the *strong* sense, to say not only that the person is reliable, but also that they have a good moral character or admirable motivation.

The professions position themselves as a group who can be trusted in the strong sense. Their members claim that they are not simply reliable but are also people of upstanding character and motivated by non-selfish interests. For many observers and providers, this strong sense of trust is an indispensable feature of professional work. It is important that professionals are of outstanding moral character, and put the interests of the recipients of their work ahead of their own. More formally, and under law, many professionals owe a fiduciary duty or an obligation of good faith to the recipients of their work. It is this strong sense of trust that has been extended and popularized in the phrase 'trusted adviser', used by many professional firms. It denotes professionals who not only enjoy deep personal relationships with those they guide but also display a wealth of experience of business issues.[7] In concept, the 'trusted adviser' has much in common with the 'man of affairs', the incorruptible, personal business counsellor of yesteryear.

The *trust objection* suggests that the professions, and our ability to trust in them in the strong sense, are the only way to resolve our fundamental challenge (that we all have problems for which we do not personally have the expertise to resolve). Yet we think this is mistaken. Our primary need is only for a *reliable* outcome. Of course, we do not want the people and systems that meet this need to be dishonest or criminal. But neither do we necessarily need them to be motivated by an altruistic regard for others. That would be too onerous a requirement. Our primary concern need not be with altruism or the achievement of the highest ethical ideals but to make sure that our problems are resolved reliably, efficiently, and effectively.

When we consider why the professions established their reputations for trustworthiness in the first place, they likely did so to meet this primary concern. Put another way, they established a reputation for trustworthiness not as an end in itself, but as a useful way to signal their reliability to others. To the extent that this is true, when we then see other people and systems effectively signalling their reliability *without* professing also to being motivated by some special moral character, we ought to question whether this additional demand is unnecessarily burdensome. This appears to be the case in the technology-based Internet society—enterprises like Khan Academy and LegalZoom operate reliably and to a high level of user satisfaction without feeling the need to address explicitly whether they are altruistic or ethically superior.

Quasi-trust

What will replace this strong form of trust and traditional concept of professional ethics? We can draw examples from the cases laid out in this and the previous chapter. Consider existing online services, from interactive advisory systems through to communities of experience. When users consult and rely on the guidance, insight, or service offered by these systems, it does not seem to us that they can 'trust' these systems as they would a village doctor, family lawyer, or local teacher. Rather, there is a diluted sense of trust at play here, which can be better equated with confidence than with fiduciary duty. As practical expertise becomes increasingly available through online service, as this becomes a popular channel through which service is delivered, we expect that users will find ways of seeking reassurance that what is on offer is reliable. This may come from the provider being a highly reputable brand; it could stem from clear endorsement for a service by, say, a government or leading charity; or it might derive from positive past experience of the site, or from recommendations by satisfied users. In any event, this confidence will not be rooted in the kind of interpersonal connection that arises when two human beings are in contact.

We refer to this future confidence in online services as 'quasi-trust' (this is unrelated to the legal use of this term). To have quasi-trust in an online service is to have confidence in the reliability of its output and in the honesty of its provider.

Without prejudice to the foregoing, as lawyers would say, there is no expectation, however, that this provider will put his users' interests ahead of his own. Confidence and honesty fall short of a duty of good faith. (When we speak here of 'honesty', our emphasis is, therefore, more on an absence of dishonesty rather than a demand for exceptional moral probity.)

Quasi-trust will have an important role in the context of decomposed tasks that are sourced by providers who are not traditional, mainstream professionals. For example, if a major project is broken down and tasks are passed, say, to third-party outsourcers or indeed to para-professionals, what level of trust will we have in these organizations and individuals? Will we expect them to owe us a duty of good faith, even though we may never meet or communicate with them and they may be conducting, frankly, fairly low-level, process-based, administrative work for us? Again, we predict we will want a relationship of quasi-trust to be in place—we will want to be assured of, and so confident in, their reliability (competence and experience) and in their honesty. We would want to be sure that they can deliver work to the standard we require, but we will not expect them to take a metaphorical bullet for us.

Many traditional professionals may feel a deep sense of unease at this line of thinking. In response, in the spirit of the new, bias-free, mindset that we advocate in sections 1.8 and 1.9, we encourage that a step back be taken. More fundamental questions can usefully be asked. What purpose does trust serve? To what problem is trust the solution? We maintain that trust plays a vital, but secondary, role when our way of making expertise available is through the gatekeepers we call the professions. When professionals no longer stand at the gate, we will no longer have use for their traditional conception of trust. Quasi-trust, backed by contract or even regulation, will be sufficient.

6.2. The moral limits of markets

In considering the *trust objection*, we argue that for the purpose of resolving our fundamental problem—of making practical expertise more widely available in society—the moral character and motivations of those involved are less important than whether the work they carry out can be relied upon. Of course, this is not to say that we are indifferent to the nature of the process. We do not want to see dishonesty or criminality. We may require regulation or the imposition of contract. But our primary need is for reliable, effective, and efficient outcomes. The character and motivations of those involved are important to the extent that they meet this primary need. And given that there is a vanguard today that do not profess to being motivated by, say, altruism, but yet manage reliably to achieve better outcomes, these motivations now seem to us less important than they once were.

Professional norms and market norms

The *moral limits objection* argues that this focus on outcomes (where by outcomes we mean access to different types of affordable practical expertise) is too narrow. To value a process only to the extent that it demonstrates that a person or system will reliably meet our needs for practical expertise is too limiting. There are additional reasons to value the moral character and motivations of the professions beyond their influence on these outcomes. Some possible reasons are explored in this section.

One way to think more formally about the moral character and motivations of the professions is in terms of the 'norms' that govern and shape their members' behaviour. *Professional* norms are the sets of beliefs, values, and customs that are shared by those who work in the professions. In contrast, *market* norms are those shared by those outside the professions, working in the market. As we note in section 1.5, writers and thinkers have distinguished these two sets of norms in various ways—such as a concern for client welfare rather than selfinterest alone, an ethic of personal service rather than an ethic of impersonal service, and a 'collectivity-orientation' instead of a 'self-orientation'. These contrasts are reflected in our everyday language—when we talk about being 'professional' in what one does, or behaving 'professionally', we are appealing to a pattern of behaviour that is distinctive and worthy of praise. The professions, in contrast to many other occupations, have this normative dimension.

Sandel's arguments

Michael Sandel, the political philosopher, in *What Money Can't Buy: The Moral Limits of Markets*, sets out a clear version of the *moral-limits objection.*[8] His case is framed in terms of this language of norms. His focus is broader than just *professional* norms—he looks at all *non-market* norms as opposed to *market* norms. But given that professional norms are a particular type of non-market norm, his arguments matter for our purpose as well.

Sandel's case, in short, is that market norms are increasingly replacing non-market norms—more and more things are bought and sold on the market and according to market values. Many people (including Sandel himself) feel uncomfortable about this. His project is to tease out why we might feel this sense of discomfort, and to encourage a public conversation on the appropriate limits of market norms. His concern is that the current boundary between what should and what should not be bought and sold on the market has crept up on us without adequate discussion and consent. His arguments bear directly on our discussion, since they help explain why we might be uncomfortable with a decline in professional norms (and a corresponding rise in market norms) following the liberalization of the professions, by which we mean when a widening range of tasks, by law, are no longer the exclusive preserve of professionals (see section 3.8).

Sandel's story begins with the claim that we live in an 'Era of Market Triumphalism,'[9] a society in which more and more can be bought and sold.[10] Sandel gives several examples. You can buy prison-cell upgrades in California for $82 a night and purchase the right to immigrate to the United States for $500,000. You can sell yourself to drug-safety trials for $7,500 (or more, depending on how invasive, or uncomfortable, the trial is), and can sell your time by waiting in a queue on Capitol Hill for a lobbyist who will pay you up to $20 an hour. Sandel suggests that there is something objectionable about this increasing reach of markets and this spread of market norms. We may be comfortable when market values determine how sports-cars or luxury yachts are produced and distributed. But when market values determine how severe a prison sentence is, or who holds US citizenship, or who has access to political decision-making, we feel less relaxed.

But what is it that makes us feel uncomfortable? What is wrong about the spread of market norms? Sandel provides two objections. The first he calls the Corruption Objection. Certain goods and services themselves have a moral character, an intrinsic virtue that distinguishes them from other things. When they are valued in a market and bought and sold, then that moral character can be 'degraded'. When markets are established for US citizenship and access to the political process, their distinctive value might be undermined. We might think that they are in some sense not as 'special'; that they have been corrupted.[11]

The second he calls the Inequality Objection. Market choices are often not truly free or voluntary choices. People may be poor, and so compelled to sell something they do not want to sell, or unable to buy something that they want to buy. Or people may be unable to bargain as effectively as others in the market, and so get a worse deal. And yet the case for markets is often based on an appeal to the principle that markets offer equal footing for the free exercise of choice. In short, if inequality is large enough, markets may lead to a lack of adequate or 'meaningful consent' in the choices people make. As Sandel puts it, 'in a society where everything is for sale, life is harder for those of modest means'.[12]

To tease out the distinction between these two objections, consider the idea of establishing a market for human organs. For example, the buying and selling of kidneys is currently illegal in the United States and United Kingdom. But demand for kidneys outstrips the supply of kidneys. More people want transplants than can be provided. To bring supply and demand into balance, some economists have called for the establishment of a market for kidneys. Since the supply is less than the demand, a higher price would encourage more donors to come forward and increase supply, and since some individuals would find the price beyond their means, it would also decrease demand. The imbalance between demand and supply would be resolved.

But many people might find this solution objectionable, and Sandel's two objections explain why.[13] On the one hand, in thinking of the human body as simply a store of 'spare parts', we might corrupt what many take to be its unique moral character. The human body ought to be inviolable, and not freely cut up for cash. This is the Corruption Objection. Second, there is the fear that those who do sell their kidneys may not have a meaningful choice in their decision-making. Those who are poorer may be more inclined to put their kidneys up for sale. In exercising choice over whether to sell their kidneys, people may not be on an equal footing. This is the Inequality Objection.

What is important about these two arguments is that they are not framed in terms of outcomes. The *moral limits objection* is not that the quantity or quality of what is produced is worse when non-market norms are replaced by market norms. Instead, it argues that we have other things to value, alongside any changes in these outcomes. The question for us is whether, in the particular context of the professions, these objections matter. Just as Sandel argues that market norms are increasingly displacing non-market norms (and this may be objectionable), so too in our particular case it appears that the liberalization of the professions could result in market norms displacing professional norms (a particular case of non-market norms). Is this a phenomenon we should resist?

Responding to the objections

While we find Sandel's arguments to be compelling in general, in relation to the professions in particular there are sound reasons to resist his objections. Consider the Inequality Objection. First, given the case built in this book, there are grounds for believing that the consequence of liberalization will be *greater*, not less, access to affordable expertise (due in particular to the nature of knowledge—see section 5.1). This runs entirely contrary to the spirit of the Inequality Objection.

There is a second difficulty with the Inequality Objection—in criticizing the market and its norms, it does not distinguish between who *produces* a good or service and who *pays* for a good or service. There is a difference between privately owned companies competing to *produce* a good or service, and private individuals *paying* for a good or service out of their own earnings. The Inequality Objection conflates production and payment. But its real quarrel is only with the latter—when people, due to inequality, do not have the same ability to exercise choice freely in a market. The question of how to *pay* for a good or service is quite separate, though, from the main concern of this book—liberalizing the professions, and using different people and systems in a market to *produce* and distribute practical expertise. The fundamental point is that we can use the market and its norms without falling foul of the Inequality Objection.

To see this more clearly, consider who provides and who pays for healthcare in the United Kingdom through the National Health Service (NHS). The guiding principle of the NHS is that it is free at the point of use—access should not depend upon an individual's ability to pay. The state always pays for the service. The market is not involved in *paying*—whether you personally can afford it has no bearing on whether you have access to healthcare. However, the market *is* involved in *producing* healthcare. Over the past few decades there has been a move away from healthcare in the NHS being provided solely by the public sector, to provision with, and by, competing private companies. Liberalization has taken place, and market systems and market values play a growing role in the NHS. But this marketization has not undermined access. In contrast to the fear of the Inequality Objection, inequality in society does not limit meaningful choice in the NHS, despite the presence of market norms. Contrary to the objection, we can liberalize certain services and still offer genuine choice even if there is wider inequality in society.

Let us turn now to the Corruption Objection. There are two basic reasons why we might also resist this—either because we do not think that the professions in fact have a special moral character, or because we do not think that this character is degraded in the market. But suppose instead that both are true—that the professions do have this character and that it is degraded in some way if their work is done according to market norms. In that case, there is a trade-off—we must strike a balance between the value we place on protecting this moral character and the value we place on the pursuit of greater access to affordable practice expertise. The Corruption Objection is clear on how to resolve this trade-off—the pursuit of the latter comes at the price of the former, but that price is too high and ought to be resisted. In contrast, we believe, for two reasons, that a diminution in the moral character of professional work is a price worth paying.

First, the professions, unlike many other occupations, are responsible for many of the most important functions and services in society. It was recognition of the importance of their work that drove the initial 'grand bargain' (see section 1.4). Secondly, levels of access and affordability to the practical expertise that the professions provide fall well short of acceptable (see section 1.7). The combination of these two reasons—the importance of what they provide and the current inadequacy of the provision—overwhelms the case to protect the status quo. This is not to deny the value of the moral character. Instead, it is to argue that, in the professions, there is another competing value, providing affordable access to practical expertise, that we ought to prioritize.

6.3. Lost craft

Across the professions, people make use of different skills and crafts—the teacher artfully herding a class of distracted students, an architect finessing drawings, a preacher inspiring a congregation, the lawyer drafting a fiendish warranty, a surgeon restoring life with strokes of a scalpel. These skills and crafts are valued. People take pride in mastering their craft. They feel a sense of self-worth and dignity when putting them into service, and they enjoy the status and prestige in demonstrating their talents to others. The *lost-craft objection* is rooted in a fear that by moving from bespoke production of practical expertise to more commoditized processes—by standardizing, systematizing, and externalizing—we will somehow lose these traditional crafts.

Lessons from coffee-making

The philosopher Julian Baggini explores a similar fear in a simple study of the decline of the craft of traditional coffee-making.[14] Traditionally, baristas were talented artisans in a richly human process—the soft, aromatic breath of the beans as a fresh bag was popped open, the crackle and crunch of the grinder, the soft pad of the tamper, the purr of the machine, the gentle double trickle of coffee into the cup. According to Baggini, creativity and flair were essential in making fine coffee. There was something of an art to it all.

However, the past few years have seen the emergence of automated capsule-based coffee production—the Nespresso and Lavazza systems, for example. As a result, coffee-making is reduced to the process of inserting a vacuum-sealed coffee pod into a machine. The human element is restricted to the flick of a switch or the pull of a lever. What was once a craft has become automated. This is unsurprising, Baggini argues, because coffee-making is well suited to automation. All variables involved, from the temperature and flow of the water to the coarseness of the grind of the beans, can, through careful experimentation and research, be optimally determined in advance and then fixed. The result is a cup of coffee of a consistently high quality, that can beat the best classic coffee in blind-taste tests.

These systems were first introduced as time-saving tools for homes and cafés. But now some of the leading restaurants in the world are employing them. The Nespresso machine, for example, is used by fifteen Michelin-starred restaurants in the United Kingdom, by over 100 in France, and in Italy, arguably the home of coffee, by more than twenty. In response, many diners have expressed dissatisfaction. The coffee may win in blind tests, but they feel that the restaurants are somehow cutting corners. In restaurants where trainees spend years washing vegetables and cleaning pots before being allowed to pick up a paring-knife, they dislike the idea that their coffee has been made by a waiter simply pressing a button on a machine.

Baggini's point is not simply about disgruntled customers. Many baristas themselves also lament the loss of their craft. Nor is his point only about the coffee-making process. It is a deeper and more general insight that extends to the computerization of other crafts as well. For any given process, many of us care both about the outcomes of that process (for example, a deeply satisfying, rich taste of coffee) *and*, in addition, we also care about the nature of the process itself (for example, whether the cup of coffee is the result of the press of a button, or of some more involved, bespoke activity). In other words, when considering a process, there are two phenomena that we may have reason to value—the outcome of the process, and the skill and craft involved, independently of the outcome. And whenever a craft is replaced by a form of systematization, we may feel that, leaving outcomes to one side, we are losing something that we value for good reason.

This has implications for the professions. The transformation we anticipate in their work is away from bespoke production and towards commoditization, in the form of standardization, systematization, and externalization. Traditional professional jobs will increasingly be decomposed into their constituent tasks, and in turn each of these tasks will be carried out in the most efficient way. It follows that some tasks will be computerized and people will—crudely—be replaced by machines. It also follows that, just as with the decline of traditional coffee-making, if a teacher's classroom instruction is replaced by online learning platforms, if an architect's hand-drawn sketches are replaced by CAD software, if a doctor's diagnosis is replaced by IBM's Watson, then in displacing the professional crafts involved, we may be losing something worth valuing. Indeed, we might still regret the loss of the human craft even if outcomes improve—if an online lesson is more effective, if a blueprint is more precise, if a contract is tighter, or if a medical diagnosis is more accurate.

Process or outcomes?

How seriously should we take this objection? One response is to argue that this tension between two sets of values—the intrinsic value of the process itself and the value of any improvement in outcomes it brings about—is illusory. The best way to improve outcomes is not to change, but to continue to rely on the traditional crafts and skills of the professions. Any change would not only lead to a loss of the crafts, but a worsening of outcomes as well. There is no trade-off between protecting the crafts and improving outcomes. This response is not persuasive. Indeed, it is mistaken. It is clear from the illustrations in Chapter 2, and the arguments of this book more generally, that in a technology-based Internet society we can increase access to affordable practical expertise by embracing production and distribution models that are quite different from the approach of the traditional professions. There is clearly, therefore, at least a trade-off between continuing with the inherited approach, namely the traditional professions, and improving outcomes by working differently. At the same time, it is not clear that working differently necessarily leads to a decline in all professional crafts. It is true that, over time, many tasks that are currently carried out by professions will be undertaken in different ways. It is also true that, in some circumstances, these tasks will be computerized, professionals will be disintermediated, and certain crafts will fade. But it is also possible that new tasks will emerge, and so new crafts will need to be mastered—for example, building expert systems, curating communities of experience, managing the support systems for para-professionals. These new crafts may be unfamiliar to today's professionals and have a stronger technological character than professional work of the past, but they are crafts to be mastered nonetheless.

Suppose, though, that the transformation that we anticipate does lead to a decline in human craft. Then we do face a trade-off—do we preserve the processes underpinning craft but forgo improvements in outcomes, or do we sacrifice those processes for improvements in outcomes? In the particular case of the professions, our own inclination is to favour the second option, for two reasons. These are the same as in the *moral-limits objection.* The professions are responsible for many of the most important functions and services in society. Yet levels of access and affordability to the practical expertise that the professions provide fall short of acceptable. The combination of these two reasons—the importance of what they provide, and the current inadequacy of the provision—overwhelms the case to protect the craft. We may value these human crafts, but while so many people in our world are deprived of access to affordable legal advice, a decent education, and basic medical care, this (often nostalgic) preference for craft is trumped by the need for an improvement in outcomes. We are in a state of necessity, and the luxury of protecting a craft for its own sake without regard for the outcomes it secures is an indulgence we cannot afford. The professions must remain, for now, a means to an end and not an end in themselves.[15]

Comparing human and machine performance

In time, we will become more troubled by this objection. We can imagine a day when machines will not just make coffee, but will write wonderful poetry, compose splendid symphonies, paint stunning landscapes, sing beautifully, and even dance with remarkable grace. We are likely to judge these contributions in two ways. On the one hand, we might take a view on their relative merits as machine-generated achievement, marvelling perhaps at the underpinning natural language processing or robotics. Our interest will be in comparing like with like—machine performance with machine performance. On the other hand, we might compare their output with the creative expressions of human beings. It may well be that we will concede that, in terms of outcomes, the machine is superior. Yet this will be to contrast apples with pears, so that this comparison may turn out to be wrong-headed.

We marvel today at world-class runners, even though our cars are faster. In the future we may race our robots (or perhaps they will race their human beings), but we will find little purpose in pitting human athletes against androids on the track. Indeed, we will still marvel at the physical prowess of the high-performance human beings who are not robotically enhanced. Likewise, in literature and the humanities, in music and in the performing arts, we will surely still have deep respect and admiration for human creation that is native, shorn of any digital support. We will regard and evaluate these creations as engagement, communication, and expression amongst human beings alone. We will value them precisely because they are the product of flesh and blood, toil and anguish, inspiration and exhilaration of fellow human beings. We will value not only the outcome but also the human imagination and effort that were expended in the creative process. How things are done will matter too.

And so, even if the machine outperforms the human being, we may, in the pursuit of certain activities, have less interest in non-human output. A similar argument may be run in the context of professionals. Even if a machine can match the finest doctor, lawyer, actuary, or consultant, we may nonetheless prefer to seek the services of the human being, because we like the idea of securing the services of first-rate practitioners; we even revel in the sheer brilliance of the minds of other human beings. We may relish and pursue the vicarious excitement gained from witnessing the best professionals at the top of their game. It might follow, therefore, that we deny ourselves high-performance machines in favour of engagement with human beings whose prowess we admire and with which we want to connect.

But, again, there are two problems with this line of thinking. First, if machines substantially outperform the best human experts, it would be bizarre, on the grounds of fellow feeling alone, to reject machines in favour of less capable human beings. Second, even if there is little to choose, in performance terms, between human and machines, engaging people to undertake tasks that systems can perform is an extravagance that we cannot support in the world of professional work. Again, professional work is too important and current levels of affordable access to it are too low. Deploying a leading human expert may well be regarded as the Rolls-Royce of professional work. The reality, however, as we say in section 1.7, is that only a few have the privilege of receiving such work, and the rest of us are walking.

6.4. Personal interaction

The traditional professions, to varying degrees, are based on one-to-one, often face-to-face, interaction between the professional and those with whom they are working. The *personal-interaction objection* represents the apprehension that the transformations that we have set out will bring this face-to-face engagement to a regrettable end. The personal touch involved in many of our current interactions with professionals is something to value and protect, and so, the objection goes, we ought to be wary of any changes that threaten to undermine it.

An immediate challenge to this objection is that it is tendentiously based on the presumption that new technologies necessarily reduce personal interaction. In many cases, though, the reverse appears to be true. For some professions, where personal interaction has historically been limited, like journalism, we see these new technologies making greater personal interaction an integral part of the role. Consider the high frequency of interaction (even if not face-to-face) between many journalists and their followers on Twitter. At the same time, in other professions, where personal interaction has historically been more important, we see new technologies helping professionals to make more effective use of the limited time they have for any face-to-face exchange. We find an example here in relation to doctors and the medical profession. Online platforms like WebMD and NHS Choices, where people can review their symptoms and receive guidance on likely problems and sensible courses of action, help slow the flow of avoidable personal interactions that otherwise consume doctors' time. Computerizing certain tasks, for example, by replacing simple routine check-ups with remote monitoring devices, again can help to free up doctors. Other platforms, like HealthTap, ZocDoc, and BetterDoctor, where people can ask doctors medical questions online or arrange appointments, help these physicians make better use of otherwise idle time. Teleprofessionalism means that personal interaction is no longer constrained by geography or a patient's mobility—the use of video links, from Skype to telepresence, provides a real-time, 'face-to-face' interaction of a sort.

Where new technologies do disintermediate traditional professionals, such that face-to-face time with traditional doctors and teachers and accountants does decline, this does not necessarily lead to the end of personal interaction. Often, it will be paraprofessionals who take the place of the traditional professionals: these are people with less formal training, but empowered by new technologies to carry out tasks once reserved for the professions (see section 5.7). Indeed, this sort of re-intermediation of providers could allow us to enhance any personal interaction that does take place. Consider, for example, a surgeon who may be a deft technical hand with a scalpel but lacks the sort of empathy that the best interactions with patients require. By decomposing the work that a surgeon does, we could introduce para-professionals who are expert in precisely the sort of comforting human interaction that a surgeon might lack and critics worry we might lose. We expand on the question of empathy in the next section.

Nevertheless, in some situations the objection will stand. Human interaction will be lost as increasingly capable systems replace people. But to determine whether or not this is a consequence worth defying, we should consider why we actually value personal interaction. We believe there are two broad reasons. The first is that many people think that personal interaction is valuable because it is the best possible way to deliver practical expertise—be it healthcare, legal counsel, spiritual guidance, and so on. This is very largely a consequentialist argument, that outcomes would be worse when there are fewer face-to-face interactions. The second is that personal interaction is valuable not because it improves outcomes, but because it is an experience to be valued in and of itself. Communicating with other people, in this case our doctors, teachers, lawyers, clergy and so on, is worth protecting whether or not outcomes improve.

If the resistance to change is of the first type (that a loss in personal interaction is expected to lead to a decline in outcomes), our immediate reaction is to point to the contrary argument and evidence set out in this book. In a technology-based Internet society there are new ways to produce and share practical expertise that greatly improve access and affordability, with no loss in the quality of the work. If outcomes really are the issue, critics should embrace the changes of the kind set out in Chapter 2. We suggest that the theoretical and empirical case is already compelling. If the resistance falls under the second heading (that a loss in personal interaction is deemed valuable whether or not it affects outcomes), our reaction is twofold. On the one hand, the primary purpose of the professions is not actually to provide personal interaction. The professions are our current solution to the challenge in society of supporting people who need access to practical expertise. Yet affordable access to this expertise remains inadequate. If the price of keeping the personal interaction is maintaining this status quo, then the personal touch is also an indulgence we cannot afford.

On the other hand, there is a more general point here. Many professionals seem to have lost sight of the reasons why we have personal interaction in the first place. It is a feature of the one-to-one nature of the traditional approach. As a consequence of its long-standing presence, it has gained an aura of indispensability. But we have to remember its origins—only as a feature, albeit an important one, of one way of sharing practical expertise in society. If, however, we can find better ways of sharing expertise that require less personal interaction, then we should not defend this interaction for its own sake.

6.5. Empathy

A special case of the *personal-interaction objection* is the *empathy objection*. It is so frequently advanced that it merits a detailed response of its own. As we say in the previous section, many professionals insist that human-to-human interaction is at the heart of their daily activity—the sick patient, the troubled client, the distraught student, and the beleaguered businessman surely deserve nothing less than a face that they can face. This is a call not just for a trusted adviser but, as important, for an empathetic expert, someone who can readily perceive the emotional state of others—and more, can feel and share their anguish and joy. But no machine, the argument runs, will ever be able to feel and share the anguish and joy of a human being, and so no machine can ever fully replace human professionals. Even if we concede that machines will never have feelings—although some experts will challenge this[16]—there is a danger that the empathy card is overplayed. Please note that we are not about to suggest that empathy, expressed from one human being to another, is not valuable or important. It is a phenomenon to be cherished. What we are instead suggesting is that the role and significance of empathy in the professions is often exaggerated.

In the first instance, it is a regrettable truth that a great number of professional experts are deeply lacking in empathy. Countless tales are relayed of the surgeon with zero bedside manner, the lawyer with no client-handling ability, the brutally insensitive teacher, and so on. Apparently, on average, doctors interrupt patients within eighteen seconds of beginning their story.[17] When we tell lawyers about this, they wonder why their medical friends wait so long. We jest, but no one can seriously maintain that all professionals are great listeners and truly empathetic. Accordingly, we must be cautious about asking more of our machines than we currently secure from people. And even if we accept that human empathy is often needed in the context of professional work, it does not follow that subject matter experts are the people best placed to be involved. When there is bad news to impart—a disease is incurable, a huge tax payment is due, a child is not making the grade, a pet is fading, a liability is unavoidable—it is not self-evident that we should lean towards the technical specialist to dispense the comforting words. Instead, we might turn, for example, to a para-professional, someone with sufficient insight into the area of expertise as well as the genuine capacity to empathize. By disengaging the application of expertise from the communication with the recipient (this itself is a type of decomposition—see section 5.6), this moves us, in part, away from the traditional model of production and distribution of practical expertise towards the 'paraprofessional' model (section 5.7). In both cases, though, human beings are still involved.

More generally, it should not be assumed that machines and systems on their own will never be capable, in some sense, of exhibiting empathy. There are two dimensions to empathy—cognitive and affective.[18] The cognitive element refers to the mental processes by which the emotional state of another is recognized and understood. As we explain in section 4.6, work is already well under way to enable machines to detect and express emotions. Early successes suggest that it is entirely conceivable that systems will eventually be better than people in gauging the mood of human beings. More, by using advanced speech synthesis (ensuring a kindly voice, perhaps), drawing on large databases of triggers and appropriate responses (a collection of *mots justes*), and by reference to users' psychological and emotional profiles, it is foreseeable that machines will be equipped to respond to their users in a manner that would *appear* to be *more* empathetic than a human being. This does not mean, of course, that machines can actually put themselves in the emotional shoes of their users and vicariously share their pain and pleasure. This would require some kind of realization of the affective component of empathizing, and would presuppose that machines could enjoy some form kind of consciousness. We are not ready to grant that this is possible, even if others are.

The cynic may instead pounce and assert that the affective element of empathy is the obligatory core of professional work. But this would be too ambitious a claim. Our research over the years suggests that some hard-nosed recipients of professional service do not in fact care about empathy; others do care, but only to the extent that their mood is recognized; while there are only some for whom full-blown empathy is pivotal, especially in the caring professions. Our cynic here does not, therefore, have a knock-down objection to the substitution of human experts by systems or machines. In any event, we can respond by questioning whether we can ever really be sure when human professionals who appear to be empathetic are in fact feeling and sharing our emotions. They could be exaggerating their apparent empathy, or acting, or performing unconsciously, in accordance with their training. In truth, we cannot know for certain whether anyone ever actually has feelings for us. It often seems most probable that they do, but, in the end, we cannot know the content of what philosophers call 'other minds'. Either way, it could well transpire that machines are superior at simulating empathy than insincere people. More, machines may even engender a preferable emotional state amongst their users than sincere human beings.

Another difficulty with the empathy argument is evidence that suggests people might sometimes actually prefer to confide in machines than human beings, especially when there are sensitive or embarrassing issues involved. In the mid-1990s this notion so unsettled Joseph Weizenbaum that he felt compelled to write what remains one of the finest books on the relationship between human beings and machines, *Computer Power and Human Reason.*[19] Then a professor of artificial intelligence at MIT, Weizenbaum had written a program, as something of a joke, that simulated an interaction with a human psychotherapist. When he invited his secretary to test the system, he was horrified when she asked him to leave the room so that she could, as it were, confess in private. Weizenbaum worried deeply about this reaction, and his book warns passionately of the perils of increasingly capable machines and their impact on human beings. Nonetheless, it is easy to see the appeal in the anonymity and privacy that machines can afford, and that this, on some occasions, might trump the desire to share a problem with a fellow person.

The final doubt we cast on the alleged indispensability of empathy in the delivery of professional work is the practical observation we have made elsewhere. Most individuals and businesses cannot afford the services of first-rate—and, we may add, empathetic—professionals. Affordable access to practical expertise is not as great as it ought to be. Policymakers and consumers may therefore face a stark choice between some kind of online provision of access to guidance and, frankly, no help at all. Doubters may complain that this online provision will be delivered either non-empathetically or with simulated empathy. We say that this provision—yielding, say, an accurate diagnosis, opinion, or computation—will invariably be a better outcome than proceeding without any assistance.

6.6. Good work

Many commentators and recipients of professional work might reasonably be attracted to change in the professions if this gives rise to greater access to affordable practical expertise. The *good-work objection* is the fear that by focusing too heavily on this and other beneficial consequences of change for those who use the professions, we may be neglecting the harmful impact of this change on the nature and quality of the work for professionals themselves. To put it differently, we run the risk of throwing the baby out with the bathwater if we focus on the benefits of technological change to consumers to the exclusion of the likely costs to producers.

When we talk about producers we have in mind those who are currently employed in the professions, as well as the new providers who might replace them. The weight of the *good-work objection* is increased by the fact that the current global complement of professionals likely extends to several hundreds of millions of individuals. In 2009 a report from the British Government estimated that almost half of the UK working population was in the professions (around 11 million people).[20] Although their definition of 'the professions' was notably broad (including most of the 'creative industry' and much of the public sector), even if their estimate is twice as large as it ought to be, it nonetheless remains a significant number of people (around 5.5 million in the United Kingdom alone). It would be strange to disregard the consequences of change on this workforce and fixate only on improvements in outcomes for others.

The fear that technological change could erode the quality of work in an economy is not new. It worried the earliest economists and social theorists. Karl Marx, for example, is known for his writings on the misery that technology could bring. Even Adam Smith, the political economist and philosopher who is held out as the standard-bearer for unfettered markets and innovation, recognized the downside, eighty years before Marx. Today, of course, the conditions in the professions are very different from those in the factories and mills that occupied the thoughts of these classical theorists. Workers in industrial Britain in the eighteenth and nineteenth centuries were systematically exploited and oppressed, and had little legal protection. To draw a direct comparison between their plight and the prospects for our professions would be to overstate the case. Yet we can still learn, albeit indirectly, from the insights of Smith and Marx.

In 1776, Adam Smith published *The Wealth of Nations*.[21] He was trying to understand what made some countries rich and others poor. His answer, in short, was that different countries had undergone different degrees of 'division of labour'. This explained why some countries enjoyed a 'universal opulence' and others did not. The rationale underlying this division of labour was that by dividing up any given piece of work into its constituent tasks, and then reallocating particular tasks as specialties for specific people, productivity would be much greater than when one person is spread thinly across a range of tasks. If the division of labour were broader (spread across more areas of work) and deeper (each area of work broken down more comprehensively into constituent tasks), then productivity would be higher too.

Smith illustrated his thesis with the now well-known case study of the pin-making trade.[22] One 'workman', he wrote, 'could scarce, perhaps, with his utmost industry, make one pin a day, and certainly could not make twenty'. But if the work was broken down into its tasks, and allocated to different workmen such that 'one man draws out the wire, another straights it, a third cuts it, a fourth points it, a fifth grinds it at the top for receiving the head', and so on for 'about eighteen distinct operations', then ten people (Smith claimed, on the basis of what he had witnessed) could produce upwards of 48,000 pins in a day, and so each individual effectively produced a tenth of that, namely, 4,800 pins: 'the division of labour, by reducing every man's business to some one simple operation, and by making this operation the sole employment of his life, necessarily increased very much the dexterity of the workman.'[23] The cumulative effect of this division of labour beyond the particular case of the pin trade, across all trades that make up an economy, explained why some countries were rich and others were poor. Technological change was at the core of Smith's thesis, driving a broader and deeper division of labour.

For the consumers of the goods resulting from Smith's division of labour, this increase in productivity was useful—it drove down their costs, and yet improved quality. But Smith recognized that for those who produced these goods this change could lead to widespread gloom and despair. The dull monotony of the work would cause people, in his words, to become 'as stupid and ignorant as it is possible for a human creature to become'. It appeared to Smith that a worker's 'dexterity at his own particular trade seems…to be acquired at the expense of his intellectual, social and martial virtues'.[24] Although Smith is generally regarded as a leading proponent of free markets, he recognized that what might be good for consumers was not necessarily good for producers.

Eighty years on, Karl Marx extended the argument. He saw the division of labour as oppressive, exploitative, and dehumanizing. When people are working, they do not feel they are themselves, or feel they are in control, a young Marx wrote. Only when they are not working do they feel 'at home'.[25] Confined to the conduct of isolated tasks in distinct and separate processes, and contributing only a small part of some larger output, people feel detached from the things being made, not properly part of the enterprise, estranged from other people who are involved, and ill at ease with themselves.[26]

Smith and Marx cast light on the prospects for today's professionals. It is clear from their writings that the *good-work objection* has some pedigree and history—even in the earliest moments of contemporary capitalism, people worried that what was good for consumers might not align with what was good for producers. The mechanics of the nineteenth-century division of labour bear a disconcerting resemblance to what we are seeing unfold for professionals of the twenty-first century. To understand this, reflect on how professional work is increasingly decomposed into its constituent tasks, and then reallocated through multi-sourcing to the most efficient provider (see Chapter 2 and section 3.5). In our current professions, some increases in productivity are being secured through techniques that are very similar to those that Smith described in the pin-making trade. The result is the possibility of far greater access to affordable practical expertise (just like the far greater production of pins). This is the transformation we anticipate—a shift away from professional work as an inescapably and irreducibly bespoke process towards various kinds of commoditization. Until recently the professions have been insulated from this industrialization. No longer.

The result of this division of labour is a loss of old jobs, but also the emergence of new ones. The problem here is that while these new jobs are clearly not exploitative and dehumanizing in the manner of nineteenthcentury factories, they do nonetheless sound duller and less substantial than the roles presently enjoyed in the professions. Most professionals now aspire to work that not only gives them a stable income but is also interesting and fulfilling. Max Weber, the classical social theorist, described in *The Protestant Ethic and the Spirit of Capitalism* how work could be a 'calling', a task 'given by God'.[27] Albeit with diluted religious overtones, the notion that professional work has some higher purpose survives in many professions today. People hope that work will fulfil a dual function—to provide a livelihood as well as purpose and meaning in our lives. The fear of the *good-work objection* is that this second element is under threat.

One initial weakness with this objection is that precisely the sorts of task at risk of computerization, at least in the short and medium term, are the least fulfilling aspects of what we do today. They tend to be routine tasks—by definition, repetitive and mundane relative to others. The corollary here is that the tasks that are *least* threatened by computerization, and so are likely to compose the majority of tomorrow's jobs, are the non-mundane tasks. Isaac Asimov put the point neatly, noting that 'any job that is so simple and repetitive that a robot can do it as well as, if not better than, a person is beneath the dignity of the human brain'.[28]

More generally, though, the *good-work objection* unfolds into two concerns. The first is that some tasks and activities that are currently found by professionals to be satisfying and stimulating will no longer be part of their portfolio in the future. Objectors regret that this good work will no longer be undertaken by professionals in years to come. This argument in part laments the passing of some individual tasks that hitherto have been handcrafted. But this argument is also put forward in opposition to the very idea of decomposition—as Marx said of division of labour in the factories, if we ask people to be involved in sub-components of some overall activity, they are likely to find it alienating to be somehow excluded from the overall process. It is not much fun being a cog in a wheel whose rotation you cannot watch.

The second concern, often not articulated up front, is that the new roles and tasks that are emerging for professionals of the future (see section 6.8) look a lot less interesting, fulfilling, and prestigious than those of today. This modernization is all very well, we hear professionals say, but it leaves us with a less interesting working life.

Both concerns run the risk of allowing the tail to wag the dog. We can sympathize with professionals whose work may be destined to be less stimulating than in the past, but it is hard to sustain the position that we should not modernize for this reason alone. It is not the *purpose* of ill-health, lack of education, religious belief, bad teeth, legal disputes, human beings' appetite for news, and the tax system to keep professionals in stimulating employ-ment. Our professions are solutions to these problems or chal-lenges. What, then, should we do if we can find better, quicker, cheaper, and less forbidding ways of meeting these problems and challenges that, at the same time, diminish the excitement or motivation for the human professionals who will be involved? Here again we find the tension between good work for producers and affordable access for consumers. Once more we need to strike a balance between the two. The value of maintaining the traditional way of working has to be weighed against the promise of far greater access to affordable practical expertise for others.

Our strong inclination is to favour consumers and to ask professionals to rethink how they work and how they might best contribute in a technology-based Internet society. We are asking no more than has been asked of countless other sectors and industries that have been deeply affected by new technology.

6.7. Becoming expert

In the course of our research, and in conversations with professionals, we were frequently questioned about the ways in which young professionals might learn their trade in the coming years. According to our broad hypothesis, much of the routine and repetitive work of today's aspiring professionals will be undertaken in new ways, for example, by para-professionals, offshoring, or online service. Are we not therefore depriving young professionals of the work upon which they currently cut their teeth? If we source much of the basic work in alternative ways, on what ground will young professionals take their early steps towards becoming expert?

Maintaining a pipeline of experts

This *becoming-expert objection* is clearly an important one. If we accept that expert professionals will be needed for the foreseeable future, it would be counter-productive to overhaul our professions today in a way that would inhibit or even eliminate our future pipeline of human experts. However, the challenge levelled here is, we suggest, a serious but not fatal one. In the first instance, it is clear that most paying recipients have little sympathy with this problem. The hard-nosed recipient of professional work regards the conundrum as a training problem. If there is realistic promise of professional work being delivered at a substantially higher level and substantially lower cost, then, just as we are overhauling the work of the professions, so similarly we should reinvent the way we train our professionals. We should apply as much creative energy in rethinking how our young professionals are immersed in their trade. It would be both premature and unimaginative to strangle at birth the whole enterprise of transforming the production and distribution of practical expertise in society on the grounds that traditional methods of training do not sit comfortably with modernization. Most recipients of professional work, if offered the option, would select lower-cost work and guidance from an institution that has to redesign its training over a higher-price service from an institution that is unwilling to revisit its methods of education. There is a related point here—that in this era of cost-consciousness, when recipients of professional work are asking for more professional work at less cost, they are not as willing as in previous years to pay for the time of budding professionals who are learning their trade by working with the recipients of their work. In short, recipients are increasingly unhappy about paying for the training of their external providers.

In the course of our consulting work we have spoken to aspiring young professionals in many disciplines and invited their views. Commonly they have responded that they are able to grasp many of the tasks they undertake in the name of training after a handful of experiences, and that many months of repetition were unnecessary: 'we get it after a couple of days; we don't need to do this for a couple of years.' In the context of professional organizations, this can be phrased in another way—we should not confuse training with exploitation. The commercial reality is that young professionals in these businesses undertake routine work because this is at the heart of the pyramidic model of profitability that requires the 'leveraging' (as is said) of junior professionals. On this model, these novices are paid much less than they are charged to clients; and it is too often disingenuous to claim that this practice is conducted in the name of training or education.

Focusing still on professional firms, if clients refuse to pay for the work of professionals in training, then two significant consequences are likely to follow. The first is that firms are likely to recruit far fewer graduates. Although firms that are committed to the health of their profession may feel an obligation to bring through a new generation, this may not incline them to take on as much 'talent' as their business model encouraged them to do in the past. Secondly, young professionals may well get paid substantially less in the future. If their work cannot command sufficient fee income, their market value and salary expectations may drop accordingly. There might be an exception here for the supremely talented, over whom recruitment wars could well continue to be waged for many years yet.

Returning to the training problem, we suggest that there are alternative ways of training professionals that do not demand years of effort on routine and repetitive tasks. In the confines of this book we can only sketch an outline of an alternative approach, one we believe should have three fundamental components. The first is reinstatement of apprenticeship. Feedback from the wide range of professionals with whom we engaged suggests that, once young aspirants have secured their formal qualifications, then there is no better way to learn any trade in question than by sitting at the feet of a seasoned practitioner. This may involve sharing a room, being positioned nearby in open-plan areas, observing surgery first-hand, sitting in on classes, or accompanying journalists out in the field. The young professional should have the opportunity to learn, absorb, and emulate the daily working habits and methods of an experienced master. In this way, and with appropriate supporting technologies, tyros can watch closely the ways in which successful professionals solve problems, offer reassurance, communicate with those they help, and help pre-empt future difficulties. This approach contrasts markedly with the dispatch of young professionals, in the name of training, to basements of large buildings to undertake routine and repetitive work which clients, remarkably, have only recently been disinclined to pay for at high hourly rates. Best practice is rarely absorbed in basements.

Secondly, although this may seem duplicative and inefficient, when large collections of tasks are being sourced beyond an organization, young professionals may be required, in parallel, to take on samples of these tasks themselves. Even though this work could be undertaken more quickly, to a higher quality, and at lower cost by some alternative provider (human or machine), some exposure to the manual conduct of this work can be a vital learning experience. Just as we insist that our schoolchildren learn to perform arithmetic by hand and in head, despite the existence of calculators, so too with young professionals. In part, this will help them to learn their trade. In part, this could perhaps be integrated within working practice as some form of quality-control mechanism. In any event, and in contrast with today, no longer will recipients of professional services be willing to pay for this parallel learning process.

The final piece of our alternative jigsaw is e-learning. Elsewhere in this book we speak of great advances in e-learning, developments that are radically improving the quality and greatly extending the reach of educational experience (see section 2.2). These tools and methods are as applicable in the professions as in any other environment. And, of course, this should extend beyond the first generation of e-learning systems, such as online lectures, e-tutorials, and virtual supervision. The step change in professional education will come from the second and succeeding generations of e-learning, and especially through immersion of students in online simulations of professional activity. Before being unleashed on fellow human beings, trainee professionals will, say, treat patients and guide clients in ever more sophisticated virtual learning environments.

The analysis above is limited in its scope because its focus is on the route to becoming expert on the traditional approach to professional service. In other words, its focus is largely on our first and second models for the production and distribution of practical expertise in society—the 'traditional' and 'networked experts' models (see section 5.7). It constitutes our response to concerns about the viability of the next generation of professionals;

however, we do counsel that the population of this category itself, although needed for many years yet, will diminish in number as the alternative models take hold.

What are we training young professionals to become?

This leads us to a more fundamental training issue. If the central arguments of this book are correct, or even just persuasive, they raise questions about the way in which we currently educate and train our aspiring and young professionals. If professional craftsmanship is fading and will be replaced over time by para-professionalism, knowledge engineering, communities of experience, embedded knowledge, and machine-generated expertise, then one vital question must be asked: what are we currently training large numbers of young professionals to become? Our concern is that our elaborate and sophisticated methods and institutions for the development of professionals are configured today to bring through a new generation of twentieth-century professionals, rather than a cohort of individuals and teams who are equipped to function in a technology-based Internet society in which online service will dominate over human service and ever more capable machines will carry out tasks that used to be the preserve of human professionals. We should worry that we are training professionals to undertake work that lay people, para-professionals, or indeed machines will take on, not many years from now. There is a related concern—not just that we are training professionals for tasks for which they will no longer be required, but that policymakers are not alive to this issue. By and large, these policymakers belong to an older generation, who are often sceptical about fundamental change and yet are responsible for education policy.

Two principal questions fall for consideration. The first is: '*How* are we training the next generation of professionals?' and the second is: '*What* are we teaching tomorrow's professionals?'

The answer to the first question is, to some extent, peppered across the pages of this book that are concerned with the future of education. The numerous techniques that we mention in section 2.2 for example, such as SPOCs (small private online courses) and personalized learning systems, should be brought to bear directly in the training of professionals. The revolution in education is not confined to high schools or undergraduate teaching. The changes that we note apply across all learning environments, and the growing wealth of online resources puts at the disposal of educators much more powerful techniques for educating aspiring professionals than were available in the past, exposing them to a wide range of problems and solutions, and immersing them in the culture and values of their chosen fields.

The second question cannot yet be answered in full. We cannot today ascertain definitively the full range of new jobs and tasks that might flow in the world we predict. We cannot second-guess the entrepreneurs who will no doubt identify new opportunities for innovative services that complement the new environment. Nonetheless, in light of our six new models for the production and distribution of practical expertise, we can identify a handful of central tasks for tomorrow's professionals, tasks which we should already be equipping the next generation to perform. To these we turn in the next section.

6.8. No future roles

It is a central thesis of this book that, over time, there will be a decline in demand for the traditional professions and the conventional professional worker. In Chapter 7 we consider whether, in the very long term, this will or ought to lead to the disappearance of professionals altogether. For the purposes of this section, if it is assumed that there will be fewer traditional professionals, what are the implications of this decline for the careers of the current generation of aspiring professionals? People who pose this question are often articulating the *no-future-roles objection*. The worry here is that there will be no work or roles for tomorrow's professionals.

Our inclination is not to tackle this issue by providing a new set of job descriptions for people in and around the traditional professions. As we explain in section 5.6, we are not convinced that the concept of a 'job' will of itself be coherent in decades to come. Certainly, in an era of radical and ongoing change, the notion of a 'single job for life' will be regarded as quaint, if not misconceived. It is tempting to conclude, therefore, that future generations may have several jobs in the course of their lives. However, with the increasing decomposition of professional work, the growing impact of increasingly capable machines, and the rapidity with which we expect the job market to change, we anticipate that people will tend to be trained on a task-based basis rather than for undertaking jobs. With this in mind, informed by our analysis of the six new models of the production and distribution of practical expertise (see section 5.7), we can begin to describe, if only tentatively, the types of role, task, and activity for which human beings will be required in a post-professional society. We express these in terms of twelve 'roles' for the future, as summarized in Box 6.1 and then sketched briefly in the pages that follow.

For many years yet we will still need *craftspeople*—talented and expert individuals who can undertake tasks that can be sourced in no other ways, not even by highly capable machines. These human beings, the best and the brightest, will continue to be able to bring value to their activities that cannot be replicated or simulated, for example, by para-professionals, or be collaboratively sourced by large numbers of well intentioned lay people. And, notwithstanding our responses in this chapter to various

BOX 6.1. ***Future roles***

Craftspeople
Assistants
Para-professionals
Empathizers
R&D workers
Knowledge engineers
Process analysts
Moderators
Designers
System providers
Data scientists
Systems engineers

objections—for example, the *lost-craft* and *good-work objections*—we expect that there will still also be a nostalgic demand for professional craftspeople, even when it is no longer necessary to retain them rather than machines.

These craftspeople, operating under the 'traditional' or 'networked experts' models (section 5.7) will sometimes require *assistants*. These will be individuals who are knowledgeable and skilled in their particular professions but are not experts. For some years to come, but not as many as for experts, human assistance will still be needed to support the bespoke work of the master craftspeople. There are many tasks that do indeed require experience and knowledge, and until these can be undertaken in other ways, there will still be demand for traditional professional assistants (for example, registrars in hospitals, associates in law firms, managers in tax and audit practices). But the half-life of these individuals is steadily decreasing.

Assistants will also be needed in a different context. Some tasks are relatively rare, and so it may not be viable to systematize them; nor might they be sufficiently recurrent for there to be collaboratively generated resources available online. For such tasks, even though they may not require deep expertise, there will still be a need for professionals. This class of task may itself diminish over time if these assistants make their work product available for reuse by others (perhaps through some online service).

Many tasks that today require handcrafting by seasoned specialists will in the future be undertaken by a whole new class of professional worker—the *para-professional*. With the support of standard processes and systems, these generalists will be able to perform at a level that today requires leading specialists. This is the 'para-professional' model (section 5.7). It is tempting to regard para-professionals as bright young people who are passing through a given profession. This is greatly to understate the skills and talents of many of today's para-professionals and to misinterpret the abilities and impact of the next generation.

A crucial, but often neglected, skill of professionals and para-professionals is to listen to and empathize with those they help—for example, to impart bad news sensitively and to share appropriately in the good fortunes of, say, patients and clients. In the future there will be a need for wise and empathetic, discipline-independent individuals—*empathizers*—who can provide the reassurance to recipients of their work that is often as important as the correct answer. Empathizing of itself will be a decomposed part of some professional services. In the long run, as our response to the *empathy objection* suggests (see section 6.5), we expect machines to be play a role here, but we acknowledge this may be some years in the future.

As discussed throughout the book, there will be ongoing change and developments in the way in which practical expertise is made available in society. Just as consumer electronics and pharmaceutical companies continually have to invent new offerings, so too will providers of practical expertise. Quite aside from keeping up to date with specialist areas of knowledge, professionals and other providers will need to develop new capabilities, techniques, and technologies to deliver practical expertise in the new ways that are envisaged. This will require a body of *R&D workers*.

Many of today's students who are training to be traditional professionals will, in due course, be engaged as *knowledge engineers*.

These new professionals will specialize in designing certain kinds of online service—we call this the 'knowledge engineering' model (section 5.7). They will need to be skilled in the analysis of areas of expertise, both in textbooks and elicited from the heads of specialists, and techniques for representing this knowledge in online systems in a way that can be used directly by lay people or para-professionals. In contrast with professional work of today, which tends to focus on the particular circumstances of the individual recipient, knowledge engineering is a task that requires the development of models of knowledge that are more generic, that can be deployed and applied to solve problems, offer advice, and provide guidance in a wide range of circumstances.

We write frequently in this book about decomposing professional work into constituent tasks and sourcing these tasks in new ways. However, the job of analysing professional work, subdividing it into meaningful and manageable chunks, and identifying the most appropriate way of handling each, itself requires professional insight and experience. This will be the work of *process analysts*. These specialists will also be involved in compiling the procedures and processes that will support para-professionals. The content here will be a mix of substantive knowledge and 'know-how'—the distillation of expertise and experience in a form (including flowcharts, checklists, and decision trees) that para-professionals can apply.

Although many wikis and collaboration sites of today are subject to minimal editing, one central task in relation to resources and communities that build up bodies of practical expertise (the 'communities of experience' model—section 5.7) will be more structured and systematic moderation by domain specialists. Given that users will be relying on these systems where in the past they were dependent on professionals, it is important that there is oversight and quality control of much of the content. This task will require individuals—*moderators*—with practical experience as well as sound technical grasp.

The online provision of practical expertise will of itself become a central task and important specialism in the future. It is early days in our thinking about the design and content of online services, and people in the future will no doubt look back on current efforts (for example, to provide medical or business advice) as naive in presentation, structure, and substance. Over time, however, online services will become intuitive, simple to use, designed for users with varying degrees of knowledge, and will focus both on solving problems painlessly as well as avoiding them in the first place. Experts in online provision—we think of them as *designers*—will be those who conceive and design the systems themselves.

Those who actually bring about the delivery of online professional services may not be subject matter experts, knowledge engineers, or designers. They will be the *system providers*. Sometimes these will be individuals with charitable intent. Often they will be businesspeople who will find ways, whether by subscription or more oblique methods, of generating revenue from their work.

Yet another new group of professionals will be the *data scientists*—the data experts who will have mastery of the tools and techniques that are required to capture and analyse large bodies of information with the intent of identifying correlations, trends, and causal insights. Like many of the new roles we identify, this will require an interdisciplinary background: experience and understanding not just of various technologies but also of the professional disciplines involved.

Finally we will need *systems engineers*, specialists who will devote their energies to developing the machines that, as we predict, will themselves directly generate practical expertise. In today's terms, these might be AI systems, Big Data systems, or intelligent search systems. These engineers are the human beings (for now) who build the systems, operating under the 'embedded knowledge' or 'machine-generated' models. Looking forward, as we stress periodically in this book, it is likely that many of the techniques that will underpin machine-generated practical expertise have not yet been conceived.

Of course, it must be asked whether these new roles and tasks that we have identified will themselves survive in the very long term. The next generation of machines, it can be argued, will threaten tomorrow's professionals as surely as they are displacing the work of today's. This may be so. In the next chapter we consider this, and confront the implications of technology displacing most of the work of human beings.

6.9. Three underlying mistakes

Each of the eight objections in this chapter, in different ways, challenges the wisdom of allowing our professions to fade from society. Some of the arguments are more compelling than others. But none of them unsettles our own belief, as explained in the next chapter and the Conclusion, that the transformation of the professions we describe is the preferred direction of travel.

Looking across the objections laid out in this chapter, we perceive three broad classes of underlying mistake.

The first is a tendency, as time passes, increasingly to confuse the means with the end. In various ways in the course of this book, we seek to disentangle the professions themselves from the problems and complications that they have evolved to address. The fundamental role of the professions is to provide access to knowledge and experience that non-specialists lack. They help overcome human beings' limited understanding. The professions are the means; and the end is making practical expertise available to those who need it. And yet consider, for example, the *personal-interaction objection*. In a print-based industrial society, it did seem to be the case that the most effective way of sharing practical expertise was through face-to-face interaction. However, over time, this personal interaction *itself* is something that many have come to value in the professions, quite apart from the usefulness of these interactions in offering access to practical expertise. In a technology-based Internet society, where there are more effective ways to produce and distribute practical expertise that make less use of personal interaction, the error is to let this veneration for tradition (quite apart from its effect on output) inhibit important change. There are myriad other opportunities in life for human beings to enjoy face-to-face interaction with one another—there is no obvious reason why our apparent need for interpersonal contact should have to be satisfied by our accountants and doctors.

The second mistake is a failure to strike the best balance between competing values. The promise of the transformation set out in this book is greater access to affordable practical expertise. We have good reason to value this outcome very highly. Yet this transformation will require us to abandon many aspects of our traditional professions—for example, losing the dimension of craft from professional work. Of course, we should question whether we ought to value the phenomena that we will jettison (for example, personal interaction), and we should ask whether these phenomena are actually under threat (as in the case of empathy, and the possibility of more, not less, empathy). But for the moment let us concede these doubts—that they ought to be valued and that the transformation does indeed threaten them. If so, we face a trade-off between competing values—the value of greater access to affordable expertise, and the value of maintaining some desirable characteristics of the status quo. To determine the appropriate pace and scale of the transformation, we must strike the best balance between these values. In our view, this balance falls in favour of transformation. And we have explained why at various points in this chapter. The professions are responsible for many of the most important functions and services in society. Yet levels of access and affordability to the practical expertise that the professions provide are woefully low. We stress once again that the combination of these two reasons—the importance of what they provide, and the current inadequacy of the provision—must invariably trump the case to protect the current set-up.

The third mistake is to expect more of our machines than we expect of ourselves. If we hear, for example, that an online diagnostic system is capable of making a correct diagnosis 80 per cent of the time, our instinct seems to be to declare that the 20 per cent of incorrect diagnoses is intolerable, rather than to compare that error level with human beings' current capabilities.

We see this spirit in many of the objections of this chapter. Those who object often demand that the people and systems that replace the professions should attain a level of moral virtuosity, for example, or a degree of empathy that palpably outstrips those who currently work in the professions. As Voltaire would caution, in reforming or transforming the professions, we should not let the best be the enemy of the good.[29] Frequently, the question that should be asked of a proposed new system or service is not how it compares to traditional service, but whether it would be better than nothing at all.

7

After the Professions

When we started working on this book in 2010, our principal focus was on what the future might hold for the professions. In the course of our research and writing, however, we realized that to confine our attention to our current professions would, for two related reasons, be too limiting. In the first instance, when we gave thought to why we have the professions at all, and when we explored theories of the professions in trying to make sense of the work of professionals, we unearthed a more basic and important question that had to be answered: *How do we share practical expertise in society?* It became clear to us that 'through the professions' was only one answer to this question.

In a print-based industrial society the professions have emerged as the standard solution to one shortcoming of human beings, namely, that we have 'limited understanding'. When people need help in certain kinds of situation in life, those that call for specific types of specialist knowledge, then we naturally turn to professionals. But we cannot assume that this current answer is the only or best answer for all time. We should be alive to the possibility, as we move from a print-based industrial society into a technology-based Internet society, that there are alternatives. And we should also want to investigate these.

Which leads to our second reason for concluding that our current professions are too limited an object of study. When we undertook our research at the vanguard, we found that technology and the Internet are not just improving old ways of working; they are also enabling us to bring about fundamental change. They are providing new ways to make practical expertise far more widely available. And so, what is coming over the horizon are not just better ways of handling the work within the current remit of the professions, but systems that are greatly extending our capacity to sort out problems that arise from insufficient access to practical expertise.

In short, therefore, we concluded in the early stages of our work that to concentrate only on the future of the professions would be to let the tail wag the dog. It would be to focus in a self-limiting way on past and current institutions, and to ignore new possibilities and capabilities for sharing practical expertise.

In all, then, we decided that our book should look both at the prospects for our current professions and also at what will replace them.

In relation to our current professions, we argue that the professions will undergo two parallel sets of changes. The first will be dominated by automation. Traditional ways of working will be streamlined and optimized through the application of technology. The second will be dominated by innovation. Increasingly capable systems will transform the work of professionals, giving birth to new ways of sharing practical expertise. In the long run this second future will prevail, and our professions will be dismantled incrementally. As we note in Chapters 5 and 6, there will still be a need in certain circumstances for traditional professionals, but even this need itself is likely to diminish over time. Moreover, as we describe in section 6.8, some new roles for professionals will also arise, although today's professionals may query whether these roles deserve the descriptor 'professional', and, as also suggested, many of these new roles might themselves in due course be superseded by new systems and different people. For the professions, there is no way of softening the blow. Decades from now, today's professions will play a much less prominent role in society.

What about after the professions? What people and systems will replace them in the very long term? Answering these questions raises a further series of difficult issues that we consider in this chapter. Before we go further, we must issue a health warning. Readers who are interested only in the next decade or so should jump immediately to the Conclusion. Likewise, those who strongly prefer practicalities to theory may also prefer to skip this chapter in its entirety.

We now invite our remaining readers (both of you) to join us on a journey that will involve no visits to doctors in hospitals, lawyers in courtrooms, or teachers in classrooms. Instead, we confront three supertanker topics. The first of these is the nature and limitations of the intelligence of our future machines. Will these machines think and enjoy consciousness like human beings? And for which, if any, of the tasks that the professions have traditionally undertaken will human beings still be needed in years to come? These questions carry us into our second topic, which is 'technological unemployment', the notion that, crudely, machines will put humans out of work. Finally, we respond to the challenge that what we say about liberating practical expertise and making it available online is all very well, but it is frankly neither practical nor feasible.

7.1. Increasingly capable, non-thinking machines

A central theme of this book is that our machines and systems are becoming increasingly capable and, over time, that they will outperform human professionals at many tasks. In the race for the uptake and use of technology, there is, we say again, no finishing-line. Instead, we are seeing an apparently relentless flow of advances, driven by market forces and human ingenuity, with each invention fuelled by the exponential increase in the power and capacity of the underpinning technologies.

Understandably, this leads many observers to ask just how 'intelligent' our systems will become, and whether machines of the future might even be conscious in much the same way as human beings are. These are fascinating questions that have been pondered by AI specialists since the middle of the twentieth century,[1] and they raise fundamental conundrums that have exercised philosophers for thousands of years. Readers should not be surprised to learn that we do not crack these questions in what remains of this book. But we do reflect in this chapter on various aspects of them, and in so doing return to a common confusion—the AI fallacy—that obscures our view of the future of the professions.

In section 4.6 we point to a variety of existing techniques and technologies that are already achieving remarkable levels of performance in a wide range of tasks. Perhaps the most dramatic is IBM's Watson, the computer system that was catapulted to fame by its appearance in 2011 on *Jeopardy!*, a TV quiz show, on which, in a live broadcast, it beat the two best-ever human contestants (see section 4.6). Much has been said and written about this feat, but nothing perhaps as witty and insightful as a headline in the *Wall Street Journal* to an opinion piece by the philosopher John Searle. It read: 'Watson Doesn't Know It Won on "Jeopardy!"'[2] We could add that Watson, after its great triumph, had no apparent inclination to laugh or cry, to go for a celebratory drink, to share the moment with a close friend, to chat about what it felt like, or to commiserate with its vanquished opponents. Nor indeed did Watson dream about victory before or after the event. IBM could, of course, build in some appropriately timed whoops, laughs, and expressions of sentiment and recall, but this output would not imbue the system with consciousness and feelings. Watson is an astounding system, but even its biggest fans do not claim that it enjoys thoughts and emotions akin to those experienced by human beings.

Does it matter that Watson cannot think? Trying to answer this question unearths a whole set of motivations for being involved with AI. When we started our work in the AI field in the early 1980s, we identified various groups of researchers. There were psychologists and other AI scientists who hoped that the study of artificial intelligence would lead to better understanding of the human brain.[3] There were computer scientists who felt that the best way to create AI systems was to base these on models of thought and brain function that neuroscientists and psychologists had evolved.[4] There were philosophers who brought to the table centuries of past thinking about the mind.[5] Finally, there were expert systems workers who—generally—were trying to represent the decision-making processes of human specialists as bodies of 'if–then' rules and embody these in complex decision trees that non-expert users could navigate.[6] We belonged to this final school, and were involved with the development of expert systems in law, audit, tax, and, more remotely, in medicine. However, we took a keen interest in the work of the other three groups, largely because their writing was fascinating, and not because it helped us to develop live systems. We co-engineered the world's first commercially available expert system in law,[7] but we never based this on a sophisticated model of brain function, nor did we regard our system as a contribution to psychology or philosophy. Still less did we believe that the system was conscious or had thoughts. But we did claim that it was useful and that it could outperform any human lawyer.

Like Watson, although vastly less ambitious, ours was a non-thinking, high-performing system. In the language of some AI scientists and philosophers of the 1980s, these systems would be labelled, perhaps a little pejoratively, as 'weak AI' rather than 'strong AI'.[8] Broadly speaking, 'weak AI' is a term applied to systems that appear, behaviourally, to engage in intelligent human-like thought but in fact enjoy no form of consciousness; whereas systems that exhibit 'strong AI' are those that, it is maintained, do have thoughts and cognitive states. On this latter view, the brain is often equated with the digital computer.

Today, fascination with 'strong AI' is perhaps more intense than ever, even though really big questions remain unanswered and unanswerable. How can we know if machines are conscious in the way that human beings are? How, for that matter, do we know that consciousness feels the same for all of us as human beings? Or indeed, how can we be confident that anyone (other than 'I') is conscious (the problem, again, of 'other minds')? Undeterred by these philosophical challenges, books and projects abound on building brains and creating minds.[9]

In the 1980s, in our speeches, we used to joke about the claim of one of the fathers of AI, Marvin Minsky, who reportedly said that 'the next generation of computers will be so intelligent, we will be lucky if they keep us around as household pets'.[10] Today, it is no longer laugh-worthy or science-fictional[11] to contemplate a future in which our computers are vastly more intelligent than us—this prospect is discussed at length in *Superintelligence* by Nick Bostrom, who runs the Future of Humanity Institute at the Oxford Martin School at the University of Oxford.[12]

Ironically, this growth in confidence in the possibility of 'strong AI', at least in part, has been fuelled by the success of Watson itself. The irony here is that Watson in fact belongs in the category of 'weak AI', and it is precisely because it cannot meaningfully be said to think that the system is not deemed very interesting by some AI scientists, psychologists, and philosophers. For pragmatists (like us) rather than purists, whether Watson is an example of 'weak' or 'strong' AI is of little moment. Pragmatists are interested in high-performing systems, whether or not they can think. Watson did not need to be able to think to win.

Nor does a computer need to be able to think or be conscious to pass the celebrated 'Turing Test'. This test requires, crudely, that a machine can fool its users into thinking that they are actually interacting with a human being.[13] A 'weak AI' system can, in principle, pass the 'Turing Test', because success in this test is confirmation of 'intelligence' in a behavioural sense only. The responses of the machine may, on the face of it, be indistinguishable from those generated by a sentient being, but this does not allow us to infer that the computer is conscious or thinking.

It turns out, then, that 'weak AI' is not so weak after all. Its putative weakness lies in AI's inability to replicate the human brain together with consciousness. But some weak systems are becoming increasingly capable and can outperform human beings, even though they do not 'think' or operate in the same way as we think we do.

We learned this many years ago in the context of speech recognition, another branch of AI (or at least it was regarded as such in the early days). As we explain in section 4.9, the challenge of developing systems that could recognize human speech was eventually met through a combination of brute-force processing and statistics. An advanced speech recognition system that can distinguish between 'abominable' and 'a bomb in a bull' does so not by understanding the broader context of these utterances in the way that human beings do, but by statistical analysis of a large database of documents that confirm, for instance, other words that are likely to be collocated or associated with 'bull'.

The upshot of all of this is that we can create remarkable, high-performing machines that do not think and are not modelled on human intelligence. This point was anticipated, with characteristic flair, by Nobel Laureate Richard Feynman, as far back as 1985:

Some people look at the activity of the brain in action and see that in many respects it surpasses the computer of today, and in many other respects the

> computer surpasses ourselves. This inspires people to design machines that can do more. What often happens is that an engineer makes up how the brain works in his opinion, and then designs a machine that behaves that way. This new machine may in fact work very well. But, I must warn you that that does not tell us anything about how the brain actually works, nor is it necessary to ever really know that in order to make a computer very capable. It is not necessary to understand the way birds flap their wings and how the feathers are designed in order to make a flying machine. It is not necessary to understand the lever system in the legs of a cheetah, that is an animal that runs fast, in order to make an automobile with wheels that goes very fast. It is therefore not necessary to imitate the behavior of Nature in detail in order to engineer a device which can in many respects surpass Nature's abilities.[14]

Garry Kasparov, the grandmaster chess-player, makes the same point, although he was more personally affected than Feynman. In 1997, when he was world champion, Kasparov was roundly beaten by Deep Blue, a chess-playing system that was developed by IBM. In a sense, they were playing a different game. In Kasparov's words:

> The AI crowd, too, was pleased with the result and the attention, but dismayed by the fact that Deep Blue was hardly what their predecessors had imagined decades earlier when they dreamed of creating a machine to defeat the world chess champion. Instead of a computer that thought and played chess like a human, with human creativity and intuition, they got one that played like a machine, systematically evaluating 200 million possible moves on the chess board per second and winning with brute number-crunching force.[15]

The lesson should be clear—we can develop high-performing, non-thinking machines that can outperform the best human experts, even though they go about their business in quite unhuman ways. The lesson for professionals should also be clear. We will not need to understand and then replicate the way human experts work, nor will we need to develop thinking machines to replace much of the work currently undertaken by human professionals. We showed this in practice in 1988, when we developed our expert system in law.[16] And Chapter 2 of this book provides many further illustrations. Yet we find that scholars, practitioners, and journalists frequently fail to recognize this, and so commit the AI fallacy.[17]

7.2. The need for human beings

Many years from now, then, high-performing, non-thinking machines will outperform the best human experts, and do so in quite unhuman ways. Given this, for which tasks that the professions currently perform, if any, will human beings be needed in the very long term? In a world packed with increasingly capable systems, what role will human professionals play? Will there be anything left for people to do when we are fully settled in a technology-based Internet society in which non-thinking, high-performing systems are commonplace?

There are two questions tucked away here. The first is whether future systems will be able to undertake all tasks to a standard higher than the best human experts. The second is whether there are any tasks that we feel should always be undertaken by human beings, even if they could be carried out to a higher standard by autonomous machines.

The capabilities of professionals and machines

One way of tackling the first question above is to consider four capabilities that professionals seem to bring to bear in their daily work. The first is cognitive capability—the ability to think, understand, analyse, reason, solve problems, and reflect. The second is affective capability—the capacity to have feelings and emotions, both introspective and in response to others. The third is manual capability—physical and psychomotor aptitude. And the fourth is moral capability—the faculty to distinguish right from wrong (good from bad, just from unjust, and so on), to reason about what right or wrong means, and, more than this, to take responsibility for the choices, decisions, guidance, and actions that they take (whose rightness or wrongness we may have weighed). Psychologists and philosophers would no doubt be inclined to suggest a different classification or to break down each category into further subdivisions and to quibble about the overlaps. Our approach is admittedly simplified, but we think it captures the most important features of the debate.

Scepticism about the role of machines is perhaps most compelling when expressed in human terms; when, for example, it is asserted that, 'of course, machines will never actually think or have feelings or have a craftsman's sense of touch, or decide what is the right thing to do'. Framed in this way, this sort of claim appears convincing. It is indeed hard to imagine a machine thinking with the clarity of a judge, empathizing in the manner of a psychoanalyst, extracting a molar with the dexterity of a dental surgeon, or taking a view on the ethics of a tax-avoidance scheme. However, there is a problem here, and it is one that our choice of language itself perpetuates. In choosing terms such as 'think', 'feel', 'touch', or 'moralize', because these words refer to human capabilities we run the risk of excluding machines before we have the chance to debate the issue fully. If we believe or assert that thinking, feeling, touching, and moralizing are uniquely human experiences then it must be true that no non-humans can engage. However, this is only true, as philosophers would say, by definition. It is a circular argument. If we define tasks as uniquely human tasks, then it is no great surprise that machines cannot undertake them. This line of thinking takes us nowhere.

Lurking here once again, in fact, is our old friend the AI fallacy. The particular danger here is that of being excessively anthropocentric. In contemplating the potential of future machines to outperform human beings, what really matters is not *how* the systems operate but whether, in terms of the outcome, the end product is superior. In other words, whether machines will replace human professionals is not about the capacity of systems to perform tasks as people do. It is about whether systems can outperform human beings—full stop. And so, when IBM's Watson beat the best-ever human champions on a TV quiz show, what mattered was not whether Watson had cognitive states in common with its flesh-and-blood opponents, but whether its score was higher.

To be more precise, then, the fundamental question to be asked and answered is whether machines and systems can undertake tasks that for human beings require cognitive, affective, manual, and moral capabilities, even if they discharge these tasks by quite different means.

As for cognitive tasks, a plausible opening position runs as follows—that machines will be able to take on fairly straightforward reasoning and problem-solving, but more involved challenges will still need human experts. Most professionals are comfortable with this broad statement: 'routine' work can be handed over to machines, but human experts will still be needed for the tricky stuff that calls for creativity, innovation, and strategic insight. However, there are two problems with this. The first is that professionals, unconsciously or otherwise, are prone to exaggerate the number of occasions on which deep expertise is genuinely required. Often the creative, innovative, and strategic input, if needed at all, is only a modest component—in terms of time consumed, if not of the value provided—of the work that has to be done. Professionals who doubt this should spend just one day analysing the full range of activities and tasks with which they are involved, and then ask which of those could actually have been passed to someone less expert. It is disconcerting for how little of the day experts are actually needed. The second problem is that some tasks that today require human expertise (for example, in law, tax, and medicine) are undoubtedly complex and yet can still be routinized. In particular, when the knowledge required for a given professional service is an intimate familiarity with a large, complex web of interrelated rules—as often it is—then systems are often better placed than human experts to meet the need.[18]

This suggests that what are left for human experts are tasks that demand the exercise of some kind of cognitive capability that are not routinizable, that is, capable of being reduced to some routine form (section 3.5), whether by some protocol, algorithm, decision tree, checklist, or the like. Is this, then, the reserved area for human professionals? Is it here that people can bring unique value? It is in answering this question that we will likely differentiate machines from many professionals. Our hypothesis is that systems will increasingly become more capable at performing even those tasks that are regarded today as not routinizable. We stress again that the non-thinking, high-performing machine does not operate in the same way as a human being works. Increasingly capable machines (whether using AI, Big Data techniques, or techniques not yet invented) will arrive at conclusions and offer guidance that in human beings we would regard as creative or innovative. Systems will make connections, identify patterns and correlations, and find solutions in ways that will appear ingenious to us, and often well beyond our own cognitive capabilities.

And so, when the full range of professional work is considered, we suggest, first, that the genuinely innovative work represents a small class of task, and second, as machines become more capable it will be a class that will steadily shrink as the exclusive preserve of human experts.

What about the affective capability of human professionals? Is this similarly threatened? Again, a credible opener might be that some situations are so significant, sensitive, or emotional that only a fellow human being is qualified or appropriately placed to offer the help needed. Once more, this is comforting for the professional at the heart of whose current work is high-touch, interpersonal interaction with the recipients of their service. But it assumes that there is no substitute for human engagement.

We address this issue more fully in section 6.5, when we discuss systems that might empathize. We recognize there that empathy is a phenomenon to cherish, but we argue that: many human experts are lacking in empathy, and so we should not ask more of our systems than we get from our experts; systems may eventually become more accurate than people in gauging the mood of, and responding to, human beings; machines may become superior at simulating empathy than insincere people, and even engender preferable emotional states amongst their users than sincere human beings; when embarrassing or sensitive issues are involved, some people may prefer the anonymity and privacy of interacting with a system; and, in any event, in an era when traditional service is often unaffordable, low- or no-cost online guidance without human empathy is a more attractive option than no assistance whatsoever. There are problems, therefore, with the argument that the only way practical expertise can be dispensed is through human beings with feelings and emotions.

The flow of our argument should be apparent. Machines (non-thinking, high-performing systems—see section 7.1) can already discharge many tasks that, not many years ago, we thought were beyond their capabilities; and, as machines become increasingly capable, the number of tasks they can take on will grow, and their execution will become better and quicker. This is the general direction of travel. And so too, in relation to the third capability, manual skills, advances in robotics will steadily reduce the range of physical activities that we regard as uniquely requiring human dexterity.

Turning finally to the moral faculty, this is more difficult, because what is involved here is not simply the ability to distinguish right from wrong, and the ability to justify this distinction by reference to some higher or broader principle, but also the capacity to take responsibility for moral judgements that are made. It is entirely possible that future systems (modelled, for example, on traditional, rule-based expert systems) could articulate and balance moral arguments, identify consistencies and illogicalities, point out assumptions and presuppositions of given lines of debate, and identify conclusions that can validly be drawn from some set of premises. Such systems would be a special kind of moral philosopher, capable of clear and structured reasoning about ethical issues.

However, it is harder to grapple with the notion that the buck actually stops at a robot, that a machine might be regarded as in some sense responsible for important moral decisions, such as whether to switch off a lifesupport system, put down a household pet, concede custody in a divorce action, or positively discriminate in favour of a minority applicant to a university. The point is not just that we like to have someone to hold responsible (blame or praise) when things go awry or splendidly. It is that we tend to want another human being to have reflected, and perhaps agonized, over decisions and advice that matter to us. Somehow, in some circumstances, it feels inappropriate, or wrong, to abnegate responsibility and pass it along to a machine, no matter how high-performing.[19]

Moral constraints

This leads us, then, to the second question that arises when we consider how professional work might be distributed between human beings and machines—are there tasks that only human beings should be permitted to undertake?

In turn, this takes us into the normative realm of life, as distinct from the factual realm: what we 'ought' to do rather than what 'is' the case. And, in the context of professional work, when right and wrong are being balanced and recommendations on significant issues are made as a result, our sense may well be that there must be human intervention and involvement.

This dilemma is already present in modern warfare. For professional soldiers (the profession of arms), there is ongoing debate about the extent to which computerized and robotic weapons should be autonomous. Our strong intuition may well be, for instance, that no missile should be fired at people unless another human being has made an informed choice to select this course of action and will take responsibility for the consequences. Here, we may think, we have found the limits of our machines. But in the heat of the battle, and under enemy fire, it may be that there is insufficient time to pass the decision to a human being, which is why, by analogy, soldiers in the field are given some autonomy to make life-taking decisions without reference up their chain of command. This delegation is not open-ended—it is constrained by training and protocol. Similarly, autonomous weapons can have built-in checks that embody and reflect some principled, ethical views that have been settled in advance and embodied in the systems. But it is also possible that sophisticated systems with massive data-analysis capability can make more informed real-time choices than a human being to whom a decision might be referred.

We use a military example to highlight that none of this is at all straightforward. Although it is superficially plausible to say that all moral decisions must be made by human beings and not by machines, this may lead to worse outcomes when measured against common moral requirements (for example, to minimize harm to noncombatants), or it might not be practical. Moreover, even if we wish to proscribe certain uses of machines, what is the best way to prevent their development and use?

We have no easy answers here. Nor do we believe there are general principles that we can lay down for application across the professions. Often in this discussion we find professionals advocating that we invoke the three 'laws of robotics', as expounded by the science-fiction author Isaac Asimov. Genius though he was and elegant though they are, they do not provide sufficient detail. For example, his first law, that '[a] robot may not injure a human being, or, through inaction, allow a human being to come to harm',[20] does not really help us to pinpoint what constitutes 'injury' and 'harm', or to resolve difficult moral trade-offs where both action and inaction have consequences. (An example of such a trade-off—should a doctor remove an organ from a patient who is slowly dying, hastening his death, to save another critically ill patient in need of an organ, who will die if there is no transplant?)[21] In the context of the professions, we need to proceed beyond generalities to particular debate over the realistic limits, on moral grounds, of practical expertise being made available to lay people without the possibility of intervention or supervision by experts.

We see an analogy here with the debate in the United Kingdom, in the early 1980s, over the moral implications of emerging techniques such as in-vitro fertilization and test-tube babies. A national inquiry and consultation was launched, leading to an influential report by the philosopher Mary (later Baroness) Warnock.[22] The subject generated great attention amongst the media, the public, the academic world, and scientific community. The inquiry substantially raised the level of general understanding of the central issues, and the main problems were clarified, if not resolved. We suggest, before our systems become much more capable, that there is a need for a similar scale of debate on the moral constraints we should impose on the use of models for the distribution of practical expertise that do not involve professionals or para-professionals.

Needless to say, we regard the activity of demarcating those tasks that only human beings should be permitted to undertake as being too important to be left solely to professionals. Their conflict of interest here is incontestable. Professionals must be heavily involved in the debate, because their insight and experience is vital. But, to repeat a phrase from the Introduction, to leave it to professionals to decide to what extent their work can and should be displaced by technology would be to invite the rabbits to guard the lettuce.

Overall, though, it is hard to resist the conclusion that, at least to some extent, machines can already undertake tasks that in human beings require cognitive, affective, manual, and moral capabilities. As machines become increasingly capable, in response to the question 'What will be left for human professionals to do?', it is also hard to resist the conclusion that the answer must be, 'less and less'.

However, as we discuss in section 6.3, for certain kinds of activity we may prefer to engage human beings *even if* they perform less impressively than machines. We may do so because we value the effort and imagination expended by fellow human beings over the outcome. Precisely because it was crafted by a human being, we may prefer to buy a sculpture by a person, even though a robot could do a better and cheaper job. In the professions, though, our general view is that this (often nostalgic) preference for the old ways of working will be too high a price to pay, especially if the quality of service is demonstrably lower than that provided by a machine.

7.3. Technological unemployment?

In 1930, speculating about 'the economic possibilities for our grandchildren', John Maynard Keynes introduced the concept of 'technological unemployment'.[23] The basic idea is simple—that new technologies might put people out of work. The question to which we now turn is whether there will be technological unemployment in the professions in the very long term. The short answer is, 'there will'. We can find no economic law that will somehow secure employment for professionals in the face of increasingly capable machines.[24] However, it is *uncertain* how extensive the job-loss will be. In this and the following section we explain why there is uncertainty here, and we provide a new framework for thinking in a systematic way about technological unemployment in the professions.

By way of preface, we need to be careful with the term 'employment'. Our interest is not simply in whether technology might put professionals out of work, but also how *well paid* any work is. A future where there is full employment but with wages below subsistence level would be a worry. Our focus, then, is on the future of what we call 'reasonably-paid' employment.

Hotdogs

To tackle the question of technological unemployment, we find it helpful to work with a simplified story, one that we base on a discussion of 'hotdogs' by Paul Krugman, a Nobel Laureate in economics.[25] Imagine a company that hires people to make hotdogs, and that this involves just three tasks—preparing the sausage, baking the bun, and putting the hotdog together. Each person hired to make hotdogs specializes in just one of these tasks—a job at this company, therefore, can only be one of sausage-preparer, or bun-baker, or hotdog-compiler. At first, assume that there are no machines. This means that the company must hire people to do the three different jobs. Next, consider that a machine is invented to automate the preparation of sausages, and does so more productively and at a far lower cost than a person. For a profit-seeking company, it would make commercial sense to install machines and use them to prepare sausages, rather than use people. The result would be that sausage-preparers would lose their jobs.

Two possibilities (of many) might follow. First, the former sausage-preparers might try to get their old jobs back by taking a cut in their wages and trying to compete with the machines. Alternatively, they might try to get different jobs, by learning new skills and competing with bun-bakers and hotdog-compilers for their jobs. In that event, the wages of the bun-bakers and hotdog-compilers would be driven down instead. In both these cases, 'technological unemployment' is possible. The former sausage-preparers might stay unemployed if they cannot cut their wages to compete with the machines or cannot learn new skills to secure a different job. Equally, the bun-bakers and hotdog-compilers might lose their jobs if their wages are dramatically undercut by the former sausage-preparers. However, unemployment is not the only possible outcome. There is an alternative where everyone ends up in work—former sausage-preparers learn new skills and join the bun-bakers and hotdog-compilers, but everyone has lower wages.

A further consequence is likely, although it is often ignored by those who write on technological unemployment. If using the machines reduces the cost of preparing each sausage, it will also lower the overall cost of producing each hotdog. If, in turn, the company chooses to lower its hotdog prices to reflect this, and the demand for hotdogs is sensitive to this reduction, then the demand for hotdogs will rise, and the company will respond by producing *more* hotdogs to meet this upsurge in appetite. This effect is critical. It means that, after the machine is introduced, there is more work to be done—to make more hotdogs, the company will need more sausages to be prepared, more buns to be baked, and more hotdogs to be put together. And so, while there may no longer be jobs for sausage-preparers (those have been lost to machines), there will be more jobs for bun-bakers and hotdog-compilers, because the machines have given rise to an increase in the overall output of hotdogs. If enough of these new jobs are created to balance the loss of jobs in preparing sausages, and if the old sausage-preparers can learn the skills required for these new jobs, we do not need to worry about the future of work at this company. The newly created jobs can absorb those whose jobs were destroyed.

We concede that the hotdog story is a simplification of this corner of the food industry.[26] But it does demonstrate that technology can be both destructive, by displacing people from their jobs, and creative, in that it can give rise to new jobs.

The next step in this story is the important one. So far we have assumed that each job is made up of only one task. In practice, the job of a person in the hypothetical hotdog business would more likely involve some *combination* of each of the three types of task. Indeed, when we think about the nature of any job, it will more probably be made up of many different tasks rather than one particular task. This echoes a theme of this book, that jobs or pieces of work in the professions can be decomposed into a diverse set of constituent tasks (see, for example, section 5.6). Many discussions of technological unemployment ignore this point, assuming that jobs are made up of single tasks. In reality, systems do not tend to completely displace people from their jobs. Rather, they take on particular *tasks* for which humans are no longer required. Jobs do not vanish in an instant. They wither more gradually. An entire job disappears only if the full bundle of tasks that make it up are lost and not replenished with new ones.

If we now assume that all hotdog jobs involve some combination of all three different tasks, it still makes sense for the company to install the machine to improve the efficiency of one task (sausage-preparation). However, the impact on the workers is different. They will all stop preparing sausages (this is now done by machines) and instead will turn their efforts to baking buns and compiling hotdogs (since there is no machine to do these tasks). In effect, the new machine changes the bundle of tasks that make up their jobs.

This brings a new worry, however. Once the remaining tasks are bundled up into redefined jobs, will there also be fewer jobs available overall? On the one hand, people are performing fewer types of task than before (two, rather than three). But on the other hand, it also costs less to prepare each sausage and so less to produce each hotdog. If the company again reflects this in lower prices, and the demand for hotdogs rises in response, then the company will again have to produce more hotdogs to meet this greater hunger. This would mean, critically, an increase in the number of all three tasks. As a result, although machines and not people are preparing sausages, there are now more tasks to be carried out in baking buns and compiling hotdogs, and a corresponding need for more human involvement.

Of course, if new machines are then developed that can bake buns and even compile hotdogs, then the picture shifts again. But the central question remains—whether the creative effect of the new technology outweighs its destructive effect on jobs that are made up of tasks.

Three central questions

The hotdog story helps us to consider more systematically the general concept of technological unemployment, because it leads us to recognize that we must always distinguish three different questions.

First: *What is the new quantity of tasks that have to be carried out?* ('Question 1'). In the hotdog story, introducing a more efficient machine means that the overall cost of producing each hotdog falls. If the company lowers its prices to reflect this, and demand is sensitive to a fall in price, then more hotdogs will have to be produced. When more efficient machines are installed throughout an economy rather than in a single company, the output of the economy increases—with these new machines, individuals and companies can achieve more with the same resources. In this bigger economy, a larger number of tasks have to be carried out.

Second: *What is the nature of these tasks?* ('Question 2'). In the hotdog story there are only three types of task. But in a wider economy, there are many more types of task. When new machines are introduced, and the output of the economy increases, a new set of tasks will have to be carried out in addition to the existing set of tasks. All of these tasks, the existing ones and the new ones, will each be of a certain type.

Third: *Who has the advantage in carrying out these tasks?* ('Question 3'). There are certain tasks that are more efficiently carried out by people, and other tasks that are more efficiently carried out by machines. The boundary of advantage, as between people and machines, is constantly changing.[27]

Those who are pessimistic about the future of employment fear that new technologies are able to perform too many tasks that were once done by people alone. Their worry is that this means there is or will be less left for people to do. The pessimists are often called 'Neo-Luddites'.[28] However, their account only looks at Question 3—whether people or machines have the advantage at some type of task. They ignore Questions 1 and 2. They do not consider whether a new technology would increase output and the quantity of tasks to be undertaken (Question 1), and whether the new tasks created are of a type in which people retain an advantage (Question 2). The pessimists are *right* to recognize that people will not do some of the types of task that they took on in the past. But they are *wrong* to ignore the fact that new tasks might have to be undertaken, and these new tasks might be of a type in which people still have the advantage; and, if this is the case, then there is new work for people to do.

Now consider the optimists. They argue that the pessimists' account relies on the 'lump of labour fallacy'—a term given by economists to the belief that there is some fixed quantity of reasonably-paid work, a given 'lump' of labour that is to be divided up and parcelled out either to people or to machines. The optimists rightly note that this is wrong, and make an argument based on Question 1. If a new technology is more productive, it will increase output, there will be more work that has to be done, and so more tasks for people to do. There is no fixed 'lump' of labour, and instead the quantity of reasonably-paid work will grow over time. However, the optimists only look at Question 1—whether the improvement in productivity will increase output, and create more tasks. They ignore Questions 2 and 3. They do not seem to recognize that unless the new tasks are of a type (Question 2) in relation to which people continue to retain an advantage over machines (Question 3), then there is little cause for celebration. The new machines will simply do these new tasks as well. The optimists are *right* to recognize that there will be more to be done. But they are *wrong* to ignore the fact that machines might be better placed than people to undertake these fresh tasks.

Whether as optimist or pessimist, however, we suggest that it is only when we consider all three questions together that can we say anything reliable about the consequences of increasingly capable machines on reasonably-paid employment. Taken together, our three questions lead us to the crux of the debate on technological unemployment. If new technologies create a large quantity of new additional tasks, and these are of a type in which people rather than machines have the advantage, then concerns about technological unemployment are misplaced. On the other hand, if new technologies do not create many additional tasks, or if the tasks that they do create are of a type in which machines, rather than people, have the advantage, then technological employment, to a greater or lesser extent, will follow.

7.4. The impact of technology on professional work

What does this mean for the professions in the very long term? No doubt, the future for which most professionals hope is that there will continue to be reasonably-paid employment for most doctors, lawyers, teachers, and so forth. Is this realistic?

Technological unemployment in the professions

Bearing in mind our three questions, if we expect that the range of types of task in which professionals will retain an advantage over machines to shrink, then to avoid technological unemployment we have to have sufficient growth in the types of task in which human beings still retain an advantage. In fact, we would need the volume of these tasks to grow at an accelerating rate—as professionals are left with an advantage in fewer types of task, each time an additional type of task is ceded to a machine, it is likely not only to affect more and more professionals, but will also put increasing strain on the shrinking set of tasks left for people to do. To put this another way, an increasing number of professionals must be absorbed in a decreasing range of types of task (namely, those in which professionals still have the advantage). In short, it will become ever more difficult, as time passes and machines become increasingly capable, to ensure that there is enough reasonably-paid employment for professionals.

To put some flesh on these bones, consider each of our three questions in more detail. First of all, then, what is the likely volume of professional tasks involved in the future? Broadly speaking, we expect the number of tasks to increase. In part, this is because our economies are likely to grow and develop, incomes will rise, and so there will be growing demand for practical expertise. It is also because there is, we believe, a great 'latent demand' for professional work—there is a vast reservoir of need for practical expertise that is currently unmet (see section 3.7). The professions, as they are currently constituted, do not and cannot provide affordable access to all who want to benefit from their services. The new production and distribution models that we identify are likely to make practical expertise far more affordable. These new models, that is, are likely to realize and fulfil the latent demand. For both these reasons, there will be substantial new workloads to be handled and a far larger number of professional tasks to be carried out.

Secondly, what type of professional tasks will there be? In so far as the traditional tasks of professionals are concerned, the gut feeling of many practitioners is that much of their daily endeavour is more complex and challenging than the work done by non-professionals elsewhere in the economy.

This book seeks to show that this intuition is often misplaced, and to 'demystify' the professions and the work that they do. Our main argument here is that once professional work is decomposed or disaggregated into more basic tasks, then a great many of these are similar to those in other, non-professional occupations. But it is also true that some of the tasks do indeed call upon more complex cognitive, manual, and affective capacities. Moreover, 'moral' tasks may well feature more prominently in professional work than they do in other sectors. Again, though, it is important not to exaggerate this dimension of professional activity. It would be disingenuous to suggest that all professional work involves matters of the gravest ethical significance. We believe that this analysis extends equally to the new jobs that we anticipate in section 6.8. We predict that these new jobs will also, in their turn, be susceptible to decomposition, and that, as with traditional professional tasks, some of these will be straightforward and others will be complex.

Thirdly, who will have the advantage in carrying out the old and new professional tasks—people or machines? As in the wider economy, the advantage in performing most types of task, as the analysis of technology in this book suggests, will continue to shift towards machines and away from people. This is because many apparently non-routine tasks can in fact be routinized, and many genuinely non-routinizable tasks can still be undertaken by machines. However, an important exception is that people are likely to retain the advantage in making or supporting important moral decisions because, as we argue in section 7.2, these are unlikely to be passed over to a machine.

Taken together, what do these three responses mean for the future of reasonably-paid employment in the professions? Our expectation is that, over time—by which we mean decades, rather than overnight—there will be technological unemployment in the professions. In other words, there will not be sufficient growth in the types of professional task in which people, not machines, have the advantage to keep most professionals in full employment. Because we cannot provide exact answers to the three questions, the scale of the job-loss is uncertain. Yet, when we take the findings of this book into account, there are three main reasons to think that job-loss will indeed be the general direction of travel. First, as machines continue to become increasingly capable, they will go on eroding any advantage that people have today in performing certain types of task. Secondly, professionals cannot rely on new or latent demand, largely because most of the new tasks to which it gives rise are themselves likely to be better and more efficiently undertaken by machines. Thirdly, although we envisage that there are tasks, which involve moral deliberation and moral responsibility, that ought always to be undertaken by human beings rather than machines, we do not expect a large enough volume of these to keep professionals in employment on today's scale.

The best and the brightest professionals will endure the longest—those who can perform tasks that cannot or ought not to be replaced by machines, and tasks that we prefer to leave in the hands of human beings. But there will not be a sufficiency of these tasks to keep armies of professionals in gainful employment.

We cannot emphasize strongly enough that we are not predicting that the professions will disappear over the next few years.

We are looking decades ahead in this chapter, and anticipating an incremental transformation and not an overnight revolution.

In the meantime, there is one other phenomenon to note. When we say that a machine has the 'advantage' in performing some type of task, we do not mean simply that the machine is more *productive,* that it can produce more output with less input than a person. We also have to look at the relative *cost* of using a machine or a person—how expensive is it to use. For example, even if a piece of medical diagnostic equipment were ten times as productive as a person, if it was a hundred times more expensive to use then it would not be *efficient* for doctors to use it. In the language of economists, we have to look at both quantities (how productive) and the prices (how expensive). Many of today's new technologies are extraordinarily productive, but they are also very expensive. And so it is not efficient to adopt them—yet.

Why we might be wrong

Our conclusions about long-term technological unemployment will be unpalatable for most professionals. It is possible, of course, that we might be wrong. A number of criticisms could be levelled at our thesis. Below, we summarize and respond to those we most commonly encounter.

Pragmatists often respond to our ideas with the claim that professional jobs cannot easily be decomposed into tasks. And they are given some academic support for this claim by the MIT economist David Autor, who suggests that 'many of the tasks currently bundled into these jobs cannot readily be unbundled...without a substantial drop in quality'.[29] However, this is simply not the experience of those who are working at the vanguard of the professions (see Chapter 2), nor of the current work of 'process analysts' (see section 6.8).

Others argue that the most efficient future lies with machines and human beings working together. Human beings will always have value to add as collaborators with machines. This is one of the central arguments of Erik Brynjolfsson and Andrew McAfee in *The Second Machine Age*,[30] and is also in the spirit of Garry Kasparov, the former chess world champion, who claims that a strong human player with a modest laptop can beat an extraordinarily powerful supercomputer.[31] This position also aligns with IBM's work on Watson. They speak of a 'new partnership between people and computers'.[32] We accept the force of this position in 2015. However, as machines become increasingly capable, it is not at all clear why professionals will be able to secure their place indefinitely in these joint ventures. These partnerships between professionals and machines are just as much at risk from being conducted entirely by machines as those involving people alone. As time goes by, surely tomorrow's high-performing, increasingly capable, nonthinking machines will have less need of professionals as collaborators.

A different claim, touched upon earlier, is that new jobs for professionals will no doubt emerge in years to come, even if we currently have no sense of what these might be. New technologies, this argument goes, have often displaced workers, but new job opportunities have always arisen to meet new demands. For example, in 1900 41 per cent of the US workforce worked in agriculture. Today that figure has plummeted to less than 2 per cent.[33] Nobody could have predicted in 1900 'that one hundred years later, health care, finance, information technology, consumer electronics, hospitality, leisure and entertainment would employ far more workers than agriculture'.[34] Likewise, two decades ago nobody could have predicted that today many thousands of people would be employed as 'search-engine optimizers' (specialists who help website providers to secure high ranking on the results pages of systems like Google).

This chapter suggests that professionals should be cautious in taking too much comfort from this line of thinking. Of course, in the future, new demands will arise, and these will call for new services. Some might lead to entirely new industries. But we have to be clear why new services and new industries might lead to new jobs for professionals. In the past, it was not because the service *itself* was new; it was because *providing* the service required new tasks to be performed in which people, and not machines, had the advantage. So too for the future—people will demand new services, but we cannot assume that professionals, rather than machines, will be best placed to undertake the new tasks that will be involved.

But *surely*, despite what we say, there will always be some tasks that will remain forever the inescapable preserve of professionals. This is a common response to those who predict technological unemployment for professionals. And it is often supported by the view that professional jobs contain tasks that are 'not susceptible' to computerization, because they are 'non-routine' and so always have to be undertaken by people.[35] But this again is to make the unwarranted assumption that non-routine tasks will never be performed by machines.[36] We challenge that view in this book, and suggest that it is often rooted in the AI fallacy—in this context, to suppose that the only way to develop systems that perform non-routine tasks is to replicate the thinking processes of human specialists, and because we are unlikely to replicate human brains, then these tasks will always be the province of human beings. But, as we say repeatedly, machines can perform very demanding tasks, and often outperform human beings, by operating in entirely different ways from human beings (see Chapter 4). Increasingly capable machines, we conclude, will gradually take on more and more non-routine tasks; and so the intuition that there will always be tasks left that only humans can perform will prove to be ill-founded.

Finally on technological unemployment, although the emphasis of our analysis has been on the professions, our conclusions extend across most, if not all, types of work. Indeed, we regard the professions as likely to last longer in their current form than most other occupations. We are therefore raising fundamental questions for society in general. Before too long, we will need to revisit our ideas about full-time employment, the purpose of work, and the balance between work and leisure.

7.5. The question of feasibility

Perhaps the most penetrating challenge to the thesis of this book is practical—that while the ideal of 'liberating' practical expertise is a worthy one, the ideas we set out will not work in practice. This raises what we call the 'feasibility question'.

It runs like this: of course we want as many people as possible to benefit from the best practical expertise—the newest medical discoveries, the clearest legal advice, the best educational experience, the most insightful news and reporting, and so on. But we also have to be practical. This seems to mean two things. First, we have to make sure that there are incentives in place so that people want to produce new practical expertise. Secondly, we have to make sure that they have the financial ability to do so. If we do not, the production of practical expertise will dry up and people will have nothing online from which to benefit.

The incentive argument has much force. Would a lawyer, for example, be sufficiently incentivized to learn how to draft wonderful letters of advice if she knew she would never be paid for her advice? Would a software developer be motivated to build an online symptom assessor or health diagnostic system if patients could use these without paying? And suppose that, even in the absence of the promise of any financial reward, the lawyer and the developer still wanted to write words and software—that they are driven by some *non*-financial motivation. In that event, how would these people afford to perform these tasks? Who would pay their wages, and who would fund their training and research, given that their efforts would yield little profit today or in the future?

On this account, liberating practical expertise is problematic—both for the professions and the people and systems that will replace them. It weakens everyone's incentives to produce practical expertise and, in turn, reduces their financial ability to do so even if they still wanted to. Rather than liberating practical expertise, the feasibility question leads us to wonder whether we ought to do the opposite. We must surely allow those who intend to invest their time and money in the production of practical expertise to maintain some *exclusivity* over their work, to keep control over those who can access their practical expertise, and so retain some capacity to charge, or in some other way be paid, for its production and distribution.

This, of course, is precisely what the grand bargain achieves. The professions are granted exclusivity over their respective bodies of practical expertise so that they can enjoy the fruit of their efforts. This might be financial profit, or some other kind of funding or support. This payback means that people and institutions can cover their past costs, and the promise of future payback means that they have healthy incentives to continue to make new investments (in training and research, for example). This ensures that their respective bodies of practical expertise are refreshed and kept up to date. Without the grand bargain, it can be argued, the whole edifice would crumble.

The feasibility question leads us to confront a trade-off. On the one hand, we are keen to share our current practical expertise as widely as possible. But, on the other hand, we want to make sure that we provide the necessary incentives and financial wherewithal for people to produce new practical expertise in the future. If we liberate the practical expertise we have today, we might undermine the production of new practical expertise tomorrow.

The further problems of the 'commons'

And there is another potential problem. Part of our thesis is that some practical expertise should be held in a 'commons'. It will be recalled that this means the ownership and control of practical expertise is taken out of the hands of a few large institutions (for example, professional institutions, corporations, and governments) and shared among those who participate. The very idea of a commons approach might prompt three additional worries about feasibility.

The first is the most basic—why on earth would people or institutions give up ownership or control of their valuable practical expertise and willingly share it with others in the commons? For the reasons just discussed, would they not want to maintain exclusivity? Would this not be to forgo an opportunity for profit?

The second misgiving is that the practical expertise, if held in a commons, might be overused. Garrett Hardin, an ecologist, called this phenomenon the 'tragedy of the commons'. In a widely cited article in *Science* in 1968, Hardin invited readers to imagine a group of shepherds who share a pasture, where each shepherd must decide how many sheep to put out to graze. If shepherds act out of self-interest alone, the result would be a 'tragedy'—each shepherd would enjoy the *full* benefit of putting each extra sheep out to graze (plumper and healthier sheep), but only suffer *part* of the cost of doing so (more arid and slightly less verdant pasture, the full cost of which would be borne by all the shepherds, and not just by one). Not considering the full cost of their actions, each shepherd would therefore put too many sheep out to graze, the pasture would fall into disrepair, and, as Hardin put it, 'ruin is the destination toward which all men rush'.[37] Similarly, we might expect that practical expertise, shared in a commons, would be overused by a rushing throng of users, narrowly preoccupied with their interests alone.

The third is a fear of underproduction of new practical expertise in a commons. When one institution owns and controls practical expertise, it is clear that the costs of its maintenance and growth must fall on them. That is one justification for the grand bargain. But in a commons, when ownership and control is spread more widely, who covers these costs? Intuitively, it might be supposed that expenses should be shared amongst all the different owners. But this of itself presents a problem. When people grasp that they will not be excluded from the commons by failing to cough up for their share of the cost, will they not then plan to 'free-ride' or 'piggy-back' on the contributions of others? After all, not paying will not stop them from using and benefiting from the practical expertise. However, the more people that keep their hands in their pockets, the less new practical expertise will be produced. The more that people rely on the contributions of others in this way, the smaller the overall contribution made by the community, and the less likely it is that any costs will be adequately covered.

Arguments in favour of feasibility

We suggest that the previous paragraphs capture the main objections of those who argue that our ideas about sharing practical expertise are impractical. To reduce the critique to its core, the concern is that, without the exclusivity provided by the grand bargain, there will be no prospect of the profit or gain that would naturally incentivize people to produce and share their expertise, and in turn provide them with the financial means to do so.

One common way to answer the feasibility question is to focus only on the *marginal* costs of producing and sharing 'information goods' (see section 5.4). Jeremy Rifkin explores this argument in his book *The Zero Marginal Cost Society*.[38] In our context, the information good is 'practical expertise'. And it is true that the marginal costs of producing and sharing practical expertise are very low—it costs almost nothing to let one more person watch an online educational video, or duplicate an article and e-mail it to a friend, or run an online diagnostic system and check his health, or use online legal document assembly software. This is because of the economic characteristics of practical expertise that we introduce in section 5.1.

Like Rifkin, we cannot accept this argument uncritically. It is incomplete and misleading to focus only on marginal costs—because marginal costs are not the only costs incurred in the production and distribution of practical expertise. Importantly, there are also the initial fixed costs that must be met before the marginal costs arise. And these fixed costs can be very high. Someone has to direct and produce the online educational video in the first place, or draft the initial article, or write the code for the online diagnostic system and the online legal document assembly software. Perhaps, in the future, machines will carry out these initial tasks as well (software has been generating software for decades, but the field is still in its infancy). But, even then, someone will have to cover the set-up costs of building the first machine. Of course, once these tasks have been completed, once the video is finished and the article has been drafted and the code has been written, then the end products can be reproduced and distributed at very little expense. But before we can enjoy these low marginal costs, the fixed costs of the initial set-up have to be funded by someone. When we take account of these set-up costs, it might indeed appear that we have to allow those who invest to maintain some exclusivity over their product. They should then be able to charge for their service, or in some other way raise revenue to cover all of their costs, and therefore be able to continue producing and distributing practical expertise.

Another common way to try to respond to the feasibility question is to argue that not everyone is driven by financial reward. It does not matter that liberating expertise is less profitable, the argument goes, because people are not always motivated by financial gain. Very often they are driven some by other, non-financial motivation—they want to make better legal guidance and medical advice available because, for example, it is intrinsically good to do so. Yochai Benkler explores this phenomenon in detail in his book *The Penguin and the Leviathan*. And he is infused with optimism:

> For the commons has finally come into its own. Because in today's knowledge economy, the most valuable resources—information and knowledge—are themselves a public good, and the best way to develop and maximise this good is through millions of networked people pooling that knowledge and working together to create new products, ideas, and solutions.[39]

And again:

> Once you open up the possibility that people are not only using the Web as a platform to produce their own individual content, but also to pool their efforts, knowledge and resources without expecting any sort of payment or compensation, the possibilities for what they can create are astounding.[40]

This evidence goes some way to addressing the 'free-rider' problem. If people were to behave in the selfless way that Benkler describes, then they would be less likely to try to take advantage of each other. A prime illustration here is Wikipedia, which attracts a great deal of donations and effort from its users, without threatening exclusivity by making access conditional on payment.

Applying Benkler's arguments to practical expertise, they are most convincing in the context of lay people who choose to share their experiences from being helped by professionals, or pass along insights into the ways in which they have sorted out problems for themselves. The problem, however, is when we think about professionals—they might be expected to be as enthusiastic about externalizing their practical expertise as encyclopedia publishers might have been to provide entries for Wikipedia when it was first launched.

We should be cautious here. Many professionals are also driven by objectives other than profit. They do not always rely on selling their practical expertise to cover their costs. Many, for example, are focused on delivering the most effective service, *given* some fixed level of funding, raised not from direct charging but from elsewhere—from the state or through philanthropy, for instance. Consider the NHS or state education in the United Kingdom. Recipients enjoy these services at no charge at the point of delivery. There is no direct sales revenue involved. The focus in these services is, or at least ought to be, on how best to make the most of falling marginal costs and to share practical expertise more widely.

What about those professionals who are driven solely by financial rewards? One possibility here is that very large 'latent demand' (see section 3.7) might incentivize large firms, for example, to make their practical expertise available far more widely but at far lower cost. This would be a low-cost rather than a no-cost service. Revenues would be generated by providing help to a great many people and organizations who were unable to afford traditional service in a print-based industrial society. However, even if this latent demand does exist, the basic challenge regarding the commons surely still obtains—why would these firms give up ownership and control of their practical expertise? They might externalize their knowledge at lower cost but stop short of handing their expertise over to a commons.

Finally, there is a further reason why profit-seeking professionals might concede their practical expertise to a commons. Recall our model of the evolution of professional service, introduced in section 5.3. We suggest that professional work moves from being handcrafted to being standardized, systematized, and then in some way externalized. We also explain that as work evolves in this way, from left to right on Figure 5.1, its value reduces—the cost of the service comes down and the competition likely intensifies. At a certain stage in this process of evolution it may be that profit-seeking professionals will recognize that the practical expertise involved can no longer yield a profit and yet may still be of great use to the communities within which they work. In that event, they may choose to make this expertise available on a commons on a pro-bono or charitable basis.

What, then, of the 'tragedy' of the commons? On closer inspection, Hardin's classical account of the 'tragedy' does not map easily onto a commons of practical expertise. His analysis focused on physical goods, and his story was about a pasture that is depleted by a surfeit of sheep. In the language of section 5.1, his focus is on goods that are 'rival' in consumption—the more a shepherd uses it, the less fertile it becomes for the shepherds who follow. But our analysis confirms that practical expertise is very different from physical goods. Not only is practical expertise 'non-rival'—it does not get worn down with use—but it is often 'cumulative', becoming more and more valuable with use and reuse. Hardin feared that a commons would lead to overuse and so to 'tragedy', but the notion of overuse makes little sense in respect of practical expertise. Far from eroding with use, expertise often increases in value. Rather than our commons leading to a 'tragedy of the commons', then, it appears that it might lead instead to what Carol Rose describes as the 'comedy of commons'.[41] The commons lets us take advantage of the special economic characteristics of practical expertise.

Exclusivity revisited

It may be that we are too bullish. The latent market might not be as large as we expect, or the commons of practical expertise may turn out to be less feasible than we argue. In either of these events, we should then concede that some exclusivity is needed—both to create strong incentives to produce practical expertise, and to provide the necessary financial means.

However, this need not catapult us back to the grand bargain, under which human professionals are currently granted remarkable monopolies over numerous areas of human activity. Instead, we would require the minimum level of exclusivity that would be needed to incentivize providers of practical expertise.

In other words, our concession leads to a *general* case for exclusivity rather than an automatic default to the grand bargain. As elaborated in our Conclusion, we maintain that it is preferable to liberate practical expertise wherever we can, and so encourage our six alternative ways of producing and distributing practical expertise to flourish. We welcome the involvement of alternative providers who would otherwise be excluded by the grand bargain. If new forms of exclusivity must emerge, these should be premised, perhaps, on the exceptional quality or reliability of the practical expertise provided, and not on the artificiality of the outmoded grand bargain. We take the view that providers of practical expertise should survive and thrive because they bring value and benefits not offered by others; and not because actual and potential competitors are excluded by regulation.

In any event, our concession to some minimum exclusivity is a case for *temporary* exclusivity. It is not an argument for granting permanent rights over bodies of practical expertise. Rather, we envisage this exclusivity as a short-term arrangement to allow providers to recoup their set-up costs. Otherwise, we worry that any new forms of exclusivity might become entrenched and, in turn, we would witness the emergence of 'new gatekeepers' in place of the professions.

Finally, this is only a case for exclusivity over *particular* parts of the work that the professions and potential new providers currently undertake. In the spirit of decomposition (section 5.6), we should not treat the work as an indivisible monolithic whole, but ask in respect of each component part whether the sort of exclusivity that is traditionally required is necessary.

In summary, we suggest that it should indeed be feasible to make some practical expertise available on a commons basis, and this need not require the elaborate or extensive granting of exclusivity to future providers. Lurking behind this conclusion and much that we say throughout this chapter is our clear preference for what we call the 'liberation' of expertise. In the remainder of the book, we explain why we take this position.

Conclusion

What Future Should We Want?

In the long run, increasingly capable machines will transform the work of professionals, giving rise to new ways of sharing practical expertise in society. This is the central thesis of our book. We cannot commit to time-frames, in large part because the speed of change is not in our hands. But we are confident that the change will constitute an incremental transformation rather than an overnight revolution. In the language of the book, the shift itself can be characterized in many ways: as the industrialization and digitization of the professions; as the routinization and commoditization of professional work; as the disintermediation and demystification of professionals. Whatever terminology is preferred, we foresee that, in the end, the traditional professions will be dismantled, leaving most (but not all) professionals to be replaced by less expert people and high-performing systems. We expect new roles will arise, but we are unsure how long they will last, because these too, in due course, may be taken on by machines.

In the post-professional society, we predict that practical expertise will be available online. Our strong inclination is to encourage the removal of current and future gatekeepers, and to provide people with as much access as is feasible to this collective knowledge and experience. The final step in our argument is to explain why we think that it is desirable to liberate practical expertise in this way.

When we speak above and throughout about technology and its impact on the professions, we are conscious that it might sound as though we believe the future is already mapped out in detail and is somehow inevitable—that we are hardline 'determinists'. Our analysis in Chapter 4, for example, makes it clear that we expect machines to become increasingly capable, that devices will be increasingly pervasive, and that human beings will be increasingly connected. And we certainly do anticipate an exponential growth in information technology. While we do not foresee these developments unfolding as a matter of necessity, we do regard them as extremely probable (barring asteroids, nuclear wars, pandemics, or the like). However—and this is where we part company with determinists—this does not mean that human beings have no control over future direction. On the contrary, we take the view that how we use technology in the professions is very much in our own hands.

It is not simply that we *can* shape our own future; more than this, we believe that we *ought* to, from a moral point of view. Two major moral questions arise in this book. The first is whether there are any likely uses of technology—by the professions or by those who replace them—that we regard as morally unacceptable. Should we seek to impose moral constraints on the march of technology across the professions? We address this issue in section 7.2, where we suggest that it would be inappropriate for some decisions, such as whether to turn off a life-support system, to be handed over to a machine, no matter how high-performing it might be. We call for public debate on the moral issues arising from models for the production and distribution of practical expertise that do not directly involve professionals or para-professionals. And we ask that this debate be held sooner rather than later, before our machines become much more capable.

The second moral question is this—who should own and control practical expertise in a technology-based Internet society? Although this question belongs to the field of political philosophy, it also raises intensely practical issues. The future of the professions rests largely on the answer we prefer. In print-based industrial societies, the professions generally own and control practical expertise, a state of affairs that is supported by the grand bargain. But if we imagine a future in which much practical expertise can be made available online, it is less obvious that the professions, or indeed anyone, should be entitled to act as its gatekeepers.

We have encountered a range of views in response to this question about the future ownership and control of practical expertise. At one end of this spectrum, there are those who argue compellingly for a full-scale 'liberation', while at the other, there are those who would much prefer 'enclosure'.

Those who call loudest for liberation demand that practical expertise should be common property and in the public domain, available and shared by all on an online basis at no or low cost, without any gatekeepers controlling access to it.[1] They point to the shortcomings of our current professions (see section 1.7), especially that for most people they are unaffordable and inaccessible. They also point to the economic characteristics of knowledge (non-rival, non-excludable, cumulative, and digitizable) which mean that practical expertise can be reproduced and distributed at negligible cost using increasingly capable machines. Their view is that, by disintermediating the professions, and by spreading practical expertise more widely, we have the capacity to improve the lives of a great many people—to provide better healthcare, superior education, greater access to justice, and so on. At the same time, the liberators worry that wresting ownership from the professions may not be sufficient to ensure liberation. They argue that we should also be alert to the emergence of new gatekeepers.[2] New monopolies might arise that take ownership and control over practical expertise, and exclude people, for example, through the imposition of prohibitive charging regimes.

Those who instead argue for enclosure take an entirely different view.[3] They maintain that practical expertise should be fenced off and controlled by providers, rather than held as a shared resource. Some invoke the conventional law of intellectual property to establish and maintain this enclosure. Many current professionals are advocates of this position. They argue that much of the practical expertise we are discussing is their property, the fruits of their own labour and talent, and that only they have the knowledge to curate and exploit it. Others point to the related questions of feasibility that we set out in section 7.5. In chargeable online service they therefore find a reassuring continuity with traditional professional work. They concede that some of their practical expertise will need to be externalized (see section 5.5), but understandably, they want to convert this into a new source of income. At the same time, they regard themselves as uniquely qualified to take sole responsibility for curating the content that is being made available online. Other proponents of enclosure are online content and service providers. They see huge commercial opportunities in moving from conventional professional service to online practical expertise. These providers are joined by some government agencies in calling for enclosure. The motivation of these public bodies is generally not income. Rather, there is a strong sense that practical expertise is too valuable a resource to be left to lay people to manage. One role of government, on this view, is to oversee and control the quality of the expertise that is made available.

What future should we want? Are there irreconcilable differences between those who would liberate and those who would enclose? One of the main difficulties in deciding between competing moral or political positions of this kind is that it is hard to prevent personal preferences from exerting undue influence. In this context, many who might be disposed to express a view—professionals, most notably—are far from impartial. Most professionals will naturally and understandably oppose a new arrangement, under which their own status or wealth might diminish.

To help us with this dilemma, we borrow a technique developed by the political philosopher John Rawls, in his influential book *A Theory of Justice*.[4] In developing his ideas about what constitutes a just society, Rawls asks us to imagine a hypothetical situation in which nobody knows his or her personal and social circumstances. People have no idea of their natural talents and abilities—whether, for example, they are smart, good-looking, or physically strong. Nor do they have any idea of their class or social status. In fact, they know no 'particular information' about themselves—they do not know their age, their gender, their race, or even what generation they belong to. When we imagine ourselves in this hypothetical situation of unknowing cluelessness, we are behind what Rawls calls the 'veil of ignorance'. And only when we are behind this 'veil' can we be genuinely impartial.

We ask our readers, especially professionals, to place themselves behind a veil of ignorance and ponder how we should share practical expertise in a technology-based Internet society. We are *not* asking readers to consider the future of the professions. That would immediately limit the imagination—inviting views on how the professions should evolve suggests that the professions must have a central role to play. In contrast, this book suggests that increasingly capable, non-thinking machines will displace much of the work of human professionals. Our question, instead, is whether, from behind the veil of ignorance, we should prefer these systems and machines to be held in common for many or controlled by a few, whether we should prefer practical expertise to be made available at little cost or at greater expense, whether it should be liberated or enclosed.

This question is, of course, one for the long term, and we can frame it another way. Beyond the professions, there will lie a fork in the road, with two possible routes stretching out. One leads to a society in which practical expertise is a shared online resource, freely available and maintained in a collaborative spirit. The other route leads to a society in which this knowledge and experience may be available online, but is owned and controlled by providers, so that recipients will generally pay for access to this resource and our collective practical expertise is enclosed and traded, most likely by new gatekeepers. The first route leads us to a type of commons where our collective knowledge and experience, in so far as is feasible, is nurtured and shared without commercial gain, while the second takes us to an online marketplace in which practical expertise is invariably bought and sold. From behind the veil of ignorance, which route would readers take?

We oversimplify, of course. The options are unlikely to be so stark. And hybrid possibilities could be fashioned. But having to choose one over the other is a revealing discipline, because the spirit of each option is very different, and, as we plan and build our technology-based Internet society, we should be clear and principled in the choices we make.

Our sense is that, from behind a veil of ignorance, most people would choose to liberate rather than enclose. By and large, it would be better to live in a society in which most medical help, spiritual guidance, legal advice, the latest news, business assistance, accounting insight, and architectural know-how is widely available, at low or no cost. This is certainly what we believe—that, over the next decade or two, we have an opportunity to begin this transformation in our world.

We feel a great sense of excitement in imagining human beings across the world—rich and poor—having direct access to living, evolving treasure troves of help, guidance, learning, and insight that will empower them to live healthier and happier lives. But this shift will not come about spontaneously. It is a goal to which we must actively strive. We must remember that inaction, as well as action, is a choice. If we choose to do nothing, and we decide to default to our traditional ways and discard the promise of technological change for fear, say, of rocking the boat, then this is a decision for which later generations can hold us accountable. In the words, again, of Anthony Kenny, technology 'puts sins of omission as immediately and inevitably within our power as it puts sins of commission'.[5] The potential sins of omission here are too profound to ignore. We now have the means to share expertise much more widely across our world. We should also have the will.

ENDNOTES

New Preface – An Update

1. Hannah Kuchler, 'Google AI system beats doctors in detection tests for breast cancer', *Financial Times,* 1 Jan 2020 <https://www.ft.com/content/3b64fa26-28e9-11ea-9a4f-963f0ec7e134>; David Brookes, 'How Artificial Intelligence Can Save Your Life', *The New York Times,* 24 June 2019 <https://www.nytimes.com/2019/06/24/opinion/artificial-intelligence-depression.html?searchResultPosition=20>; Brian Resnick, 'How data scientists are using AI for suicide prevention', *Vox,* 9 June 2018 <https://www.vox.com/science-and-health/2018/6/8/17441452/suicide-prevention-anthony-bourdain-crisis-text-line-data-science> (accessed 3 Nov 2021).
2. Ewen Callaway, '"It will change everything": DeepMind's AI makes gigantic leap in solving protein structures', *Nature,* 30 Nov 2020 <https://www.nature.com/articles/d41586-020-03348-4> (accessed 3 Nov 2021).
3. Madhumita Murgia, 'AI-design drug to enter human clinical trial for first time', *Financial Times,* 30 Jan 2020 <https://www.ft.com/content/fe55190e-42bf-11ea-a43a-c4b328d9061c> (accessed 3 Nov 2021).
4. Sarah Neville and Richard Waters, 'Novartis and Microsoft join forces to develop drugs using AI', *Financial Times,* 1 October 2019 https://www.ft.com/content/93e532ee-e3a5-11e9-b112-9624ec9edc59 (accessed 3 Nov 2021).
5. *Deep Medicine: How Artificial Intelligence Can Make Healthcare Human Again* (New York: Basic Books, 2019).
6. NHS, 'Preparing the healthcare workforce to deliver the digital future', February 2019, at https://topol.hee.nhs.uk/ (accessed 3 November 2021).
7. p.6.
8. p.82.
9. Natasha Singer, 'Learning Apps Have Boomed in the Pandemic. Now Comes the Real Test', *The New York Times,* 17 March 2021 <https://www.nytimes.com/2021/03/17/technology/learning-apps-students.html> (accessed 3 Nov 2021).

10. 'COVID-19 fuelling education's tech disruption, deepening digital divide', *Reuters*, 11 Jan 2021 <https://www.reuters.com/article/us-education-future-idUSKBN29G2LR> (accessed 3 November 2021).
11. Peter Diamandis, 'Dreamscape: 21st Century Education', 23 May 2021 <https://www.diamandis.com/blog/science-age-reversal-o> (accessed 3 Nov 2021).
12. Peter Holley, 'Meet 'Mindar', the robotic Buddhist priest', *Washington Post*, 22 August 2019 <https://www.washingtonpost.com/technology/2019/08/22/introducing-mindar-robotic-priest-that-some-are-calling-frankenstein-monster/> (accessed 3 Nov 2021).
13. Gabriele Trovato et al., 'Communcating with SanTO – the first Catholic Robot', 2019. *28th IEEE International Conference on Robot and Human Interactive Communication (RO-MAN)*, 1–6.
14. Diana Löffler, Jörn Hurtienne, and Ilona Nord, 2021, 'Blessing Robot BlessU2: A Discursive Design Study to Understand the Implications of Social Robots in Religious Contexts', *International Journal of Social Robotics*, 13 569–586.
15. Mark Bridge, 'Gender-neutral robot priests to take on patriarchy', *The Times*, 20 Sept 2019 <https://www.thetimes.co.uk/article/gender-neutral-robot-priests-to-take-on-patriarchy-r3sqkgm2k> (accessed 3 Nov 2021).
16. Alan Cooperman, 'Will the coronavirus permanently convert in-person worshippers to online streamers? They don't think so', *Pew Research Center*, 17 August 2020 <https://www.pewresearch.org/fact-tank/2020/08/17/will-the-coronavirus-permanently-convert-in-person-worshippers-to-online-streamers-they-dont-think-so/> (accessed 3 Nov 2021).
17. 'Millions join worship online as churches bring services into the home in pandemic year', The Church of England, 16 March 2021 <https://www.churchofengland.org/news-and-media/news-releases/millions-join-worship-online-churches-bring-services-home-pandemic> (accessed 3 Nov 2021).
18. Aiden Pink, 'Some Orthodox rabbis permit phone use on holidays, citing pandemic's mental health risks', *Forward*, 7 April 2020 <https://forward.com/fast-forward/443428/some-orthodox-rabbis-permit-phone-use-on-holidays-citing-pandemics-mental/> (accessed 3 Nov 2021).
19. William Macaraan, 'The sacrament of confession during Covid-19 pandemic', *Journal of Public Health (Oxf)*, 34(3) e531–e532.

20. Michael Jensen et al., 2018. 'The Use of Social Media by United States Extremists', START Research Brief <https://www.start.umd.edu/pubs/START_PIRUS_UseOfSocialMediaByUSExtremists_ResearchBrief_July2018.pdf>. For the UK case, see Jonathan Kenyon, Jens Binder, and Christopher Baker-Beall, 2021. 'Exploring the role of the Internet in radicalisation and offending of convicted extremists', Ministry of Justice Analytical Series. <https://assets.publishing.service.gov.uk/government/uploads/system/uploads/attachment_data/file/1017413/exploring-role-internet-radicalisation.pdf> (accessed 3 Nov 2021).
21. https://remotecourts.org/ (accessed 3 November 2021) and Richard Susskind, *Online Courts and the Future of Justice* (Oxford: Oxford University Press, paperback, 2020).
22. See Richard Susskind, *Online Courts and the Future of Justice*, Part IV.
23. An almost daily update of these and emerging systems is given at https://www.artificiallawyer.com/ (accessed 3 November 2021).
24. Clive Cookson, 'Computer algorithms beat humans at predicting reoffending rates', *Financial Times*, 14 Feb 2000 <https://www.ft.com/content/a496d49a-4f6f-11ea-95a0-43d18ec715f5> (accessed 3 Nov 2021).
25. Hugh Son, 'JPMorgan software does in seconds what took lawyers 360,000 hours', *The Independent*, 28 Feb 2017 <https://www.independent.co.uk/news/business/news/jp-morgan-software-lawyers-coin-contract-intelligence-parsing-financial-deals-seconds-legal-working-hours-360000-a7603256.html> (accessed 3 November 2021).
26. <https://www.allenovery.com/en-gb/global/expertise/advanced_delivery/scaled_solutions> (accessed 3 November 2021).
27. https://www.legalzoom.com (accessed 3 November 2021).
28. https://technation.io/lawtechuk/ (accessed 3 November 2021).
29. 'ABC figures: Newspapers will no longer have to publish sales', *BBC News*, 21 May 2020 <https://www.bbc.co.uk/news/entertainment-arts-52754762> (accessed 3 Nov 2021).
30. Clara Hendrickson, 2019. 'Local Journalism in Crisis: Why America Must Revive its Local Newsrooms', *The Brookings Institution* <https://www.brookings.edu/wp-content/uploads/2019/11/Local-Journalism-in-Crisis.pdf> (accessed 3 Nov 2021).
31. There were 2.3m subscribers in 2015 – see the figure in Hanaa' Tameez, 'For the first time, The New York Times' digital subscriptions generate

more revenue than its print ones', *Nieman Lab,* 5 Nov 2020 <https://www.niemanlab.org/2020/11/for-the-first-time-the-new-york-times-digital-subscriptions-generate-more-revenue-than-its-print-ones/>; there were 7.8 million in 2021 - see Edmund Lee, 'The New York Times Tops 7.8 Million Subscribers as Growth Slows', *The New York Times,* 5 May 2021 <https://www.nytimes.com/2021/05/05/business/media/nyt-new-york-times-earnings-q1-2021.html> (accessed 3 Nov 2021).

32. Nic Newman, 'Journalism, media, and technology trends and predictions 2021', Reuters Institute, 7 January 2021 <https://reutersinstitute.politics.ox.ac.uk/journalism-media-and-technology-trends-and-predictions-2021> (accessed 3 November 2021).
33. See 'Future of Big Data in Management Consulting', in Jeremy Curuksu, *Data Driven: An Introduction to Management Consulting in the 21st Century* (New York: Springer, 2018), Chapter 2.
34. Barry Libert and Megan Beck, 'AI May Soon Replace Even the Most Elite Consultants', *Harvard Business Review,* 24 July 2017 <https://hbr.org/2017/07/ai-may-soon-replace-even-the-most-elite-consultants>. That paper's central theme was substantially echoed in a report in *The Economist* - 'AI providers will increasingly compete with management consultancies', 28 March 2017 <https://www.economist.com/special-report/2018/03/28/ai-providers-will-increasingly-compete-with-management-consultancies> (accessed 3 November 2021).
35. See https://www.mckinsey.com/solutions (accessed 3 November 2021).
36. Sir Donald Brydon, 'Assess, Assure and Inform', December 2019, p.4, at <https://assets.publishing.service.gov.uk/government/uploads/system/uploads/attachment_data/file/852960/brydon-review-final-report.pdf> (accessed 3 November 2021).
37. Brydon (2019), 8.
38. See, for example, a joint report by the global Association of Chartered Certified Accountants and Chartered Accountants Australia and New Zealand, 'Audit and Technology', June 2019, via <https://www.charteredaccountantsanz.com/news-and-analysis/insights/research-and-insights/how-technology-will-allow-audit-to-look-forwards-not-backwards> (accessed 3 November 2021).

39. Naveen Kalia, 'How the pandemic is accelerating the future of audit', 19 October 2020 <https://home.kpmg/ca/en/home/insights/2020/10/how-the-pandemic-is-accelerating-the-future-of-audit.html> (accessed 3 November 2021).
40. Ben Moore, 'Most Americans File Their Taxes Online, But May Still Worry About Security', *PCMag*, 14 July 2020 <https://uk.pcmag.com/tax-software/127750/most-americans-file-their-taxes-online-but-many-still-worry-about-security> (accessed 3 November 2021).
41. Michael Rapoport and Vipal Monga, 'General Electrics's Novel Tax Deal Could Lead the Way', *The Wall Street Journal*, 30 January 2017 <https://www.wsj.com/articles/general-electrics-novel-tax-deal-could-lead-the-way-1485781202> and announcement at <https://sellercentral-europe.amazon.com/forums/t/deloitte-new-tax-service-provider-for-vat-services-on-amazon/442628> (accessed 3 November 2021).
42. Heather Sandlin, 'Deloitte and Taxamo to launch new tax compliance service', *Accountancy Today*, 31 March 2020 <https://www.accountancytoday.co.uk/2020/03/31/deloitte-and-taxomo-to-launch-new-tax-compliance-service/ (accessed 3 November 2021)>. Our thanks to Conrad Young for his guidance on developments in Tax.
43. HMRC, 'Overview of Making Tax Digital', November 2020 <https://www.gov.uk/government/publications/making-tax-digital/overview-of-making-tax-digital> (accessed 3 November 2021).
44. Peter Handlykken, 'Rethinking the Tax Collection Process in Norway', in IOTA, 'Transforming Tax Administration and Involving Shareholders' (2017, Budapest), pp.1320, at <https://www.iota-tax.org/system/files/transforming-tax-administration.pdf> (accessed 3 November 2021).
45. OECD, 'Tax Administration 3.0: The Digital Transformation of Tax Administration', November 2020 <https://www.oecd.org/tax/forum-on-tax-administration/publications-and-products/tax-administration-3-0-the-digital-transformation-of-tax-administration.pdf> (accessed 3 November 2021).
46. Kors Kool, 'Tax Administration and the Role of Third Parties', in IOTA, 'Transforming Tax Administration and Involving Shareholders' (2017, Budapest), p.45, at <https://www.iota-tax.org/system/files/transforming-tax-administration.pdf> (accessed 3 November 2021).

47. See, for instance, Higharc, Finch 3D, Archistar, TestFit, discussed in Daniel Davis, 'Can Algorithms Design Buildings?', 24 June 2019 <https://www.architectmagazine.com/technology/can-algorithms-design-buildings_o> (accessed 3 November 2021).
48. Daniel Susskind, *A World Without Work*, (London: Allen Lane, 2020), pp. 71–72.
49. See, for example, Hypar at <https://hypar.io/> (accessed 3 November 2021).
50. See <https://fologram.com/> (accessed 3 November 2021).
51. Quoted in David McClean et al, 'Mental health in UK architecture education: An analysis of contemporary student wellbeing', February 2020, an initial study funded by RIBA research grant, at <https://www.architecture.com/-/media/files/Education/Former-bursary-winners/David-McClean-Peter-Holgate-Mental-Health-in-UK-architecture-education#:~:text=More%20specifically%20at%20subject%20level,Waite%2C%202017)%20and%2033%25> (accessed 3 November 2021).
52. Philip Kennicott, 'Designing to Survive', *The Washington Post Magazine*, 13 July 2020 <https://www.washingtonpost.com/magazine/2020/07/13/pandemic-has-shown-us-what-future-architecture-could-be/> (accessed 3 November 2021).
53. India Block, 'Coronavirus "disaster" sees 45 per cent of architects lose income in UK, 7 April 2020 <https://www.dezeen.com/2020/04/07/coronavirus-architects-lost-income-uk/> (accessed 3 November 2021).
54. 'The stockmarket is now run by computers, algorithms and passive managers', *The Economist*, 5 October 2019 <https://www.economist.com/briefing/2019/10/05/the-stockmarket-is-now-run-by-computers-algorithms-and-passive-managers> (accessed 3 November 2021).
55. David Bholat and Daniel Susskind, 'The assessment: artificial intelligence and financial services', *Oxford Review of Economic Policy*, 2021, vol. 37, issue 3, 417–434; Stephen Morris, 'Fitch invests in AI start-up to improve bank misconduct', *Financial Times*, 18 January 2021 <https://www.ft.com/content/4bf67e86-84ff-4616-ab40-36fd25fc71b7> (accessed 3 November 2021).
56. Jaclyn Peiser, 'The Rise of the Robot Reporter', *The New York Times*, 5 February 2019 <https://www.nytimes.com/2019/02/05/business/media/artificial-intelligence-journalism-robots.html; Michael Mackenzie, 'Morningstar unleashes robots to write fund research', *Financial Times*, 26 March 2021 <https://www.ft.com/content/3f3d4f09-b579-4649-90f4-44709c475991> (accessed 3 November 2021).

57. Frank Arute et al, 'Quantum supremacy using a programmable superconducting processor', *Nature*, 574, 505–510 (2019); and Han-Sen Zhong et al, 'Quantum computational advantage using photons', *Science*, 370, 1460-1463 (2020).
58. Kate Crawford, 'Time to regulate AI that interprets human emotions', *Nature*, 6 April 2021 https://www.nature.com/articles/d41586-021-00868-5 (accessed 3 November 2021).
59. 'How have Covid-19 vaccines been made quickly and safely?', *Welcome*, 21 January 2021 <https://wellcome.org/news/quick-safe-covid-vaccine-development> (accessed 3 November 2021).
60. Natasha Singer, 'The Hard Part of Computer Science? Getting Into Class', *The New York Times*, 24 January 2019 <https://www.nytimes.com/2019/01/24/technology/computer-science-courses-college.html> (accessed 3 November 2021).
61. CVPR, ICJAI, AAAI, NeurIPS, ICML, and ICRA – from 11,816 to 27,396. IROS is omitted due to missing data for 2018. See https://aiimpacts.org/ai-conference-attendance/ (accessed 3 November 2021).
62. Zachary Arnold et al, 'Tracking AI Investment', Center for Security and Emerging Technology, September 2020 <https://cset.georgetown.edu/research/tracking-ai-investment/> (accessed 3 November 2021).
63. Matthew Hutson, 'Robo-writers: the rise and risks of language-generating AI', *Nature*, 3 March 2021 <https://www.nature.com/articles/d41586-021-00530-0> (accessed 3 November 2021).
64. 'GPT-3 Powers the Next Generation of Apps', 25 March 2021 <https://openai.com/blog/gpt-3-apps/> (accessed 3 November 2021).
65. Daniel Susskind, *A World Without Work* (London: Allen Lane, 2020).
66. Richard Susskind, *Online Courts and the Future of Justice* (Oxford: Oxford University Press, paperback, 2020).
67. A slightly updated version was posted on LinkedIn on 14 April 2020: <https://www.linkedin.com/pulse/five-phases-recovery-from-covid-19-richard-susskind-daniel-susskind/> (accessed 3 November 2021).
68. See the preface to the paperback edition of Richard Susskind, *The End of Lawyers?* (Oxford: Oxford University Press, 2010).
69. See Richard Susskind, *The End of Lawyers?* (2010), p.86.

Introduction

1. See Chapters 2 and 3 for references and further details of these examples.
2. We use the terms 'increasingly capable systems' and 'increasingly capable machines' interchangeably throughout the book. More generally, unless the context indicates otherwise, we also use 'systems' and 'machines' interchangeably.

1. The Grand Bargain

1. Robert Pear, 'After Slow Growth, Experts Say, Health Spending Is Expected to Climb', *New York Times*, 3 Sept. 2014 <http://www.nytimes.com> (accessed 27 March 2015).
2. 'Business Register and Employment Survey (BRES) 2013 – Table 1: Broad Industry Group', Office for National Statistics, 25 Sept. 2014. <http://www.ons.gov.uk/ons/taxonomy/index.html?nscl=Employment+by+Industry+ Sector#tab-data-tables> (accessed 27 March 2015).
3. 'Legal profession and the EU', The Law Society, 11 June 2013 <https://www.lawsociety.org.uk/policy-campaigns/government-parliamentary-affairs/miscellaneous-briefings/legal-profession-and-the-eu/> (accessed 27 March 2015).
4. Independent Reviewer on Social Mobility and Child Poverty, *Fair Access to Professional Careers: A Progress Report* (2012), 32 and 4. [Full publication details for book titles are provided in the Bibliography.]
5. Social Mobility and Child Poverty Commission, *Elitist Britain?* (2014), 10 at <https://www.gov.uk/government/publications/elitist-britain> (accessed 27 March 2015).
6. Independent Reviewer on Social Mobility and Child Poverty, *Fair Access to Professional Careers* (2012), 44.
7. *Chariots of Fire* (1981), at <http://www.imdb.com/title/tt0082158>.
8. Panel on Fair Access to the Professions, *Unleashing Aspiration* (2009), 14. Our thanks to Professor Alan Paterson for drawing this report to our attention. See Alan Paterson, *Lawyers and the Public Good* (2012), 7.
9. Eliot Freidson, *Professional Powers* (1988), 31. Freidson offers 'A Semantic History' of 'Profession' in ch. 2.
10. See Robin Downie, 'Professions and Professionalism', *Journal of Philosophy of Education*, 24 (1990), 147–59.

11. David Sciulli, *Professions in Civil Society and the State* (2009), 1.
12. Andrew Abbott, *The System of Professions* (1988), 318.
13. Moreover, the 'characteristics of professional status' change over time, as can be seen in Roy Lewis and Angus Maude, *Professional People in England* (1953), 72–3, where one of their characteristics is a 'Ban on Advertising of Services'.
14. For readers interested in whether prostitutes have a claim to be regarded as professionals, see Jethro Lieberman, *The Tyranny of the Experts* (1970), 64–6. The phrase the 'oldest profession' is probably derived from Rudyard Kipling's reference to the 'most ancient profession'.
15. See Christopher McKenna, *The World's Newest Profession* (2006).
16. We borrow this term from Ivan Illich. See Ivan Illich, 'Disabling Professions', in Ivan Illich *et al.*, *Disabling Professions* (1977).
17. In thus characterizing the professions, critics may choose to brand us as members of the 'trait' school of theorists—see sect. 1.5. We think our isolation of 'broad features' falls well short of being traitist.
18. Ludwig Wittgenstein, *Philosophical Investigations* (1958), See also Downie, 'Professions and Professionalism', 147.
19. We use the term 'lay people' throughout the book. It is not ideal. But we find it the best of a bad bunch of possible terms. For example, we do not like 'ordinary people', 'non-professionals', or indeed the lawyer's 'man on the Clapham Omnibus'.
20. As Freidson puts it: 'the claims, values, and ideas that provide the rationale for . . . professionalism.' See Eliot Freidson, *Professionalism* (2001), 105.
21. William Wickenden, *A Professional Guide for Young Engineers* (1949), 16.
22. Talcott Parsons, 'The Professions and Social Structure', *Social Forces*, 17: 4 (1939), 457.
23. See e.g. David Maister, *Managing the Professional Service Firm* (1993), and Charles Ellis, *What It Takes* (2013).
24. Thomas Marshall, 'The Recent History of Professionalism in Relation to Social Structure and Social Policy', *Canadian Journal of Economics and Political Science*, 5 (1939), 325.
25. Lewis and Maude, *Professional People in England*, 17–19.
26. See e.g. Alexander Carr-Saunders and Paul Wilson, *The Professions* (1933), and Harold Perkin, *The Rise of Professional Society* (1989).

27. Abbott, *The System of Professions*, 3.
28. Lewis and Maude, *Professional People in England*, 16.
29. For a discussion of professionalizing, see Harold Wilensky, 'The Professionalization of Everyone?', *American Journal of Sociology*, 70: 2 (1964), 137–58.
30. The new Company enjoyed interesting privileges, such as the annual allocation of the bodies of four executed criminals for dissection—see <http://barberscompany.org>.
31. Everett Hughes, *Men and Their Work* (1964), 7.
32. Keith MacDonald, *The Sociology of the Professions* (1995), 10.
33. Donald Schön, *Educating the Reflective Practitioner* (1987), 7.
34. William Alford, Kenneth Winston, and William Kirby (eds.), *Prospects for the Professions in China* (2011), 1.
35. Schön, *Educating the Reflective Practitioner*, 7, where he is citing Everett Hughes.
36. Atul Gawande, *Better* (2007), 148.
37. Everett Hughes, 'The Study of Occupations', in *Sociology Today*, Vol. II, ed. Robert Merton, Leonard Broom, and Leonard Cottrell (1959), 449.
38. Adam Smith, *Wealth of Nations* (1998), 101.
39. Richard Susskind, *Tomorrow's Lawyers* (2013), 6.
40. Abbott, *The System of Professions*, 1.
41. See e.g. Abbott, *The System of Professions*, 86–7: 'For Parsons a professional's power over clients was necessary to successful treatment and did not prevent other professional powers. It was grounded in expertise, guaranteed by professional control, and offset by the trust between professional and client.'
42. Marshall, 'The Recent History of Professionalism in Relation to Social Structure and Social Policy', 331–2.
43. Paul Halmos, 'The Personal Service Society', *British Journal of Sociology*, 18 (1967), 13. Halmos, in fact, divides the professions into those who provide a 'personal' service, and those who provide an 'impersonal' one.
44. Talcott Parsons, *The Social System* (1951), ch. 2.
45. Alexander Carr-Saunders and Paul Wilson, *The Professions* (1933), 471, quoted in Geoff Mungham and Philip Thomas, 'Solicitors and Clients: Altruism or Self-Interest?' in *The Sociology of the Professions*, ed. Robert Dingwall and Philip Lewis (1983), 136.

46. Richard Tawney, *The Acquisitive Society* (1921), 35.
47. Émile Durkheim, *The Division of Labor in Society* (1997), p. xxxix. As Larson points out, Durkheim had in mind a broader conception of the 'professions' than we are using in this book (perhaps 'occupation' is a more fitting word for the translation of the French word *profession* that Durkheim uses). Yet the similarity between his thinking and that of the later theorists is still clear. These ideas reoccur in Durkheim's work. In *On Suicide*, reflecting on how to resolve escalating waves of suicide in Europe, Durkheim proposed the professions as a remedy, describing them as the best way to 'reawaken our moral sensibility'. See Émile Durkheim, *On Suicide* (2006), esp. bk. 3, ch. 3.
48. Talcott Parsons, *Essays in Sociological Theory* (1964), 382 (original emphasis).
49. Carr-Saunders and Wilson, *The Professions*, 497.
50. Durkheim, *On Suicide*, 426.
51. Terence Johnson, *Professions and Power* (1972), 22.
52. Geoffrey Millerson, 'Dilemmas of Professionalism', *New Society*, 4 June 1964, quoted in Johnson, *Professions and Power*, 23.
53. Schön, *Educating the Reflective Practitioner*, 7.
54. Macdonald, *The Sociology of the Professions*, p. xii.
55. Max Weber, *Economy and Society* (1978), 342.
56. Max Weber, 'Bureaucracy', in *Max Weber: Essays in Sociology*, ed. Hans Heinrich Gerth and Charles Wright Mills (1947), 233.
57. William Goode, 'Encroachment, Charlatanism and the Emerging Profession: Psychology, Sociology, and Medicine', *American Sociological Review*, 25: 6 (1960), 902.
58. See e.g. Wilensky, 'The Professionalization of Everyone?', 137–58.
59. Magali Larson, *The Rise of Professionalism* (2013).
60. Larson, *The Rise of Professionalism*, 5–6.
61. Everett Hughes, 'The Study of Occupations', 447.
62. George Bernard Shaw, *The Doctor's Dilemma* (1954), 16.
63. Jethro Lieberman, *The Tyranny of the Experts* (1970).
64. Stanley Fish, *Doing What Comes Naturally* (1989), 200–1.
65. See Illich, 'Disabling Professions', 11–12.
66. See Illich, 'Disabling Professions', 19.

67. See Illich, 'Disabling Professions', 19–20. One antidote to the professions, in this spirit, are 'counterprofessionals'. In the words of Donald Schön, these are 'advocates and adversaries who can effectively resist professionally engineered subversion of the public interest and the rights of clients': Schön, *The Reflective Practitioner*, 340.
68. Macdonald, *The Sociology of the Professions*, 22.
69. Elliott Krause, *Death of the Guilds* (1996), p. ix.
70. Krause, *Death of the Guilds*, 281. Krause is discussing Weber in the quotation. See also Hughes, *Men and Their Work*, 131–2.
71. Compare this with the proposition that 'the professions should be uniquely sensitive to the dangers surrounding conflicts of interest': John Coffee, *Gatekeepers* (2006), 365.
72. More than this, it can even be argued, in the very specific sense that Lawrence Lessig identifies, that there is institutional 'corruption' in some of the professions. See Lawrence Lessig, *Republic, Lost* (2011), 16–17.
73. Marshall, 'The Recent History of Professionalism in Relation to Social Structure and Social Policy', 325.
74. See Abbott, *The System of Professions*, 324.
75. Abbott, *The System of Professions*, 315.
76. Abbott, *The System of Professions*, 323.
77. There are some references. For example, Paul Halmos, *The Personal Service Society* (1970), 9–10, on 'automation', and William Scott, 'Lords of the Dance: Professionals as Institutional Agents', *Organization Studies*, 29: 2 (2008), 230, on 'mechanization and routinization'. But the literature can be very dismissive. See e.g. MacDonald, *The Sociology of the Professions*, 62, where the possibility that artificial intelligence might have a role in the professions is written off as implausible.
78. Aristotle, *Politics*, part XI, at <http://classics.mit.edu/Aristotle/politics.3.three.html>, (accessed 28 March 2015). Jethro Lieberman, a law professor, puts it similarly: 'The time for heresy is overdue: The expert is the wrong person to define his job or to evaluate how well it is performed.' See Lieberman, *The Tyranny of the Experts*, 275.
79. Anthony Kenny, *What I Believe* (2006), 123.
80. <http://www.kpmg.com>.
81. Our thinking on asymmetry of knowledge aligns to some extent with that of Durkheim, Parsons, and Abbott.

82. Herbert Hart, *The Concept of Law* (1994), 197. Original emphasis.
83. On the distinction between 'knowing that' and 'knowing how', see Gilbert Ryle, *The Concept of Mind* (1949), 28–32.
84. On tacit knowledge, see Michael Polanyi, 'The Logic of Tacit Inference', *Philosophy*, 41: 155 (1966), 1–18.
85. See e.g. Amos Tversky and Daniel Kahneman, 'Judgment under Uncertainty: Heuristics and Biases', *Science*, 185: 4157 (1974), 1124–31. They explore the problems with some of these rules of thumb.
86. Note the correspondence here with philosophical and psychological concepts of practical reason and practical reasoning. See Joseph Raz, *Practical Reason and Norms* (1999).
87. We are alive to a sophisticated challenge to this conception of knowledge, namely, a concern over what might be called the objectification of knowledge. In standardizing practical expertise or representing it in computer systems, the charge here is that this oversimplifies and fails to acknowledge that knowledge is dependent on social factors, such as culture, custom, tradition, and so forth. We find it hard to reconcile this view with the daily experience of professionals in action. They often work with informal, approximations of fields of knowledge. The purist may find these untenable (and they may be theoretically flawed), but they do seem to work in practice. For a stimulating related discussion, see David Bloor, *Knowledge and Social Imagery* (1991).
88. Abraham Maslow, *The Psychology of Science* (1966), 15.
89. Richard Feynman, *The Feynman Lectures on Physics*, Vol. 1 (1964), ch. 3.7 <http://www.feynmanlectures.caltech.edu/I_toc.html> (accessed 27 March 2015).
90. Discussed in Alex Frame, *Salmond: Southern Jurist* (1995), 30.

2. From the Vanguard

1. 'After forty years one begins to be able to distinguish an ephemeral surface ripple from a deeper current or an authentic change.' A quotation from Antonio Weiss, 'Harold Bloom, The Art of Criticism No. 1', *Paris Review*, 118 (Spring, 1991) <http://www.theparisreview.org> (accessed 23 March 2015).
2. Eric Topol, *The Patient Will See You Now* (2015), 5.

3. 'Policy: Improving quality of life for people with long term conditions', Department of Health, 25 Mar. 2013 <https://www.gov.uk/government/policies/improving-quality-of-life-for-people-with-long-term-conditions> (accessed 6 March 2015).
4. Atul Gawande, *The Checklist Manifesto* (2010).
5. The OECD estimates that per capita visits to US doctors is 4 per annum (a 2010 figure). If US population is ~320 million (a 2014 figure), then average visits are 1.28bn per annum, and 107m per month (assuming the per capita visits have changed little). In contrast, the WebMD network has 190m unique users per month (and over 1bn pages views a month). For the data, see 'Doctors' consultations: Number per capita', Health: Key Tables from OECD No.40, OECD, 30 June 2014 <http://dx.doi.org/10.1787/doctorconsult-table-2014-1-en> (accessed 25 March 2015). 'WebMD Announces Fourth Quarter and Year End Financial Results', WebMD, 24 February 2015, <http://investor.shareholder.com/wbmd/releasedetail.cfm?ReleaseID=898072&CompanyID=WBM> (accessed 6 March 2015).
6. 'Our intelligent monitoring of GP practices', Care Quality Commission, 13 January 2015, <http://www.cqc.org.uk/content/our-intelligent-monitoring-gp-practices> (accessed 6 March 2015).
7. Christopher Steiner, *Automate This* (2012), 154.
8. 'Memorial Sloan Kettering Trains IBM Watson to Help Doctors Make Better Cancer Treatment Choices', Memorial Sloan Kettering Cancer Center, 11 April 2014 <http://www.mskcc.org/blog/msk-trains-ibm-watson-help-doctors-make-better-treatment-choices> (accessed 6 March 2015).
9. Mohana Ravindranath, 'VA signs $6 million contract for IBM Watson to advise PTSD treatment', *Washington Post*, 15 Dec. 2014.
10. According to Medline, there were 765,850 new citations in 2014. On average, that is 1.46 a minute. That is ~2098 on average each day which, if 2 percent are relevant, is 42 papers. If they take 30 minutes each to skim read, that is 21 hours a day. Data from 'Detailed Indexing Statistics: 1965–2014', U.S. National Library of Medicine, 3 March 2015 <http://www.nlm.nih.gov/bsd/index_stats_comp.html> (accessed 6 March 2015).
11. Trish Greenhalgh, 'Is Evidence-Based Medicine Broken?', *Project Syndicate*, 8 Oct. 2014, <http://www.project-syndicate.org> (accessed 6 March 2015).

12. Mark L. Graber, Robert M. Wachter, and Christine K. Cassel, 'Bringing Diagnosis into the Quality and Safety Equations', *Journal of the American Medical Association*, 208: 12 (2012), 1211–12.
13. Steiner, *Automate This*, 155.
14. 'About Aethon: Company Background', Aethon <http://www.aethon.com/about/> (accessed 6 March 2015).
15. '2015 Physician's Desk Reference, 69th Edition' <http://www.amazon.com> (accessed 6 March 2015).
16. Glenna Picton, 'Study shows promise in automated reasoning, hypothesis generation over complete medical literature', Baylor College of Medicine, 25 August 2014 <https://www.bcm.edu/news/research/automated-reasoning-hypothesis-generation> (accessed 9 March 2015).
17. Bill Saporito, 'IBM's Startling Cancer Coup', *Time*, 28 Aug. 2014.
18. Scott Spangler *et al.*, 'Automated hypothesis generation based on mining scientific literature', *Proceedings of the 20th ACM SIGKDD international conference on knowledge discovery and data mining* (2014), 1877–86.
19. 'Computer says "try this"', *Economist*, 4 Oct. 2014.
20. <http://www.ukapa.co.uk> (accessed 9 March 2015).
21. See e.g. 'Doctor, Doctor?', leader in *The Times*, 22 Aug. 2014.
22. For a comprehensive treatment of the nursing profession, see Institute of Medicine, *The Future of Nursing* (2011).
23. '"OPERATION LINDBERGH" A World First in TeleSurgery: The Surgical Act Crosses the Atlantic!', IRCAD, Press Conference 19 Sept. 2001 <http://www.ircad.fr/wp-content/uploads/2014/06/lindbergh_presse_en.pdf> (accessed 23 March 2015).
24. 'VA Telehealth Services Served Over 690,000 Veterans In Fiscal Year 2014', US Department of Veteran Affairs, 10 Oct. 2014 <http://www.va.gov/opa/pressrel/pressrelease.cfm?id=2646> (accessed 6 March 2015).
25. Sarah Neville, 'Hospital takes the pulse of nursing by video', *Financial Times*, 5 Oct. 2014 <http://www.ft.com/> (accessed 6 March 2015).
26. Mark Scott, 'Novartis Joins With Google to Develop Contact Lens That Monitors Blood Sugar', *New York Times*, 15 July 2014 <http://www.nytimes.com> (accessed 27 March 2015).
27. <https://www.bluestardiabetes.com>.
28. <http://www.eyenetra.com> (accessed 6 March 2015).

29. 'Mobile Medical Applications', FDA, 6 Apr. 2014 <http://www.fda.gov/MedicalDevices/ProductsandMedicalProcedures/ConnectedHealth/MobileMedicalApplications/ucm255978.htm> (accessed 6 March 2015).
30. Roy Kessels, 'Patients memory for medical information', *Journal of the Royal Society of Medicine*, 96: 5 (2003), 219–22.
31. David Cutler and Wendy Everett, 'Thinking Outside the Pillbox—Medication Adherence as a Priority for Health Care Reform', *New England Journal of Medicine*, 362: 17 (2010), 1553–5.
32. Tara Hovarth *et al.*, 'Mobile phone text messaging for promoting adherence to antiretroviral therapy in patients with HIV infection', *Cochrane Database of Systematic Reviews*, 3 (2012): <doi: 10.1002/14651858.CD009756> (accessed 27 March 2015).
33. Caroline Jones et al., '"Even if You Know Everything You Can Forget": Health Worker Perceptions of Mobile Phone Text-Messaging to Improve Malaria Case-Management in Kenya' *PLoS ONE*, 7: 6 (2012): <doi: 10.1371/journal.pone.0038636> (accessed 27 March 2015).
34. David Rose, *Enchanted Objects: Design, Human Desire, and the Internet of Things* (2014). It increases drug adherence by 23 percentage points (to 94%) compared with standard vials. See p. 130.
35. 'Emory University Hospital Explores "Intensive Care Unit of the Future"', IBM, 4 November 2013 <http://www-03.ibm.com/press/us/en/pressrelease/42362.wss> (accessed 6 March 2015).
36. Nick Bilton, 'Disruptions: Medicine that Monitors You', *New York Times*, 23 June 2013 <http://www.nytimes.com> (accessed 27 March 2015).
37. <http://www.patientslikeme.com> (accessed 27 March 2015).
38. Christina Farr and Alexei Oreskovic, 'Exclusive: Facebook plots first steps into healthcare', *Reuters*, 3 Oct. 2014 <http://www.reuters.com> (accessed 27 March 2015).
39. David Bray et al., 'Sermo: A Community-Based, Knowledge Ecosystem' (2008), <http://dx.doi.org/10.2139/ssrn.1016483> and <http://www.sermo.com> (accessed 27 March 2015).
40. <https://secure.quantiamd.com> (accessed 27 March 2015).
41. <https://www.doximity.com> (accessed 27 March 2015).
42. Daniel Gaitan, 'Crowdsourcing the answers to medical mysteries', *Reuters*, 1 Aug. 2014 <http://www.reuters.com> (accessed 27 March 2015).
43. <http://www.innocentive.com>.

44. <https://watsi.org>.
45. Jerome Groopman, 'Print Thyself: How 3-D Printing is Revolutionizing Medicine', *New Yorker*, 24 Nov. 2014.
46. e.g. 'vascular networks' in Luiz Bertassoni et al., 'Hydrogel bioprinted microchannel networks for vascularization of tissue engineering constructs', *Lab on a Chip*, 14: 13 (2014), 2202–11.
47. <http://www.organdonor.gov> and 'Fact Sheets: Transplants save lives', NHS website, Aug. 2014 <http://www.organdonation.nhs.uk/newsroom/fact_sheets/transplants_save_lives.asp> (accessed 9 March 2015).
48. Erika Check Hayden, 'Technology: The $1,000 Genome', *Nature*, 19 Mar. 2014.
49. Francis S. Collins, *The Language of Life: DNA and the Revolution in Personalized Medicine* (2010), p. xviii discusses the services, but their costs are now far lower. See e.g. the $99 service at <https://www.23andme.com> (accessed 27 March 2015).
50. Richard P. Feynman, 'Plenty of Room at the Bottom', talk to the American Physical Society at Caltech, Dec. 1959, p. 5 <http://www.pa.msu.edu/~yang/RFeynman_plentySpace.pdf> (accessed 27 March 2015).
51. Miguel Helft, 'Google's Larry Page: The Most Ambitious CEO in the Universe', *Fortune Magazine*, 13 Nov. 2014 <http://fortune.com> (accessed 27 March 2015).
52. David L. Jaffe, Drew Nelson, and John Thiemer, 'Perspectives in Assistive Technology', Stanford University Slides for ENGR110/210 <https://web.stanford.edu/class/engr110/2012/04b-Jaffe.pdf> (accessed 6 March 2015).
53. <http://www.media.mit.edu/research/groups/biomechatronics> (accessed 6 March 2015).
54. 'Difference Engine: The Caring Robot', *Economist*, 14 May 2013.
55. David Feil-Seifer and Maja J. Matarić, 'Defining Socially Assistive Robotics', *Proceedings of the 2005 IEEE 9th International Conference on Rehabilitation Robotics*, (2005).
56. Andrew Griffiths, 'How Paro the robotic seal is being used to help UK dementia patients', *Guardian*, 8 July 2014 <http://www.theguardian.com/> (accessed 27 March 2015).
57. 'Introducing Kaspar', University of Hertfordshire, <http://www.herts.ac.uk/kaspar/introducing-kaspar> (accessed 6 March 2015). Also see John-John Cabibihan et al., 'Why Robots? A Survey on the Roles and

Benefits of Social Robots in the Therapy of Children with Autism', *International Journal of Social Robotics*, 5: 4 (2013), 593–618.

58. We are grateful to Professor Yasunori Kasai for this insight.
59. <https://ai-therapy.com>.
60. 'Blended Learning', Rocketship Education, <http://www.rsed.org/Blended-Learning.cfm> (accessed 7 March 2015).
61. <http://newclassrooms.org>.
62. <http://www.matchbooklearning.com>.
63. <http://www.ednovate.org>.
64. Adam Newman, 'Learning to Adapt: Understanding the Adaptive Learning Supplier Landscape', *Tyton Partners*, 15 Apr. 2013. <http://tytonpartners.com/library/understanding-the-adaptive-learning-supplier-landscape/> (accessed 27 March 2015).
65. Benjamin S. Bloom, 'The 2 Sigma Problem: The Search for Methods of Group Instruction as Effective as One-to-One Tutoring', *Educational Researcher*, 13: 6 (1984), 4–16.
66. <https://www.edmodo.com> (accessed 7 March 2015).
67. <http://www.edudemic.com>, <http://www.edutopia.org>, <http://www.sharemylesson.com>.
68. <http://moodle.com>, <http://www.brightspace.com> (accessed 7 March 2015).
69. 'Khan Academy', *EdSurge* <https://www.edsurge.com/khan-academy> (accessed 7 March 2015).
70. 'Research on the Use of Khan Academy in Schools', *SRI Education*, Mar. 2014 <http://www.sri.com/sites/default/files/publications/2014-03-07_implementation_briefing.pdf> (accessed 7 March 2015).
71. In 2012 there were 3,912,540 pupils in state-funded primary schools, 3,225,540 in state-funded secondary schools, and private schools ~7 percent of total. From 'School capacity: academic year 2011 to 2012', *Department for Education*, 1 March 2013 <https://www.gov.uk/government/statistics/school-capacity-academic-year-2011-to-2012> (accessed 7 March 2015).
72. 'TED reaches its billionth video view!', TEDBlog, 13 Nov. 2013 <http://blog.ted.com/ted-reaches-its-billionth-video-view/> (accessed 7 March 2015).
73. <https://www.youtube.com/t/education> (accessed 7 March 2015).

74. 'Research on the Use of Khan Academy in Schools', *SRI Education*, Mar. 2014 <http://www.sri.com/sites/default/files/publications/2014-03-07_implementation_briefing.pdf> (accessed 7 March 2015).
75. 'Let's use video to reinvent education', a TED talk from Salman Khan, Mar. 2011 <http://www.ted.com/talks/salman_khan_let_s_use_video_to_reinvent_education?language=en> (accessed 7 March 2015).
76. 3.4 per cent in 2012, up from 1.7 per cent in 1999. 'Fast Facts', US Center for National Education Statistics <http://nces.ed.gov/fastfacts/display.asp?id=91> (accessed 7 March 2015).
77. 'The Digital Revolution and Higher Education', Pew Research Center, 28 Aug. 2011 <http://www.pewinternet.org/files/old-media//Files/Reports/2011/PIP-Online-Learning.pdf> (accessed 7 March 2015).
78. Precisely, there was an enrolment of 314,159 in Udacity's CS101 course. See e.g. <https://twitter.com/udacity/status/340643280528211968> (accessed 7 March 2015).
79. <https://www.coursera.org>, <https://www.edx.org> (accessed 7 March 2015).
80. Sean Couglan, 'Harvard plans to boldly go with "Spocs"', *BBC News*, 24 Sept. 2013 <http://www.bbc.co.uk/news/business-24166247> (accessed 7 March 2015).
81. <https://www.udemy.com>, <https://www.udacity.com>
82. 'Teachers' workload diary survey', Department for Education, Feb. 2014 <https://www.gov.uk/government/uploads/system/uploads/attachment_data/file/285941/DFE-RR316.pdf> (accessed 7 March 2015).
83. Caroline Porter and Melissa Korn, 'Can this Online Course Get Me a Job?', *Wall Street Journal*, 4 Mar. 2014 <http://www.wsj.com> (accessed 27 March 2015).
84. 'Apple: most popular app store categories 2015', Statista <http://www.statista.com/statistics/270291/popular-categories-in-the-app-store/> (accessed 7 March 2015).
85. John Doerr, 'Smart Phones for Smart Kids', *Wall Street Journal*, 21 Aug. 2014 <http://www.wsj.com> (accessed 27 March 2015).
86. See e.g. <http://www.coursesmart.com> and <https://www.classdojo.com>.

87. 'Feedback', 'individualization', and 'prediction' are the three possibilities for Big Data in education, set out in Viktor Mayer-Schönberger and Kenneth Cukier, *Learning with Big Data: The Future of Education* (2014).
88. <http://www.wikipedia.org> (accessed 7 March 2015).
89. The Directory of Open Access Journals, <http://doaj.org> (accessed 7 March 2015). Peer review is itself being challenged, for example, by Kathleen Fitzpatrick, *Planned Obsolescence: Publishing, Technology, and the Future of the Academy* (2011), and others who argue for more open 'peer-to-peer review' by larger, online communities of scholars.
90. Susannah Locke, 'The Gates Foundation pushes to make more academic research free and open to the public', *Vox*, 24 Nov. 2014 <http://www.vox.com> (accessed 7 March 2015).
91. 'Faculty Advisory Council Memorandum on Journal Pricing', Harvard University Library, 17 Apr. 2012 <http://isites.harvard.edu/icb/icb.do?keyword=k77982&tabgroupid=icb.tabgroup143448> (accessed 7 March 2015).
92. <https://www.duolingo.com>.
93. Larry Summers, 'What You (Really) Need to Know', *New York Times*, 20 Jan. 2012 <http://www.nytimes.com> (accessed 27 March 2015).
94. Saad Rizvi, Katelyn Donnelly, and Michael Barber, 'An Avalanche is Coming', *IPPR*, 11 Mar. 2013.
95. Jonathan Rose, *The Intellectual Life of the British Working Classes* (2001), 13.
96. Marc MacWilliams, 'Techno-Ritualization—The Gohonzon Controversy on the Internet', *Heidelberg Journal of Religions on the Internet*, 2.01 (2006) <http://archiv.ub.uni-heidelberg.de/volltextserver/6959/> (accessed 7 March 2015).
97. <https://twitter.com> (accessed 7 March 2015).
98. Bianca Bosker, 'Hook of Mormon: Inside the Church's Online-Only Missionary Army', *Huffington Post*, 4 Sept. 2014 <http://www.huffingtonpost.co.uk> (accessed 7 March 2015).
99. Rick Gladstone and Vindu Goel, 'ISIS Is Adept on Twitter, Study Finds', *New York Times*, 5 Mar. 2015 <http://www.nytimes.com> (accessed 7 March 2015).
100. Brian Johnson, 'This Week in the Future: Religion & Tech: A Match Made in Heaven', Shelly Palmer Blog, 13 Dec. 2012 <http://www.

shellypalmer.com/2012/2012/12/twtf-religion-and-tech> (accessed 27 March 2015).

101. We are grateful to Rabbi Gideon Sylvester for this point. Thus, the orthodox rabbi can never be 'disintermediated' (see Ch. 3).
102. Heidi Campbell (ed.), *Digital Religion: Understanding Religious Practice in New Media Worlds* (2013).
103. Heidi Campbell, 'Considering the Performance of Religious Indentity Online', Presentation at Faith 2.0: Religion and the Internet, The Royal Society of Arts, 14 Apr. 2011.
104. The Anglican Cathedral of Second Life <https://slangcath.wordpress.com> (accessed 14 April 2015).
105. Heinz Scheifinger, 'Hindu Worship Online and Offline', in *Digital Religion*, ed. Heidi Campbell.
106. 'OnIslam.net's Virtual Hajj on Second Life', OnIslam, 6 Nov. 2010 <http://www.onislam.net/english/news/global/449652-onislamnets-virtual-hajj-on-second-life.html> (accessed 7 March 2015).
107. John Micklethwait and Adrian Wooldridge, *God is Back: How the Global Revival of Faith is Changing the World* (2009), 268.
108. Casey N. Cep, 'Big Data for the Spirit', *New Yorker*, 5 Aug. 2014.
109. 'Catholic Church gives blessing to iPhone app', *BBC News*, 8 Feb. 2011 <http://www.bbc.co.uk/news> (accessed 27 March 2015).
110. Susan Elizabeth Prill, 'Sikhi through Internet, Films and Videos', in *The Oxford Handbook of Sikh Studies*, ed. Pshaura Singh and Louis E. Fenech (2014).
111. Micklethwait and Wooldridge, *God is Back*, 268.
112. <http://www.askmoses.com>.
113. <http://www.christianmingle.com>, <http://jdate.com>, <http://www.muslima.com>.
114. Emily Greenhouse, 'Treasures in the Wall', *New Yorker*, 1 Mar. 2013.
115. Lior Wolf et al., 'Identifying Join Candidates in the Cairo Genizah', *International Journal of Computer Vision*, 94: 1 (2011), 118–35.
116. Lior Wolf and Nachum Dershowitz, 'Automatic Scribal Analysis of Tibetan Writing', abstract for panel at the International Association for Tibetan Studies 2013 <http://www.cs.tau.ac.il/~wolf/papers/genizahijcv.pdf> (accessed 7 March 2015).

117. Adiel Ben-Shalom et al., 'Where is my Other Half?', *Digital Humanities* (2014). <http://www.genizah.org/professionalPapers/MyOtherHalf.pdf> (accessed 7 March 2015).
118. Idan Dershowitz et al., 'Computerized Source Criticism of Biblical Texts', published online (2014). <http://www.cs.tau.ac.il/~nachumd/ComputationalHumanities.html > (accessed 7 March 2015).
119. <http://www.beliefnet.com/Online-Media-Kit/Company-Profile.aspx> (accessed 7 March 2015).
120. <http://www.patheos.com/About-Patheos/Advertising.html> (accessed 7 March 2015).
121. Susan Elizabeth Prill, 'Sikhi through Internet, Films and Videos', in *The Oxford Handbook of Sikh Studies*, ed. Singh and Fenech.
122. e.g. <http://www.plumline.org>.
123. <http://en.wikipedia.org/wiki/Sangat_(term)> (accessed 7 March 2015).
124. Jennifer Preston, 'Facebook Page for Jesus, With Highly Active Fans', *New York Times*, 4 Sept. 2011 <http://www.nytimes.com> (accessed 27 March 2015).
125. Douglas E. Cowan and Jeffrey K. Hadden, 'Virtually Religious: New Religious Movements and the World Wide Web' in *The Oxford Handbook of New Religious Movements*, ed. James R. Lewis (2008).
126. Laurie Goodstein, 'Some Mormons Search the Web and Find Doubt', *New York Times*, 30 July 2013 <http://www.nytimes.com> (accessed 27 March 2015).
127. Dave Lee, 'How Scientology changed the internet', *BBC News*, 17 July 2013 <http://www.bbc.co.uk/news> (accessed 7 March 2015).
128. 'How Technology is Changing Millennial Faith', Barna, 15 October 2013 <https://www.barna.org/barna-update/millennials/640-how-technology-is-changing-millennial-faith> (accessed 7 March 2015).
129. Jonathan Zittrain and Benjamin Edelman, 'Documentation of Internet Filtering in Saudi-Arabia', 12 Sept. 2002 <http://cyber.law.harvard.edu/filtering/saudiarabia/> (accessed 7 March 2015).
130. Nathan Jeffay, 'Kosher Smart Phone Arrives as Ultra-Orthodox Tech Taboo Shifts', *Jewish Daily Forward*, 18 Sept. 2013 <http://www.forward.com> (accessed 7 March 2013).
131. Richard Susskind, *Tomorrow's Lawyers* (2013), p. xiii.

132. See e.g. Bruce MacEwen, *Growth Is Dead: Now What?: Law Firms on the Brink* (2013), Steven Harper, *The Lawyer Bubble: A Profession in Crisis* (2013), Mitch Kowalski, *Avoiding Extinction: Reimagining Legal Services for the 21st Century* (2012), George Beaton (ed.), *New Law New Rules* (2013), Jordan Furlong, 'The New World of Legal Work' (2014), at <http://www.lod.co.uk/media/pdfs/The_New_World_Of_Legal_Digital_Download.pdf> (accessed 25 March 2015).
133. Charles Dickens, *Bleak House* (1996), 14.
134. These changes are permitted in England and Wales under the Legal Services Act 2007, which has been in force since 2011.
135. This research was carried out in 2004. See <http://www.which.co.uk>. Also see various articles in *Consumer Policy Review*, 16: 6 (Nov.–Dec. 2006).
136. These and many other examples of alternative providers are discussed in <http://www.legalfutures.co.uk>.
137. <http://www.integreon.com>, <http://www.novuslaw.com>.
138. <http://thomsonreuters.com>. Two examples of new legal businesses acquired by Thomson Reuters are Pangea 3 (<http://www.pangea3.com>) and Practical Law (<http://uk.practicallaw.com>).
139. <http://www.riverviewlaw.com>. Alternative business structures were created by and are permitted under the Legal Services Act 2007.
140. <http://www.axiomlaw.com>.
141. <http://www.lod.co.uk>, <http://www.pinsentmasonsvario.com>.
142. e.g. Allen & Overy, Herbert Smith Freehills, and Simmons & Simmons. These and many others are described at <http://www.legalfutures.co.uk>.
143. This was anticipated in 1992 in Richard Susskind, 'Why Lawyers Should Consider Consultancy', *Financial Times*, 13 Oct. 1992.
144. <http://uk.westlaw.com> and <https://www.lexisnexis.com>.
145. Two useful periodicals on legal technology can be found at <http://www.legaltechnology.com>, <http://www.legaltechnews.com>.
146. <http://www.business-integrity.com> (ContractExpress), <http://www.exari.com>.
147. <http://www.epoq.co.uk>.
148. <http://www.docracy.com>.
149. <http://www.shakelaw.com>.
150. <http://www.austlii.edu.au>.

151. <http://www.legalzoom.com>, <https://www.rocketlawyer.com>.
152. <http://www.allenovery.com/online-services>.
153. <http://www.neotalogic.com>.
154. See e.g. <https://www.intralinks.com>, <http://www.digitalwarroom.com>.
155. See Maura Grossman and Gordon Cormack, 'Technology-Assisted Review in E-Discovery Can be More Effective and More Efficient Than Exhaustive Manual Review', *Richmond Journal of Law and Technology*, 17: 3 (2001), 1–48.
156. <https://lexmachina.com>.
157. Daniel Katz, Michael Bommarito, and Josh Blackman, 'Predicting the Behavior of the Supreme Court of the United States: A General Approach', 21 July 2014, at <http://dx.doi.org/10.2139/ssrn.2463244> (accessed 25 March 2015).
158. <https://kirasystems.com>, <http://ebrevia.com>.
159. Susskind, *Tomorrow's Lawyers*, 99–100.
160. Richard Susskind, 'Online disputes: is it time to end the "day in court"?', *The Times*, 26 Feb. 2015. The proposals can be found in Civil Justice Council, 'Online Dispute Resolution', Feb. 2015, at <https://www.judiciary.gov.uk/wp-content/uploads/2015/02/Online-Dispute-Resolution-Final-Web-Version1.pdf> (accessed 26 March 2015).
161. See John Ramseyer and Eric Rasmusen, 'Comparative Litigation Rates', The Harvard John M. Olin Discussion Paper Series, Discussion Paper No. 681, 7 Nov. 2010 <http://www.law.harvard.edu/programs/olin_center/papers/pdf/Ramseyer_681.pdf> (accessed 25 March 2015). They estimate ~5,806 suits per 100,000 people in the USA. If the US population is ~ 320m, then that is ~ 18.6m suits overall. On eBay's ODR, see Civil Justice Council, 'Online Dispute Resolution', Feb. 2015, at <https://www.judiciary.gov.uk/wp-content/uploads/2015/02/Online-Dispute-Resolution-Final-Web-Version1.pdf> (accessed 26 March 2015).
162. <http://www.modria.com>.
163. <http://www.paymd.com>.
164. <http://www.resolver.co.uk>.
165. <https://www.legalonramp.com>.
166. Susskind, *Tomorrow's Lawyers*, 89.
167. <http://www.avvo.com> (accessed 7 March 2015).
168. See e.g. <https://www.comparelegalcosts.co.uk>.

169. <https://www.priorilegal.com>.
170. See Paul Hodkinson, 'E-auctions: reviewing the review', *Legal Week*, 9 June 2005.
171. Richard Susskind, *The End of Lawyers?* (2008), 2.
172. It is true that in some parts of the world newspaper circulation is high and growing. But these tend to be less developed countries, and the current US experience remains a useful insight into where these industries might find themselves in the future.
173. Robert W. McChesney and John Nichols, *The Death and Life of American Journalism* (2010), 3.
174. Print circulation (000s) down from 54,626 to 40,420 from 2004 to 2014 (data from NAA, <http://www.naa.org/>). Population (m) up from 293.6 to 318.9 (data from US Census Bureau, <http://www.census.gov>). And so print circulation per capita is down from 0.186 to 0.127, around 32% (accessed 4 May 2015).
175. From 54,200 to 36,700 full-time daily newspaper journalists 2004–14. Total workforce data from American Society of News Editors <http://asne.org/> (accessed 7 March 2015).
176. 'The Late Edition', *Economist*, 26 Apr. 2014.
177. George Brock, *Out of Print: Newspapers, Journalism, and the Business of News in the Digital Age* (2013), 149.
178. 'Internet Overtakes Newspapers as News Outlet', Pew Research Center, 23 Dec. 2008 <http://www.people-press.org> (accessed 7 March 2015).
179. Andrea Caumot, '12 trends shaping digital news', Pew Research Center, 16 Oct. 2013 <http://www.pewresearch.org> (accessed 7 March 2015).
180. 'Internet Access—Households and Individuals 2014', Office for National Statistics, 7 Aug. 2014 <http://www.ons.gov.uk/ons/index.html> (accessed 7 March 2015).
181. 'The Internet Economy on the Rise: Progress since the Seoul Declaration', OECD, Sept. 2013.
182. 'Digital News Report 2014', Reuters Institute for the Study of Journalism <http://www.digitalnewsreport.org> (accessed 7 March 2015).
183. Eric Alterman, 'Out of Print: The Death and Life of the American Newspaper', *New Yorker*, 31 Mar. 2008.
184. 'The Late Edition', *Economist*, 26 Apr. 2014.

185. 'Amid Criticism, Support for Media's "Watchdog" Role Stands Out', Pew Research Center, 8 Aug. 2013 <http://www.pewresearch.org> (accessed 7 March 2015).
186. Clay Shirky, 'Last Call: The End of the Printed Newspaper', *Medium*, 19 Aug. 2015 <https://medium.com> (accessed 7 March 2015).
187. The *Evening Standard* in London, for example, was making annual losses of £30 million before 2009. It became a free paper and made a £2.5 million profit in 2013. Arif Durrani, 'London Evening Standard profits double in 2013', *Media Week*, 17 Jan. 2014 <http://www.mediaweek.co.uk> (accessed 8 March 2015).
188. Kenneth Olmstead, Amy Mitchell, and Tom Rosensteil, 'The Top 25', Pew Research Center, 9 May 2011 <http://www.journalism.org> (accessed 8 March 2015).
189. Mark Sweney, 'The Guardian overtakes New York Times in comScore traffic figures', *Guardian*, 21 Oct. 2014 <http://www.theguardian.com/> (accessed 20 March 2015).'ABCs: National daily newspaper circulation September 2014', *Guardian*, 10 Oct. 2014 <http://www.theguardian.com/> (accessed 20 March 2015).
190. $3.42bn of $37.59bn. From 'Business model evolving, circulation revenue rising', Newspaper Association of America, 18 April 2014 <http://www.naa.org/Trends-and-Numbers/Newspaper-Revenue/Newspaper-Media-Industry-Revenue-Profile-2013.aspx> (accessed 8 March 2015).
191. 'Digital News Report 2014', Reuters Institute for the Study of Journalism <http://www.digitalnewsreport.org> (accessed 7 March 2015).
192. Facebook Newsroom, <http://newsroom.fb.com/company-info/> (accessed 8 March 2015).
193. <https://twitter.com> (accessed 8 March 2015).
194. <https://www.youtube.com> (accessed 8 March 2015).
195. 'Digital News Report 2014', Reuters Institute for the Study of Journalism <http://www.digitalnewsreport.org> (accessed 7 March 2015).
196. Nic Newman, 'Journalism, Media, and Technology Predictions 2013', accessed online <https://docs.google.com/file/d/0B-whYpjV6DzWUER1VjgySzB1OG8/edit> (8 March 2015).
197. David Carr, 'Facebook Offers Life Raft, but Publishers Are Wary', *New York Times*, 26 Oct. 2014 <http://www.nytimes.com> (accessed 8 March 2015).

198. Lauren Goode, 'Susan Wojcicki Wants to Sell You Youtube Video Subscriptions (Video)', re/code, 27 Oct. 2014 <http://recode.net> (accessed 8 March 2015).
199. 1.39bn total monthly users, 1.19bn mobile monthly users. From <http://newsroom.fb.com/company-info/> (accessed 27 March 2015).
200. Nic Newman, 'Mainstream media and the distribution of news in the age of social discovery', Reuters Institute for the Study of Journalism, Sept. 2011 <https://reutersinstitute.politics.ox.ac.uk> (accessed 8 March 2015).
201. John Reynolds, 'Three-fifth's of Twitter's UK users follow a newspaper or journalist', *Guardian*, 4 Mar. 2014 <http://www.theguardian.com/> (accessed 8 March 2015).
202. 'ABCs: National daily newspaper circulation September 2014', *Guardian*, 10 Oct. 2014 <http://www.theguardian.com/> and <https://twitter.com> (accessed 8 March 2015).
203. David Carr, 'Facebook Offers Life Raft, but Publishers Are Wary', *New York Times*, 26 Oct. 2014 <http://www.nytimes.com> (accessed 8 March 2015).
204. Lizzie Widdicombe, 'From Mars', *New Yorker*, 23 Sept. 2013.
205. Scott E. Gant, *We're All Journalists Now* (2007).
206. Roy Greenslade, 'Huffington Post beats the New York Times to top news website chart', *Guardian*, 10 June 2011 <http://www.theguardian.com/> (accessed 8 March 2015).
207. Christian Caryl, 'Why Wikileaks Changes Everything', *New York Review of Books*, 13 Jan. 2011.
208. The New York Times Innovation Report, retrieved from Jason Abbruzzese, 'The Full New York Times Innovation Report', *Mashable*, 16 May 2014 <http://mashable.com> (accessed 8 March 2015).
209. Derek Thompson, 'The Facebook Effect on the News', *Atlantic*, 12 Feb. 2014 <http://www.theatlantic.com> (27 March 2015).
210. <http://www.vox.com>, <https://www.themarshallproject.org>, <http://www.realclearpolitics.com>, <http://fivethirtyeight.com>.
211. <https://chartbeat.com>.
212. Kenneth Olmstead et al., 'News Video on the Web', Pew Research Center, 26 Mar. 2014 <http://www.journalism.org> (accessed 8 March 2014).
213. Nicholas Negroponte, *Being Digital* (1995), 152–4.

214. The New York Times Innovation Report, retrieved from Jason Abbruzzese, 'The Full New York Times Innovation Report', *Mashable*, 16 May 2014 <http://mashable.com> (accessed 8 March 2015).
215. Ravi Somaiya, 'How Facebook is Changing the Way Its Users Consume Journalism', 26 Oct. 2014 <http://www.nytimes.com> (accessed 8 March 2015).
216. <http://www.storyful.com> (accessed 8 March 2015).
217. <https://www.grammarly.com>, <https://www.evernote.com>.
218. Paul Colford, 'A Leap Forward in Quarterly Earnings Stories', The Definitive Source blog at Associated Press, 30 June 2014 <http://blog.ap.org/2014/06/30/a-leap-forward-in-quarterly-earnings-stories/> (accessed 8 March).
219. <http://www.forbes.com> See e.g. 'Earnings Increase Expected for Dick's Sporting Goods', *Forbes*, 3 Feb. 2015. The author on that piece is 'Narrative Science', an algorithm. (accessed 27 March 2015).
220. Timothy Aeppel, 'This Wasn't Written by an Algorithm, But More and More Is', *Wall Street Journal*, 15 Dec. 2014 <http://www.wsj.com> (accessed 8 March).
221. Christer Clerwall, 'Enter the Robot Journalist', *Journalism Practice*, 8: 5 (2014), 519–31.
222. Clayton Christensen, Dina Wang, and Derek van Bever, 'Consulting on the Cusp of Disruption', *Harvard Business Review*, Oct. 2013 <https://hbr.org> (accessed 8 March 2015).
223. Duff McDonald, *The Firm: The Story of McKinsey and Its Secret Influence on American Business* (2013), 325.
224. Lucy Kellaway, 'McKinsey's airy platitudes bode ill for its next half-century', *The Financial Times*, 14 Sept. 2014 <http://www.ft.com/> (accessed 8 March 2015).
225. Christopher D. McKenna, *The World's Newest Profession: Management Consulting in the Twentieth Century* (2010).
226. Sophie Christie, 'Tesco Clubcard vs Nectar: Best loyalty schemes', *Telegraph*, 30 Aug. 2013 <http://www.telegraph.co.uk> (accessed 8 March 2015).
227. Walter Kiechel, *The Lords of Strategy: The Secret Intellectual History of the New Corporate World* (2010), 65.

228. See 'Q1 2014 Revenue up 2.3 percent Crossed the 50,000 Employee Threshold in India', CapGemini Newsroom, 29 April 2014 <http://www.capgemini.com/investor/press/q1-2014-revenue-up-23-crossed-the-50000-employee-threshold-in-india> (accessed 8 March 2015); Mini Joseph Tejaswi, 'Accenture to hire aggressively in India', *Times of India*, 18 July 2012 <www.timesofindia.indiatimes.com> (accessed 8 March 2015).
229. Clayton Christensen, Dina Wang, and Derek van Bever, 'Consulting on the Cusp of Disruption', *Harvard Business Review*, Oct. 2013 <https://hbr.org> (accessed 8 March 2015).
230. <http://www.deloittemanagedanalytics.com> (accessed 8 March 2015).
231. Clayton Christensen, Dina Wang, and Derek van Bever, 'Consulting on the Cusp of Disruption', *Harvard Business Review*, Oct. 2013 <https://hbr.org> (accessed 8 March 2015).
232. <http://www.behaviouralinsights.co.uk>.
233. Hal R. Varian, 'Computer Mediated Transactions', *American Economic Review*, 100: 2 (2010), 1–10.
234. <http://glg.it>, <http://www.guidepointglobal.com> (accessed 8 March 2015).
235. <http://www.edenmccallum.com>, <http://www.businesstalentgroup.com>, <http://www.castprofessionals.com> (accessed 8 March 2015).
236. <http://www.10eqs.com> (accessed 8 March 2015).
237. <http://www.expert360.com>, <http://www.skillbridge.co>, <http://vumero.com> (accessed 8 March 2015).
238. <http://www.executiveboard.com> (accessed 8 March 2015).
239. 'Become an Analyst', Wikistrat <http://www.wikistrat.com/become-an-analyst/> (accessed 8 March 2015).
240. <http://www.kaggle.com> (accessed 8 March 2015).
241. Derrick Harris, 'Has Ayasdi turned machine learning into a magic bullet?', Gigaom, 16 Jan. 2013 <https://gigaom.com> (accessed 8 March 2015).
242. Tom Simonite, 'Watson Groomed as C-Suite Advisor', *MIT Technology Review*, 4 Aug. 2014 <http://www.technologyreview.com> (accessed 8 March 2015).
243. Tracy Alloway and Arash Massoudi, 'Goldman Sachs leads $15m financing of data service for investors', *Financial Times*, 23 Nov. 2014 <http://www.ft.com> (accessed 8 March 2015).

244. Clayton Christensen, Dina Wang, and Derek van Bever, 'Consulting on the Cusp of Disruption', *Harvard Business Review*, Oct. 2013 <https://hbr.org> (accessed 8 March 2015).
245. Jerry Useem, 'Business School, Disrupted', *New York Times*, 31 May 2014 <http://www.nytimes.com> (accessed 8 March 2015).
246. Erika Andersen, 'Why Writing a Book is Good Business', *Forbes*, 12 Oct. 2012 <http://www.forbes.com> (accessed 8 March 2015).
247. <https://itunes.apple.com/us/app/minto/id538500088?mt=8> (accessed 8 March 2015).
248. See both 'Management Consulting: To the Brainy, the Spoils', *Economist*, 11 May 2013 and 'Consultancy Firms: Strategic Moves', *Economist*, 9 Nov. 2013.
249. Michael Rapoport, 'Big Four Firms to Be Questioned on Push into Consulting', *Wall Street Journal*, 9 Dec. 2013 <http://www.wsj.com> (accessed 8 March 2015).
250. 'Deloitte 2012 Global Report', Deloitte <http://public.deloitte.com/media/0564/pdfs/DTTL_2012GlobalReport.pdf> (accessed 8 March 2015), and 'Deloitte Global Impact 2013', Deloitte <http://public.deloitte.com/media/0565/downloads/2013GlobalImpact.pdf> (accessed 8 March 2015).
251. See also Charles D. Ellis, *What It Takes: Seven Secrets of Success from the World's Greatest Professional Firms* (2013), ch. 1.
252. 'Our experts describe you as an appallingly dull fellow, unimaginative, timid, lacking in initiative, spineless, easily dominated, no sense of humor, tedious company, and irrepressibly drab and awful, and whereas in most professions, these would be considerable drawbacks, in chartered accountancy, they're a positive boon!' See <http://www.ibras.dk/montypython/episode10.htm> (accessed 8 March 2015).
253. '2012 Annual Report to Congress—Volume 1', Taxpayer Advocate Service at the IRS, 9 January 2013 <http://www.taxpayeradvocate.irs.gov/2012-Annual-Report/FY-2012-Annual-Report-To-Congress-Full-Report.html> (accessed 8 March 2015).
254. <https://turbotax.intuit.com/>, <http://www.hrblock.com>, <http://www.taxact.com>.
255. These were 47,946,000 self-prepared e-filing receipts, 125,821,000 total e-filing receipts, and 149,684,000 total individual income tax returns

(online and paper). '2014 Filing Season Statistics', IRS, 26 December 2014 <http://www.irs.gov/uac/Dec-26-2014> (accessed 27 March 2015).

256. <https://ttlc.intuit.com/>, <http://community.hrblock.com/>.
257. <http://quickbooks.intuit.com>, <https://www.xero.com/>, <http://www.kashflow.com>.
258. See HM Revenue & Customs, 'Making Tax Easier', March 2015, <https://www.gov.uk/government/uploads/system/uploads/attachment_data/file/413975/making-tax-easier.pdf> (accessed 14 March 2015).
259. 'Record to report cycle—tax compliance and reporting', Deloitte, 2014, <https://www2.deloitte.com/content/dam/Deloitte/global/Documents/Tax/dttl-tax-tmc-technology-landscape-2014.pdf> (accessed 8 March 2015).
260. 'European VAT refund guide 2014', Deloitte Global Tax Center (Europe), 2014 <http://www2.deloitte.com/content/dam/Deloitte/global/Documents/Tax/dttl-tax-vat-refund-guide-gtce-2014.pdf> (accessed 8 March 2015).
261. 'Electronic Arm Twisting', *Economist*, 17 May 2014.
262. Elisabetta Povoledo, 'Italians Have a New Tool to Unearth Tax Cheats', *New York Times*, 27 Jan. 2013 <http://www.nytimes.com> (accessed 8 March 2015).
263. Reed Albergotte, 'IRS, States Call on IBM, LexisNexis, SAS to Fight Fraud', *Wall Street Journal*, 22 July 2013 <http://www.wsj.com> (accessed 8 March 2015).
264. Abbi Hobbs, 'Big Data, Crime and Security', Houses of Parliament Postnote no. 470, July 2014 <http://www.parliament.uk> (accessed 8 March 2015).
265. Lucy Warwick-Ching and Vanessa Houlder, 'Ten Ways HMRC Checks if You're Cheating', *Financial Times*, 16 Nov. 2012 <http://www.ft.com> (accessed 8 March 2015).
266. Carl Benedikt Frey and Michael Osborne, 'The Future of Employment: How Susceptible Are Jobs to Computerisation', 17 Sept. 2013 <http://www.oxfordmartin.ox.ac.uk/downloads/academic/The_Future_of_Employment.pdf> (accessed 23 March 2015).
267. '2012 Annual Report to Congress—Volume 1', Taxpayer Advocate Service at the IRS, 9 January 2013 <http://www.taxpayeradvocate.irs.gov/2012-Annual-Report/FY-2012-Annual-Report-To-Congress-Full-Report.html> (accessed 8 March 2015).

268. See Richard Susskind, *Expert Systems in Law* (1987), 208–13.
269. 'Key Facts and Trends in the Accountancy Profession', Financial Reporting Council, June 2014 <https://www.frc.org.uk/Our-Work/Publications/FRC-Board/Key-Facts-and-Trends-in-the-Accountancy-Profession.pdf> (accessed 8 March 2015).
270. 'Our Audit Methodology', KPMG, <https://www.kpmg.com/eg/en/services/audit/pages/ourauditmethodology.aspx> (accessed 8 March 2015), 'Transparency Report 2014', EY Global, <http://www.ey.com/Publication/vwLUAssets/EY-Global-Transparency-Report-2014/$FILE/EY-Global-Transparency-Report-2014.pdf> (accessed 8 March 2015).
271. 'Transparency Report: Building trust through assurance', PwC UK, 30 June 2014 <http://www.pwc.co.uk/en_UK/uk/transparencyreport/assets/pdf/transparency-report-fy14.pdf> (accessed 8 March 2015).
272. John C. Coffee, *Gatekeepers: The Role of the Professions and Corporate Governance* (2006), 15.
273. 'The Dozy Watchdogs', *Economist*, 13 Dec. 2014.
274. James Shanteau, 'Cognitive Heuristics and Biases in Behavioral Auditing: Review, Comments, and Observations', *Accounting, Organizations, and Society*, 14: 1 (1989), 165–77.
275. James P. Liddy, 'The Future of Audit', *Forbes*, 4 Aug. 2014 <http://www.forbes.com> (accessed 8 March 2015).
276. Viktor Mayer-Schönberger and Kenneth Cukier, *Big Data: A Revolution That Will Transform How we Live, Work, and Think* (2013), 26.
277. Mayer-Schönberger and Cukier, *Big Data*, 32.
278. Mayer-Schönberger and Cukier, *Big Data*, and James Surowiekcki, 'A Billion Prices Now', *New Yorker*, 30 May 2011.
279. Michael Andersen, 'Four crowdsourcing lessons from the Guardian's (spectacular) expenses-scandal experiment', NiemanLab, 23 June 2009 <http://www.niemanlab.org> (accessed 8 March 2015).
280. <https://www.xbrl.org>.
281. For instance, 'the long shadow of the gentleman architect still hangs over the profession', in Dickon Robinson et al., 'The Future for Architects?', *Building Futures*, 25 Feb. 2011 <http://www.buildingfutures.org.uk/assets/downloads/The_Future_for_Architects_Full_Report_2.pdf> (accessed 8 March 2015).

282. 'Pathways and Gateways: the structure and regulation of architectural education', UK Architectural Education Review Group, April 2013 <http://people.bath.ac.uk/absaw/files/> (accessed 8 March 2015).
283. See 'The RIBA Education Review—updated August 2014', RIBA Education Department, August 2014 <http://www.architecture.com/Files/RIBA ProfessionalServices/Education/Validation/RIBAEducationReviewAugust 2014update.pdf> (accessed 8 March 2015); 'Becoming a solicitor—Costs of qualifying', The Law Society, Mar. 2015 <http://www.lawsociety.org.uk/law-careers/becoming-a-solicitor/costs-of-qualifying/> (accessed 8 March 2015); and 'Debt "putting off" medical students, BMA warns', *BBC News*, 19 May 2012 <http://www.bbc.co.uk/> (accessed 8 March 2015).
284. Oliver Wainwright, 'Pressure builds for change in Britain's schools of architecture', *Guardian*, 27 June 2013 <http://www.theguardian.com/> (accessed 8 March 2015).
285. Dana Cuff and John Wriedt (eds.), *Architecture from the Outside In: Selected Essays by Robert Gutman* (2010), 229.
286. Rory Stott, 'Does the Cost of Architectural Education Create a Barrier to the Profession?', *ArchDaily*, 29 May 2013 <http://www.archdaily.com> (accessed 8 March 2015).
287. David Ross Scheer, *The Death of Drawing* (2014).
288. This is taken from Scheer, *The Death of Drawing*, 139–45, a clear exposition of the different types of computational design.
289. 'Project Dreamcatcher', Autodesk, 2015. <http://autodeskresearch.com/projects/dreamcatcher> (accessed 8 March 2015).
290. <http://www.sketchup.com>, <http://www.chiefarchitect.com>, <http://www.mattermachine.com>.
291. Steven Kurutz, 'Computer Programs Help Users Bypass the Architect', *New York Times*, 20 June 2012 <http://www.nytimes.com> (accessed 8 March 2015).
292. <http://www.webuildhomes.nl/en> (accessed 8 March 2015).
293. <http://www.arcbazar.com>.
294. See both 'WikiHouse 4.0', WikiHouse website, <http://www.wikihouse.cc/news-2/> (accessed 8 March 2015), and also Rory Stott, 'WikiHouse Unveils World's First Two-Storey Open-Source House at London Design Festival', *ArchDaily*, 22 Sept. 2014 <http://www.archdaily.com/> (accessed 8 March 2015).
295. <http://www.paperhouses.co>.

296. <http://openarchitecturenetwork.org> (accessed 9 March 2015).
297. Andrew Blackman, 'Real-Estate Crowdfunding Finds Its Footing', *Wall Street Journal*, 13 Apr. 2014 <http://www.wsj.com> (accessed 9 March 2015).
298. <http://www.luchtsingel.org/en/> (accessed 9 March 2015).
299. Naushad Forbes, 'India's Higher Education Opportunity', in *Economic Reform in India: Challenges, Prospects, and Lessons*, ed. Nicholas C. Hope et al. (2014), 261.
300. Marcus Fairs, 'In the future we might print not only buildings, but entire urban sections', 21 May 2013, *Dezeen magazine*, <http://www.dezeen.com> (accessed 27 March 2015).
301. Rory Olcayto, 'How 3D printing could transform building design', *Financial Times*, 30 May 2014 <http://www.ft.com/> (accessed 8 March 2015).
303. Kelly Smith, 'Minnesota man builds castle with 3-D concrete printer', *Minnesota Star Tribune*, 2 Sept. 2014 <http://www.startribune.com> (accessed 9 March 2015).
304. Chris Anderson, *Makers: The New Industrial Revolution* (2012), 52.
305. Norman Hack and Willi Viktor Lauer, 'Mesh-Mould: Robotically Fabricated Spatial Meshes as Reinforced Concrete Formwork', *Architectural Design*, 84: 3 (2014), 44–53.
306. AKT II, *deliverance of Design* (2013) and 'UK Pavilion: Shanghai Expo 2010', Heatherwick Studio website <http://www.heatherwick.com/uk-pavilion/> (accessed 9 March 2015).
307. <http://brickdesign.rob-technologies.com>.
308. <http://gramaziokohler.arch.ethz.ch/web/e/forschung/221.html> (accessed 9 March 2015).
309. Matthias Kohler, Fabio Gramazio, and Jan Williamson, *The Robotic Touch: How Robots Change Architecture* (2014), 310–23.
310. Justin Werfel, 'Collective Construction with Robot Swarms', in *Morphogenetic Engineering: Understanding Complex Systems*, ed. René Doursat, Hiroki Sayama, and Olivier Michel (2012).
311. Michael Rubenstein, Alejandro Cornejo, and Radhika Nagpal, 'Programmable self-assembly in a thousand-robot swarm', *Science*, 345: 6198 (2014), 795–9.
312. Neri Oxman et al., 'Towards Robotic Swarm Printing', *Architectural Design*, 84: 3 (2014), 108–15.

313. <https://3dwarehouse.sketchup.com>, <https://grabcad.com> (accessed 9 March 2015).
314. <http://www.grasshopper3d.com/forum>.
315. <http://archinect.com>, <http://architizer.com>, <https://www.pinterest.com>.
316. 'archdaily.com', Alexa, <http://www.alexa.com/siteinfo/archdaily.com> (accessed 9 March 2015).
317. We have used this quotation from Gibson in two earlier books. See Susskind, *The End of Lawyers?*, 21, and *Tomorrow's Lawyers*, 90.

3. Patterns across the Professions

1. David H. Maister, *Managing the Professional Service Firm* (1993), p. xv.
2. As noted in Chapter 1, we take the term 'post-professional society' from Illich. See Ivan Illich, 'Disabling Professions' in *Disabling Professions*, ed. Irving K. Zola et al. (2000).
3. W. Chan Kim and Renée Mauborgne, *Blue Ocean Strategy* (2005).
4. Clayton Christensen, *The Innovator's Dilemma* (1997).
5. Paul Geroski and Constantinos Markides, *Fast Second* (2005).
6. Philip Augar, *The Death of Gentlemanly Capitalism: The Rise and Fall of London's Investment Banks* (2008).
7. Richard Susskind, *Tomorrow's Lawyers* (2013), 19–22.
8. This is an updated version of the distinction between 'automation' and 'innovation' in Richard Susskind, *The Future of Law* (1996), 49–50.
9. Richard Susskind, *Tomorrow's Lawyers, The End of Lawyers?* (2010), and *The Future of Law*.
10. See Clayton Christensen, *The Innovator's Dilemma* (1997), and Jill Lepore, 'The Disruption Machine', *New Yorker*, 23 June 2014.
11. See e.g. Clayton Christensen and Henry Eyring, *The Innovative University* (2011).
12. Joseph Schumpeter describes the process of 'creative destruction' in *Capitalism, Socialism and Democracy* (1994), foreshadowing this contemporary literature. See part II, ch. VII.
13. See e.g. <http://www.data.gov> for the USA, <http://data.gov.uk> for the UK, and <http://www.data.go.jp> for Japan.

14. Erik Brynjolfsson and Andrew McAfee, *The Second Machine Age* (2014), ch. 12.
15. Most notably, the Sarbanes–Oxley Act of 2002 (enacted 30 July 2002), known also as the 'Public Company Accounting Reform and Investor Protection Act'. This is part of the federal law of the USA.
16. See e.g. *Glasgow Herald*, 18 Nov.1985, p. 15.
17. <http://www.ey.com> (accessed 23 March 2015).
18. Atul Gawande, *The Checklist Manifesto* (2010), 34.
19. Gawande, *The Checklist Manifesto*, 36.
20. See Yochai Benkler, *The Wealth of Networks—How Social Production Transforms Markets and Freedom* (2006).
21. <http://www.tripadvisor.co.uk>.
22. See Eric Topol, *The Patient Will See You Now* (2015), on driverless cars and doctorless patients.
23. Penelope Eckert, 'Communities of Practice', in *The Encyclopedia of Language and Linguistics*, ed. Keith Brown (2006).
24. James Surowiecki, *The Wisdom of Crowds* (2004).
25. See e.g. David Maister, *Managing the Professional Service Firm* (1993).
26. See e.g. the Sarbanes–Oxley Act of 2002 in the USA (n. 15 above).
27. Directive 2014/56/EU of the European Parliament and of the Council of 16 April 2014 amending Directive 2006/43/EC on statutory audits of annual accounts and consolidated accounts.
28. With original emphasis, from Herbert L. A. Hart, 'Bentham and the Demystification of the Law', *Modern Law Review*, 36: 1 (1973), 2.
29. Harold J. Laski, *The Limitations of the Expert*, Fabian Tract 235 (1931), 14.

4. Information and Technology

1. We first introduced this concept in the mid-1990s, in Richard Susskind, *The Future of Law* (1996).
2. Walter Ong, *Orality and Literacy* (1982).
3. We can anticipate a fifth stage, but it is beyond the scope of this book—this is the likely stage in the development of humanity when human beings become digitally enhanced, when machines and human beings

become entwined and even indistinguishable. Some of these themes are touched on in Nick Bostrom, *Superintelligence* (2014).

4. Ong, *Orality and Literacy*, Marshall McLuhan, *Understanding Media* (2002), Luciano Floridi, *The Philosophy of Information* (2013), James Gleick, *The Information* (2011), and the works to which they refer.
5. Ong, *Orality and Literacy*, 31.
6. Gleick, *The Information*, and his discussion of Plato, who spoke of the 'forgetfulness' of those who do 'not practice their memory' (p. 30). See also Ong, *Orality and Literacy*, 79–81.
7. See our discussion of 'retrospective modernism' in section 1.9.
8. Ong, *Orality and Literacy*, 83–4.
9. Ong, *Orality and Literacy*, 7.
10. Gleick, *The Information*, 31.
11. Susskind, *The Future of Law*, 58.
12. Susskind, *The Future of Law*, 96. Original emphasis.
13. Susskind, *The Future of Law*, 96.
14. Peter Drucker, *Management: Tasks, Responsibilities, Practices* (1993), 44.
15. Mathematically, we mean something precise when we say that a variable is growing 'exponentially'—that the variable is changing at a rate that is proportional to the current value of that variable. The particular constant of proportionality that describes the pattern of growth is called 'growth rate'. As a result, growth can be 'exponential', but also take place at different 'rates'.
16. Gordon E Moore, 'Cramming More Components onto Integrated Circuits', *Electronics*, 38: 8 (1965), 114–17.
17. Ray Kurzweil, *The Singularity is Near* (2005), 111–12, and Ralph Cavin, Paolo Lugli, and Viktor Zhirnov, 'Science and Engineering Beyond Moore's Law', *Proceedings of the IEEE*, 100 (2012), 1720–49.
18. On the assumption that the piece of paper is 0.06 mm thick. See e.g. Adrian Paenza, 'How folding paper can get you to the moon', Ted-Ed video, <http://ed.ted.com/lessons/how-folding-paper-can-get-you-to-the-moon> (accessed 27 March 2015).
19. Ray Kurzweil, *How to Create a Mind* (2012), 249. Also see Kurzweil, *The Singularity is Near*, chs. 2 and 3.
20. Kurzweil, *The Singularity is Near*, 7–8.
21. Kurzweil, *The Singularity is Near*, 22–6.

22. Kurzweil, *The Singularity is Near*, 127.
23. Kurzweil, *How to Create a Mind*, 248–61.
24. The economic impact of this network effect is discussed by Michael Spence in his Nobel Prize lecture of 2001. See Michael Spence, 'Signaling in Retrospect and the Informational Structure of Markets', Nobel Prize Lecture, 8 Dec. 2001.
25. Jonathan Koomey et al., 'Implications of Historical Trends in the Electrical Efficiency of Computing', *Annals of the History of Computing*, 33: 3 (2011), 46–54.
26. See ongoing discussions on Kurzweil's website <www.kurzweilai.net>. Also see Bill Joy, 'Why the Future Doesn't Need Us', *Wired* (Apr. 2000). Kurzweil checks his own homework in 'How My Predictions are Faring', Oct. 2010 <http://www.kurzweilai.net/images/How-My-Predictions-Are-Faring.pdf> (accessed 27 March 2015).
27. See e.g. Joel Garreau, *Radical Evolution* (2005), and 'Coming To an Office Near You', *Economist*, 18 Jan. 2014.
28. See e.g. the work of Singularity University at <http://singularityu.org> (accessed 23 March 2015).
29. For a clear introduction to the cloud and cloud computing, and a clear indication of its mounting signifiance, see Kuan Hon and Christopher Millard, 'Cloud Technologies and Services', in *Cloud Computing Law*, ed. Christopher Millard (2013).
30. John Kelly and Steve Hamm, *Smart Machines* (2013).
31. Nick Bostrom, *Superintelligence* (2014).
32. See e.g. Tim Bradshaw, 'Scientists and Investors Warn on AI', *Financial Times*, 12 Jan. 2015.
33. Kelly and Hamm, *Smart Machines*, and Kieron O'Hara et al., *Web Science: Understanding the Emergence of Macro-Level Features of the World Wide Web* (2013).
34. Soshana Zuboff, *In the Age of the Smart Machine* (1988), 9.
35. Zuboff, *In the Age of the Smart Machine*, 10.
36. Some writers treat 'machine learning' as yet another synonym. See e.g. Eric Siegel, *Predictive Analytics* (2013). We find this unhelpful, because 'machine learning' is a term that is used in a different sense by AI scientists, referring (approximately) to systems that can learn from experience.
37. Tim Harford, 'Big Data: Are We Making a Big Mistake?', *Financial Times*, 28 Mar. 2014 <http://www.ft.com> (accessed 23 March 2015). On the

other hand, for a sophisticated and broadly supportive introduction to Big Data, although admittedly from Google's Chief Economist, see Hal Varian, 'Big Data: New Tricks for Econometrics', *Journal of Economic Perspectives*, 28: 2 (2014), 3–28.

38. Marshall Kirkpatrick, 'Google CEO Eric Schmidt: "People Aren't Ready For The Technology Revolution"' <http://www.huffingtonpost.com/> (accessed 23 March 2015). There has been some debate over how much information was generated up to 2003. While Schmidt said 5 exabytes, 23 exabytes has been said to be nearer the mark. See e.g. Klint Finley, 'Was Eric Schmidt Wrong About the Historical Scale of the Internet?' <http://readwrite.com/2011/02/07/are-we-really-creating-as-much> (accessed 23 March 2015). The currently accepted tally is that 3 exabytes is currently created each day.
39. Kelly and Hamm predict that, by 2020, there will be 'a data universe of 40 zettabytes of digital stuff': *Smart Machines*, 44. It is explained there that a 'zettabyte is a decidely *big* number: a 1 followed by 21 zeros. One zettabyte of storage would hold 250 billion two-hour HD movies' (p. 44); original emphasis. An exabyte is a mere 1 followed by 18 zeros.
40. Kelly and Hamm, *Smart Machines*, 69.
41. Viktor Mayer-Schönberger and Kenneth Cukier, *Big Data* (2013), 53–4 and 191.
42. Jacques Bughin and James Manyika. *Internet Matters: Essays in Digital Transformation* (2011), 102–3.
43. Mayer-Schönberger and Cukier, *Big Data*, 12–13.
44. Siegel, *Predictive Analytics*, 3; original emphasis.
45. Siegel, *Predictive Analytics*, 3.
46. Personal correspondence. Our thanks to Nigel Shadbolt for drawing our attention to this quotation. Also see Patrick Winston, *Artificial Intelligence* (1993).
47. For a detailed introduction to the history of Watson, see Stephen Baker, *Final Jeopardy: Man vs Machine and the Quest to Know Everything* (2011).
48. See IBM's website <http://www.ibm.com/smarterplanet/us/en/ibmwatson/> (accessed 19 February 2015).
49. Tim Cocks, 'IBM starts rolling out Watson supercomputer in Africa', 26 Feb. 2014 <http://www.reuters.com/> (accessed 27 March 2015).
50. See the Preface to Mark Elling Rosheim, *Leonardo's Lost Robots* (2006).

51. Jon Bing, 'The Riddle of the Robots', *Journal of International Commercial Law and Technology*, 3: 3 (2008), 197–206.
52. For a comprehensive account of the literary and cinematic treatment of intelligent machines, see Despina Kakoudaki, 'Affect and Machines in the Media', in *The Oxford Handbook of Affective Computing*, ed. Rafael Calvo et al. (2015).
53. This was epitomized in television advertisements for the Fiat Strada in the late 1970s and early 1980s, carrying the strapline, 'handbuilt by robots', and then amusingly satirized by the TV comedy show *Not the Nine o'clock News*—a sketch depicting a factory full of people called 'Bob', ending with the tagline, 'hand built by Roberts': <https://www.youtube.com/watch?v=FU-tuYoZ7nQ> (accessed 24 March 2015).
54. Frank Levy and Richard Murnane, *The New Division of Labour* (2004), 1–2, for the upheaval, and 20–30 for the truck-driver discussion.
55. Alison Sander and Meldon Wolfgang, 'The Rise of Robotics', 27 Aug. 2014, at <https://www.bcgperspectives.com/content/articles/business_unit_strategy_innovation_rise_of_robotics> (accessed 23 March 2015).
56. See <http://cyberlaw.stanford.edu/wiki/index.php/Automated_Driving:_Legislative_and_Regulatory_Action> (accessed 27 March 2015).
57. Guy Ryder, 'Labor in the Age of Robots', *Project Syndicate*, 22 Jan. 2015 <http://www.project-syndicate.org/> (accessed 23 March 2015).
58. Sam Frizell, 'Meet the Robots Shipping Your Amazon Orders', *Time*, 1 Dec. 2014, <http://time.com/3605924/amazon-robots/> (accessed 23 March 2015).
59. See <http://allaboutroboticsurgery.com/zeusrobot.html> (accessed 23 March 2015).
60. David Rose, *Enchanted Objects* (2014), 23–4; original emphasis.
61. See Julian Savulescu and Nick Bostrom, *Human Enhancement* (2011), on the technologies and the ethical questions they raise.
62. Malcolm Peltu and Yorick Wilks, 'Close Engagements with Artificial Companions: Key Social, Psychological, Ethical and Design Issues', *OII/e-Horizons Discussion Paper*, No. 14 (2008). Also see Timothy Bickmore, 'Relational Agents in Health Applications: Leveraging Affective Computing to Promote Health and Wellness', in *Oxford Handbook of Affective Computing*, ed. Calvo *et al.*
63. See 'Difference Engine: The Caring Robot', *Economist*, 14 May 2014.

64. Compare David Maister, Charles Green, and Robert Galford, *The Trusted Advisor* (2002).
65. Alison Sander and Meldon Wolfgang, 'The Rise of Robotics', 27 Aug. 2014, at <https://www.bcgperspectives.com/content/articles/business_unit_strategy_innovation_rise_of_robotics/> (accessed 23 March 2015).
66. Yasunori Kasai, 'In Search of the Origin of the Notion of aequitas (*epieikeia*) in Greek and Roman Law', *Hiroshima Law Journal*, 37: 1 (2013), 543–64.
67. Rose, *Enchanted Objects*, 37.
68. Rosalind Picard, *Affective Computing* (1997), 250.
69. Raffi Khatchadourian, 'We Know How You feel', *New Yorker*, 19 Jan. 2015.
70. Woody Allen, 'Mechanical Objects', *Standup Comic, 1964–1968*, transcript at <http://www.ibras.dk/comedy/allen.htm#Mechs> (accessed 23 March 2015).
71. Calvo *et al.* (eds.), *Oxford Handbook of Affective Computing*, 1.
72. Calvo *et al.* (eds.), *Oxford Handbook of Affective Computing*, sect. 4.
73. Calvo *et al.* (eds.), *Oxford Handbook of Affective Computing* (2015), ch. 29.
74. 'The Truly Personal Computer', *Economist*, 28 Feb. 2015.
75. See William Dutton, Grant Blank, and Darja Groselji, 'Cultures of the Internet: The Internet in Britain', Oxford Internet Survey 2013 Report, OII OxIS, 2013. This analysis of Internet usage shows that 78% of the British population are now users. While the balance of 22% is significant, only a small percentage of these non-users 'definitely' have no one who could assist them in using the Internet. This suggests that less than 5% of adults are out of reach of the Internet today, which is a smaller percentage than is often presumed.
76. Rose, *Enchanted Objects*, Adrian McEwen and Hakim Cassimally, *Designing the Internet of Things* (2014), Daniel Kellmereit and Daniel Obodovski, *The Silent Intelligence* (2013), and Michael Porter and James Heppelman, 'How Smart, Connected Products are Transforming Competition', *Harvard Business Review* (Nov. 2014), 63–104.
77. Rose, *Enchanted Objects*, and Porter and Heppelman, 'How Smart, Connected Products are Transforming Competition', 76.
78. Rose, *Enchanted Objects*, 50.
79. Porter and Heppelman, 'How Smart, Connected Products are Transforming Competition', *Harvard Business Review*, 81.

80. Rose, *Enchanted Objects*, 27.
81. On 15 January 2015 Google announced that it was to stop producing Google Glass as a prototype but that they are still committed to its further development.
82. See e.g. <http://www.magicleap.com>.
83. Marco Iansiti and Karim Lakhani, 'Digital Ubiquity', *Harvard Business Review* (Nov. 2014), 91–9.
84. Gil Press, 'Internet of Things By The Numbers: Market Estimates and Forecasts', *Forbes*, 22 Aug. 2014, and 'More than 50 Billion Connected Devices', *Ericsson White Paper*, Feb. 2011 at <http://www.akos-rs.si/files/Telekomunikacije/Digitalna_agenda/Internetni_protokol_Ipv6/More-than-50-billion-connected-devices.pdf> (accessed 23 March 2015).
85. Discussed in Richard Susskind, *The End of Lawyers?* (2008), p. 59.
86. International Telecommunications Union, 'The World in 2014: ICT Fact and Figures' at <http://www.itu.int/en/ITU-D/Statistics/Documents/facts/ICTFactsFigures2014-e.pdf> (accessed 29 March 2015).
87. Sara Radicati, 'Email Statistics Report, 2014–2018', at <http://www.radicati.com/wp/wp-content/uploads/2014/01/Email-Statistics-Report-2014-2018-Executive-Summary.pdf> (accessed 19 March 2015).
88. On sites such as <https://www.flickr.com>, <http://www.slideshare.net>, <https://www.youtube.com> (accessed 23 March 2015).
89. <http://www.youtube.com/yt/press/statistics.html> (accessed 23 March 2015).
90. <http://www.nielsen.com/us/en/insights/news/2012/buzz-in-the-blogosphere-millions-more-bloggers-and-blog-readers.html> (accessed 23 March 2015).
91. <https://about.twitter.com/company> (accessed 19 March 2015).
92. <http://www.statista.com/statistics/274050/quarterly-numbers-of-linkedin-members/> (accessed 19 March 2015).
93. <http://wikipedia.org> (accessed 23 March 2015).
94. A important literature on mass collaboration emerged in the mid-2000s. See e.g. Yochai Benkler, *The Wealth of Networks* (2006), Don Tapscott and Anthony Williams, *Wikinomics* (2006), Charles Leadbetter, *We-Think* (2008), and Cass Sunstein, *Infotopia* (2006). For a more critical view of the subject at that time, see Andrew Keen, *The Cult of the Amateur* (2007).

95. Greg Kroath-Hartman, Jonathan Corbet, and Amanda McPherson, 'Linux Kernel Development: How Fast it is Going, Who is Doing It, What They are Doing, and Who is Sponsoring it', Sept. 2013 <http://www.linuxfoundation.org/publication/linux-foundation/who-writes-linux-2013> (accessed 24 March 2015).
96. Daren Brabham, *Crowdsourcing* (2013).
97. Yochai Benkler, *The Penguin and the Leviathan* (2011), 23.
98. Benkler, *The Penguin and the Leviathan*, 182.
99. See <http://www.retailresearch.org/onlineretailing.php> (accessed 24 March 2015).
100. <http://www.ebay.com>.
101. Trefis Team, 'eBay: The Year 2013 In Review', 26 December 2013, at <http://www.forbes.com/sites/greatspeculations/2013/12/26/ebay-the-year-2013-in-review/> (accessed 24 March 2015).
102. See Dov Seidman, *How* (2007), 39; original emphasis.
103. Some popular texts of that era were Patrick Winston, *Artificial Intelligence* (1984), Edward Feigenbaum and Pamela McCorduck, *The Fifth Generation* (1983), Donald Michie and Rory Johnston, *The Creative Computer* (1984), and Edward Feigenbaum, Pamela McCorduck, and Penney Nii, *The Rise of Expert Company* (1988).
104. Richard Susskind, *Expert Systems in Law* (1987).
105. Phillip Capper and Richard Susskind, *Latent Damage Law—The Expert System* (1988).
106. Richard Susskind and Chris Tindall, 'VATIA: Ernst && Whinney's VAT Expert System', in *Proceedings of the Fourth International Expert Systems Conference* (1988).
107. We have answered this question at length in Richard Susskind, 'Artificial Intelligence and the Law Revisited', in *Jon Bing: A Tribute*, ed. Dag Wiese Schartum, Lee A.Bygrave, and Anne Gunn Berge Bekken (2014).
108. Note, incidentally, that the allegations of failure are rarely formally published. They tend to be expressed orally and anecdotally. We know of no scholarly study of the long-term impact on the professions of the expert systems work undertaken in law during the 1980s.
109. Richard Susskind, *Transforming the Law* (2000), 209.
110. Frederick Hayes-Roth, Donald Waterman, and Douglas Lenat, *Building Expert Systems* (1983).

5. Production and Distribution of Knowledge

1. See e.g. Elinor Ostrom, 'Beyond Markets and States: Polycentric Governance of Complex Economic Systems', Nobel Prize Lecture, 8 Dec. 2009 <http://www.nobelprize.org/nobel_prizes/economic-sciences/laureates/2009/ostrom:lecture.pdf> (accessed 25 March 2015), and Joseph Stiglitz, 'Knowledge as a Public Good', in *Global Public Goods: International Cooperation in the 21st Century*, ed. Inge Kaul, Isabelle Grunberg, and Marc Stern (1999) <doi: 10.1093/0195130529.003.0015> (accessed 25 March 2015).
2. See Paul Samuelson, 'The Pure Theory of Public Expenditure', *Review of Economics and Statistics*, 36: 4 (1954), 387–9, and 'Diagrammatic Exposition of a Pure Theory of Public Expenditures', *Review of Economics and Statistics*, 37: 4 (1955), 350–6.
3. Economists call goods with both of these two characteristics, non-rival and non-excludable, 'public goods'. If we were being more precise, we might call knowledge an 'impure' public good, since it is often, but not necessarily, non-excludable. One source of confusion with this term is that many 'public goods' also turn out to be good for the public—things like clean air, street-lighting, and national security, are public goods in the formal economic sense, and in the more general sense.
4. Yochai Benkler, *The Wealth of Networks: How Social Production Transforms Markets and Freedom* (2006), 37.
5. Kenneth Neil Cukier and Viktor Mayer-Schönberger, 'The Rise of Big Data', *Foreign Affairs* (May–June 2013) <http://www.foreignaffairs.com> (accessed 25 March 2015).
6. Hal Varian, 'Markets for Information Goods', University of California, Berkeley, 16 Oct. 1998 <http://people.ischool.berkeley.edu/~hal/Papers/japan/> (accessed 25 March 2015).
7. This is a heavily revised version of the model laid out in Richard Susskind, *The End of Lawyers?* (2008), ch. 2.
8. See previous reference in Ch. 2, n. 252.
9. Atul Gawande, *The Checklist Manifesto* (2010), 13.
10. Gawande, *The Checklist Manifesto*, 19.
11. See e.g. James Boyle, *The Public Domain* (2010).
12. Lawrence Lessig, *The Future of Ideas* (2001), 20.

13. Elinor Ostrom, *Governing the Commons: The Evolution of Institutions for Collective Action* (1990), 14.
14. Hal Varian, 'Versioning: The Smart Way to Sell Information', in *Markets of One*, ed. James Gilmore and Joseph Pine (2000), 134.
15. See e.g. Langdon Winner, who writes: 'the basic conceit is always the same: new technology will bring universal wealth, enhanced freedom, revitalized politics, satisfying community, and personal fulfillment.' Langdon Winner, 'Technology Today: Utopia or Dystopia?', in *Technology and the Rest of Culture*, ed. Arien Mack (2001), 59.
16. See e.g. Adam Smith, *An Inquiry into the Nature and the Causes of the Wealth of Nations* (1998) and Karl Marx, *Capital: Critique of Political Economy*, vol. 1 (1992).
17. David Autor, 'The "Task Approach" to Labor Markets: An Overview', Institute for the Study of Labour Discussion Paper Series, No. 7178, Jan. 2013 <http://ftp.iza.org/dp7178.pdf> (accessed 25 March 2015).
18. Richard Susskind, *Transforming the Law* (2000), 47. We went on: 'In the real world, clients' problems will very rarely belong exclusively to one category alone; as purely high-end or entirely routine, for instance. In a complex deal in the future, for example, a vital task at the outset will be to assess which modes of service (whether human, unbundled, or online) are best suited for particular tasks required by the deal. The product to the client will be a blend of these different channels of service delivery.' 49.
19. Susskind, *The End of Lawyers?*, 43. Also see Richard Susskind, *Tomorrow's Lawyers* (2013), 29–31.
20. 'Workers on Tap', *Economist*, 3 Jan. 2015.
21. Yochai Benkler, 'The Battle between Capital and Labour', *Financial Times*, 23 Jan. 2015.
22. <http://creativecommons.org>. On creative commons generally, see Lawrence Lessig, *The Future of Ideas* (2001).
23. We first discussed agents in Susskind, *Transforming the Law*, 93.

6. Objections and Anxieties

1. See e.g. Christopher Millard (ed.), *Cloud Computing Law* (2013) and Ian Lloyd, *Information Technology Law* (2014).

2. See Misha Glenny, *DarkMarket: Cyberthieves, Cybercops and You* (2011), or Jamie Bartlett, *The Dark Net* (2014).
3. A classic difficulty in relation to professional service is that the value derived from any advice or guidance drawn from professional work can be unclear and difficult for recipients to figure out for themselves. Does a student succeed at school because of the support of a particular teacher, or was his or her own ability and effort the cause? Is a patient feeling better because of the doctor's advice, or in spite of it? (For Voltaire, this state of not knowing was in fact the cure: 'the art of medicine consists in amusing the patient while nature cures the disease.' We are grateful to our good friend Dr Michael Ingram for drawing our attention to this quotation.) Economists speak in this context of 'credence' goods—where the seller knows more about the good than the buyer, and the latter lacks the knowledge to judge the value of what is being provided. As a consequence, there is a possibility that people could be exploited. See Gillian K. Hadfield, 'The Price of Law: How the Market for Lawyers Distorts the Justice System', *Michigan Law Review*, 98: 4 (2000), 953–1006, and Uwe Dulleck and Rudolf Kerschbamer, 'On Doctors, Mechanics, and Computer Specialists: The Economics of Credence Goods', *Journal of Economic Literature*, 44: 1 (2006), 5–42.
4. 'Charlatanism', *Lancet*, 226: 5856 (1935), 1187.
5. '2014 Business Plan and Budget', General Medical Council, 10 Dec. 2013 <http://www.gmc-uk.org/06___2014_Business_Plan_and_Budget.pdf_54299995.pdf> (accessed 23 March 2015).
6. Natalie Gold, 'Trustworthiness and Motivations', in *Capital Failure: Rebuilding Trust in Financial Services*, ed. Nicholas Morris and David Vines (2014), 129–53.
7. David H. Maister, Charles H. Green, and Robert M. Galford, *The Trusted Advisor* (2001).
8. Michael J. Sandel, *What Money Can't Buy: The Moral Limits of Markets* (2012). An earlier set of lectures by Sandel, on which the book draws, is a more formal exposition. These are 'What Money Can't Buy: The Moral Limits of Markets', The Tanner Lectures on Human Values, delivered 11 and 12 May 1998 <http://tannerlectures.utah.edu/_documents/a-to-z/s/sandel00.pdf> (accessed 23 March 2005).
9. Sandel, *What Money Can't Buy*, 6.

10. Whether this observation is true is a challenge that critics make, pointing to e.g. the abolition of slavery and an end to a market in forced human labour.
11. Sandel, *What Money Can't Buy*, 110–11.
12. Sandel, *What Money Can't Buy*, 8.
13. The case of human organs and the two objections is set out in Sandel, *What Money Can't Buy*, 110.
14. Julian Baggini, 'Joy in the Task', *Aeon Magazine*, 9 Jan. 2013 <http://aeon.co/magazine/culture/julian-baggini-coffee-artisans/> (accessed 23 March 2015).
15. James C. Klagge, 'Marx's Realms of "Freedom" and "Necessity"', *Canadian Journal of Philosophy*, 16: 4 (1986), 769–78.
16. See e.g. Antonio Regalado, 'What It Will Take for Computers to Be Conscious', *MIT Technology Review*, 2 Oct. 2014 <http://www.technologyreview.com> (accessed 30 March 2015).
17. Jerome Groopman, *How Doctors Think* (2008), 17.
18. Simon Baron-Cohen, *The Essential Difference: Male and Female Brains and the Truth About Autism* (2004).
19. Joseph Weizenbaum, *Computer Power and Human Reason: From Judgment to Calculation* (1984).
20. The Panel on Fair Access to the Professions, *Unleashing Aspiration: The Final Report of the Panel on Fair Access to the Professions* (2009). <http://webarchive.nationalarchives.gov.uk/+/http:/www.cabinetoffice.gov.uk/media/227102/fair-access.pdf> (accessed 23 March 2015).
21. Adam Smith, *An Inquiry into the Nature and Cause of the Wealth of Nations* (1998).
22. Smith, *The Wealth of Nations*, 12–15.
23. Smith, *The Wealth of Nations*, 429.
24. Smith, *The Wealth of Nations*, 430.
25. 'He is at home when he is not working and when he is working he is not at home': 'Economic and Philosophical Manuscripts', in *Karl Marx: Selected Writings*, ed. Lawrence Simon (1994), 62.
26. Marx, 'Economic and Philosophical Manuscripts', *passim*.
27. Max Weber, *The Protestant Ethic and the Spirit of Capitalism* (2011), 99.
28. Isaac Asimov, *Robot Visions* (1990), 341.

29. 'Le mieux est l'ennemi du bien' ('the best is the enemy of the good'), in Voltaire, 'La Bégueule' (1772) <http://fr.wikisource.org/wiki/La_Bégueule> (accessed 23 March 2015).

7. After the Professions

1. Three influential publications are Alan Turing, 'Computing Machinery and Intelligence', *Mind*, 59: 236 (1950), 433–60; Margaret Boden, *Artificial Intelligence and Natural Man* (1977); and Douglas Hoftstadter and Daniel Dennett (eds.), *The Mind's I* (1982). The term 'artificial intelligence' was coined by John McCarthy in 1955.
2. John Searle, 'Watson Doesn't Know It Won on "Jeopardy!"', *Wall Street Journal*, 23 Feb. 2011.
3. See e.g. Boden, *Artificial Intelligence and Natural Man*.
4. See e.g. Terry Winograd, *Language as a Cognitive Process* (1982).
5. See e.g. John Searle, *Minds, Brains and Science* (1984) and Hubert Dreyfus and Stuart Dreyfus, *Mind Over Machine* (1986).
6. See e.g. Donald Waterman, *A Guide to Expert Systems* (1986), Frederick Hayes-Roth, Donald Waterman, and Douglas Lenat, *Building Expert Systems* (1983).
7. Phillip Capper and Richard Susskind, *Latent Damage Law—The Expert System* (1988).
8. See John Searle, 'Minds, Brains, and Programs', in *The Mind's I*, ed. Hoftstadter and Dennett. See also Searle, *Minds, Brains and Science*, ch. 2.
9. See e.g. Ray Kurzweil, *How to Create a Mind* (2012), Michio Kaku, *The Future of the Mind* (2014), John Brockman (ed.), *Thinking* (2013). Also relevant is the Human Brain Project at <https://www.humanbrainproject.eu/en_GB> (accessed 23 March 2015).
10. Quoted in Searle, *Minds, Brains and Science*, 30.
11. For a discussion of relevant science-fiction work, see Jon Bing, 'The Riddle of the Robots', *Journal of International Commercial Law and Technology*, 3: 3 (2008), 197–206.
12. Nick Bostrom, *Superintelligence* (2014).
13. See Turing, 'Computing Machinery and Intelligence'. In 2014 it was claimed by researchers at Reading University that their computer program had passed the Turing Test by convincing judges it was a 13-year-old boy.

See Izabella Kaminska, 'More Work to Do on the Turing Test', *Financial Times*, 13 June 2014 <http://www.ft.com> (accessed 23 March 2015).

14. See Richard P. Feynman, 'The Computing Machines in the Future', in *Nishina Memorial Lectures* (2008), 110.
15. See Garry Kasparov, 'The Chess Master and the Computer', *New York Review of Books*, 11 Feb. 2010.
16. Capper and Susskind, *Latent Damage Law—The Expert System.*
17. By way of illustration, the fallacy is committed by a prominent journalist in Philip Collins, 'Computers Won't Outsmart Us Any Time Soon', *The Times*, 23 Mar. 2104, and by the leading cognitive scientist Douglas Hofstadter, interviewed in William Herkewitz, 'Why Watson and Siri Are Not Real AI', *Popular Mechanics*, 10 Feb. 2014 <http://www.popularmechanics.com> (accessed 23 March 2015).
18. This is a running theme of Richard Susskind, *Expert Systems in Law* (1987). This is a revised version of a doctoral thesis, submitted to the University of Oxford in 1986.
19. An interesting area for further research emerges here. When we hold professionals responsible and call them to account, we invariably ask them for explanations of how they came to their conclusions and decisions. How will we be able to secure explanations from our high-performing machines, when they work in ways that are quite unlike the reasoning processes of human beings? In the 1980s one characteristic of expert systems work was that these systems should be 'transparent', which meant they could explain their lines of reasoning. It is not clear that the second wave of AI systems will be able to explain themselves, as it were, in the way that the AI scientists of the 1980s had hoped. On the other hand, it is also clear that many of our highest-performing experts are also unable to explain how they work, often putting it down to 'gut reaction' or 'experience'.
20. The other two are: 'A robot must obey the orders given it by human beings except when such orders would conflict with the First Law', and 'A robot must protect its own existence as long as such protection does not conflict with First or Second Laws'. These are discussed in Bing, 'The Riddle of the Robots'. According to Jon Bing, the pioneering academic computer lawyer who was also Norway's leading science-fiction writer,

Asimov himself attributed the three laws to a discussion, on 23 December 1940, with the science-fiction editor John W. Campbell.

21. There is an analogy here with John Stuart Mill's 'harm principle'. The vast literature generated on the question of what constitutes 'harm to others' gives some sense of where the practical application of Asimov's laws might take us. See John Stuart Mill, *On Liberty* (1974).
22. Mary Warnock, *Report of the Committee of Inquiry into Human Fertilisation and Embryology* (1984). <http://www.hfea.gov.uk/docs/Warnock_Report_of_the_Committee_of_Inquiry_into_Human_Fertilisation_and_Embryology_1984.pdf> (accessed 23 March 2015).
23. John Maynard Keynes, *Essays in Persuasion* (1963), 364.
24. Larry Summers says similarly: 'There is nothing in the logic of the market or human experience to suggest that it must necessarily be so that there will be jobs for all at acceptable wages, no matter how technology evolves.' See Sarah O'Connor, 'Larry Summers: "Robots are already taking your jobs"', *Financial Times*, 27 May 2014 <http://blogs.ft.com/money-supply/2014/05/27/larry-summers-robots-are-already-taking-your-jobs/> (accessed 10 March 2015).
25. Paul Krugman, 'The Accidental Theorist', *Slate Magazine*, 24 Jan. 1997. In fact, our story is based on a story that is in turn based on Krugman's story. This is found in Maarten Goos, Alan Manning, and Anna Salomons, 'Explaining Job Polarization in Europe: The Roles of Technology, Globalization and Institutions', *CEP Discussion Paper*, No. 1026 (2010). They instead thought in terms of hamburgers, but we find Krugman's unit of analysis to be marginally more palatable.
26. Many other changes have been left out of the hotdog story. For example, there might be a 'general equilibrium' effect—hotdog prices have changed relative to the price of other goods in the economy, and this may have consequences for demand. Similarly, there might be an 'innovation' effect—the new machine may spark an entirely new industry ('hotburgers', perhaps) that did not exist before. Incomes have risen, too, and that might affect what people demand. Each of these effects would have consequences for jobs. We leave these effects, and others, to one side for simplicity. Again, Goos, Manning, and Salomons, in their paper 'Explaining Job Polarization in Europe', make this point well. See n. 25.
27. This model is, of course, a simplification of the problem. This boundary of advantage, for example, is in fact 'endogenous', depending not

only upon the productivity of the people and machines but, for instance, on their wages and rents, which in turn depend upon the prices of the goods and services that the tasks they carry out produce, which in turn depend upon the nature of consumer demand and the form of production in the economy, and so on. We abstract from this in this simple model. A more complex model is the subject of research by Daniel Susskind at the University of Oxford. That model builds on the 'Ricardian model of the labor market', set out in Daron Acemoglu and David Autor, 'Skills, Tasks and Technologies: Implications for Employment and Earnings', in *Handbook of Labor Economics*, Volume 4, Part B, ed. David Card and Orley Ashenfelter (2011), 1043–171.

28. The spirit of their anxieties is shared with the original nineteenth-century 'Luddities' (whose name derives from their declared support for Ned Ludd, an East Midlands weaver who smashed a set of framing machines in anger and in fear in the early tremors of the Industrial Revolution). The Luddites viewed James Hargreaves's spinning jenny in the nineteenth century with the same anxious suspicion that today's pessimists view Tim Berners-Lee's World Wide Web in the twenty-first century. See Eric Hobsbawm and George Rudé, *Captain Swing* (2001).
29. David Autor, 'Polanyi's Paradox and the Shape of Employment Growth', *NBER Working Paper* 20485, National Bureau of Economic Research (2014).
30. Erik Brynjolfsson and Andrew McAfee, *The Second Machine Age: Work, Progress, and Prosperity in a Time of Brilliant Technologies* (2014). Also see Erik Brynjolfsson and Andrew McAfee, *Race Against the Machine* (2011).
31. Kasparov, 'The Chess Master and the Computer'.
32. <http://www.ibm.com/smarterplanet/us/en/ibmwatson/> (accessed 23 March 2015). Also see John Kelly and Steve Hamm, *Smart Machines* (2013).
33. Autor, 'Polanyi's Paradox and the Shape of Employment Growth', 38.
34. Autor, 'Polanyi's Paradox and the Shape of Employment Growth', 38.
35. David Autor, Frank Levy, and Richard J. Murnane first developed this idea over a decade ago, in 'The Skill Content of Recent Technological Change: An Empirical Exploration', *Quarterly Journal of Economics*, 118: 4 (2003), 1279–333, and a more popular book by the latter two authors a few years later, *The New Division of Labour* (2004), put this line of thinking into wider currency. An updated version of their thinking is found in

'Dancing with Robots' (2013), at <http://content.thirdway.org/publications/714/Dancing-With-Robots.pdf> (accessed 25 March 2015).

36. What we say here is consistent with the observation by Frey and Osborne, in a much-discussed paper, that 'Computer capital can now equally substitute for a wide range of tasks commonly defined as non-routine.' See Carl Benedikt Frey and Michael Osborne, 'The Future of Employment: How Susceptible Are Jobs to Computerisation', 17 Sept. 2013 <http://www.oxfordmartin.ox.ac.uk/downloads/academic/The_Future_of_Employment.pdf> (accessed 23 March 2015).
37. Garrett Hardin, 'The Tragedy of the Commons', *Science*, 162: 3859 (1968), 1243–8.
38. Jeremy Rifkin, *The Zero Marginal Cost Society* (2014).
39. Yochai Benkler, *The Wealth of Networks* (2006), 153.
40. Benkler, *The Wealth of Networks*, 221–2.
41. Carol Rose, 'The Comedy of the Commons: Commerce, Custom, and Inherently Public Property', *University of Chicago Law Review*, 53: 3 (1986), 711–81.

Conclusion

1. This is the strongest version of liberation discussed in section 5.5.
2. The 'new gatekeeper' theme echoes concerns about the future of the Internet in other works, such as Jonathan Zittrain, *The Future of the Internet: And How to Stop It* (2009), Andrew Keen, *The Internet Is Not the Answer* (2015), and Evgeny Morozov, *The Net Delusion* (2012), and *To Save Everything, Click Here* (2013).
3. The term 'enclosure' is borrowed from James Boyle. He defines it as 'the process of fencing off common land turning it into private property'. See James Boyle, 'The Second Enclosure Movement and the Construction of the Private Domain', *Law and Contemporary Problems*, 66 (2003), 33–4. Boyle writes also of a 'second enclosure movement', which he characterizes as 'the enclosure of the intangible commons of the mind' (p. 37). This, essentially, is the enclosure of intellectual property. See also Boyle's *The Public Domain* (2010).
4. John Rawls, *A Theory of Justice* (1999). See also John Rawls, *Justice as Fairness: A Restatement* (2001).
5. Anthony Kenny, *What I Believe* (2006), 123. Also see section 1.7.

BIBLIOGRAPHY

The following is a list of all books and articles referenced in the text and contained in the endnotes, as well as a selection of further reading. For websites and online data tables, please refer to the endnotes. Here and in the endnotes, the dates of last access to the websites are given only when the references relate to data and facts that might be subject to change over time.

Abbott, Andrew, *The System of Professions* (Chicago: University of Chicago Press, 1988).

Abbruzzese, Jason, 'The Full New York Times Innovation Report', *Mashable*, 16 May 2014 <http://mashable.com> (accessed 8 March 2015).

Abel, Richard, 'The Decline of Professionalism', *Modern Law Review*, 49: 1 (1986), 1–41.

Acemoglu, Daron, 'Technical Change, Inequality, and the Labor Market', *Journal of Economic Literature*, 40: 1 (2002), 7–72.

Acemoglu, Daron, and David Autor, 'Skills, Tasks and Technologies: Implications for Employment and Earnings', in *Handbook of Labor Economics*, Volume 4, Part B, ed. David Card and Orley Ashenfelter (North-Holland: Elsevier, 2011), 1043–171.

Adler, Paul, Seok-Woo Kwon, and Charles Heckscher, 'Professional Work: The Emergence of Collaborative Community', *Organization Science*, 19: 2 (2008), 359–76.

Aeppel, Timothy, 'This Wasn't Written by an Algorithm, But More and More Is', *Wall Street Journal*, 15 Dec. 2014 <http://www.wsj.com> (accessed 8 March 2015).

Agus, David, *The End of Illness* (London: Simon & Schuster, 2012).

Ahonen, Tomi, and Alan Moore, *Communities Dominate Brands* (London: Futuretext, 2005).

AKT II, *Deliverance of Design* (London: akt II, 2013).

Albergotte, Reed, 'IRS, States Call on IBM, LexisNexis, SAS to Fight Fraud', *Wall Street Journal*, 22 July 2013 <http://www.wsj.com> (accessed 8 March 2015).

Alford, William, Kenneth Winston, and William Kirby (eds.), *Prospects for the Professions in China* (Abingdon: Routledge, 2011).

Allen, Woody, 'Mechanical Objects', *Standup Comic, 1964–1968*, transcript at <http://www.ibras.dk/comedy/allen.htm#Mechs> (accessed 23 March 2015).

Alloway, Tracy, and Arash Massoudi, 'Goldman Sachs leads $15m financing of data service for investors', *Financial Times*, 23 Nov. 2014 <http://www.ft.com> (accessed 8 March 2015).

Alterman, Eric, 'Out of Print: The Death and Life of the American Newspaper', *New Yorker*, 31 Mar. 2008.

Andersen, Erika, 'Why Writing a Book is Good Business', *Forbes*, 12 Oct. 2012 <http://www.forbes.com> (accessed 8 March 2015).

Andersen, Michael, 'Four crowdsourcing lessons from the Guardian's (spectacular) expenses-scandal experiment', NiemanLab, 23 June 2009 <http://www.niemanlab.org> (accessed 8 March 2015).

Anderson, Chris, *Makers: The New Industrial Revolution* (London: Random House, 2012).

Aristotle, *Politics*, Part XI <http://classics.mit.edu/Aristotle/politics.3.three.html> (accessed 28 March 2015).

Asimov, Isaac, *Robot Visions* (London: Victor Gollancz, 1990).

Aubert, Vilhelm, *Sociology of Law* (Harmondsworth: Penguin Books, 1969).

Augar, Philip, *The Death of Gentlemanly Capitalism* (London: Penguin Books, 2001).

Autodesk, 'Project Dreamcatcher', 2015 <http://autodeskresearch.com/projects/dreamcatcher> (accessed 8 March 2015).

Autor, David, 'The "Task Approach" to Labor Markets: An Overview', Institute for the Study of Labour Discussion Paper Series, No. 7178, Jan. 2013 <http://ftp.iza.org/dp7178.pdf>(accessed 25 March 2015).

Autor, David, 'Polanyi's Paradox and the Shape of Employment Growth', NBER Working Paper 20485, National Bureau of Economic Research (2014).

Autor, David, Frank Levy, and Richard Murnane, 'The Skill Content of Recent Technological Change: An Empirical Exploration', *Quarterly Journal of Economics*, 118: 4 (2003), 1279–333.

Awan, Nishat, Tatjana Schneider, and Jeremy Till, *Spatial Agency: Other Ways of Doing Architecture* (New York: Routledge, 2011).

Ayres, Ian, *Super Crunchers*, paperback edn. (London: John Murray, 2008).

Baker, Stephen, *Final Jeopardy: Man vs. Machine and the Quest to Know Everything* (New York: Houghton Mifflin Harcourt, 2011).

Barker, Richard, *2030: The Future of Medicine* (Oxford: Oxford University Press, 2011).

Barna, 'How Technology is Changing Millennial Faith', 15 Oct. 2013 <https://www.barna.org/barna-update/millennials/640-how-technology-is-changing-millennial-faith> (accessed 7 March 2015).

Baron-Cohen, Simon, *The Essential Difference*, paperback edn. (London: Penguin 2004).

Barrat, James, *Our Final Invention* (New York: St Martin's Press, 2013).

Bartlett, Jamie, *The Dark Net* (London: William Heinemann, 2014).

Battelle, John, *The Search* (London: Nicholas Brealey, 2005).

BBC, 'Catholic Church gives blessing to iPhone app', *BBC News*, 8 Feb. 2011 <http://www.bbc.co.uk/news> (accessed 27 March 2015).

BBC, 'Debt "putting off" medical students, BMA warns', *BBC News*, 19 May 2012 <http://www.bbc.co.uk/> (accessed 8 March 2015).

Beaton, George (ed.), *New Law New Rules* (Sydney: Beaton Capital, 2013).

Ben-Shalom, Adiel, Yaacov Choueka, Nachum Dershowitz, Roni Shweka, and Lior Wolf, 'Where is my Other Half?', *Digital Humanities* (2014). <http://www.genizah.org/professionalPapers/MyOtherHalf.pdf> (accessed 7 March 2015).

Benkler, Yochai, *The Wealth of Networks* (New Haven: Yale University Press, 2006).

Benkler, Yochai, *The Penguin and the Leviathan* (New York: Crown Business, 2011).

Benkler, Yochai, 'The Battle between Capital and Labour', *Financial Times*, 23 Jan. 2015.

Berlin, Isaiah, *Karl Marx* (New York: Oxford University Press, 1996).

Bertassoni, Luiz, Martina Cecconi, Vijayan Manoharan, Mehdi Nikkhah, Jesper Hjortnaes, Ana Luiza Cristino, Giada Barabaschi, Danilo Demarchi, Mehmet Dokmeci, Yunzhi Yang, and Ali Khademhosseini, 'Hydrogel bioprinted microchannel networks for vascularization of tissue engineering constructs', *Lab on a Chip*, 14: 13 (2014), 2202–11.

Bickmore, Timothy, 'Relational Agents in Health Applications: Leveraging Affective Computing to Promote Health and Wellness', in *The Oxford*

Handbook of Affective Computing, ed. Rafael Calvo, Sidney D'Mello, Jonathan Gratch, and Arvid Kappas (Oxford: Oxford University Press, 2015).

Bilton, Nick, 'Disruptions: Medicine that Monitors You', *New York Times*, 23 June 2013 <http://www.nytimes.com> (accessed 27 March 2015).

Bing, Jon, 'The Riddle of the Robots', *Journal of International Commercial Law and Technology*, 3: 3 (2008), 197–206.

Blackman, Andrew, 'Real-Estate Crowdfunding Finds its Footing', *Wall Street Journal*, 13 Apr. 2014 <http://www.wsj.com> (accessed 9 March 2015).

Bledstein, Burton, *The Culture of Professionalism* (New York: W.W. Norton & Co., 1976).

Bloom, Benjamin, 'The 2 Sigma Problem: The Search for Methods of Group Instruction as Effective as One-to-One Tutoring', *Educational Researcher*, 13: 6 (1984), 4–16.

Bloor, David, *Knowledge and Social Imagery* (Chicago: University of Chicago Press, 1991).

Boden, Margaret, *Artificial Intelligence and Natural Man* (Brighton: Harvester Press, 1977).

Bosker, Bianca, 'Hook of Mormon: Inside the Church's Online-Only Missionary Army', *Huffington Post*, 4 Sept. 2014 <http://www.huffingtonpost.co.uk> (accessed 7 March 2015).

Bostrom, Nick, *Superintelligence* (Oxford: Oxford University Press, 2014).

Boyle, James, 'The Second Enclosure Movement and the Construction of the Private Domain', *Law and Contemporary Problems*, 66 (2003), 33–74.

Boyle, James, *The Public Domain* (New Haven: Yale University Press, 2010).

Brabham, Daren, *Crowdsourcing* (Cambridge, Mass.: MIT Press, 2013).

Bradshaw, Tim, 'Scientists and Investors Warn on AI', *Financial Times*, 12 Jan. 2015.

Bray, David, Karen Croxson, William Dutton, and Benn Konsynski, 'Sermo: A Community-Based, Knowledge Ecosystem', OII Distributed Problem-Solving Networks Conference, Feb. 2008 <http://dx.doi.org/10.2139/ssrn.1016483> (accessed 28 March 2015).

Brock, George, *Out of Print* (London: Kogan Page, 2013).

Brockman, John (ed.), *Is the Internet Changing the Way You Think?* (New York: HarperCollins, 2011).

Brockman, John (ed.), *Thinking* (New York: HarperCollins, 2013).

Broderick, Maureen, *The Art of Managing Professional Services* (New Jersey: Prentice Hall, 2011).

Brynjolfsson, Eric, and Andrew McAfee, *Race Against the Machine* (Lexington: Digital Frontier Press, 2011).

Brynjolfsson, Eric, and Andrew McAfee, *The Second Machine Age* (New York: W.W. Norton & Co., 2014).

Bughin, Jacques, and James Manyika, *Internet Matters: Essays in Digital Transformation*, Volume 3 (McKinsey, 2011).

Bughin, Jacques, and James Manyika, *Internet Matters: The Rise of Digital Economy. Essays on Digital Transformation*, Volume 5 (McKinsey, 2014).

Cabibihan, John-John, Hifza Javed, Marcelo Ang, Jr., and Sharifah Mariam Aljunied, 'Why Robots? A Survey on the Roles and Benefits of Social Robots in the Therapy of Children with Autism', *International Journal of Social Robotics*, 5: 4 (2013), 593–618.

Calvo, Rafael, Sidney D'Mello, Jonathan Gratch, and Arvid Kappas (eds.), *The Oxford Handbook of Affective Computing* (Oxford: Oxford University Press, 2015).

Campbell, Heidi, 'Considering the Performance of Religious Indentity Online', Presentation at Faith 2.0: Religion and the Internet, The Royal Society of Arts, 14 Apr. 2011.

Campbell, Heidi (ed.), *Digital Religion: Understanding Religious Practice in New Media Worlds* (London: Routledge, 2013).

CapGemini, 'Q1 2014 Revenue up 2.3% Crossed the 50,000 Employee Threshold in India', CapGemini Newsroom, 29 Apr. 2014 <http://www.capgemini.com/investor/press/q1-2014-revenue-up-23-crossed-the-50000-employee-threshold-in-india> (accessed 8 March 2015).

Capper, Phillip, and Richard Susskind, *Latent Damage Law—The Expert System* (London: Butterworths, 1988).

Care Quality Commission, 'Our Intelligent Monitoring of GP Practices', 13 Jan. 2015, <http://www.cqc.org.uk/content/our-intelligent-monitoring-gp-practices> (accessed 6 March 2015).

Carey, John, *The Faber Book of Utopias* (London: Faber & Faber, 1999).

Carpo, Mario (ed.), *The Digital Turn in Architecture 1992–2012* (Chichester: John Wiley & Sons, 2013).

Carr, David, 'Facebook Offers Life Raft, but Publishers Are Wary', *New York Times*, 26 Oct. 2014 <http://www.nytimes.com> (accessed 8 March 2015).

Carr, Nicholas, *The Glass Cage* (London: Bodley Head, 2015).

Carr-Saunders, Alexander, and Paul Wilson, *The Professions* (Oxford: Clarendon Press, 1933).

Caryl, Christian, 'Why Wikileaks Changes Everything', *New York Review of Books*, 13 Jan. 2011.

Castells, Manuel, *The Rise of the Network Society*, 2nd edn. (Oxford: Blackwell Publishing, 2000).

Cavin, Ralph, Paolo Lugli, and Victor Zhirnov, 'Science and Engineering beyond Moore's Law', *Proceedings of the IEEE*, 100 (2012), 1720–49.

Caumot, Andrea, '12 Trends Shaping Digital News', Pew Research Center, 16 Oct. 2013 <http://www.pewresearch.org> (accessed 7 March 2015).

Cep, Casey, 'Big Data for the Spirit', *New Yorker*, 5 Aug. 2014.

Cheetham, Graham, and Geoff Chivers, *Professions, Competence and Informal Learning* (Cheltenham: Edward Elgar, 2005).

Christensen, Clayton, and Henry Eyring, *The Innovative University* (San Francisco: Jossey-Bass, 2011).

Christensen, Clayton and Michael Raynor, *The Innovator's Solution* (Boston: Harvard Business School Press, 2003).

Christensen, Clayton, and Anthony Scott, 'Cheaper, Faster, Easier: Disruption in the Service Sector', *Strategy & Innovation*, 2: 1 (2004), 3–6.

Christensen, Clayton, Dina Wang, and Derek van Bever, 'Consulting on the Cusp of Disruption', *Harvard Business Review*, Oct. 2013 <https://hbr.org> (accessed 8 March 2015).

Christie, Sophie, 'Tesco Clubcard vs Nectar: Best Loyalty Schemes', *Telegraph*, 30 Aug. 2013 <http://www.telegraph.co.uk> (accessed 8 March 2015).

Civil Justice Council, 'Online Dispute Resolution', Feb. 2015, at <https://www.judiciary.gov.uk/wp-content/uploads/2015/02/Online-Dispute-Resolution-Final-Web-Version1.pdf> (accessed 26 March 2015).

Clerwall, Christer, 'Enter the Robot Journalist', *Journalism Practice*, 8: 5 (2014), 519–31.

Cocks, Tim, 'IBM Starts Rolling Out Watson Supercomputer in Africa', 26 Feb. 2014 <http://www.reuters.com/> (accessed 27 March 2015).

Coffee, John, *Gatekeepers* (Oxford: Oxford University Press, 2006).

Colford, Paul, 'A Leap Forward in Quarterly Earnings Stories', The Definitive Source blog at Associated Press, 30 June 2014 <http://blog.ap.org/2014/06/30/a-leap-forward-in-quarterly-earnings-stories/> (accessed 8 March 2015).

Collins, Francis, *The Language of Life* (London: Profile Books, 2010).

Collins, Harry, *Artificial Experts* (Cambridge, Mass.: MIT Press, 1990).

Cope, David, *Computer Models of Musical Creativity* (Cambridge, Mass.: MIT Press, 2005).

Couglan, Sean, 'Harvard Plans to Boldly Go with "Spocs"', *BBC News*, 24 Sept. 2013 <http://www.bbc.co.uk/news/business-24166247> (accessed 7 March 2015).

Cowan, Douglas, and Jeffrey K. Hadden, 'Virtually Religious: New Religious Movements and the World Wide Web', in *The Oxford Handbook of New Religious Movements*, ed. James R. Lewis (Oxford: Oxford University Press, 2008).

Cowen, Tyler, *Average is Over* (New York: Dutton, 2013).

Craig, John (ed.), *Production Values* (London: Demos, 2006).

Cuff, Dana, and John Wriedt (eds.), *Architecture from the Outside In* (New York: Princeton Architectural Press, 2010).

Cukier, Kenneth Neil, and Viktor Mayer-Schönberger, 'The Rise of Big Data', *Foreign Affairs*, May–June 2013 <http://www.foreignaffairs.com> (accessed 25 March 2015).

Cutler, David, and Wendy Everett, 'Thinking Outside the Pillbox—Medication Adherence as a Priority for Health Care Reform', *New England Journal of Medicine*, 362: 17 (2010), 1553–5.

Damon, William, Anne Colby, Kendall Bronk, and Thomas Ehrich, 'Passion and Mastery in Balance: Toward Good Work in the Professions', *MIT Press*, 134: 3 (Summer 2005), 27–35.

Davidson, Cathy, and David Goldberg, *The Future of Learning Institutions in a Digital Age* (Cambridge, Mass.: MIT Press, 2009).

Dawson, Lorne, and Douglas Cowan (eds.), *Religion Online* (New York: Routledge, 2004).

Deloitte, 'Record to Report Cycle—Tax Compliance and Reporting', 2014 <https://www2.deloitte.com/content/dam/Deloitte/global/Documents/Tax/dttl-tax-tmc-technology-landscape-2014.pdf> (accessed 8 March 2015).

Deloitte, 'Deloitte 2012 Global Report' <http://public.deloitte.com/media/0564/pdfs/DTTL_2012GlobalReport.pdf> (accessed 8 March 2015).

Deloitte, 'Deloitte Global Impact 2013' <http://public.deloitte.com/media/0565/downloads/2013GlobalImpact.pdf> (accessed 8 March 2015).

Deloitte Global Tax Center, (Europe), 'European VAT refund guide 2014' <http://www2.deloitte.com/content/dam/Deloitte/global/Documents/Tax/dttl-tax-vat-refund-guide-gtce-2014.pdf> (accessed 8 March 2015).

Dennett, Daniel, *Intuition Pumps and Other Tools for Thinking* (London: Allen Lane, 2013).

Department of Health, 'Policy: Improving Quality of Life for People with Long Term Conditions', 25 Mar. 2013 <https://www.gov.uk/government/policies/improving-quality-of-life-for-people-with-long-term-conditions> (accessed 6 March 2015).

Dershowitz, Idan, Moshe Koppel, Navot Akiva, and Nachum Dershowitz, 'Computerized Source Criticism of Biblical Texts', published online (2014) <http://www.cs.tau.ac.il/~nachumd/ComputationalHumanities.html> (accessed 7 March 2015).

Diamandis, Peter, and Steven Kotler, *Abundance* (New York: Free Press, 2012).

Dickens, Charles, *Bleak House* (London: Penguin, 1996).

Dingwall, Robert, and Philip Lewis, *The Sociology of the Professions* (London: Macmillan, 1983).

Doerr, John, 'Smart Phones for Smart Kids', *Wall Street Journal*, 21 Aug. 2014 <http://www.wsj.com> (accessed 27 March 2015).

Donkin, Richard, *The History of Work* (Hampshire: Palgrave Macmillan, 2010).

Downie, Robin, 'Professions and Professionalism', *Journal of Philosophy of Education*, 24: 2 (1990), 147–59.

Dreyfus, Hubert, *What Computers Still Can't Do* (Cambridge, Mass.: MIT Press, 1992).

Dreyfus, Hubert, and Stuart Dreyfus, *Mind over Machine* (Oxford: Basil Blackwell, 1986).

Drucker, Peter, *Management: Tasks, Responsibilities, Practices* (New York: Harper & Row, 1993).

Dulleck, Uwe, and Rudolf Kerschbamer, 'On Doctors, Mechanics, and Computer Specialists: The Economics of Credence Goods', *Journal of Economic Literature*, 44: 1 (2006), 5–42.

Durkheim, Émile, *The Division of Labor in Society*, paperback edn. (New York: Free Press, 1997).

Durkheim, Émile, *On Suicide* (London: Penguin Books, 2006).

Durrani, Arif, 'London Evening Standard Profits Double in 2013', *Media Week*, 17 Jan. 2014 <http://www.mediaweek.co.uk> (accessed 8 March 2015).

Dutton, William, 'The Fifth Estate Emerging through the Network of Networks', *Prometheus*, 27: 1 (2009), 1–15.

Dutton, William, Grant Blank, and Darja Groselj, 'Cultures of the Internet: The Internet in Britain', *Oxford Internet Survey 2013 Report*, OII OxIS (2013).

Eckert, Penelope, 'Communities of Practice', in *Encyclopedia of Language and Linguistics*, ed. Keith Brown, 2nd edn. (Amsterdam: Elsevier Science, 2006).

The Economist, 'Consultancy Firms: Strategic Moves', *Economist*, 9 Nov. 2013.

The Economist, 'Difference Engine: The Caring Robot', *Economist*, 14 May 2013.

The Economist, 'Management Consulting: To the Brainy, the Spoils', *Economist*, 11 May 2013.

The Economist, 'Coming to an Office Near You', *Economist*, 18 Jan. 2014.

The Economist, 'Computer says "Try This"', *Economist*, 4 Oct. 2014.

The Economist, 'The Dozy Watchdogs', *Economist*, 13 Dec. 2014.

The Economist, 'Electronic Arm Twisting', *Economist*, 17 May 2014.

The Economist, 'The Late Edition', *Economist*, 26 Apr. 2014.

The Economist, 'Workers on Tap', *Economist*, 3 Jan. 2015.

EdSurge, 'Khan Academy', *EdSurge* <https://www.edsurge.com/khan-academy> (accessed 7 March 2015).

Ellis, Charles, *What It Takes* (Hoboken, NJ: John Wiley & Sons, 2013).

Ericsson, 'More than 50 Billion Connected Devices', *Ericsson White Paper*, Feb. 2011 at <http://www.akos-rs.si/files/Telekomunikacije/Digitalna_agenda/Internetni_protokol_Ipv6/More-than-50-billion-connected-devices.pdf> (accessed 23 March 2015).

EY Global, 'Transparency Report 2014' <http://www.ey.com/Publication/vwLUAssets/EY-Global-Transparency-Report-2014/$FILE/EY-Global-Transparency-Report-2014.pdf> (accessed 8 March 2015).

Fairs, Marcus, 'In the future we might print not only buildings, but entire urban sections', 21 May 2013, *Dezeen magazine* <http://www.dezeen.com> (accessed 27 March 2015).

Farr, Christina, and Alexei Oreskovic, 'Exclusive: Facebook plots first steps into healthcare', *Reuters*, 3 Oct. 2014 <http://www.reuters.com> (accessed 27 March 2015).

Feigenbaum, Edward, and Pamela McCorduck, *The Fifth Generation* (London: Addison-Wesley, 1983).

Feigenbaum, Edward, Pamela McCorduck, and Penney Nii, *The Rise of the Expert Company* (London: Macmillan, 1988).

Feil-Seifer, David, and Maja J. Matarić, 'Defining Socially Assistive Robotics', *Proceedings of the 2005 IEEE 9th International Conference on Rehabilitation Robotics* (2005).

Feynman, Richard, 'Plenty of Room at the Bottom', Talk to the American Physical Society at Caltech, Dec. 1959 <http://www.pa.msu.edu/~yang/RFeynman_plentySpace.pdf> (accessed 27 March 2015).

Feynman, Richard, *The Feynman Lectures on Physics*, Volume 1 (1964), <http://www.feynmanlectures.caltech.edu/I_toc.html> (accessed 27 March 2015).

Feynman, Richard, *'Surely You're Joking, Mr. Feynman'* (London: Unwin, 1986).

Feynman, Richard, *The Pleasure of Finding Things Out* (London: Penguin Books, 2001).

Feynman, Richard, 'The Computing Machines in the Future', Lecture Notes in Physics (*Nishina Memorial Lectures*) 746 (2008), 99–114.

Financial Reporting Council, 'Key Facts and Trends in the Accountancy Profession', Financial Reporting Council, June 2014 <https://www.frc.org.uk/Our-Work/Publications/FRC-Board/Key-Facts-and-Trends-in-the-Accountancy-Profession.pdf> (accessed 8 March 2015).

Finley, Klint, 'Was Eric Schmidt Wrong About the Historical Scale of the Internet?' <http://readwrite.com/2011/02/07/are-we-really-creating-as-much> (accessed 23 March 2015).

Fish, Stanley, *Doing What Comes Naturally* (Oxford: Oxford University Press, 1989).

Fitzpatrick, Kathleen, *Planned Obsolescence* (New York: New York University Press, 2011).

Floridi, Luciano, *The Philosophy of Information*, paperback edn. (Oxford: Oxford University Press, 2013).

Floridi, Luciano, *The Fourth Revolution* (Oxford: Oxford University Press, 2014).

Food and Drug Administration, 'Mobile Medical Applications', 6 Apr. 2014 <http://www.fda.gov/MedicalDevices/ProductsandMedicalProcedures/ConnectedHealth/MobileMedicalApplications/ucm255978.htm> (accessed 6 March 2015).

Foray, Dominique, *The Economics of Knowledge*, paperback edn. (Cambridge, Mass.: MIT Press, 2006).

Forbes, Naushad, 'India's Higher Education Opportunity', in *Economic Reform in India: Challenges, Prospects, and Lessons*, ed. Nicholas C. Hope, Anjini

Kochar, Roger Noll, and T. N. Srinivasan (Cambridge: Cambridge University Press, 2014).

Ford, Martin, *The Lights in the Tunnel* (Acculant Publishing, 2009).

Foxell, Simon (ed.), *The Professionals' Choice* (London: Building Futures, 2003).

Frame, Alex, *Salmond: Southern Jurist* (Wellington: Victoria University Press, 1995).

Freidson, Eliot, *Professional Powers*, paperback edn. (Chicago: University of Chicago Press, 1988).

Freidson, Eliot, *Professionalism*, 3rd edn. (Oxford: Polity Press, 2001).

Frey, Carl Benedikt, and Michael Osborne, 'The Future of Employment: How Susceptible Are Jobs to Computerisation', 17 Sept. 2013 <http://www.oxfordmartin.ox.ac.uk/downloads/academic/The_Future_of_Employment.pdf> (accessed 23 March 2015).

Friedman, Thomas, *The World is Flat*, updated and expanded edn. (London: Penguin, 2006).

Frizell, Sam, 'Meet the Robots Shipping Your Amazon Orders', *Time*, 1 Dec. 2014 <http://time.com/3605924/amazon-robots/> (accessed 23 March 2015).

Furlong, Jordan, 'The New World of Legal Work', published online, 2014 <http://www.lod.co.uk/media/pdfs/The_New_World_Of_Legal_Digital_Download.pdf> (accessed 28 March 2015).

Gaitan, Daniel, 'Crowdsourcing the answers to medical mysteries', *Reuters*, 1 Aug. 2014 <http://www.reuters.com> (accessed 27 March 2015).

Gant, Scott, *We're All Journalists Now* (New York: Free Press, 2007).

Gardner, Howard, 'Compromised Work'. *MIT Press*, 134: 3 (Summer 2005), 42–51.

Gardner, Howard, *5 Minds for the Future* (Boston: Harvard Business Press, 2008).

Gardner, Howard, and Lee Shulman, 'The Professions in America Today: Crucial but Fragile', *Daedalus*, 134: 3 (2005), 13–18.

Garreau, Joel, *Radical Evolution* (New York: Doubleday, 2004).

Gawande, Atul, *Better* (London: Profile, 2007).

Gawande, Atul, *The Checklist Manifesto* (London: Profile Books, 2010).

Gawande, Atul, 'Big Med', *New Yorker*, 13 Aug. 2012.

Gawande, Atul, *Being Mortal* (London: Profile Books, 2014).

General Medical Council, '2014 Business Plan and Budget', 10 Dec. 2013 <http://www.gmc-uk.org/06___2014_Business_Plan_and_Budget.pdf_54299995.pdf> (accessed 23 March 2015).

Giddens, Anthony, *Capitalism and Modern Social Theory* (Cambridge: Cambridge University Press, 1994).

Gilmore, James, and Joseph Pine (eds.), *Markets of One* (Boston: Harvard Business School Press, 2000).

Gladstone, Rick, and Vindu Goel, 'ISIS Is Adept on Twitter, Study Finds', *New York Times*, 5 Mar. 2015 <http://www.nytimes.com> (accessed 7 March 2015).

Gleick, James, *The Information* (London: Fourth Estate, 2011).

Glenny, Misha, *DarkMarket: Cyberthieves, Cybercops and You* (London: Bodley Head 2011).

Goetz, Thomas, *The Decision Tree* (New York: Rodale, 2010).

Gold, Natalie, 'Trustworthiness and Motivations', in *Capital Failure: Rebuilding Trust in Financial Services*, ed. Nicholas Morris and David Vines (Oxford: Oxford University Press, 2014), 129–53.

Goldin, Claudia, and Lawrence Katz, *The Race between Education and Technology* (Cambridge, Mass.: Harvard University Press, 2009).

Goldman, Harvey, 'Good Work, from Homer to the Present', *Daedalus*, 134: 3 (Summer 2005), 36–41.

Goode, Lauren, 'Susan Wojcicki Wants to Sell You Youtube Video Subscriptions (Video)', re/code, 27 October 2014 <http://recode.net> (accessed 8 March 2015).

Goode, William, 'Encroachment, Charlatanism and the Emerging Profession: Psychology, Sociology, and Medicine', *American Sociological Review*, 25: 6 (1960), 902–65.

Goodstein, Laurie, 'Some Mormons Search the Web and Find Doubt', *New York Times*, 30 July 2013 <http://www.nytimes.com> (accessed 27 March 2015).

Goos, Maarten, Alan Manning, and Anna Salomons, 'Explaining Job Polarization in Europe: The Roles of Technology, Globalization and Institutions', *CEP Discussion Paper*, No. 1026 (2010).

Graber, Mark, Robert Wachter, and Christine Cassel, 'Bringing Diagnosis into the Quality and Safety Equations', *Journal of the American Medical Association*, 208: 12 (2012), 1211–12.

Graham, Mark, and William Dutton (eds.), *Society and the Internet* (Oxford: Oxford University Press, 2014).

Gramazio, Fabio, and Matthias Kohler, *The Robotic Touch* (Zurich: Park Books, 2015).

Gray, John, *How To Get Better Value Healthcare*, 2nd edn. (Oxford: Offox Press, 2011).

Greenhalgh, Trish, 'Is Evidence-Based Medicine Broken?', *Project Syndicate*, 8 Oct. 2014, <http://www.project-syndicate.org> (accessed 6 March 2015).

Greenhouse, Emily, 'Treasures in the Wall', *New Yorker*, 1 Mar. 2013.

Greenslade, Roy, 'Huffington Post Beats the New York Times to Top News Website Chart', *Guardian*, 10 June 2011 <http://www.theguardian.com/> (accessed 8 March 2015).

Griffiths, Andrew, 'How Paro the Robotic Seal is Being Used to Help UK Dementia Patients', *Guardian*, 8 July 2014 <http://www.theguardian.com/uk> (accessed 27 March 2015).

Groopman, Jerome, *How Doctors Think* (New York: First Mariner Books, 2008).

Groopman, Jerome, 'Print Thyself: How 3-D Printing is Revolutionizing Medicine', *New Yorker*, 24 Nov. 2014.

Grossman, Maura, and Gordon Cormack, 'Technology-Assisted Review in E-Discovery Can be More Effective and More Efficient than Exhaustive Manual Review', *Richmond Journal of Law and Technology*, 17: 3 (2011), 1–48.

Gulati, Ranjay, *Reorganise for Resilience* (Boston: Harvard Business Press, 2009).

Hack, Norman, and Willi Viktor Lauer, 'Mesh-Mould: Robotically Fabricated Spatial Meshes as Reinforced Concrete Formwork', *Architectural Design*, 84: 3 (2014), 44–53.

Hadfield, Gillian, 'The Price of Law: How the Market for Lawyers Distorts the Justice System', *Michigan Law Review*, 98: 4 (2000), 953–1006.

Halmos, Paul, 'The Personal Service Society', *British Journal of Sociology*, 18 (1967), 13–28.

Halmos, Paul, *The Personal Service Society* (London: Constable, 1970).

Handy, Charles, *The Age of Unreason* (London: Random House, 2002).

Harari, Yuval, *Sapiens* (London: Harvill Secker, 2014).

Hardin, Garrett, 'The Tragedy of the Commons', *Science*, 162: 3859 (1968), 1243–8.

Harford, Tim, 'Big Data: Are We Making a Big Mistake?' *Financial Times*, 28 Mar. 2014 <http://www.ft.com> (accessed 23 March 2015).

Harper, Steven, *The Lawyer Bubble: A Profession in Crisis* (New York: Basic Books, 2013).

Harris, Derrick, 'Has Ayasdi Turned Machine Learning into a Magic Bullet?', *Gigaom*, 16 Jan. 2013 <https://gigaom.com> (accessed 8 March 2015).

Hart, Herbert, 'Bentham and the Demystification of the Law', *Modern Law Review*, 36: 1 (1973), 2–17.

Hart, Herbert, *Essays on Bentham* (New York: Oxford University Press, 1982).

Hart, Herbert, *The Concept of Law*, 2nd edn. (New York: Oxford University Press, 1994).

Harvard University Library, 'Faculty Advisory Council Memorandum on Journal Pricing', 17 Apr. 2012 <http://isites.harvard.edu/icb/icb.do?keyword=k77982&tabgroupid=icb.tabgroup143448> (accessed 7 March 2015).

Hayden, Erika Check, 'Technology: The $1,000 Genome', *Nature*, 19 Mar. 2014 <doi:10.1038/nature.2014.14530> (accessed 30 March 2015).

Hayes-Roth, Frederick, Donald Waterman, and Douglas Lenat (eds.), *Building Expert Systems* (London: Addison-Wesley, 1983).

Heatherwick Studio, 'UK Pavilion: Shanghai Expo 2010' <http://www.heatherwick.com/uk-pavilion/> (accessed 9 March 2015).

Helft, Miguel, 'Google's Larry Page: The Most Ambitious CEO in the Universe', *Fortune Magazine*, 13 Nov. 2014 <http://fortune.com> (accessed 27 March 2015).

Herkewitz, William, 'Why Watson and Siri Are Not Real AI', *Popular Mechanics*, 10 Feb. 2014 <http://www.popularmechanics.com> (accessed 23 March 2015).

Hess, Charlotte, and Elinor Ostrom, *Understanding Knowledge as a Commons* (Cambridge, Mass.: MIT Press, 2011).

Higgs, Eric, Andrew Light, and David Strong (eds.), *Technology and the Good Life* (Chicago: University of Chicago Press, 2000).

Hildebrandt, Mireille, and Antoinette Rouvroy, *Law, Human Agency and Autonomic Computing*, paperback edn. (London: Routledge, 2013).

Himanen, Pekka, *The Hacker Ethic and the Spirit of the Information Age* (London: Secker & Warburg, 2001).

Hirschman, Albert, *The Rhetoric of Reaction* (Cambridge, Mass.: Harvard University Press, 1991).

HM Revenue and Customs, 'Making Tax Easier', Mar. 2015, <https://www.gov.uk/government/uploads/system/uploads/attachment_data/file/413975/making-tax-easier.pdf> (accessed 14 March 2015).

Hobbs, Abbi, 'Big Data, Crime and Security', Houses of Parliament Postnote no. 470, July 2014 <http://www.parliament.uk> (accessed 8 March 2015).

Hobsbawm, Eric, and George Rudé, *Captain Swing* (London: Phoenix Press, 1969).

Hodkinson, Paul, 'E-auctions: Reviewing the Review', *Legal Week*, 9 June 2005.

Hoftstadter, Douglas, and Daniel Dennett (eds.), *The Mind's I* (New York: Basic Books, 1982).

Holmes, Andrew, *Commoditization and the Strategic Response* (Aldershot: Gower, 2008).

Hon, Kuan, and Christopher Millard, 'Cloud Technologies and Services', in *Cloud Computing Law*, ed. Christopher Millard (Oxford: Oxford University Press, 2013).

Horn, Michael, and Curtis Johnson, *Disrupting Class* (New York: McGraw-Hill, 2008).

House, Patrick, 'The Electronic Holy War', *New Yorker*, 15 Mar. 2014.

Tara Hovarth, Hana Azman, Gail Kennedy, and George Rutherford, 'Mobile phone text messaging for promoting adherence to antiretroviral therapy in patients with HIV infection', *Cochrane Database of Systematic Reviews*, 3 (2012): <doi: 10.1002/14651858.CD009756> (accessed 27 March 2015).

Huerta, Ignacio (ed.), *In 100 Years* (Cambridge, Mass.: MIT Press, 2013).

Hughes, Everett, 'The Study of Occupations', in *Sociology Today*, Vol. II, ed. Robert Merton, Leonard Broom, and Leonard Cottrell (New York: Harper-Row, 1959).

Hughes, Everett, *Men and Their Work* (Toronto: Free Press, 1964).

Hyde, Rory, *Future Practice* (New York: Routledge, 2012).

Iansiti, Marco, and Karim Lakhani, 'Digital Ubiquity', *Harvard Business Review* (Nov. 2014), 91–9.

IBM, 'Emory University Hospital Explores "Intensive Care Unit of the Future"', 4 Nov. 2013 <http://www-03.ibm.com/press/us/en/pressrelease/42362.wss> (accessed 6 March 2015).

Illich, Ivan, *Toward a History of Needs* (New York: Pantheon Books, 1978).

Illich, Ivan, Irving Zola, John McKnight, Jonathan Caplan, and Harley Shaiken, *Disabling Professions* (London: Marion Boyars, 1977).

Independent Reviewer on Social Mobility and Child Poverty, *Fair Access to Professional Careers* (London: Cabinet Office, 2012).

Institute of Medicine, *The Future of Nursing* (Washington, DC: National Academies Press, 2011).

International Telecommunications Union, 'The World in 2014: ICT Fact and Figures', 2014 <http://www.itu.int/en/ITU-D/Statistics/Documents/facts/ICTFactsFigures2014-e.pdf> (accessed 28 March 2015).

IRCAD, '"OPERATION LINDBERGH" A World First in TeleSurgery: The Surgical Act Crosses the Atlantic!', IRCAD, Press Conference 19 Sept. 2001 <http://www.ircad.fr/wp-content/uploads/2014/06/lindbergh_presse_en.pdf> (accessed 23 March 2015).

Isaacson, Walter, *The Innovators* (London: Simon & Schuster, 2014).

Jackson, John (ed.), *Professions and Professionalization* (Cambridge: Cambridge University Press, 1970).

Jaffe, David, Drew Nelson, and John Thiemer, 'Perspectives in Assistive Technology', Stanford University Slides for ENGR110/210 <https://web.stanford.edu/class/engr110/2012/04b-Jaffe.pdf> (accessed 6 March 2015).

Jarvis, Jeff, *What Would Google Do?* (New York: HarperCollins, 2009).

Jeffay, Nathan, 'Kosher Smart Phone Arrives as Ultra-Orthodox Tech Taboo Shifts', *Jewish Daily Forward* 18 Sept. 2013 <http://www.forward.com> (accessed 7 March 2013).

Jenkins, Brian, Richard Susskind, Mike Warburg, and John Carrington, *Focus on IT in the City* (London: The Worshipful Company of Information Technologists, 1995).

Johnson, Brian, 'This Week in the Future: Religion & Tech: A Match Made in Heaven', Shelly Palmer Blog, 13 Dec. 2012 <http://www.shellypalmer.com/2012/2012/12/twtf-religion-and-tech> (accessed 27 March 2015).

Johnson, Steven, *Future Perfect* (London: Allen Lane, 2012).

Johnson, Terence, *Professions and Power* (London: Macmillan, 1972).

Jones, Caroline, Beatrice Wasunna, Raymond Sudoi, Sophie Githinji, Robert Snow, and Dejan Zurovac, '"Even if You Know Everything You Can Forget": Health Worker Perceptions of Mobile Phone Text-Messaging to Improve Malaria Case-Management in Kenya' <http://www.ft.com> (accessed 23 March 2015). *PLoS ONE*, 76: 6 (2012): doi: 10.1371/journal.pone.0038636 (accessed 27 March 2015).

Joy, Bill, 'Why the Future Doesn't Need Us', *Wired* (Apr. 2000).

Kaku, Michio, *The Future of the Mind* (London: Allen Lane, 2014).

Kaminska, Izabella, 'More Work to Do on the Turing Test', *Financial Times*, 13 June 2014, <http://www.ft.com/> (accessed 23 March 2015).

Kaplan, Ari, *Reinventing Professional Services* (Hoboken, NJ: John Wiley & Sons, 2011).

Kara, Hanif, and Andreas Georgoulias (eds.), *Interdisciplinary Design* (Barcelona: Actar Publishers, 2013).

Kasai, Yasunori, 'In Search of the Origin of the Notion of aequitas (*epieikeia*) in Greek and Roman Law', *Hiroshima Law Journal*, 37: 1 (2013), 543–64.

Kasparov, Garry, 'The Chess Master and the Computer', *New York Review of Books*, 11 Feb. 2010.

Katsh, Ethan, *Law in a Digital World* (New York: Oxford University Press, 1995).

Katsh, Ethan, and Janet Rifkin, *Online Dispute Resolution* (San Francisco: Jossey-Bass, 2001).

Katz, Daniel, Michael Bommarito, and Josh Blackman, 'Predicting the Behavior of the Supreme Court of the United States: A General Approach', 21 July 2014 <http://dx.doi.org/10.2139/ssrn.2463244> (accessed 25 March 2015).

Keen, Andrew, *The Cult of the Amateur* (London: Nicholas Brealey Publishing, 2011).

Keen, Andrew, *The Internet Is Not The Answer* (London: Atlantic Books, 2015).

Kellaway, Lucy, 'McKinsey's Airy Platitudes Bode Ill for its Next Half-century', *Financial Times*, 14 Sept. 2014 <http://www.ft.com/> (accessed 8 March 2015).

Kellmereit, Daniel, and Daniel Obodovski, *The Silent Intelligence* (San Francisco: DnD Ventures, 2013).

Kelly, John, and Steve Hamm, *Smart Machines* (New York: Columbia University Press, 2013).

Kelly, Kevin, *What Technology Wants* (London: Penguin Books, 2011).

Kenny, Anthony, *What I Believe* (London: Continuum, 2006).

Kessels, Roy, 'Patients' Memory for Medical Information', *Journal of the Royal Society of Medicine*, 96: 5 (2003), 219–22.

Kessler, Andy, *The End of Medicine* (New York: HarperCollins, 2006).

Keynes, John Maynard, *Essays in Persuasion* (New York: Norton & Co., 1963).

Khan, Salman, 'Let's Use Video to Reinvent Education', TED talk, Mar. 2011 <http://www.ted.com/talks/salman_khan_let_s_use_video_to_reinvent_education?language=en> (accessed 7 March 2015).

Khatchadourian, Raffi, 'We Know How You Feel', *New Yorker*, 19 Jan. 2015.

Kiechel, Walter, *The Lords of Strategy* (Boston: Harvard Business Press, 2010).

Kim, W. Chan, and Renée Mauborgne, *Blue Ocean Strategy* (Boston: Harvard Business School Press, 2005).

Kirkpatrick, Marshall, 'Google CEO Eric Schmidt: "People Aren't Ready For The Technology Revolution"' (4 August 2010) <http://www.huffingtonpost.com/> (retrieved on 23 March 2015).

Kluge, Jurgen, Wolfram Stein, and Thomas Licht, *Knowledge Unplugged* (Aldershot: Palgrave, 2001).

Kohler, Matthias, Fabio Gramazio, and Jan Williamson, *The Robotic Touch: How Robots Change Architecture* (Chicago: Park Books, 2014).

Koomey, Jonathan, Stephen Berard, Marla Sanchez, and Henry Wong, 'Implications of Historical Trends in the Electrical Efficiency of Computing', *Annals of the History of Computing*, 33: 3 (2011), 46–54.

Kowalski, Mitch, *Avoiding Extinction: Reimagining Legal Services for the 21st Century* (Chicago: American Bar Association, 2012).

KPMG, 'Our Audit Methodology', <https://www.kpmg.com/eg/en/services/audit/pages/ourauditmethodology.aspx> (accessed 8 March 2015).

Krause, Elliott, *Death of the Guilds* (New Haven: Yale University Press, 1996).

Kreiss, Daniel, Megan Finn, and Fred Turner, 'The Limits of Peer Production: Some Reminders from Max Weber for the Network Society', *New Media & Society*, 13: 2 (Mar. 2011), 243–59.

Kroah-Hartman, Greg, Jonathan Corbet, and Amanda McPherson, 'Linux Kernel Development: How Fast it is Going, Who is Doing it, What They are Doing, and Who is Sponsoring it', Sept. 2013 <http://www.linuxfoundation.org/publications/linux-foundation/who-writes-linux-2013> (accessed 24 March 2015).

Krugman, Paul, 'The Accidental Theorist', *Slate Magazine*, 24 Jan. 1997 <http://www.slate.com> (accessed 29 March 2015).

Kurutz, Steven, 'Computer Programs Help Users Bypass the Architect', *New York Times*, 20 June 2012 <http://www.nytimes.com> (accessed 8 March 2015).

Kurzweil, Ray, *The Singularity is Near* (New York: Viking, 2005).

Kurzweil, Ray, 'How My Predictions Are Faring', Oct. 2010 <http://www.kurzweilai.net/images/How-My-Predictions-Are-Faring.pdf> (accessed 27 March 2015).

Kurzweil, Ray, *How to Create a Mind* (New York: Viking Penguin, 2012).

The Lancet, 'Charlatanism', *Lancet*, 226: 5856 (1935), 1187.

Lanier, Jaron, *Who Owns the Future?* (London: Allen Lane, 2013).

Larson, Magali, *The Rise of Professionalism* (New Brunswick: Transaction Publishers, 2013).

LaRusso, Nicholas, Barbara Spurrier, and Gianrico Farrugia, *Think Big, Start Small, Move Fast* (New York: McGraw-Hill, 2015).

Laski, Harold, 'The Limitations of the Expert', *Fabian Tract*, 235 (1931).

The Law Society, 'Legal Profession and the EU', 11 June 2013 (accessed 27 March 2015).

The Law Society, 'Becoming a Solicitor—Costs of Qualifying', Mar. 2015 <http://www.lawsociety.org.uk/law-careers/becoming-a-solicitor/costs-of-qualifying/> (accessed 8 March 2015).

Leadbetter, Charles, *We-Think* (London: Profile, 2008).

Lee, Dave, 'How Scientology Changed the Internet', *BBC News*, 17 July 2013 <http://www.bbc.co.uk/news> (accessed 7 March 2015).

Lepore, Jill, 'The Disruption Machine', *New Yorker*, 23 June 2014.

Lessig, Lawrence, *The Future of Ideas* (New York: Random House, 2001).

Lessig, Lawrence, *Code: Version 2.0* (New York: Basic Books, 2006).

Lessig, Lawrence, *Republic, Lost* (New York: Twelve, 2011).

Levitt, Theodore, 'Production-line Approach to Service' *Harvard Business Review* (Sept. 1972), 41–52.

Levitt, Theodore, *Marketing Myopia* (Boston: Harvard Business School Publishing, 2008).

Levy, Frank and Richard Murnane, *The New Division of Labour* (New York: Russell Sage Foundation, 2004).

Levy, Frank, and Richard Murnane, 'Dancing with Robots', *Third Way*, 2013 <http://content.thirdway.org/publications/714/Dancing-With-Robots.pdf> (accessed 25 March 2015).

Lewis, Roy, and Angus Maude, *Professional People in England* (Cambridge, Mass.: Harvard University Press, 1953).

Liddy, James, 'The Future of Audit', *Forbes*, 4 Aug. 2014 <http://www.forbes.com> (accessed 8 March 2015).

Lieberman, Jethro, *The Tyranny of the Experts* (New York: Walker & Co., 1970).

Lloyd, Ian, *Information and Technology Law*, 7th edn. (Oxford: Oxford University Press, 2014).

Locke, Susannah, 'The Gates Foundation Pushes to make more academic research free and open to the public', *Vox*, 24 Nov. 2014 <http://www.vox.com> (accessed 7 March 2015).

Lukes, Steven, *Émile Durkheim: His Life and Work* (New York: Harper & Row, 1972).

Macdonald, Keith, *The Sociology of the Professions* (London: Sage Publications, 1995).

MacEwen, Bruce, *Growth Is Dead: Now What?: Law Firms on the Brink* (New York: Adam Smith Esq., 2013).

Mack, Adrian (ed.), *Technology and the Rest of Culture* (Columbus, Ohio: Ohio State University Press, 1997).

MacWilliams, Marc, 'Techno-Ritualization—The Gohonzon Controversy on the Internet', *Heidelberg Journal of Religions on the Internet*, 2.01, (2006) <http://archiv.ub.uni-heidelberg.de/volltextserver/6959/> (accessed 7 March 2015).

Maharg, Paul, *Transforming Legal Education* (Aldershot: Ashgate, 2007).

Maister, David, *Managing the Professional Service Firm* (New York: Free Press, 1993).

Maister, David, *Strategy and the Fat Smoker* (Boston: Spangle Press, 2008).

Maister, David, Charles Green, and Robert Galford, *The Trusted Advisor*, paperback edn. (London: Simon & Schuster, 2002).

Maitland, Alison, and Peter Thompson, *Future Work* (Hampshire: Palgrave Macmillan, 2011).

Marcus, Gary, 'Why We Should Think About the Threat of Artificial Intelligence', *New Yorker*, 24 Oct. 2013.

Markides, Constantinos, and Paul Geroski, *Fast Second* (San Franciso: Jossey-Bass, 2004).

Marshall, Thomas, 'The Recent History of Professionalism in Relation to Social Structure and Social Policy', *Canadian Journal of Economics and Political Science*, 5: 3 (1939), 325–40.

Marx, Karl, *Capital: Critique of Political Economy*, vol. 1, Penguin Classics (London: Penguin, 1990).

Maslow, Abraham, *The Psychology of Science* (Chapel Hill, NC: Maurice Bassett, 1966).

Maslow, Abraham, *Maslow on Management* (New York: John Wiley & Sons, 1988).

Mayer-Schönberger, Viktor, and Kenneth Cukier, *Big Data* (London: John Murray, 2013).

McAfee, Andrew, and Eric Brynjolfsson, 'Big Data: The Management Revolution', *Harvard Business Review* (Oct. 2012), 1–9.

McChesney, Robert, and John Nichols, *The Death and Life of American Journalism* (Philadelphia: Nation Books, 2010).

McChesney, Robert, and Victor Pickard (eds.), *Will The Last Reporter Please Turn Out The Lights* (New York: New Press, 2011).

McDonald, Duff, *The Firm* (London: Oneworld, 2014).

McEwen, Adrian, and Hakim Cassimally, *Designing the Internet of Things* (Chichester: John Wiley & Sons, 2014).

McKenna, Christopher, *The World's Newest Profession* (New York: Cambridge University Press, 2006).

McLuhan, Marshall, *Understanding Media* (London: Routledge, 2002).

Meade, James, *Efficiency, Equality and the Ownership of Property* (Oxford: Routledge, 2012).

Memorial Sloan Kettering Cancer Center, 'Memorial Sloan Kettering Trains IBM Watson to Help Doctors Make Better Cancer Treatment Choices', 11 Apr. 2014 <http://www.mskcc.org/blog/msk-trains-ibm-watson-help-doctors-make-better-treatment-choices> (accessed 6 March 2015).

Merton, Robert, Leonard Broom, and Leonard Cottrell (eds.), *Sociology Today*, Vol. II (New York: Harper-Row, 1959).

Michie, Donald, and Rory Johnston, *The Creative Computer* (Middlesex: Viking Penguin, 1984).

Micklethwait, John, and Adrian Wooldridge, *God is Back* (London: Allen Lane, 2009).

Mill, John Stuart, *On Liberty* (Harmondsworth: Penguin, 1974).

Miller, Arthur, *Colliding Worlds* (New York: W. W. Norton & Co., 2014).

Millerson, Geoffrey, 'Dilemmas of Professionalism', *New Society*, 4 June 1964.

Moore, Gordon, 'Cramming More Components onto Integrated Circuits', *Electronics*, 38: 8 (1965), 114–17.

Morgan, Thomas, *The Vanishing American Lawyer* (New York: Oxford University Press, 2010).

Morozov, Evgeny, *The Net Delusion* (London: Penguin Books, 2012).

Morozov, Evgeny, *To Save Everything, Click Here* (New York: PublicAffairs, 2013).

Mountain, Darryl, 'Disrupting Conventional Law Firm Business Models Using Document Assembly', *International Journal of Law and Information Technology*, 15: 2 (2007), 170–91.

Mumford, Lewis, *Technics and Civilization* (Chicago: University of Chicago Press, 2010).

Nagel, Thomas, *Equality and Partiality* (New York: Oxford University Press, 1991).

Narrative Science, 'Earnings Increase Expected for Dick's Sporting Goods', *Forbes*, 3 Feb. 2015 <http://www.forbes.com> (accessed 27 March 2015).

NASA, '3D Printing: Food in Space', 23 May 2013 <http://www.nasa.gov/directorates/spacetech/home/feature_3d_food.html#.VP18-N5mjww> (accessed 9 March 2015).

Negroponte, Nicholas, *Being Digital* (London: Hodder & Stoughton, 1995).

Neville, Sarah, 'Hospital Takes the Pulse of Nursing by Video', *Financial Times*, 5 Oct. 2014 <http://www.ft.com/> (accessed 6 March 2015).

The New York Times, 'Innovation Report', retrieved from Jason Abbruzzese, 'The Full New York Times Innovation Report', *Mashable*, 16 May 2014 <http://mashable.com> (accessed 8 March 2015).

Newman, Adam, 'Learning to Adapt: Understanding the Adaptive Learning Supplier Landscape', *Tyton Partners*, 15 Apr. 2013 (accessed 27 March 2015).

Newman, Nic, 'Mainstream Media and the Distribution of News in the Age of Social Discovery', Reuters Institute for the Study of Journalism, Sept. 2011 <https://reutersinstitute.politics.ox.ac.uk> (accessed 8 March 2015).

Newman, Nic, 'Journalism, Media, and Technology Predictions 2013', accessed online <https://docs.google.com/file/d/0B-whYpjV6DzWUER1VjgySzB1OG8/edit> (8 March 2015).

NHS, 'Fact Sheets: Transplants save lives', Aug. 2014 <http://www.organdonation.nhs.uk/newsroom/fact_sheets/transplants_save_lives.asp> (accessed 9 March 2015).

Nietzsche, Friedrich, *Human, All Too Human*, tr. Gary Handwerk (Stanford: Stanford University Press, 1995).

O'Connor, Sarah, 'Larry Summers: "Robots Are Already Taking Your Jobs"', *Financial Times*, 27 May 2014 <http://blogs.ft.com/money-supply/2014/05/27/larry-summers-robots-are-already-taking-your-jobs/> (accessed 10 March 2015)

O'Hara, Kieron, Noshir Contractor, Wendy Hall, James Hendler, and Nigel Shadbolt, *Web Science: Understanding the Emergence of Macro-Level Features of the World Wide Web* (Now Publishers, 2013).

OECD, 'The Internet Economy on the Rise: Progress since the Seoul Declaration', Sept. 2013.

Office for National Statistics, 'Internet Access—Households and Individuals 2014', Office for National Statistics, 7 August 2014 <http://www.ons.gov.uk/ons/index.html> (accessed 7 March 2015).

Olcayto, Rory, 'How 3D Printing Could Transform Building Design', *Financial Times*, 30 May 2014 <http://www.ft.com/> (accessed 8 March 2015).

Ollman, Bertell, *Alienation* (London: Cambridge University Press, 1973).

Olmstead, Kenneth, Amy Mitchell, Jesse Holcomb, and Nancy Vogt, 'News Video on the Web', Pew Research Center, 26 March 2014 <http://www.journalism.org> (accessed 8 March 2014).

Olmstead, Kenneth, Amy Mitchell, and Tom Rosensteil, 'The Top 25', Pew Research Center, 9 May 2011 <http://www.journalism.org> (accessed 8 March 2015).

Ong, Walter, *Orality and Literacy* (London: Routledge, 1982).

OnIslam, 'OnIslam.net's Virtual Hajj on Second Life', 6 Nov. 2010 <http://www.onislam.net/english/news/global/449652-onislamnets-virtual-hajj-on-second-life.html> (accessed 7 March 2015).

Ostrom, Elinor, *Governing the Commons: The Evolution of Institutions for Collective Action* (New York: Cambridge University Press, 1990).

Ostrom, Elinor, 'Beyond Markets and States: Polycentric Governance of Complex Economic Systems', Nobel Prize Lecture, 8 December 2009 <http://www.nobelprize.org/nobel_prizes/economic-sciences/laureates/2009/ostrom:lecture.pdf> (accessed 25 March 2015).

Oudshoorn, Nelly, and Trevor Pinch (eds.), *How Users Matter*, paperback edn. (Cambridge, Mass.: MIT Press, 2005).

Oxford Martin Commission for Future Generations, *Now for the Long Term* (Oxford: Oxford Martin School, 2013).

Oxman, Neri, Jorge Duro-Royo, Steven Keating, Ben Peters, and Elizabeth Tsai, 'Towards Robotic Swarm Printing', *Architectural Design*, 84: 3 (2014), 108–15.

Palfrey, John, and Urs Gasser, *Born Digital* (New York: Basic Books, 2008).

Paliwala, Abdul (ed.), *A History of Legal Informatics* (Zaragoza: Prensas Universitarias de Zaragoza, 2010).

Panel on Fair Access to the Professions, *Unleashing Aspiration* (London: Cabinet Office, 2009).

Parfit, Derek, *Reasons and Persons* (Oxford: Clarendon Press, 1987).

Pariser, Eli, *The Filter Bubble* (London: Penguin Books, 2012).

Parsons, Matthew, *Effective Knowledge Management for Law Firms* (New York: Oxford University Press, 2004).

Parsons, Talcott, 'The Professions and Social Structure', *Social Forces*, 17: 4 (1939), 457–67.

Parsons, Talcott, *The Social System* (New York: Free Press, 1951).

Parsons, Talcott, *Essays in Sociological Theory* (New York: Free Press, 1964).

Parsons, Talcott, *The Structure of Social Action*, 2 vols., paperback edn. (New York: Free Press, 1968).

Pasquale, Frank, *The Black Box Society* (Cambridge, Mass.: Harvard University Press, 2015).

Paterson, Alan, *Lawyers and the Public Good* (Cambridge: Cambridge University Press, 2012).

Pear, Robert, 'After Slow Growth, Experts Say, Health Spending Is Expected to Climb', *New York Times*, 3 Sept. 2014 <http://www.nytimes.com> (accessed 29 March).

Peltu, Malcolm, and Yorick Wilks, 'Close Engagements with Artificial Companions: Key Social, Psychological, Ethical and Design Issues', *OII/e-Horizons Discussion Paper*, No.14 (Jan. 2008).

Perkin, Harold, *The Rise of Professional Society* (Abingdon: Routledge, 1989).

Pew Research Center, 'Internet Overtakes Newspapers as News Outlet', 23 Dec. 2008 <http://www.people-press.org> (accessed 7 March 2015).

Pew Research Center, 'The Digital Revolution and Higher Education', 28 Aug. 2011 <http://www.pewinternet.org/files/old-media//Files/Reports/2011/PIP-Online-Learning.pdf> (accessed 7 March 2015).

Pew Research Center, 'Amid Criticism, Support for Media's 'Watchdog' Role Stands Out', 8 Aug. 2013 <http://www.pewresearch.org> (accessed 7 March 2015).

Picard, Rosalind, *Affective Computing* (Cambridge, Mass.: MIT Press, 1997).

Picton, Glenna, 'Study shows promise in automated reasoning, hypothesis generation over complete medical literature', Baylor College of Medicine,

25 Aug. 2014 <https://www.bcm.edu/news/research/automated-reasoning-hypothesis-generation> (accessed 9 March 2015).

Pink, Daniel, *A Whole New Mind* (London: Cyan, 2005).

Polanyi, Michael, 'The Logic of Tacit Inference', *Philosophy*, 41: 155 (1966), 1–18.

Porter, Caroline, and Melissa Korn, 'Can This Online Course Get Me a Job?', *Wall Street Journal*, 4 Mar. 2014 <http://www.wsj.com> (accessed 27 March 2015).

Porter, Michael, and James Heppelman, 'How Smart, Connected Products are Transforming Competition', *Harvard Business Review* (Nov. 2014).

Porter, Michael, and Elizabeth Teisberg, *Redefining Heath Care* (Boston: Harvard Business Press, 2006).

Posen, Solomon, *The Doctor in Literature* (Oxford: Radcliffe Publishing, 2005).

Postman, Neil, *The End of Education* (New York: Vintage Books, 1996).

Povoledo, Elisabetta, 'Italians Have a New Tool to Unearth Tax Cheats', *New York Times*, 27 Jan. 2013 <http://www.nytimes.com> (accessed 8 March 2015).

Press, Gil, 'Internet of Things by the Numbers: Market Estimates and Forecasts', *Forbes*, 22 Aug. 2014 <http://www.forbes.com/> (accessed 28 March 2015).

Preston, Jennifer, 'Facebook Page for Jesus, With Highly Active Fans', *New York Times*, 4 Sept. 2011 <http://www.nytimes.com> (accessed 27 March 2015).

Prill, Susan Elizabeth, 'Sikhi through Internet, Films and Videos', in *The Oxford Handbook of Sikh Studies*, ed. Pshaura Singh and Louis E. Fenech (Oxford: Oxford University Press, 2014).

PwC UK, 'Transparency Report: Building Trust through Assurance', 30 June 2014 <http://www.pwc.co.uk/en_UK/uk/transparencyreport/assets/pdf/transparency-report-fy14.pdf> (accessed 8 March 2015).

Radicati, Sara, 'Email Statistics Report, 2014–2018', Apr. 2014 <http://www.radicati.com/wp/wp-content/uploads/2014/01/Email-Statistics-Report-2014-2018-Executive-Summary.pdf> (accessed 19 March 2015).

Rainie, Lee, and Barry Wellman, *Networked* (Cambridge, Mass.: MIT Press, 2012).

Raisel, Ethan, *The McKinsey Way* (New York: McGraw-Hill, 1999).

Ramseyer, John, and Eric Rasmusen, 'Comparative Litigation Rates', Harvard John M. Olin Discussion Paper Series, Discussion Paper No. 681 (Nov. 2010) (accessed 25 March 2015).

Rapoport, Michael, 'Big Four Firms to Be Questioned on Push into Consulting', *Wall Street Journal*, 9 Dec. 2013 <http://www.wsj.com> (accessed 8 March 2015).

Raustiala, Kal, and Christopher Sprigman, *The Knockoff Economy* (New York: Oxford University Press, 2012).

Ravindranath, Mohana, 'VA signs $6 Million Contract for IBM Watson to Advise PTSD Treatment', *Washington Post*, 15 Dec. 2014.

Rawls, John, *A Theory of Justice*, rev. edn. (Cambridge, Mass.: Harvard University Press, 1999).

Rawls, John, *Justice as Fairness: A Restatement*, 2nd edn. (Cambridge, Mass.: Harvard University Press, 2001).

Raz, Joseph, *Practical Reason and Norms*, new edn. (Oxford: Oxford University Press, 1999).

Regalado, Antonio, 'What it Will Take for Computers to Be Conscious', *MIT Technology Review*, 2 Oct. 2014 <http://www.technologyreview.com> (accessed 30 March 2015).

Regan, Milton, and Palmer Heenan, 'Supply Chains and Porous Boundaries: The Disaggregation of Legal Services', *Fordham Law Review*, 78: 5 (2010), 2137–91.

Reuters Institute for the Study of Journalism, 'Digital News Report 2014', <http://www.digitalnewsreport.org> (accessed 7 March 2015).

Reynolds, John, 'Three-fifth's of Twitter's UK Users Follow a Newspaper or Journalist', *Guardian*, 4 Mar. 2014 <http://www.theguardian.com/> (accessed 8 March 2015).

Rheingold, Howard, *The Virtual Community* (Reading, Mass.: Addison-Wesley, 1993).

Rheingold, Howard, *Smart Mobs* (Cambridge, Mass.: Perseus, 2003).

Rheingold, Howard, *Net Smart* (Cambridge, Mass.: MIT Press, 2012).

RIBA Education Department, 'The RIBA Education Review—updated August 2014' <http://www.architecture.com/Files/RIBAProfessionalServices/Education/Validation/RIBAEducationReviewAugust2014update.pdf> (accessed 8 March 2015).

Rifkin, Jeremy, *The Zero Marginal Cost Society* (New York: Palgrave Macmillan, 2014).

Rizvi, Saad, Katelyn Donnelly, and Michael Barber, 'An Avalanche is Coming', *IPPR*, 11 Mar. 2013.

Robinson, Dickon, Claire Jamieson, John Worthington, and Caroline Cole, 'The Future for Architects?', *Building Futures*, 25 Feb. 2011 <http://www.buildingfutures.org.uk/assets/downloads/The_Future_for_Architects_Full_Report_2.pdf> (accessed 8 March 2015).

Rose, Carol, 'The Comedy of the Commons: Commerce, Custom, and Inherently Public Property', *University of Chicago Law Review*, 53: 3 (1986), 711–81.

Rose, David, *Enchanted Objects* (New York: Scribner, 2014).

Rose, Jonathan, *The Intellectual Life of the British Working Classes* (New Haven and London: Yale University Press, 2001).

Rosheim, Mark, *Leonardo's Lost Robots* (New York: Springer-Verlag, 2006).

Rubenstein, Michael, Alejandro Cornejo, and Radhika Nagpal, 'Programmable Self-assembly in a Thousand-robot Swarm', *Science*, 345: 6198 (2014), 795–9.

Ryder, Guy, 'Labor in the Age of Robots', *Project Syndicate*, 22 Jan. 2015 <http://www.project-syndicate.org/> (accessed 23 March 2015).

Ryle, Gilbert, *The Concept of Mind* (Harmondsworth: Penguin, 1949).

Samuelson, Paul, 'The Pure Theory of Public Expenditure', *Review of Economics and Statistics*, 36: 4 (1954), 387–9.

Samuelson, Paul, 'Diagrammatic Exposition of a Pure Theory of Public Expenditures', *Review of Economics and Statistics*, 37: 4 (1955), 350–6.

Sandel, Michael, 'What Money Can't Buy: The Moral Limits of Markets', The Tanner Lectures on Human Values, delivered 11 and 12 May 1998.

Sandel, Michael, *What Money Can't Buy: The Moral Limits of Markets* (London: Allen Lane, 2012).

Sander, Alison, and Meldon Wolfgang, 'The Rise of Robotics', 27 Aug. 2014 <https://www.bcgperspectives.com/content/articles/business_unit_strategy_innovation_rise_of_robotics/> (accessed 23 March 2015).

Saporito, Bill, 'IBM's Startling Cancer Coup', *Time*, 28 Aug. 2014.

Savulescu, Julian, and Nick Bostrom, *Human Enhancement* (Oxford: Oxford University Press, 2011).

Schank, Roger, *Designing World-Class e-Learning* (New York: McGraw-Hill, 2002).

Scheer, David, *The Death of Drawing* (London: Routledge, 2014).

Scheifinger, Heinz, 'Hindu Worship Online and Offline', in *Digital Religion: Understanding Religious Practice in New Media Worlds*, ed. Heidi Campbell (London: Routledge, 2013).

Schmidt, Eric, and Jared Cohen, *The New Digital Age* (London: John Murray, 2013).

Schön, Donald, *Educating the Reflective Practitioner*, paperback edn. (San Francisco: Jossey-Bass, 1987).

Schön, Donald, *The Reflective Practitioner*, paperback edn. (London: Ashgate, 2009).

Schumpeter, Joseph, *Capitalism, Socialism and Democracy*, paperback edn. (London and New York: Routledge, 1996).

Sciulli, David, *Professions in Civil Society and the State* (Leiden: Koninklijke Brill, 2009).

Scotchmer, Suzanne, *Innovation and Incentive*, paperback edn. (Cambridge, Mass.: MIT Press, 2006).

Scott, Mark, 'Novartis Joins with Google to Develop Contact Lens that Monitors Blood Sugar', *New York Times*, 15 July 2014 <http://www.nytimes.com> (accessed 27 March 2015).

Scott, Richard, 'Lords of the Dance: Professionals as Institutional Agents', *Organization Studies*, 29: 2 (2008), 219–38.

Searle, John, 'Minds, Brains, and Programs', in Douglas Hoftstadter and Daniel Dennett (eds.) *The Mind's I* (New York: Basic Books, 1982).

Searle, John, *Minds, Brains and Science* (London: BBC, 1984).

Searle, John, *Mind, Language and Society* (London: Weidenfeld & Nicolson, 1999).

Searle, John, 'Watson Doesn't Know it Won on "Jeopardy!"', *Wall Street Journal*, 23 Feb. 2011 <http://www.wsj.com> (accessed 28 March 2015).

Seidman, Dov, *How* (Hoboken, NJ: Wiley, 2007).

Sennett, Richard, *The Craftsman* (London: Penguin Books, 2009).

Sennett, Richard, *Together* (London: Allen Lane, 2012).

Shadbolt, Nigel, Wendy Hall, and Tim Berners-Lee, 'The Semantic Web Revisited', *IEEE Intelligent Systems*, 21: 3 (2006), 96–101.

Shanteau, James, 'Cognitive Heuristics and Biases in Behavioral Auditing: Review, Comments, and Observations', *Accounting, Organizations, and Society*, 14: 1 (1989), 165–77.

Shapiro, Carl, and Hal Varian, *Information Rules* (Boston: Harvard Business School Press, 1999).

Shapiro, Carl, and Hal Varian, 'Versioning: The Smart Way to Sell Information', in James Gilmore and Joseph Pine (eds.), *Markets of One* (Boston: Harvard Business School Press, 2000).

Shaw, Bernard, *The Doctor's Dilemma* (New York: Penguin Books, 1954).

Shirky, Clay, *Here Comes Everybody* (London: Allen Lane, 2008).

Shirky, Clay, 'Last Call: The End of the Printed Newspaper', *Medium*, 19 Aug. 2015 <https://medium.com> (accessed 7 March 2015).

Siegel, Eric, *Predictive Analytics* (Hoboken, NJ: John Wiley & Sons, 2013).

Siegel, Lee, *Against the Machine* (London: Serpent's Tail, 2008).

Simon, Lawrence (ed.), *Karl Marx: Selected Writings* (Indianapolis: Hackett, 1994).

Simonite, Tom, 'Watson Groomed as C-Suite Advisor', *MIT Technology Review*, 4 Aug. 2014 <http://www.technologyreview.com> (accessed 8 March 2015).

Smith, Adam, *An Inquiry into the Nature and Causes of the Wealth of Nations*, paperback edn. (Oxford: Oxford University Press, 1998).

Smith, Adam, *The Theory of Moral Sentiments* (London: Penguin Books, 2009).

Smith, Kelly, 'Minnesota Man Builds Castle with 3-D Concrete Printer', *Minnesota Star Tribune*, 2 Sept. 2014 <http://www.startribune.com> (accessed 9 March 2015).

Smith, Merritt, and Leo Marx (eds.), *Does Technology Drive History* (Cambridge, Mass.: MIT Press, 1994).

Smoot, Bill, *Conversations with Great Teachers* (Bloomington, Ind.: Indiana University Press, 2010).

Social Mobility and Child Poverty Commission, *Elitist Britain?* (2014) <https://www.gov.uk/government/publications/elitist-britain> (accessed 27 March 2015).

Solis, Brian, *Business as Usual* (Hoboken, NJ: John Wiley & Sons, 2012).

Somaiya, Ravi, 'How Facebook is Changing the Way its Users Consume Journalism', *New York Times*, 26 Oct. 2014 <http://www.nytimes.com> (accessed 8 March 2015).

Spada Research, 'British Professions Today: The State of the Sector', *Spada* (2009).

Spangler Scott, Angela Wilkins, Benjamin Bachman, Meena Nagarajan, Tajhal Dayaram, Peter Haas, Sam Regenbogen, Curtis Pickering, Austin Comer, Jeffrey Myers, Ioana Stanoi, Linda Kato, Ana Lelescu, Jacques Labrie, Neha Parikh, Andreas Martin Lisewski, Lawrence Donehower, Ying Chen, and Olivier Lichtarge, 'Automated Hypothesis Generation Based on Mining Scientific Literature', *Proceedings of the 20th ACM SIGKDD International Conference on Knowledge Discovery and Data Mining* (2014), 1877–86.

Spence, Michael, 'Signaling in Retrospect and the Informational Structure of Markets', Nobel Prize Lecture, 8 Dec. 2001.

SRI Education, 'Research on the Use of Khan Academy in Schools', Mar. 2014 <http://www.sri.com/sites/default/files/publications/2014-03-07_implementation_briefing.pdf> (accessed 7 March 2015).

Steiner, Christopher, *Automate This* (New York: Portfolio/Penguin, 2012).

Stephens, Mitchell, *Beyond News* (New York: Columbia University Press, 2014).

Stevens, Mark, *The Big Eight* (New York: Macmillan, 1981).

Stewart, Thomas, *Intellectual Capital* (London: Nicholas Brealey, 1997).

Stiglitz, Joseph, 'Knowledge as a Public Good', in *Global Public Goods: International Cooperation in the 21st Century*, ed. Inge Kaul, Isabelle Grunberg, and Marc Stern (Oxford: Oxford University Press, 1999) <DOI:10.1093/0195130529.003.0015> (accessed 25 March 2015).

Stiglitz, Joseph, and Bruce Greenwald, *Creating a Learning Society* (New York: Columbia University Press, 2014).

Stott, Rory, 'Does the Cost of Architectural Education Create a Barrier to the Profession?', *ArchDaily*, 29 May 2013 <http://www.archdaily.com> (accessed 8 March 2015).

Stott, Rory, 'WikiHouse Unveils World's First Two-Storey Open-Source House at London Design Festival', *ArchDaily*, 22 Sept. 2014 <http://www.archdaily.com> (accessed 8 March 2015).

Sullivan, William, 'Markets vs. Professions: Value Added?', *MIT Press*, 134: 3 (Summer 2005), 19–26.

Summers, Larry, 'What You (Really) Need to Know', *New York Times*, 20 Jan. 2012 <http://www.nytimes.com> (accessed 27 March 2015).

Summers, Larry, 'Economic Possibilities for Our Children', NBER Reporter, no. 4, 2014 <http://www.nber.org/reporter/2013number4/2013no4.pdf> (accessed 29 March 2015).

Sunstein, Cass, *Infotopia* (New York: Oxford University Press, 2006).

Surowiecki, James, *The Wisdom of Crowds* (London: Abacus, 2004).

Surowiekcki, James, 'A Billion Prices Now', *New Yorker*, 30 May 2011.

Susskind, Richard, *Expert Systems in Law* (Oxford: Clarendon Press, 1987; paperback edn., 1989).

Susskind, Richard, 'Why Lawyers Should Consider Consultancy', *Financial Times*, 13 Oct. 1992.

Susskind, Richard, *The Future of Law* (Oxford: Oxford University Press, 1996; paperback edn., 1998).

Susskind, Richard, *Transforming the Law* (Oxford: Oxford University Press, 2000; paperback edn., 2003).

Susskind, Richard, 'From Bespoke to Commodity', *Legal Technology Journal*, 1 (2006), 4–9.

Susskind, Richard, *The End of Lawyers?* (Oxford: Oxford University Press, 2008).

Susskind, Richard, *Tomorrow's Lawyers* (Oxford: Oxford University Press, 2013).

Susskind, Richard, 'Artificial Intelligence and the Law Revisited', in *Jon Bing: A Tribute*, ed. Dag Wiese Schartum, Lee A. Bygrave, and Anne Gunn Berge Bekken (Oslo: Gyldendal, 2014).

Susskind, Richard, 'Online Disputes: Is it Time to End the "Day in Court"?', *The Times*, 26 Feb. 2015.

Susskind, Richard, and Chris Tindall, 'VATIA: Ernst & Whinney's VAT Expert System', in *Proceedings of the Fourth International Expert Systems Conference* (London: Learned Information, 1988).

Sweney, Mark, 'The Guardian overtakes New York Times in comScore Traffic Figures', *Guardian*, 21 Oct. 2014 <http://www.theguardian.com/> (accessed 20 March 2015).

Swensen, Stephen, James Dilling, Michel Harper, and John Noseworthy, 'The Mayo Clinic Value Creation System', *American Journal of Medical Quality*, 27: 1 (2012), 58–65.

Tapscott, Don, *Grown Up Digital* (New York: McGraw-Hill, 2009).

Tapscott, Don, and Anthony Williams, *Wikinomics* (New York: Portfolio, 2006).

Tawney, Richard, *The Acquisitive Society* (New York: Harcourt, Brace & Howe, 1921).

Tawney, Richard, *The Attack and Other Papers* (New York: Harcourt Brace & Co., 1953).

Tawney, Richard, *Religion and the Rise of Capitalism* (New Brunswick: Transaction Publishers, 1998).

Taxpayer Advocate Service at the IRS, '2012 Annual Report to Congress—Volume 1', 9 Jan. 2013 <http://www.taxpayeradvocate.irs.gov/2012-Annual-Report/FY-2012-Annual-Report-To-Congress-Full-Report.html> (accessed 8 March 2015).

TEDBlog, 'TED reaches its billionth video view!', 13 Nov. 2013 <http://blog.ted.com/ted-reaches-its-billionth-video-view/> (accessed 7 March 2015).

Tejaswi, Mini Joseph, 'Accenture to Hire Aggressively in India', *The Times of India*, 18 July 2012 <www.timesofindia.indiatimes.com> (accessed 8 March 2015).

Thompson, Derek, 'The Facebook Effect on the News', *Atlantic*, 12 Feb. 2014 <http://www.theatlantic.com> (27 March 2015).

The Times, 'Doctor, Doctor?', leader in *The Times*, 22 Aug. 2014.

Topol, Eric, *The Creative Destruction of Medicine* (New York: Basic Books, 2012).

Topol, Eric, *The Patient Will See You Now* (New York: Basic Books, 2015).

Trefis Team, 'eBay: The Year 2013 in Review', 26 Dec. 2013 <http://www.forbes.com/sites/greatspeculations/2013/12/26/ebay-the-year-2013-in-review/> (accessed 24 March 2015).

Tuck, Richard, *Free Riding* (Cambridge, Mass.: Harvard University Press, 2008).

Turing, Alan, 'Computing Machinery and Intelligence', *Mind*, 59: 236 (1950), 433–60.

Turkle, Sherry, *Alone Together* (New York: Basic Books, 2011).

Tversky, Amos, and Daniel Kahneman, 'Judgment under Uncertainty: Heuristics and Biases', *Science*, 185: 4157 (1974), 1124–31.

Twilley, Nicola, 'Artificial Intelligence Goes to the Arcade', *New Yorker*, 25 Feb. 2015.

UK Architectural Education Review Group, 'Pathways and Gateways: The Structure and Regulation of Architectural Education', Apr. 2013 <http://people.bath.ac.uk/absaw/files/> (accessed 8 March 2015).

University of Hertfordshire, 'Introducing Kaspar', <http://www.herts.ac.uk/kaspar/introducing-kaspar> (accessed 6 March 2015).

US Department of Veteran Affairs, 'VA Telehealth Services Served Over 690,000 Veterans In Fiscal Year 2014', 10 Oct. 2014 <http://www.va.gov/opa/pressrel/pressrelease.cfm?id=2646> (accessed 6 March 2015).

Useem, Jerry, 'Business School, Disrupted', *New York Times*, 31 May 2014 <http://www.nytimes.com> (accessed 8 March 2015).

Varian, Hal, 'Computer Mediated Transactions', *American Economic Review*, 100: 2 (2010), 1–10.

Varian, Hal, 'Big Data: New Tricks for Econometrics', *Journal of Economic Perspectives*, 28: 3 (2014), 3–28.

Varian, Hal, Joseph Farrell, and Carl Shapiro, *The Economics of Information Technology* (Cambridge: Cambridge University Press, 2004).

Wahab, Mohamed, Ethan Katsh, and Daniel Rainey (eds.), *Online Dispute Resolution: Theory and Practice* (The Hague: Eleven International, 2012).

Wainwright, Oliver, 'Pressure Builds for Change in Britain's Schools of Architecture', *Guardian*, 27 June 2013 <http://www.theguardian.com/> (accessed 8 March 2015).

Waisbord, Silvio, *Reinventing Professionalism* (Cambridge: Polity Press, 2013).

Wallach, Wendell, and Allen, Colin, *Moral Machines*, paperback edn. (New York: Oxford University Press, 2010).

Warnock, Mary, *Report of the Committee of Inquiry into Human Fertilisation and Embryology*, Department of Health and Social Security, July 1984.

Warwick-Ching, Lucy, and Vanessa Houlder, 'Ten Ways HMRC Checks if You're Cheating', *Financial Times*, 16 Nov. 2012 <http://www.ft.com> (accessed 8 March 2015).

Waterman, Donald, *A Guide to Expert Systems* (Boston: Addison-Wesley, 1986).

Weber, Max, 'Bureaucracy', in *Max Weber: Essays in Sociology*, ed. Hans Heinrich Gerth and Charles Wright Mills (New York: Oxford University Press, 1947).

Weber, Max, *Economy and Society*, Volume 1 (Berkeley and Los Angeles: University of California Press, 1978).

Weber, Max, *The Protestant Ethic and the Spirit of Capitalism*, rev. edn. (New York: Oxford University Press, 2011).

Weber, Steven, *The Success of Open Source* (Cambridge, Mass.: Harvard University Press, 2004).

WebMD, 'WebMD Announces Fourth Quarter and Year End Financial Results', 24 Feb. 2015 <http://investor.shareholder.com/wbmd/releasedetail.cfm?ReleaseID=898072&CompanyID=WBM> (accessed 6 March 2015).

Weiss, Antonio, 'Harold Bloom, The Art of Criticism No. 1', *Paris Review*, 118 (Spring 1991) <http://www.theparisreview.org> (accessed 23 March 2015).

Weizenbaum, Joseph, *Computer Power and Human Reason*, with new preface (Harmondworth: Penguin, 1984).

Werfel, Justin, 'Collective Construction with Robot Swarms', in *Morphogenetic Engineering: Understanding Complex Systems*, ed. René Doursat, Hiroki Sayama, and Olivier Michel (Berlin, Heidelberg: Springer, 2012).

West, Darrell, *Digital Schools* (Washington, DC: Brookings Institution Press, 2012).

West, Darrell, and Edward Miller, *Digital Medicine* (Washington, DC: Brookings Institution Press, 2009).

White, Lynn, *Medieval Technology and Social Change* (New York: Oxford University Press, 1964).

Wickenden, William, A *Professional Guide for Young Engineers* (New York: Engineers' Council for Professional Development, 1949).

Widdicombe, Lizzie, 'From Mars', *New Yorker*, 23 Sept. 2013.

WikiHouse, 'WikiHouse 4.0' <http://www.wikihouse.cc/news-2/> (accessed 8 March 2015).

Wikistrat, 'Become an Analyst' <http://www.wikistrat.com/become-an-analyst> (accessed 8 March 2015).

Wilensky, Harold, 'The Professionalization of Everyone?', *American Journal of Sociology*, 70: 2 (1964), 137–58.

Wilks, Yorick, 'What is the Semantic Web and What Will it Do for eScience', *Research Report*, No.12, Oxford Internet Institute, October 2006.

Winner, Langdon, *Autonomous Technology* (Cambridge, Mass.: MIT Press, 1977).

Winner, Langdon, 'Technology Today: Utopia or Dystopia?', in *Technology and the Rest of Culture*, ed. Arien Mack (Columbus, Ohio: Ohio State University Press, 2001).

Winograd, Terry, *Language as a Cognitive Process* (Boston: Addison-Wesley, 1982).

Winston, Patrick, *Artificial Intelligence*, 2nd edn. (Boston: Addison-Wesley, 1977).

Wittgenstein, Ludwig, *Philosophical Investigations*, 2nd edn. (Oxford: Basil Blackwell, 1958).

Witze, Alexandra, 'NASA to Send 3D Printer into Space', *Nature*, 513: 7517 (2014).

Wolf, Lior, and Nachum Dershowitz, 'Automatic Scribal Analysis of Tibetan Writing', abstract for panel at the International Association for Tibetan Studies 2013 <http://www.cs.tau.ac.il/~wolf/papers/genizahijcv.pdf> (accessed 7 March 2015).

Wolf, Lior, Rotem Littman, Naama Mayer, Tanya German, Nachum Dershowitz, Roni Shweka, and Yaacov Choueka, 'Identifying Join Candidates in the Cairo Genizah', *International Journal of Computer Vision*, 94: 1 (2011), 118–35.

Wootton, Richard, John Craig, and Victor Patterson (eds.), *Introduction to Telemedicine*, 2nd edn. (London: Hodder Arnold, 2011).

Zittrain, Jonathan, *The Future of the Internet—And How to Stop It* (New Haven: Yale University Press, 2009).

Zittrain, Jonathan, and Benjamin Edelman, 'Documentation of Internet Filtering in Saudi-Arabia', 12 Sept. 2002 <http://cyber.law.harvard.edu/filtering/saudiarabia/> (accessed 7 March 2015).

Zuboff, Shoshana, *In the Age of the Smart Machine*, paperback edn. (Oxford: Heinemann Professional Publishing, 1988).

INDEX